MODERN HUMANITIES RESEARCH ASSOCIATION
TUDOR AND STUART TRANSLATIONS
VOLUME 24

THOMAS ELYOT, *THE IMAGE OF GOVERNANCE* AND OTHER DIALOGUES OF COUNSEL (1533–1541)

MODERN HUMANITIES RESEARCH ASSOCIATION

TUDOR AND STUART TRANSLATIONS

texts.mhra.org.uk

Thomas Elyot,
The Image of Governance
and
Other Dialogues of Counsel
(1533–1541)

Edited by David R. Carlson

Modern Humanities Research Association
Tudor and Stuart Translations 24
2018

Published by

The Modern Humanities Research Association
Salisbury House
Station Road
Cambridge CB1 2LA
United Kingdom

First published 2018

ISBN 978-1-78188-620-5 (hardback)
ISBN 978-1-78188-621-2 (paperback)

CONTENTS

for Barker
President Bill
magistrum bibliosophos, il miglior fabbro

GENERAL EDITORS' FOREWORD

The aim of the MHRA Tudor & Stuart Translations is to create a representative library of works translated into English during the early modern period for the use of scholars, students and the wider public. The series will include both substantial single works and selections of texts from major authors, with the emphasis being on the works that were most familiar to early modern readers. The texts themselves will be newly edited with substantial introductions, notes, and glossaries, and will be published both in print and online.

The series aims to restore to view a major part of English Renaissance literature which has become relatively inaccessible and to present these texts as literary works in their own right. For that reason it will follow the same principle of modernisation adopted by other scholarly editions of canonical literature from the period. The series will have a similar scope to that of the original Tudor Translations published early in the last century, and while the great majority of the works presented will be from the sixteenth century, like the original series it will not be rigidly bound by the end-date of 1603. There will, however, be a very different range of texts with new and substantial scholarly apparatus.

The MHRA Tudor & Stuart Translations will extend our understanding of the English Renaissance through its representation of the process of cultural transmission from the classical to the early modern world and the process of cultural exchange within the early modern world.

ANDREW HADFIELD
NEIL RHODES

INTRODUCTION

Elyot's Dialogues of Counsel and Translation

Renaissance — one though not the only element of English early modern culture — was translation, always at least in the broader sense of 'cultural translation': a species of the 'transculturation' invented by anthropologists for understanding communications between disparate contemporary societies, in an ambition to attain a 'copresence of cultures'.[1] Of course, cultural translation in this broad sense invariably involves translation in the narrower, more usual sense of interlingual transfer, *uerbum e uerbo, sensus de sensu* in the late antique formulation; cultural and interlingual translation are so related that there is not one without the other, and the distinction between them proves difficult or impossible to maintain. Moreover, transculturation need not occur only amongst contemporaries. Renaissance aimed at cultural transfer — to recover Greco-Roman antiquity, in order to use the discovered knowledge on contemporary problems — and so renaissance was a transcultural contact-zone; the contact-zone was also transhistorical, however, with such 'copresense' as there was being between the living and the dead.[2] 'Emulate the dead' had been the Delphic oracle's injunction of an occasion: 'Εἰ συγχρωτίζοιτο τοῖς νεκροῖς'.[3] Following the oracle's advice in the renaissance changed both present

[1] Karlheinz Stierle, 'Translatio Studii and Renaissance: From Vertical to Horizontal Translation', in *The Translatability of Cultures*, ed. by Sanford Budick and Wolfgang Iser (Stanford, CA: Stanford University Press, 1996), pp. 55–67 (p. 64). For the conceptual background, see Peter Burke, *Lost (and Found) in Translation: A Cultural History of Translators and Translating in Early Modern Europe* (The Hague: NIAS [Netherlands Institute for Advanced Study], 2005), pp. 4–6, and 'Cultures of Translation in Early Modern Europe', in *Cultural Translation in Early Modern Europe*, ed. by Burke and R. Po-chia Hsia (Cambridge: Cambridge University Press, 2007), pp. 7–38 (pp. 8–10).

[2] A. E. B. Coldiron, 'Translation's Challenge to Critical Categories: Verses from French in the Early English Renaissance', *Yale Journal of Criticism*, 16 (2003), 315–44 (pp. 335–36), and 'Public Sphere/Contact Zone: Habermas, Early Print, and Verse Translation', *Criticism*, 46 (2004), 207–22 (pp. 214–15).

[3] Diog. Laert. 7.2, 'It is stated by Hecato and by Apollonius of Tyre in his first book on Zeno [of Citium, 335–263 BCE, the founder of Stoicism] that he consulted the oracle to know what he should do to attain the best life, and that the god's response was that he should take on the complexion of the dead. Whereafter, perceiving what was meant, he studied the ancient authors'.

and past. Early modern England's culture was altered by such translations as occurred, both broader and narrower, cultural and interlingual; but the ancient Greco-Roman culture of the Mediterranean littoral came out different-looking too.[4]

The literary work of the early Tudor counsellor and statesman Thomas Elyot (*c.* 1490–1546) was in these kinds of renaissance translation. More or less straightforward interlingual translation always figures, from ancient Greek and Latin into Early Modern English, omitting any medieval middle term.[5] Elyot also always adapted such ancient matter as he translated more freely, fitting it into modern literary constructions of his own design, amounting to proprietary authorship in most cases. The ancient matter Elyot chose to translate, sometimes under the influence of Continental contemporaries, was unusual: he did not much work with the Latin late-republican, early imperial classics — the Latin prose traditions of Caesar, Cicero, and Livy, for example, or the canonical Latin poetic tradition from Vergil to Ovid. Elyot favoured the less familiar, especially perhaps the less familiar Greek writers, even late- and post-imperial ones, as well as elusive archaic figures, Latin and Greek. He translated into English culture the dialogue-form of Lucian, cynical and irreligious, for example, and he helped disinter the fractious late imperial history, when the Roman hegemony was disintegrating — less glorious but more usefully admonitory therefore. For Elyot was concerned above all with contemporary politics, particularly the problem of counsel giving and receiving in the kind of increasingly autocratic state-monarchy in which he lived. In emulating the ancient dead, but for altering his vivid political circumstance amongst the living, Elyot translated an encyclopaedia's worth of useful antiquities into English and into English culture, in one sense and another; and these findings, assembled from a broader evidentiary sample than had been known before, he disseminated more widely, by means of print.[6]

4 Cf. Stuart Gillespie, 'Two-Way Reception: Shakespeare's Influence on Plutarch', in *English Translation and Classical Reception* (Chichester: Blackwell-Wiley, 2011), pp. 47–59.

5 Elyot knew some Chaucer: he uses *Troilus and Criseyde* for characterising Gnatho in *Pasquil* (see Seth Lerer, *Courtly Letters in the Age of Henry VIII* (Cambridge: Cambridge University Press, 1997), p. 120), and he may quote the *Pardoner's Tale* in the same dialogue, p. 39 and n. 10; he also quotes the *Reeve's Tale* in *Image*, p. 174 below. On the other hand, Elyot manifests no awareness of his Middle English antecedents on the central issue of counsel: *Confessio amantis* 7, by John Gower (d.1408), and such Langland-like poems as *Richard the Redelese* and *Mum and the Sothsegger* (both *c.* 1400–1410), or the later metropolitan tradition of Thomas Hoccleve's *Regiment of Princes* (*c.* 1411) and George Ashby's *Active Policy of a Prince* (*c.* 1463) — both writers being poet-bureaucrats — or the widely known *De laudibus legum Angliae* (*c.* 1468–1471) by the legist and public figure John Fortescue. There is analysis in Arthur B. Ferguson, *The Articulate Citizen and the English Renaissance* (Durham, NC: Duke University Press, 1965), pp. 75–129.

6 David Weil Baker, *Divulging Utopia: Radical Humanism in Sixteenth-Century England* (Amherst, MA: University of Massachusetts Press, 1999), pp. 76–77.

Elyot's Conciliar *cursus*

Thomas Elyot was born, about 1490, into a wealthy though non-noble family in the West Country of England.[7] The wealth derived from the wool trade and so depended on control of land. In addition, his father Richard Elyot (d.1522) was eminent in law. He became Serjeant-at-law in 1503, in the same call that elevated John More (*c.* 1451–1530), the father of Thomas More (1478–1535), to the same distinction; later, in 1506, Elyot senior was further promoted to King's Serjeant. From 1507, he was Justice of the Assize of the Western Circuit, and he served as Justice of the Court of Common Pleas from 1513. By virtue of this professional association, though the *Utopia* author was at least a decade older, Thomas Elyot would have known both More men, personally and over a long period, before his own entry into professional public life and during it.

The greater problem is Elyot's training in classics and contemporary humanist philology, for there are not reliable records of his college or university education.[8] He claimed to be home-schooled and self-taught, 'educated only in the house of my father and, from the time I was twelve, not instructed in letters by any preceptor any place else, being unto myself only my own guide, I fear, in both the liberal arts as well as philosophy'.[9] Rather, as Elyot later wrote to his king, he had been 'continually trained in some daily affairs of the public weal of this your most noble realm almost from my childhood'.[10] Family wealth and advocacy of the contemporary regime of property ownership — 'a conspiracy of the rich' was Thomas More's phrase for it[11] — were the determinants for Elyot's early work, and records of his legal practice remain, in 'the daily affairs of the public weal'. In 1510, the year also of his only marriage (which was to

7 For biographical information, except as indicated otherwise, I rely on the *ODNB* (and sometimes *CEBR*); for Elyot, also Lehmberg, *Sir Thomas Elyot Tudor Humanist* (Austin, TX: University of Texas Press, 1960), and Pearl Hogrefe, *Life and Times of Sir Thomas Elyot Englishman* (Ames, IA: Iowa State University Press, 1967). Kenneth J. Wilson, *Letters of Sir Thomas Elyot* (Chapel Hill, NC: University of North Carolina Press, 1976), includes transcriptions of Elyot's English-language prologues as an appendix to his edition of Elyot's surviving letters. However, this recent work does not in fact much better the literary-biographical 'Editor's Preface' of Henry Herbert Stephen Croft, in *The Boke Named the Gouernour Devised by Sir Thomas Elyot, Knight* (London: Kegan Paul, Trench, & Co., 1883), I, v–clxxxix.

8 On Elyot's possible university degrees, see Lehmberg, *Sir Thomas Elyot*, pp. 10 and 12–14.

9 'THO. ELIOTA EQVES LECTORIBVS VERE DOCTIS', in Elyot, *Dictionary* (1538), sig. A5^{r}, describing the *Dictionary*, 'id operis iam coeptum ab equite Britanno, barbarissimo scilicet, utpote in paternis tantum aedibus educato, nec ab anno aetatis duodecimo ab altero quopiam preceptore literis instructo, sibi ipsi nimirum duce tam in scientiis liberalibus quam in utraque philosophia'.

10 Elyot, *Gov.* proem (Watson, p. xxx).

11 'conspiratio diuitum', *Utopia* 2, ed. by Edward Surtz and J. H. Hexter, *Complete Works of St. Thomas More* 4 (New Haven, CT: Yale University Press, 1965), 240.20.

be childless), Elyot was admitted to Clerks' Commons of the Middle Temple, his father's inn, and he began to serve as Clerk to the Justices of Assize of his father's Western Circuit. In his own right, Thomas was several times Justice of the Peace for Oxford and Wiltshire between 1515 and 1529, and in 1527 and 1529 he served as Sheriff of the same counties.

When Elyot's father died in 1522, not only did he inherit, prodigiously as well as troublesomely (for a great deal of property was involved and litigation ensued), Elyot also changed jobs. Henry VIII's chancellor Thomas Wolsey (1470–1530) persuaded Elyot to take on the senior clerkship of the king's council, at the centre of affairs of state. Wolsey also made the scholar-poet John Skelton (*c.* 1460–1529) promises that he could not or would not keep;[12] Elyot was to be unpaid, it turned out, for discharge of the conciliar duties deputed him by Wolsey's authority. In fact, having given up his remunerative Western Circuit appointment, Elyot found that serving the king in council cost him a good deal, and he continued trying to collect what he felt was due him even well after Wolsey's disgrace in late 1529. Wolsey's destruction may also have damaged Elyot's prospects, for he did not resume the legal career that otherwise he might have followed, to the sort of eminence in the jural apparatus that his father attained. Moreover, although Wolsey's replacement as chancellor was Elyot's *amicus* Thomas More, and More's replacement was Elyot's *amicus* Thomas Cromwell (*c.* 1485–1540) — to whom Elyot directed his various pleas for relief and patronage[13] — he did not again serve the king as immediately as he had in council during the period 1523 to 1530, with one ambivalent exception.

Elyot was knighted in 1530, in recompense for his services, though of course the honour cost its recipient, rather than the crown, which received the usual fee for Elyot's distinction. He also served again as a Justice of the Peace, intermittently, and, a decade later, once as a Member of Parliament for Cambridgeshire, as a Knight of the Shire by virtue of the distinction he had paid for. Later again, Elyot purchased confiscated religious properties from the state, profitably enough, though once again so doing meant income immediately for the needy crown and only delayed benefit for Elyot.

The exceptional service he did his king came in 1531, when, again without proper recompense, he was sent as King Henry's ambassador to the Emperor Charles V (1500–1558).[14] The mission may have been designed to fail, as it did,

12 John Scattergood, *John Skelton: The Career of an Early Tudor Poet* (Dublin: Four Courts, 2014), pp. 351–55.

13 On the letters to Cromwell, see esp. Wilson, *The Letters of Sir Thomas Elyot*, pp. xi–xiii and xix–xx; on Cromwell's relations with Elyot and other writers, see R. M. Fisher, 'Thomas Cromwell, Humanism and Educational Reform', *Bulletin of the Institute of Historical Research*, 50 (1977), 151–63.

14 The parallels with the 1515 'Utopian' embassy (involving Wolsey and Wolsey's secretary Richard Pace, the translator of Lucian, to the same prince whom Elyot was to attend) and its outcomes for More, including impoverishment, are extensive: see J. H. Hexter, *More's Utopia:*

for it involved Henry's ramifying marital situation. Elyot was instructed to acquire or to provoke reassurances that the Emperor would not attack Henry's kingdom in case of his divorce from Charles's father's sister Katherine (1486–1536). Attacking England was not desirable or needful for punishing Henry, from Charles's perspective, and no such attack was ever envisaged; Henry married Ann Boleyn (d.1536) in any event. The negotiation had no point; Elyot was soon recalled, and his place was taken by another. After some Continental travel, probably also on royal mission — meant to persuade the once criminal, now of a sudden potentially useful religious reformer William Tyndale (*c.* 1494–1536)[15] to return to England: again, only the predictable failure — Elyot came home. The successor-ambassador was Thomas Cranmer (1489–1556), who did no better with the Emperor Charles, though rather well with Henry. When Cranmer's elevation to the archbishopric of Canterbury was announced in late 1532 (though he had acquired a proper wife while abroad), Elyot was incensed.

Elyot's Writing

The eve of Elyot's imperial embassy had seen the publication of *Governour* (1531): three books of counsel, for counsellors, prospective and actual members of a king's official directorate. Elyot had worked within the kind of state apparatus that *Governour* delineates; moreover, though probably conservative in religion and possibly treasonous in his support for Queen Katherine, Elyot survived the purge of council when Wolsey fell in 1529 and was able to distance himself from Thomas More too at the crucial later moment of More's resignation from the chancellorship in 1532. Elyot was adept, in other words; but he did not enjoy the sort of spectacular successes that others in the same period attained out of such manoeuvring. In any case, *Governour* is as much literary-traditional as it is derived from experience. An important part of it is translation of ancient and otherwise foreign matter, including recent Italianate humanist political analysis, into a vivid contemporary English cultural idiom.[16] Unlike whatever

The Biography of an Idea (Princeton, NJ: Princeton University Press, 1952), pp. 104–09; likewise, the 1537 embassy of Thomas Wyatt to Charles V again, when the chancellor having to be dunned for the money was Elyot's Cromwell (also formerly a secretary to Wolsey): see Robert S. Kinsman, '"The Proverbes of Salmon Do Playnly Declare": A Sententious Poem on Wisdom and Governance, Ascribed to Sir Francis Bryan', *Huntington Library Quarterly*, 42 (1979), 279–312 (pp. 310–11); also, William T. Rossiter, '*In Spayne*: Sir Thomas Wyatt and the Poetics of Embassy', in *Authority and Diplomacy from Dante to Shakespeare*, ed. by Jason Powell and Rossiter (Burlington, VT: Ashgate, 2013), pp. 101–20 (pp. 101–02).

15 Like Elyot, Tyndale was a translator of Isocrates (as well as Erasmus's *Enchiridion*): Alan Stewart, 'The Trouble with English Humanism', in *Reassessing Tudor Humanism*, ed. by Jonathan Woolfson (New York, NY: Palgrave MacMillan, 2002), pp. 78–98 (pp. 88–91).

16 Ferguson, *Articulate Citizen*, p. 168: 'Elyot set out deliberately to bring the new studies to the broad and literate group of laymen who bore the responsibility of government'. For

antecedents it may have had, Elyot's *Governour* is in English prose.

Governour begins with an apology for monarchy, making propaganda for the Tudor state in this respect as in others.[17] Arguing on the basis of considerations of 'good order' or 'degree', and implicitly against More's *Utopia* (1516) — 'where all thing is common there lacketh order, and where order lacketh there all thing is odious and uncomely'; for 'take away order from all things, what should then remain? Certes, nothing, finally, except [...] chaos' — Elyot concluded, 'there can be no perfect public weal without one capital and sovereign governor'.[18]

Governour is not a *speculum principis*, however, strictly speaking, since it is addressed not to a prince, as was the *Institutio Christiani principis* of Desiderius Erasmus (1466–1536), for example, but to princes' servant-administrators.[19] Nor is *Governour* a manual of courtly conduct, like Baldassare Castiglione's *Cortegiano* (1528).[20] Elyot himself described the book as intended for 'instructing men in such virtues as shall be expedient for them which shall have authority

the context of Elyot's political analysis, I rely on Quentin Skinner, *Foundations of Modern Political Thought* (Cambridge: Cambridge University Press, 1978), esp. I, 213–43, with the precis of much the same matter in Skinner, 'Political Philosophy', in *The Cambridge History of Renaissance Philosophy*, ed. by C. B. Schmitt and Skinner, (Cambridge: Cambridge University Press, 1988), pp. 389–452.

17 Greg Walker, *Writing Under Tyranny: English Literature and the Henrician Reformation* (Oxford: Oxford University Press, 2005), pp. 179–80; also, Fritz Caspari, *Humanism and the Social Order in Tudor England* (1954; repr. New York, NY: Columbia University Teachers College Press, 1968), pp. 186–87; F. W. Conrad, 'The Problem of Counsel Reconsidered: The Case of Thomas Elyot', in *Political Thought and the Tudor Commonwealth*, ed. by Paul A. Fideler and T. F. Mayer (London: Routledge, 1992), pp. 75–107 (p. 81); and Isabelle Bore, 'Thomas Elyot: Du courtisan disgrâcié à l'éducateur plébiscité', *Moreana*, 49 (2012), 49–75 (p. 55).

18 The quotations are *Gov.* 1.1 and 1.3 (Watson, pp. 6 and 15). On this matter of 'degree' and its implications, see Skinner, *Foundations*, I, 239–240; also, Caspari, *Humanism and the Social Order*, pp. 177–86. And on *Governour* as a reply to *Utopia*, see Ruth Mohl, *The Three Estates in Medieval and Renaissance Literature* (New York, NY: Columbia University Press, 1933), pp. 156–60.

19 Elyot praises the *Institutio Christiani principis*, nevertheless: see *Gov.* 1.11 and 3.11 (Watson, pp. 48 and 234); moreover, Croft, ed., *Boke Named the Gouernour*, II, 2, 4–5, 9, and 12–13, establishes that *Gov.* 2.1–2.2 (Watson pp. 116–17, 118–19, and 121–22) is translation of excerpts from this particular work by Erasmus. It would be difficult to overestimate Erasmus's influence on Elyot: the Isocrates and Lucian translations, as well as Erasmus's own Lucianic satires, for example; or Erasmus's various collections of *sententiae*. It is indicated below that Elyot even favoured Erasmus's edition of the *Historia augusta* (Basel: Froben, 1518), although the Aldine edition had superseded it: see below, *Image*, pp. 193, 202, 278, 284. In his epistolary preface to the edition, *Ep.* 586 (CWE 4, 373–83), Erasmus summarised his own Utopian view *de optimo reipublicae statu*, and it is much the same as Elyot's; additionally, Erasmus there delineates the value of imperial biography, singling out precisely the sort of imperial biography that Elyot was to essay in *Image*.

20 Jennifer Richards, *Rhetoric and Courtliness in Early Modern Literature* (Cambridge: Cambridge University Press, 2003), p. 44; though see also John M. Major, *Sir Thomas Elyot and Renaissance Humanism* (Lincoln, NE: University of Nebraska Press, 1964), pp. 60–73.

in a weal public'[21] — it is an essay on the ethics of public service. In its first book, *Governour* accounts 'the best form of education or bringing up of noble children', by analysis of 'the studies' ('but also the exercises' — for Elyot was an advocate of physical culture, including dance[22]) comprising 'the necessary education of noble men and other called to the governance of a public weal', to the end that, 'by the noble example of their lives and the fruit thereof coming, the public weal that shall happen to be under their governance shall not fail to be accounted happy'.[23] For the rest, *Governour* 'shall contain all the remnant', Elyot put it, 'which I can either by learning or experience find apt to the perfection of a just public weal'.[24] This remnant chiefly comprises exemplified exposition of the standard secular virtues — justice, fortitude, temperance, and sapience (as Elyot preferred to call wisdom) — as well as analysis of such ancillary considerations as the matter of majesty (including majestic apparel) and the nature of true nobility, affability, amity, and so forth, likewise all thoroughly exemplified.[25] As for the 'learning' the book advertises (in contrast to 'experience'), Elyot explains that history is 'wonderful profitable'; 'So large is the compose of that which is named history that it comprehendeth all thing that is necessary to be put in memory':

> It not only reporteth the gests or acts of princes or captains, their counsels and attemptates, enterprises, affairs, manners in living — good and bad — <and> descriptions of regions and cities, with their inhabitants; but also it bringeth to our knowledge the forms of sundry public weals, with augmentations and decays, and occasion thereof; moreover precepts, exhortations, counsels, and good persuasions, comprehended in quick sentences and eloquent orations.[26]

After leaving the king's council and completing his embassy, Elyot undertook other such propaedeutic service in other writings. During the fifteen years following, he published ten books, not counting simple reprints and revised editions. He did significantly better than he had counselling his king in

[21] *Image*, prologue, p. 172 below.

[22] The chapters on dance, esp. *Gov.* 1.20–21 (Watson, pp. 87–95) derive much from Lucian, *Salt.*; see Bore, 'Thomas Elyot', pp. 68–73.

[23] *Gov.* 1.2 and 2.1 (Watson, pp. 15 and 116). For the consequences of such an educational programme, see Skinner, *Foundations*, I, 241–43.

[24] *Gov.* 1.2 (Watson, p. 15).

[25] For the humanist promotion of this programme of virtues, see Skinner, *Foundations*, I, 228–36; also, Felix Gilbert, 'The Humanist Concept of the Prince and the *Prince* of Machiavelli', *Journal of Modern History*, 11 (1939), 449–83 (pp. 462–69).

[26] *Gov.* 3.25 (Watson, p. 281). For the learning and experience dichotomy, see Wilson, *Incomplete Fictions: The Formations of English Renaissance Dialogue* (Washington, DC: Catholic University of America Press, 1985), pp. 77–85; and on the topic of the value of history, see Skinner, *Foundations*, I, 220–21; for Elyot's use of it, see Ferguson, *Articulate Citizen*, pp. 192–94.

the publishing industry — still within the state apparatus, it may be said, though in its cultural-information department: Elyot's writings were in all cases first published by the official royal printer, Thomas Berthelet (d.1555).[27] Elyot was prescient about the new industry's benefit in this period of its institutionalisation, before the formation of the Stationers Company in 1557; for the work Elyot finished and published after his politic retirement *c.* 1532 included some remarkably successful books. A corollary of his success with the printing industry was that whatever ideas Elyot promoted in these writings enjoyed widest circulation.

With *Castle of Health* ([1537?]), a book of medicinal self-help and home-remedies, based on Italianate humanist science, Elyot opened a vein of profits that English publishers have mined ever since, one way and another. Elyot's book was reprinted in 1539, and in an augmented second edition, new and improved, in 1541 and [1544?]. His manual of child-rearing, *Education or Bringing up of Children* ([1530?], repr. [1532?]), a translation of Plutarch, was also a success in such terms.[28] Most significantly, Elyot helped the English printing industry discover the value of dictionary publishing. Elyot's Latin-English *Dictionary* was first printed in 1538 and then again — for, despite the high price of so large a book as it was, the first edition would have sold out — in a new and improved second edition, *Bibliotheca Eliotae*, in 1542 (repr. 1545). It remained in print well into the eighteenth century, though the augmented revisions published after Elyot's death in 1546 were the work of others. The 1542 title does a better job of describing the book, for it is more library than word-list.[29] Elyot also

[27] On Berthelet's work, see Daniel Wakelin, *Humanism, Reading, and English Literature 1430–1530* (Oxford: Oxford University Press, 2007), pp. 192–93; on his relations with Elyot, see Baker, *Divulging Utopia*, p. 79, and esp. Cathy Shrank, 'Sir Thomas Elyot and the Bonds of Community', in *The Oxford Handbook of Tudor Literature 1485–1603*, ed. by Mike Pincombe and Shrank (Oxford: Oxford University Press, 2009), pp. 154–69 (p. 158).

[28] See Fred Schurink, 'Print, Patronage, and Occasion: Translations of Plutarch's *Moralia* in Tudor England', *Yearbook of English Studies*, 38 (2008), 86–101 (pp. 91–93); also, Donald W. Rude, 'On the Date of Sir Thomas Elyot's *The Education or bringinge vp of children*', *Papers of the Bibliographical Society of America*, 71 (1977), 61–65. Hogrefe, *Life and Times*, pp. 221–24, argues that, with the other simply interlingual translations attributable to Elyot, including *Doctrinal*, as well as the anonymous Plutarchan *How One may take Profit of his Enemies* (London: Berthelet, [1531?]) and *A Dialogue between Lucian and Diogenes* [sc. Lucian, *Cynicus*] (London: Berthelet, [1532?]), *Education or Bringing up of Children* (London: Berthelet, [1532?]) long antedates its publication, having been made during the fifteen-twenties, when Elyot was perfecting his languages; though on the Lucian translation, see esp. Brenda M. Hosington, '"Compluria opuscula longe festivissima": Translations of Lucian in Renaissance England', in *Syntagmatia: Essays on Neo-Latin Literature*, ed. by Dirk Sacré and Jan Papy (Leuven: Leuven University Press, 2009), pp. 187–205 (pp. 189–96).

[29] Gabriele Stein, *Sir Thomas Elyot as Lexicographer* (Oxford: Oxford University Press, 2014), esp. pp. 8–9 — but with the review-article of John Considine, 'Sir Thomas Elyot Makes a Dictionary', *International Journal of Lexicography*, 27 (2014), 309–18 (esp. 313). See also Anke Bernau, 'Alphabetizing the Nation: Medieval British Origins in Thomas Elyot's

incorporated into it a biographical dictionary of Greco-Roman antiquity (from 'Alexander' to 'Zeno' in the selections included below), the biographies being assembled and translated from various ancient sources; likewise, a gazetteer of the ancient world (beginning with Abdera, 'a city in *Thracia*, which was first builded by Hercules in remembrance of his minion called *Abderitus*, which was there eaten with the horses of Diomedes. In this city were born Democritus, the great philosopher, and Protagoras, the famous rhetorician. This city was afterward called *Clazomenae*'); in addition, accounts of a number of often still obscure antiquities, for example the Roman *centumuiri*:

> Whereas the people of Rome were divided into thirty-five tribes, of every tribe were three men chosen to be judges in common matters, which company was called *Centumuiratus*; and they were called *Centumuiri*, although that there were five mo than a hundred in that company; and their judgment was named *Centum uirale iuditium* and *Centum uiralis hasta*, forasmuch as those judges, whilst they sat in judgment, had a spear pitched up before them.

'The past is a foreign country', it is said; and a foreign country is a foreign country, naturally; in consequence, the past of a foreign country is a foreign country twice over: doubly estranged and so doubly instructive.[30] More's *Utopia* makes something of such a principle, though chiefly in the realm of imagination; Elyot's later writings are the same or similar, but founded in history. For historical translation too could be a means for demonstrating that things need not be the way they were, inasmuch as other peoples, in other places, at other times, had in fact done things differently.

Image of Governance (1541) is the chief instance. *Governour* had ended with 'the last part of moral sapience and the beginning of sapience politic'; *Image* presents itself as fulfilling the implicit promise to treat of wisdom, no more in personal ethics, but in political action: it is 'a book of the form of good governance'.[31] Like the second book of More's *Utopia*, Elyot's *Image* essays

Dictionary', *Journal of Medieval and Early Modern Studies*, 47 (2017), 305–26 (pp. 306–07); Considine, 'Wisdom-Literature in Early Modern England', *Renaissance Studies*, 13 (1999), 325–42 (pp. 331–32); and DeWitt T. Starnes, 'Literary Features of Renaissance Dictionaries', *Studies in Philology*, 37 (1940), 26–50 (pp. 26 and 34–37), and 'Sir Thomas Elyot and the "Sayings of the Philosophers"', *Studies in English*, 13 (1933), 5–35 (pp. 10–12).

30 'The past is a foreign country: they do things differently there' is the initial phrase of the novel *The Go-Between* (1953), by L. P. Hartley; cf. Gillespie, *English Translation and Classical Reception*, p. 21, 'One might allow a foreign text to suggest new ways of inhabiting one's own culture or use it to explore the fault-lines within one's own identity'.

31 *Gov.* 3.30 (Watson, p. 297) and *Image* pref., p. 171 below. In *Gov.* 2.7 (Watson, p. 145), Elyot also promised to write something like *Defence*: 'But I shall forbear to speak more of Livia now, for as much as I purpose to make a book only for ladies, wherein her laud shall be more amply expressed'. In fact, *Defence* includes a *Utopia* 2-like account of an ideal polity, in its description of 'the form of good governance' in the regime of Zenobia, subject to much counsel; see *Defence*, pp. 166–67 below.

representation of an ideal polity, but in historical practice. *Image* is a dramatic narrative account of the regime of the later Roman emperor Alexander Severus (imp. 222–235), considerable parts of it translated from the *Historia augusta* (*c.* 395?).[32] After the instructively bad reign of a tyrant, next a version of Plato's philosopher-king accedes to Aristotelian royalty, in which all are subject to law, including the ruler, and, with much counsel, he reforms the state, but only for the public, common good,[33] until an uncivil military unit at the empire's German limit murders him. Elyot's work being historical and realistic, rather than ideal and imaginary, *Image* needs show that Alexander and the kind of *imperium* he tried failed and fell. For the empire in the time of Alexander Severus was neither utopic nor eutopic — not 'no place' but not simply a 'good place' either. Rather, because it was 'some place' in history, it was also imperfect.

Image of Governance remains an instruction in 'good governance', nonetheless. Elyot calls his account of Alexander Severus a *speculum* ('all his

[32] The SHA are notoriously factitious to begin with; on Elyot's relations with this source, see Mary Lascelles, 'Sir Thomas Elyot and the Legend of Alexander Severus', *Review of English Studies*, 2 (1951), 305–18, and Uwe Baumann, 'Sir Thomas Elyot's *The Image of Governance*: A Humanist's *Speculum Principis* and a Literary Puzzle', in *The Virtues of Language*, ed. by Dieter Stein and Rosanna Sornicola (Amsterdam: Benjamins, 1998), pp. 177–99 (pp. 179–92). As Lascelles and Baumann point out (with Hogrefe, *Life and Times*, pp. 323–24; William G. Crane, *Wit and Rhetoric in the Renaissance* (New York, NY: Columbia University Press, 1937), pp. 36–37 and 117–20; and Croft, *Boke Named the Gouernour*, I, cxliv–cxlv), an inspiration for Elyot's further elaborations would have been the work of his contemporary Antonio de Guevara (*c.* 1480–1545), whom he may have met. Guevara's inventive biography of Marcus Aurelius (imp. 161–180), *Libro áureo de Marco Aurelio emperador y elocuentísimo orador* (1528) — incorporating an invented account of the same sort of fictional sourcing that Elyot used for *Image*, though in fact it was based on SHA, *Marc.* — was widely circulated, including the English translation by John Bourchier, Lord Berners, published in 1535 by Elyot's publisher: *Golden Boke of Marcus Aurelius* (London: Berthelet, 1535); on it, see Joyce Boro, 'Lord Berners and His Books: A New Survey', *Huntington Library Quarterly*, 67 (2004), 236–49 (pp. 245–46). Guevara also fashioned a SHA-derived biography of Alexander Severus, included in *Una década de Césares* (1539), his collection of further imperial biographies. It is indicated below that Elyot's biography of Alexander derives independently from SHA, *Alex. Sev.*, rather than from Guevara's version; nevertheless, Guevara was much studied otherwise in England. For example, the poet Wyatt's correspondent Francis Bryan, at whose 'instant desyre' Berners made the *Libro áureo* translation, himself translated Guevara's *Menosprecio de corte y alabanza de aldea* in the same late fifteen-thirties period, though the translation was not printed for some years: *A Dispraise of the Life of a Courtier and a Commendacion of the Life of the Labouryng Man* (London: Richard Grafton, 1548); Bryan also versified selections of Elyot's *Banquet of Sapience*. On his work, see David R. Carlson, 'The Henrician Courtier Writing in Manuscript and Print', in *Companion to Tudor Literature and Culture 1485–1603*, ed. by Kent Cartwright (Chicester: Wiley-Blackwell, 2010), pp. 151–77 (pp. 158–59).

[33] For the political logic of Elyot's narration, see Skinner, *Foundations*, I, 222–28; though also Alistair Fox, 'English Humanism and the Body Politic', in *Reassessing the Henrician Age*, ed. by Fox and John Guy (Oxford: Blackwell, 1986), pp. 34–51 (pp. 45–46), and Walker, *Writing Under Tyranny*, pp. 266–67.

life is a wonderful mirror'), though it is directed expressly to governors again — 'noble lords, gentle knights, and other in the state of honour or worship, as being most ready to be advanced to governance' — intended to be 'a very true pattern, whereby they may shape all their proceedings'.[34] *Image of Governance* teaches how governors might act by imagining how they did so in a delimiting historical circumstance. For within the historiographic frame, delineating the status of a republic in the manner of *Utopia* 2, *Image* also incorporates a series of imagined dialogues, similar to the 'Dialogue of Counsel' in *Utopia* 1, which likewise purports to be historical, though of course it too cannot be.[35] Elyot's historical Alexander Severus takes counsel on counsel, debating the matter of the monarch's 'affability and familiarity' in his relations with subordinates (chaps 6–7), for example, and the problems of patronage and its corruptions (chaps 14–15). Some such episodes are historical dramatizations — 'in quick sentences and eloquent orations' — of topics treated discursively in *Governour*. There are reported debates on public health (chap. 23) and on religion, with introduction of Christian doctrines amongst a people previously unexposed (chap. 25); on the proprieties of social hierarchy — 'good order', again, or 'degree' — specifically the obligations of dominance and subservience within a class-stratified polity (chaps 27–29); on usury, detailing historical depredations of the regime of private property that the Utopians had done away with (chaps 30–32); and on the nature of true nobility, historically bodying forth the humanist

34 *Image* prol. (pp. 172–73); cf. *Image* epilogue (p. 312) the 'life may worthily be a pattern to knights, an example to judges, a mirror to princes, a beautiful image to all them that are like to be governors, whereby they may have in continual remembrance to embrace and follow his most excellent qualities'; with the comment of Baumann, 'Sir Thomas Elyot's *The Image of Governance*', p. 178.

35 Hexter, *More's Utopia*, pp. 103–55, and 'Thomas More and the Problem of Counsel', in *Quincentennial Essays on St. Thomas More*, ed. by Michael J. Moore (Boone, NC: Albion, 1978), pp. 55–66. On this problem of counsel in English humanism and its socio-political causes, see esp. Skinner, *Foundations*, I, 216–20; also, Gilbert, 'The Humanist Concept of the Prince', pp. 471–76; Lehmberg, 'English Humanists, the Reformation, and the Problem of Counsel', *Archiv für Reformationsgeschichte*, 52 (1961), 74–90; Fox, 'English Humanism and the Body Politic', in *Reassessing the Henrician Age*, ed. by Fox and Guy, pp. 34–51; A. J. Slavin, 'Platonism and the Problem of Counsel in *Utopia*', in *Reformation, Humanism and 'Revolution'*, ed. by Gordon J. Schochet (Washington, DC: Folger Shakespeare Library, 1990), pp. 207–34; John S. Guy, 'The Henrician Age', in *Varieties of British Political Thought, 1500–1800*, ed. by J. G. A. Pocock (Cambridge: Cambridge University Press, 1993), pp. 13–46 (esp. pp. 14–22), and 'The Rhetoric of Counsel in Early Modern England', in *Tudor Political Culture*, ed. by Dale Hoak (Cambridge: Cambridge University Press, 1995), pp. 292–310; Helen Barr and Kate Ward-Perkins, '"Speking for One's Sustenance": The Rhetoric of Counsel in *Mum and the Sothsegger*, Skelton's *Bowge of Court*, and Elyot's *Pasquil the Playne*', in *The Long Fifteenth Century*, ed. by Helen Cooper and Sally Mapstone (Oxford: Clarendon, 1997), pp. 249–72; and W. Scott Blanchard, 'Skelton's Critique of Wealth and the Autonomy of the Early Modern Intellectual', in *John Skelton and Early Modern Culture*, ed. by David R. Carlson (Tempe, AZ: Arizona Center for Medieval and Renaissance Studies, 2008), pp. 45–62 (pp. 55–57).

commonplace *uirtus non sanguis* (chaps 33–34).[36] Lengthy dramatization of the case of a person who is reluctant to take on conciliar responsibilities, like More's Raphael Hythlodaeus, also incorporates debate about the relative merits of book-learned theory and practical experience as qualifications for governors (chaps 34–36). For his own counsellors, it is claimed, Alexander favoured lawyers: 'he would never make decree or ordinance without twenty lawyers' (chaps 8–10). And even there is secular sanction against dicing amongst the empire's governors: Alexander promulgated law against it ('ratified by the authority of all the Senate and people'); he 'would not have any of them called either to office or council' who, 'after the said law being made, were found to be dice-players' (chap. 22).[37]

With 'his wise and virtuous mother', 'a woman of notable wisdom', Alexander debates the merits of various marriage possibilities, including the problem of taking a foreign-born woman to wife, by reason of 'the wars, which hath and mought eftsoons happen to be between us and these outward countries' (chap. 26). As with the preference for lawyers or the sanction of playing at dice, it is tempting to find allegory in such a place: to imagine that, rather than being a historically based discussion of the problem of succession in the third-century empire, the dialogue on marriage in *Image of Governance* concerns Henry VIII's particular difficulties in some strong sense.[38] Elyot's remarks on imperial

[36] On this topic, see Skinner, *Foundations*, I, 236–38 and 257–62.

[37] Cf. Elyot, *Gov.* 1.26 (Watson, pp. 108–11).

[38] Though Elyot disavows allegory, in *Gov.* proem (Watson, p. xxxi), 'Protesting unto your excellent majesty that, where I commend herein any one virtue or dispraise any one vice, I mean the general description of the one and the other without any other particular meaning to the reproach of any one person' (and cf. *Knowledge*, proem, p. 70 below), there has been much such explication. Most sustained and persuasive are the chapters on Elyot in Walker, *Writing Under Tyranny*, pp. 147–77, 181–224, 225–39, and 240–75 (including 257–58 on the 'marriage' debate in *Image*, and 268–69 on Elyot's preference for lawyers), with Walker, 'Sir Thomas Elyot and the Politics of Accomodation: The Defence of Good Women', in *Persuasive Fictions: Faction, Faith, and Political Culture in the Reign of Henry VIII* (Aldershot: Scolar, 1996), pp. 178–203; however, see also Lehmberg, 'English Humanists', pp. 79–85, and Hogrefe, *Life and Times*, pp. 193–94 (among other things, arguing that Pasquil is Elyot); Constance Jordan, 'Feminism and the Humanists: The Case of Sir Thomas Elyot's *Defence of Good Women*', *Renaissance Quarterly*, 36 (1983), 181–201 (pp. 198–201; Zenobia is Henry VIII's queen Katherine); Conrad, 'The Problem of Counsel Reconsidered', pp. 99–102 (*Pasquil*'s Harpocrates is Wolsey); and Alistair Fox, 'Sir Thomas Elyot and the Humanist Dilemma', in *Reassessing the Henrician Age*, ed. by Fox and Guy, pp. 63–73 (where Harpocrates is said to stand for Cranmer). The view herein accords instead with the anti-allegorical conclusions of Shrank, 'Sir Thomas Elyot and the Bonds of Community', e.g. p. 155: the autobiographical approach 'fails to acknowledge Elyot's continued promotion of his humanist agenda'; his writings 'were steeped with a sense of public duty, and most drew on classical material, thus displaying a key characteristic of Renaissance humanism: the application of classical learning in service of the *vita activa*'; also, Neil Rhodes, 'Introduction', in *English Renaissance Translation Theory*, ed. by Rhodes with Gordon Kendal and Louise Wilson (London: Modern Humanities Research Association, 2013), p. 35:

marriage would have interested the King, his people, and other contemporaries, of course, in consequence of the remarks' potential application to present circumstance. 'Such are the materials that history provides those who choose to make use of them', Plutarch explained.[39] Potential for application does not make the remarks stand for Henry's problems immediately, allegory-wise, however, as if the ancient Roman imperial matter were only a vehicle for conveying contemporary tenor. It is the nature of Elyot's translative undertakings never to be simply contemporary-allegorical or autobiographical. Although, by virtue of the Plutarchan principle, the writings always also carry potential for contemporary, topical application, Elyot's translating, broad and narrow, was fundamentally an education in history of the sort he espoused abstractly in *Governour.*

Elyot's translations of ancient matter provoke the same question that More's *Utopia* does, however obliquely: 'what is to be done'?[40] Moreover, Elyot's historical-educative translations provoke such questioning by the same unsettling formal means used by More in *Utopia*, as well as widely elsewhere, in other works by More and Erasmus and in contemporary drama:[41] varieties of dialogue. It is the nature of dialogue — Socratic or Ciceronian or Lucianic, Menippean or dramatic — to represent divergent points of view, most often in the absence of an obvious (or external) authority. Reader-audiences need participate in the debates. Just like the 'Dialogue of Counsel' comprising *Utopia* 1, by focusing attention on the uncertainties, Elyot's dramatizations require participative reflection.

Though the earliest of Elyot's dialogues, *Pasquil the Plain* (1533), is the least a direct interlingual translation, its conceit was translated from contemporary-historical foreign practice: at Rome, by 1509, after excavation of an ancient statue thought to represent a Roman deity, *Pasquillus* or *Pasquinus*, the custom arose of affixing to the statue and its base brief Anthesterian or Saturnalian satires, in

Elyot's 'publications had entirely pragmatic ends in view and their watchword is common profit. [...] Elyot redefined the role of translator as that of public servant'.

39 Plut., *Aem.* 5.10.

40 The quotation is from *Gov.* 3.28 (Watson, p. 291): 'The griefs or diseases which of Aristotle be called the decays of the public weal being investigate, examined, and tried, by the experience before expressed, then cometh the time and opportunity of consultation, whereby, as I said, is provided the remedies most necessary for the healing of the said griefs or reparation of decay. This thing that is called consultation is the general denomination of the act wherein men do devise together and reason what is to be done' (see Walker, *Writing Under Tyranny*, p. 147) — though it is also the title of V. I. Lenin's 1902 'dialogue of counsel', which begins with a section 'Dogmatism and "Freedom of Criticism"'.

41 An early influence of drama on Thomas More's later work with forms of dialogue is recognized, for example, in Howard B. Norland, *Drama in Early Tudor Britain, 1485–1558* (Lincoln, NE: University of Nebraska Press, 1995), pp. 111–27; the same influences as are analysed in Edward Berry, 'Thomas More and the Legal Imagination', *Studies in Philology*, 106 (2009), 316–40 (pp. 321–28), would have operated on Elyot too.

which the lowly might attack the elevated without fear of reprisal, once a year, on 25 April. The practice was institutionalised — amongst the earliest official presidents was the English cardinal-archbishop Christopher Bainbridge (d.1514), for whom Elyot's collaborator Richard Pace (d.1536) was working as a secretary at the time — and the satires were regularly put into print.[42] In his dialogue, Elyot pits Pasquil himself — the statue come to life, epitomising plain-speaking — against other types of counsellors: the proverbial flatterer Gnatho, named after the scheming, obsequious slave in Terence, like other ancient comedy; and the grave Harpocrates, a Greco-Egyptian deity of silence and restraint of speech. Which type of counsellor is best? By such means, Elyot's dialogue translates into modern English culture the model of the dialogues of the Greek Lucian of Samosata (125–180 CE), whose work Erasmus and More translated into Latin and imitated, as in *Moriae encomium*. The meeting amongst Elyot's three quasi-personifications is an unhistorical imaginative fiction, as in Lucianic dialogue; at the same time, and again as in Lucian, the problems discussed on the imaginary occasion amongst the imaginary interlocutors are historical and real: problems of counsel, as adumbrated in *Utopia* 1.[43] Occasionally drawing on historical cases — the English-born pope Adrian IV (r. 1154–1159) and Bainbridge's poisoning, trouble with the Scotist scholasticism, the 1527 sack of Rome, and so on — the argument explicates lines translated from the Greek *Choēphoroi*, with explicit attribution of it to Aeschylus (*c.* 525–455 BCE): 'I say 'twere well to bear a tongue | Full of fair silence and of fitting speech | As each beseems the time'.[44]

By contrast, *Doctrinal of Princes* ([1533?]), strictly interlingual translation,[45]

[42] See Anne Reynolds, 'Cardinal Oliviero Carafa and the Early Cinquecento Tradition of the Feast of Pasquino', *Humanistica Lovaniensia*, 34A (1985), 178–208 (esp. 184–205); also, 'The Classical Continuum in Roman Humanism: The Festival of Pasquino, the *Robigalia*, and Satire', *Bibliothèque d'Humanisme et Renaissance*, 49 (1987), 289–307; and Julia Haig Gaisser, 'The Rise and Fall of Goritz's Feasts', *Renaissance Quarterly*, 48 (1995), 41–57 (pp. 50–51 and 53). For the early English involvement, see D. S. Chambers, *Cardinal Bainbridge in the Court of Rome, 1509 to 1514* (Oxford: Oxford University Press, 1965), pp. 121–25; Bainbridge referred to Pace as 'Master Pasquil'.

[43] See Arthur E. Walzer, 'The Rhetoric of Counsel in Thomas Elyot's *Pasquil the Playne*', *Rhetorica*, 30 (2012), 1–21 (pp. 5–7). Amidst the preponderance of historical names there, in *Image*, chaps 38–39, 'Geminus', 'Moderatus', 'Rutilius Lupus', and 'Carnilius' may also be Lucianic personifications.

[44] Elyot may have known the lines from the discussion in Eras., *Apoph.*, 1 ded. ep. (= *Ep.* 2431), CWE 37, p. 12 and nn.; cf. the comments of Walzer, 'The Rhetoric of Counsel in Thomas Elyot's *Pasquil the Playne*', p. 8. Conrad, 'Problem of Counsel', p. 89, adduces instead [ps.-]Aesch., *PV* 379–382, 'OCEANUS: Do you not know then, Prometheus, that words are the physicians of a disordered temper? PROMETHEUS: If one softens the soul in season, and does not hasten to reduce its swelling rage by violence'.

[45] On Elyot's translating in *Doctrinal*, see James Wortham, 'Sir Thomas Elyot and the Translation of Prose', *Huntington Library Quarterly*, 11(1948), 219–40 (pp. 230 and 236–40). Erasmus's rather different Latin version had been printed first with the *Institutio principis*

is only implicitly dialogic. Translated from the Greek work now known as *Ad Nicoclem*, it is an address by the historical Isocrates (436–338 BCE), one of the canonical ten 'Attic Orators', to the historical king Nicocles of Cyprian Salamis (r. *c.* 374–360 BCE), son of the historical (and even more renowned) king Euagoras (411–374 BCE). The oration addresses a young monarch on the subject of right rule.[46] Elyot's chief or only significant author-like intervention is the explanatory title; for the oration consists only of platitudinous doctrine or counsel, expressed in the same form of epigrammatic *sententiae* that Elyot was to use in *Banquet of Sapience* (1539), his own English miscellany of translated doctrines, which the poet Wyatt's notorious friend Francis Bryan (*c.* 1490–1550) rendered into likewise sententious English pentameter verse. Skelton amalgamated a similar list of sentences (in Latin) for Henry when Skelton was Henry's tutor in the fifteenth century.[47] At the back of the revised second edition of Elyot's *Doctrinal*, the complementary, sententious wisdom on kingly regimen included in the 'ADDITION, TO FILL UP vacant pages' is likewise translation (with expansive periphrastic explication), but of royal-Solomonic counsel from the Bible: 'Mercy and Truth do keep the king' and so forth.[48]

Of the Knowledge Which Maketh a Wise Man (1533) is likewise historical, inasmuch as it concerns an episode in the relations amongst Plato (*c.* 429–347 BCE), the Syracusan king Dionysius I (*c.* 430–367 BCE), and the adherents and opponents of both. Plato was induced to leave Athens and to attempt to put his political ideas into practice in Dionysian Sicily; but Dionysius was interested only in decorating his regime with an appearance of sage counsel;

christiani in 1516: see Erika Rummel, *Erasmus as a Translator of the Classics* (Toronto: University of Toronto Press, 1985), pp. 103–08; Elyot would have studied it at some point or at least have seen it. Nevertheless, *Doctrinal* is held to be the first published instance of direct Greek prose to English translation: see Stephen Medcalf, 'Classical Authors', in *The Oxford History of Literary Translation in English Volume 1 to 1550*, ed. by Roger Ellis (Oxford: Oxford University Press, 2008), pp. 364–89 (pp. 384–86). In any case, there are other instances embedded in Elyot's writings, including the full English of a previously untranslated Greek prose *Fabula Aesopica* in the preface to *Image*, below, p. 173.

46 In the matched piece *Nicocles*, written after *Ad Nicoclem*, Isocrates (impersonating the king) indoctrinates a ruler's subjects on their proper duties. Elyot may not have known it, though he praises Isocrates in *Gov.* 1.11 (Watson, p. 42): 'Isocrates, concerning the lesson of orators, is everywhere wonderful profitable, having almost as many wise sentences as he hath words; and with that is so sweet and delectable to read that, after him, almost all other seem unsavoury and tedious; and in persuading as well a prince as a private person to virtue, in two very little and compendious works, whereof he made the one to King Nicocles, the other to his friend Demonicus, would be perfectly conned, and had in continual memory'; and cf. Elyot, *Bibl.*, '*Isocrates*, the name of a famous orator, of wonderful eloquence, out of whose school proceeded the most excellent orators of Greece'.

47 For Bryan's contribution, see Kinsman, '"The Proverbes of Salmon"'; for Skelton's, his *Speculum principis*, 113–151, in *Latin Writings of John Skelton* (Chapel Hill, NC: University of North Carolina Press, 1991), pp. 36–37.

48 On the 'ADDITION', see Walker, *Writing Under Tyranny*, p. 223.

Plato warned Dionysius of tyranny, and so Dionysius sold his counsel-giving philosopher into slavery. Though the historical basis of the episode is best known from the Platonic *Ep.* 7 — Morus and Hythlodaeus discuss it in *Utopia* 1, when Hythlodaeus is facing the ancient Platonic dilemma, to counsel or not to counsel — Elyot translated instead the version in the intellectual biography of Plato in the *Vitae philosophorum* of Diogenes Laertius (fl. mid-third century CE).[49] Elyot also translated from the same work parts of the life of the contemporary philosopher Aristippus (*c.* 435–350 BCE), another of Socrates's immediate followers, who also visited Dionysian Syracuse, where, being less fiercely doctrinaire than Plato, he did rather better.[50] The non-historical, imaginative conceit of Elyot's dialogue is that, having escaped his enslavement, walking home towards Athens, Plato meets Aristippus in the road and the two argue: what is the wise man's duty in such circumstance, to speak or to withhold the truth? These historical personages' imaginary conversation is markedly more maieutic in its development than Elyot's other dialogues;[51] by way of it, the philosophers conclude that 'the act of speaking truth' is 'the operation of knowledge'; knowledge being power, its possession obligates a person to speak.[52]

Defence of Good Women (1540) is also an imaginative fiction — the dialogues represented in it did not take place — except that it is historical as well, inasmuch as it pieces together a life of the West Asian emperor Zenobia (*c.* 270–272), translated from the *Historia augusta*. In addition, the dialogue incorporates brief biographical *exempla* of a number of other historical figures, translated from standard collections like Diogenes Laertius and Valerius Maximus's *Facta et dicta memorabilia* (*c.* 30 CE), though it also translates relatively more rare or recently recovered ancient sources, including the Greek Appian (*c.* 95–*c.* 165), the *Annales* of Cornelius Tacitus (*c.* 56–*c.* 120), and Quintillian's *Institutio oratoria* (*c.* 95). Elyot is only translating, while also setting his late third-century historical matter within an invented drama, another Lucianic satire like *Pasquil*

[49] More, *Utopia* 1, ed. by Surtz and Hexter, 86.16–20. The citation of 'Plato in his Epistle to Dion', in *Gov.* 3.13 (Watson, p. 313) indicates that Elyot knew the letter, or knew of it; moreover, in *Gov.* 3.14 (Watson, pp. 241–42) Elyot has another version of the story (without deportation or sale into slavery), possibly deriving from Plut., *Dion* 5.1–7.

[50] For the characterisation, see Robert Haynes, 'Plato as Protagonist in Sir Thomas Elyot's *Of the Knowledge Which Maketh a Wise Man*', in *Author as Character*, ed. by Paul Franssen and Ton Hoenselaars (Madison, NJ: Fairleigh Dickinson University Press, 1999), pp. 93–105 (esp. p. 94); Walker, *Writing Under Tyranny*, pp. 202–10; and Walzer, 'The Rhetoric of Counsel and Thomas Elyot's *Of the Knowledge Which Maketh a Wise Man*', *Philosophy and Rhetoric*, 45 (2012), 24–45 (pp. 27–28 and 30).

[51] Wilson, *Incomplete Fictions*, pp. 87–103, and Caspari, *Humanism and the Social Order*, pp. 173–74. The dialogue's structure is a better indication of Elyot's knowledge of the Platonic dialogues than the (relatively few) verbal borrowings from Plato that have been identified in Elyot's writings.

[52] Wilson, *Incomplete Fictions*, p. 97.

the Plain. Zenobia is introduced, in 274 CE precisely but as if on a stage, to settle an argument between the sort of quasi-personifications that Elyot set to action in *Pasquil*. Here Candidus, 'which may be interpreted "benign" or "gentle"', uses historical Zenobia to change the mind of a *sodalis* of his, Caninus, who, 'like a cur, at women's conditions is alway barking'.[53]

Book 1 of More's *Utopia* establishes that problems of counsel were vivid from early in the reign of Henry VIII. The issues remained vivid thereafter, especially amongst the humanist-trained scholars that England's college-schools and universities were producing in ever greater numbers, as the Tudor monarch and his governors solidified the inchoate absolutism. As one of these humanists, who had experience of counselling, Elyot returned to problems of counsel again and again, in a great part of his writings, from *Governour* to *Image of Governance*. However, Elyot was not only or simply recurring to his own personal problems. The larger context of Elyot's other writings indicates that in his several dialogues of counsel he was also popularising a humanist approach to ancient Western civilisation: importing greater knowledge of Greco-Roman historical antecedents and humanist political analysis into the English cultural ambit for the use they might be in addressing the likewise still vivid problems of *Utopia* 2, *de optimo rei publicae statu*. It may occasion regret that Elyot chose inferior ancient sources sometimes, when other, better ones were available, as in choosing to translate Diogenes Laertius, for example, when Plato's proper letters remained to be parsed for an English audience; or that Elyot preferred class-stratification to primitive communism, or absolute monarchy to modern anarcho-syndicalism. Nevertheless, by their translation of such a deal of classical matter into the contemporary English idiom, Elyot's dialogues helped orient nascent Tudor political discussion towards various possibilities latent in the ancient collocation *respublica* and its humanist analyses. His choices of English for a language and of dialogue-dramas for form vivified the discussion for relatively broad, popular participation.

[53] On the dialogue, see Jordan, 'Feminism and the Humanists', esp. pp. 184–98; Valerie Wayne, 'Zenobia in Medieval and Renaissance Literature', in *Ambiguous Realities*, ed. by Carole Levin and Jeanie Watson (Detroit, MI: Wayne State University Press, 1987), pp. 48–65 (pp. 53–54 and 57–59); Pamela Joseph Benson, *Invention of the Renaissance Woman* (University Park, PA: Pennsylvania State University Press, 1992), pp. 183–203; and Valerie Schutte, *Mary I and the Art of Book Dedications* (New York, NY: Palgrave Macmillan, 2015), pp. 25–30. Though Boccaccio, *De mul. clar.* is regularly cited in the notes to *Defence*, there is no indication that Elyot used it; Boccaccio and Elyot had recourse to the same ancient sources, and in fact Elyot used a considerable amount of material that he cannot have had from Boccaccio. On the near contemporary English prose translation, see James Simpson, 'The Sacrifice of Lady Rochford: Henry Parker's Translation of *De claris mulieribus*', in *The Triumphs of English: Henry Parker, Lord Morley*, ed. by Marie Axton and James P. Carley (London: British Library, 2000), pp. 153–69.

The Editions

No manuscripts survive. The editions of Elyot's writings herein are based on copies of the first printed editions, collated with copies of second and subsequent printed editions published during Elyot's life, for the corrections and revision of which Elyot may have been responsible, to some extent or other.[54] The editions are listed in the headnotes to each edition, with their assigned *sigla*, and the variants discovered by collation are given in textual footnotes, in the standard form: *lemma*] *variae lectiones* (the textual-footnote indication ° appearing at the beginning of the *lemmata* at issue). The abbreviations *om* and *add*, following editions-*sigla*, represent *omittit* and *addidit*, respectively, meaning that the edition indicated by *siglum* omits or adds the term or terms in question (though no judgement of error should be inferred from the abbreviations' use). The marginalia of the printed editions, generally relegated to the footnote-lists of variants, are enclosed in slashes \ /. Otherwise, all additions to the texts of the original editions (including foliations) and other departures from the texts (chiefly minor editorial corrections) are enclosed in angled brackets <>,[55] excepting the departures from the texts' spellings.

The original editions' spelling has been modernised, tacitly, chiefly by the regularisation of forms, in accordance with the headword spellings of *OED* (with the exception sometimes of variants listed in the footnotes, where the original spellings may be of heuristic value). The same procedure has been followed throughout, in all quotations of Early Modern English. No other effort to translate Elyot's (or others') writing into a later form of Modern English has been made. In practice, these procedures have meant that various word-forms obsolete after *c.* 1550 are still kept (without further comment): e.g. EME plural nouns in *-en* (*eyen* for 'eyes', *shoen* for 'shoes', etc.); EME past-tense verb forms ending in *-en* (*bounden* for 'bound', *founden* for 'found', etc.); and so on. Elyot was attentive to such figures of speech as rhythm and rhyme, and in some cases his effects depend on particular word-forms.[56] Be that as it may, the conceit is

[54] Something of an exception is *Doctrinal*, where the text is from the second edition (*c.* 1550), collated with the first ([1533?]). The second edition is more thoroughly revised (and improved) than seems usual with Elyot's writings; the second edition also adds an apologetic prologue and an appendix of scriptural translations, both supplied by Elyot, evidently both wanting in the first edition.

[55] An exception again is in the text of *Doctrinal*: the sequence of angle-bracketed numerals embedded in it, <1>–<54>, represents the standard enumeration of the periods of the Greek original, to expedite comparison with Elyot's version.

[56] Cf. Wortham, 'Sir Thomas Elyot and the Translation of Prose', pp. 227, 235, and 237–38; also, Anne Drury Hall, 'Tudor Prose Style: English Humanists and the Problem of a Standard', *English Literary Renaissance*, 7 (1977), 267–96 (pp. 283–84). Instructive illustration of Elyot's usage and its evolution is in Elisabeth Holmes, 'The Significance of Elyot's Revision of the *Gouernour*', *Review of English Studies*, 12 (1961), 352–63; and on the usage controversies, see also Massimiliano Morini, *Tudor Translation in Theory and Practice* (Burlington, VT: Ashgate, 2006), pp. 27 and 43–45.

that in context the forms' significances are readily apprehensible; and in any event, forms and terms and meanings of terms no longer in use are listed in the 'Word List' below, where the definitions and explanations have for the most part been taken or adapted from *OED*.

ELYOT CHRONOLOGY

c. 1490	birth
c. 1510	marriage to Margaret Barlow (d. 1560)
1510	London Middle Temple Clerk's Commons
1510–1526	Clerk to the Western Circuit Justices of Assize
1515–1529	Justice of the Peace, Oxfordshire and Wiltshire
1522	death of father
<1522.12	*Papyrii Gemini Eleatis Hermathena, seu De eloquentia victoria>*
1523–1530	King's Council Senior Clerk
1527	Sheriff, Oxfordshire and Wiltshire
1529	Sheriff, Oxfordshire and Wiltshire
1530	knighthood
1530–	Justice of the Peace, Cambridgeshire
[1530?]	*Education or Bringing up of Children* (trans. Plut.)
1531	*Governour*
<[1531?]	*How one may take profit of his enemies* (trans. Plut.)>
1531.09–1532.01	Ambassador to Charles V
1532.01–06	Continental travels
<[1532?]	*Dialogue between Lucian and Diogenes* (trans. Lucian)>
[1532?]	repr. *Education or Bringing up of Children*
1533	*Pasquil the Plain* and repr.
1533	*Of the Knowledge Which Maketh a Wise Man*
[1533?]	*Doctrinal of Princes* (trans. Isoc.)
1534	*Sweet and Devout Sermon of Holy Saint Cyprian* and *Rules of a Christian Life* (trans. Pico della Mirandola)
1537.07	repr. *Governour*
[1537?]	*Castle of Health*
1538	*Dictionary*
1539	MP (Knight of the Shire), Cambridgeshire
1539	repr. *Castle of Health*
1539	*Banquet of Sapience*
1539	repr. *Sweet and Devout Sermon of Holy Saint Cyprian* and *Rules of a Christian Life*
1540	*Defence of Good Women*
1540	repr. *Pasquil the Plain*
1541	2nd ed. *Castle of Health*

1541	*Image of Governance*
1542	*Bibliotheca Eliotae* (= 2nd ed. *Dictionary*)
1542	2nd ed. *Banquet of Sapience*
1544	repr. *Governour*
1544	repr. *Image of Governance*
[1544?]	repr. 2nd ed. *Castle of Health*
1545.07	*Preservative Against Death*
1545	repr. *Bibliotheca Eliotae*
1545	repr. *Defence of Good Women*
<[1545?]	repr. *How one may take profit of his enemies* (with Francis Poyntz, *Table of Cebes*)>
1545	repr. 2nd ed. *Banquet of Sapience*
1546	repr. *Governour*
1546.03.26	death

< > enclosing dubious attributions

ABBREVIATIONS

Boccaccio, *De mulier. clar.* = Boccaccio, Giovanni, *De mulieribus claris*, in *Famous Women*, ed. and trans. by Virginia Brown, I Tatti Renaissance Library (Cambridge, MA: Harvard University Press, 2001)

CEBR = *Contemporaries of Erasmus: A Biographical Register of the Renaissance and Reformation*, ed. by Peter G. Bietenholz and Thomas B. Deutscher, 3 vols (Toronto: University of Toronto Press, 1985–1987)

CWE = *Collected Works of Erasmus*, 86 vols (Toronto: University of Toronto Press, 1974–)

ESTC = *English Short Title Catalogue* online (London: British Library, 1994–) http://estc.bl.uk

OCD = *Oxford Classical Dictionary* online edition (Oxford: Oxford University Press, 2012) DOI: 10.1093/acref/9780199545568.001.0001

ODNB = *Oxford Dictionary of National Biography* online edition (Oxford: Oxford University Press, 2008–) http://www.oxforddnb.com

OED = *Oxford English Dictionary* online edition (Oxford: Oxford University Press, 2003–) http://www.oed.com

RSTC = *A Short-Title Catalogue of Books Printed in England, Scotland, & Ireland and of English Books Printed Abroad, 1475–1640*, first compiled by A. W. Pollard and G. R. Redgrave, 2nd ed., revised and enlarged, begun by W. A. Jackson and F. S. Ferguson, completed by Katharine F. Pantzer, 3 vols (London: Bibliographical Society, 1976–1991)

Watson = Elyot, Thomas, *The Boke Named the Governour*, ed. by Foster Watson (London: Dent, n. d. [1907])

Elyot's writings are cited by short titles, ordinarily the first noun, excepting *Gov.* = *Governour* and *Bibl.* = *Bibliotheca Eliotae*. The writings of Erasmus (ordinarily abbreviated 'Eras.') are cited by the short titles of CWE, excepting *Apoph.* = *Apophthegmata*. The writings of Geoffrey Chaucer are cited by the standard abbreviations, as in Larry D. Benson, gen. ed., *The Riverside Chaucer*, 3rd edn. (Boston, MA: Houghton Mifflin, 1987), p. 779. Books of the Christian Bible are cited by the abbreviations of the Colunga-Turrado edition of the Vulgate *uel sim*. Ancient writings are cited by means of the abbreviations of *OCD*. Conventions for dating early printed books are from ESTC.

BIBLIOGRAPHY

Primary Sources

Babrius and Phaedrus, ed. by Ben Edwin Perry, Loeb Classical Library 436 (Cambridge, MA: Harvard University Press, 1965)

Boccaccio, Giovanni, *De mulieribus claris*, in *Famous Women*, ed. and trans. by Virginia Brown, I Tatti Renaissance Library (Cambridge, MA: Harvard University Press, 2001)

Edward VI, *The First and Second Prayer Books*, ed. by E. C. S. Gibson (London: Dent, 1910)

Elyot, Thomas, *The Boke Named the Gouernour Deuised by Sir Thomas Elyot, Knight*, ed. by Henry Herbert Stephen Croft, 2 vols (London: Kegan Paul, Trench, & Co., 1883)

—— *The Boke Named the Governour*, ed. by Foster Watson (London: Dent, n. d. [1907])

—— *The Letters of Sir Thomas Elyot*, ed. by Kenneth J. Wilson, *Studies in Philology*, Texts and Studies 73 (Chapel Hill, NC: University of North Carolina Press, 1976)

Erasmus, Desiderius, *Collected Works of Erasmus*, 86 vols (Toronto: University of Toronto Press, 1974–)

Fabulae Aesopicae Collectae, ed. by Karl Felix Halm (Leipzig: Teubner, 1889)

Greek Elegiac Poetry, ed. by D. E. Gerber, Loeb Classical Library 258 (Cambridge, MA: Harvard University Press, 1999)

More, Thomas, *Utopia*, ed. by Edward Surtz and J. H. Hexter, Complete Works of St. Thomas More 4 (New Haven, CT: Yale University Press, 1965)

Pace, Richard, *De fructu qui ex doctrina percipitur: The Benefit of a Liberal Education*, ed. by Frank Manley and Richard S. Sylvester (New York, NY: Renaissance Society of America, 1967)

Skelton, John, *The Latin Writings*, ed. by David R. Carlson, *Studies in Philology*, Texts and Studies 88 (Chapel Hill, NC: University of North Carolina Press, 1991)

Secondary Sources

Baker, David Weil, *Divulging Utopia: Radical Humanism in Sixteenth-Century England* (Amherst, MA: University of Massachusetts Press, 1999)

Barr, Helen, and Kate Ward-Perkins, '"Speking for One's Sustenance": The Rhetoric of Counsel in *Mum and the Sothsegger*, Skelton's *Bowge of Court*, and Elyot's *Pasquil the Playne*', in *The Long Fifteenth Century: Essays for Douglas Gray*, ed. by Helen Cooper and Sally Mapstone (Oxford: Clarendon, 1997), pp. 249–72

BAUMANN, UWE, 'Sir Thomas Elyot's *The Image of Governance*: A Humanist's *Speculum Principis* and a Literary Puzzle', in *The Virtues of Language: History in Language, Linguistics and Texts: Papers in Memory of Thomas Frank*, ed. by Dieter Stein and Rosanna Sornicola, Studies in the History of the Language Sciences 87 (Amsterdam: Benjamins, 1998), pp. 177–99

BENSON, PAMELA JOSEPH, *The Invention of the Renaissance Woman: The Challenge of Female Independence in the Literature and Thought of Italy and England* (University Park, PA: Pennsylvania State University Press, 1992)

BERNAU, ANKE, 'Alphabetizing the Nation: Medieval British Origins in Thomas Elyot's *Dictionary*', *Journal of Medieval and Early Modern Studies*, 47 (2017), 305–26

BERRY, EDWARD, 'Thomas More and the Legal Imagination', *Studies in Philology*, 106 (2009), 316–40

BLANCHARD, W. SCOTT, 'Skelton's Critique of Wealth and the Autonomy of the Early Modern Intellectual', in *John Skelton and Early Modern Culture: Papers Honoring Robert S. Kinsman*, ed. by David R. Carlson (Tempe, AZ: Arizona Center for Medieval and Renaissance Studies, 2008), pp. 45–62

BORE, ISABELLE, 'Thomas Elyot: Du courtisan disgrâcié à l'éducateur plébiscité', *Moreana*, 49 (2012), 49–75

BORO, JOYCE, 'Lord Berners and His Books: A New Survey', *Huntington Library Quarterly*, 67 (2004), 236–49

BOTLEY, PAUL, *Learning Greek in Western Europe, 1396–1529: Grammars, Lexica, and Classroom Texts*, Transactions of the American Philosophical Society New Series 100.2 (Philadelphia, PA: American Philosophical Society, 2010)

BURKE, PETER, *Lost (and Found) in Translation: A Cultural History of Translators and Translating in Early Modern Europe* (The Hague: NIAS [Netherlands Institute for Advanced Study], 2005)

—— 'Cultures of Translation in Early Modern Europe', in *Cultural Translation in Early Modern Europe*, ed. by Burke and R. Po-chia Hsia (Cambridge: Cambridge University Press, 2007), pp. 7–38

CARLSON, DAVID R., 'Morley's Translations from Roman Philosophers and English Courtier Literature', in *The Triumphs of English: Henry Parker, Lord Morley, Translator to the Tudor Court*, ed. by Marie Axton and James P. Carley (London: British Library, 2000), pp. 131–51

—— 'The Henrician Courtier Writing in Manuscript and Print: Wyatt, Surrey, Bryan, and Others', in *A Companion to Tudor Literature and Culture 1485–1603*, ed. by Kent Cartwright, Blackwell Companions to Literature and Culture (Chicester: Wiley-Blackwell, 2010), pp. 151–77

CASPARI, FRITZ, *Humanism and the Social Order in Tudor England* (1954; repr. New York, NY: Columbia University Teachers College Press, 1968)

CHAMBERS, D. S., *Cardinal Bainbridge in the Court of Rome, 1509 to 1514* (Oxford: Oxford University Press, 1965)

COLDIRON, A. E. B., 'Translation's Challenge to Critical Categories: Verses from French in the Early English Renaissance', *Yale Journal of Criticism*, 16 (2003), 315–44

—— 'Public Sphere/Contact Zone: Habermas, Early Print, and Verse Translation', *Criticism*, 46 (2004), 207–22

CONRAD, F. W., 'The Problem of Counsel Reconsidered: The Case of Thomas Elyot', in *Political Thought and the Tudor Commonwealth: Deep Structure, Discourse and Disguise*, ed. by Paul A. Fideler and T. F. Mayer (London: Routledge, 1992), pp. 75–107

CONSIDINE, JOHN, 'Wisdom-Literature in Early Modern England', *Renaissance Studies*, 13 (1999), 325–42

—— 'Sir Thomas Elyot Makes a Dictionary', *International Journal of Lexicography*, 27 (2014), 309–18

CRANE, WILLIAM G., *Wit and Rhetoric in the Renaissance: The Formal Basis of Elizabethan Prose Style* (New York, NY: Columbia University Press, 1937)

FERGUSON, ARTHUR B., *The Articulate Citizen and the English Renaissance* (Durham, NC: Duke University Press, 1965)

FISHER, R. M., 'Thomas Cromwell, Humanism and Educational Reform', *Bulletin of the Institute of Historical Research*, 50 (1977), 151–63

FOX, ALISTAIR, 'English Humanism and the Body Politic', in *Reassessing the Henrician Age: Humanism, Politics, and Reform, 1500–1550*, ed. by Fox and John Guy (Oxford: Blackwell, 1986), pp. 34–51

—— 'Sir Thomas Elyot and the Humanist Dilemma', in *Reassessing the Henrician Age: Humanism, Politics, and Reform, 1500–1550*, ed. by Fox and John Guy (Oxford: Blackwell, 1986), pp. 52–73

GAISSER, JULIA HAIG, 'The Rise and Fall of Goritz's Feasts', *Renaissance Quarterly*, 48 (1995), 41–57

GILBERT, FELIX, 'The Humanist Concept of the Prince and the *Prince* of Machiavelli', *Journal of Modern History*, 11 (1939), 449–83

GILLESPIE, STUART, *English Translation and Classical Reception: Towards a New Literary History* (Chichester: Blackwell-Wiley, 2011)

GUY, JOHN S., 'The Henrician Age', in *Varieties of British Political Thought, 1500–1800*, ed. by J. G. A. Pocock with Gordon J. Schochet and Lois Schwerer (Cambridge: Cambridge University Press, 1993), pp. 13–46

—— 'The Rhetoric of Counsel in Early Modern England', in *Tudor Political Culture*, ed. by Dale Hoak (Cambridge: Cambridge University Press, 1995), pp. 292–310

HALL, ANNE DRURY, 'Tudor Prose Style: English Humanists and the Problem of a Standard', *English Literary Renaissance*, 7 (1977), 267–96

HAYNES, ROBERT, 'Plato as Protagonist in Sir Thomas Elyot's *Of the Knowledge Which Maketh a Wise Man*', in *The Author as Character: Representing Historical Writers in Western Literature*, ed. by Paul Franssen and Ton Hoenselaars (Madison, NJ: Fairleigh Dickinson University Press, 1999), pp. 93–105

HEXTER, J. H., *More's Utopia: The Biography of an Idea* (Princeton, NJ: Princeton University Press, 1952)

—— 'Thomas More and the Problem of Counsel', in *Quincentennial Essays on St. Thomas More: Selected Papers from the Thomas More College Conference*, ed. by Michael J. Moore (Boone, NC: Albion, 1978), pp. 55–66

HOGREFE, PEARL, *The Life and Times of Sir Thomas Elyot Englishman* (Ames, IA: Iowa State University Press, 1967)

HOLMES, ELISABETH, 'The Significance of Elyot's Revision of the *Gouernour*', *Review of English Studies*, 12 (1961), 352–63

HOSINGTON, BRENDA M., '"Compluria opuscula longe festivissima": Translations of

Lucian in Renaissance England', in *Syntagmatia: Essays on Neo-Latin Literature in Honour of Monique Mund-Dopchie and Gilbert Tournoy*, ed. by Dirk Sacré and Jan Papy, Supplementa Humanistica Lovaniensia 26 (Leuven: Leuven University Press, 2009), pp. 187–205

JORDAN, CONSTANCE, 'Feminism and the Humanists: The Case of Sir Thomas Elyot's *Defence of Good Women*', *Renaissance Quarterly*, 36 (1983), 181–201

KINSMAN, ROBERT S., '"The Proverbes of Salmon Do Playnly Declare": A Sententious Poem on Wisdom and Governance, Ascribed to Sir Francis Bryan', *Huntington Library Quarterly*, 42 (1979), 279–312

LASCELLES, MARY, 'Sir Thomas Elyot and the Legend of Alexander Severus', *Review of English Studies*, 2 (1951), 305–18

LEHMBERG, STANFORD E., *Sir Thomas Elyot Tudor Humanist* (Austin, TX: University of Texas Press, 1960)

—— 'English Humanists, the Reformation, and the Problem of Counsel', *Archiv für Reformationsgeschichte*, 52 (1961), 74–90

LERER, SETH, *Courtly Letters in the Age of Henry VIII: Literary Culture and the Arts of Deceit* (Cambridge: Cambridge University Press, 1997)

MAJOR, JOHN M., *Sir Thomas Elyot and Renaissance Humanism* (Lincoln, NE: University of Nebraska Press, 1964)

MEDCALF, STEPHEN, 'Classical Authors', in *The Oxford History of Literary Translation in English Volume 1 to 1550*, ed. by Roger Ellis (Oxford: Oxford University Press, 2008), pp. 364–89

MOHL, RUTH, *The Three Estates in Medieval and Renaissance Literature* (New York, NY: Columbia University Press, 1933)

MORINI, MASSIMILIANO, *Tudor Translation in Theory and Practice* (Burlington, VT: Ashgate, 2006)

NORLAND, HOWARD B., *Drama in Early Tudor Britain, 1485–1558* (Lincoln, NE: University of Nebraska Press, 1995)

REYNOLDS, ANNE, 'Cardinal Oliviero Carafa and the Early Cinquecento Tradition of the Feast of Pasquino', in *ROMA HUMANISTICA: Studia in honorem Revi adm. Dni Dni IOSAEI RUYSSCHAERT = Humanistica Lovaniensia*, 34A (1985), 178–208

—— 'The Classical Continuum in Roman Humanism: The Festival of Pasquino, the *Robigalia*, and Satire', *Bibliothèque d'Humanisme et Renaissance*, 49 (1987), 289–307

RHODES, NEIL, WITH GORDON KENDAL and LOUISE WILSON, *English Renaissance Translation Theory* (London: Modern Humanities Research Association, 2013)

RICHARDS, JENNIFER, *Rhetoric and Courtliness in Early Modern Literature* (Cambridge: Cambridge University Press, 2003)

ROSSITER, WILLIAM T., '*In Spayne*: Sir Thomas Wyatt and the Poetics of Embassy', in *Authority and Diplomacy from Dante to Shakespeare*, ed. by Jason Powell and Rossiter (Burlington, VT: Ashgate, 2013), pp. 101–20

RUDE, DONALD W., 'On the Date of Sir Thomas Elyot's *The Education or bringinge vp of children*', *Papers of the Bibliographical Society of America*, 71 (1977), 61–65

RUMMEL, ERIKA, *Erasmus as a Translator of the Classics* (Toronto: University of Toronto Press, 1985)

SCATTERGOOD, JOHN, *John Skelton: The Career of an Early Tudor Poet* (Dublin: Four Courts, 2014)

SCHURINK, FRED, 'Print, Patronage, and Occasion: Translations of Plutarch's *Moralia* in Tudor England', *Yearbook of English Studies*, 38 (2008), 86–101

SCHUTTE, VALERIE, *Mary I and the Art of Book Dedications: Royal Women, Power, and Persuasion* (New York, NY: Palgrave Macmillan, 2015)

SHRANK, CATHY, 'Sir Thomas Elyot and the Bonds of Community', in *The Oxford Handbook of Tudor Literature 1485–1603*, ed. by Mike Pincombe and Shrank (Oxford: Oxford University Press, 2009), pp. 154–69

SIMPSON, JAMES, 'The Sacrifice of Lady Rochford: Henry Parker's Translation of *De claris mulieribus*', in *The Triumphs of English: Henry Parker, Lord Morley, Translator to the Tudor Court*, ed. by Marie Axton and James P. Carley (London: British Library, 2000), pp. 153–69

SKINNER, QUENTIN, *The Foundations of Modern Political Thought*, 2 vols (Cambridge: Cambridge University Press, 1978)

—— 'Political Philosophy', in *The Cambridge History of Renaissance Philosophy*, ed. by C. B. Schmitt, Skinner, Eckhard Kessler, and Jill Kraye (Cambridge: Cambridge University Press, 1988), pp. 389–452

SLAVIN, A. J., 'Platonism and the Problem of Counsel in *Utopia*', in *Reformation, Humanism and 'Revolution'*, ed. by Gordon J. Schochet, Proceedings of the Folger Institute Center for the History of British Political Thought 1 (Washington, DC: Folger Shakespeare Library, 1990), pp. 207–34

STARNES, DEWITT T., 'Sir Thomas Elyot and the "Sayings of the Philosophers"', *Studies in English*, 13 (1933), 5–35

—— 'Literary Features of Renaissance Dictionaries', *Studies in Philology*, 37 (1940), 26–50

STEIN, GABRIELE, *Sir Thomas Elyot as Lexicographer* (Oxford: Oxford University Press, 2014)

STEWART, ALAN, 'The Trouble with English Humanism: Tyndale, More and Darling Erasmus', in *Reassessing Tudor Humanism*, ed. by Jonathan Woolfson (New York, NY: Palgrave MacMillan, 2002), pp. 78–98

STIERLE, KARLHEINZ, 'Translatio Studii and Renaissance: From Vertical to Horizontal Translation', in *The Translatability of Cultures: Figurations of the Space Between*, ed. by Sanford Budick and Wolfgang Iser (Stanford, CA: Stanford University Press, 1996), pp. 55–67

TRAPP, J. B., 'Conformity of Greek and the Vernacular: The History of a Renaissance Theory of Languages', in *Classical Influences on European Culture A. D. 500–1500*, ed. by R. R. Bolgar (Cambridge: Cambridge University Press, 1971), pp. 239–44

WAKELIN, DANIEL, *Humanism, Reading, and English Literature 1430–1530* (Oxford: Oxford University Press, 2007)

WALKER, GREG, 'Sir Thomas Elyot and the Politics of Accomodation: *The Defence of Good Women*', in *Persuasive Fictions: Faction, Faith, and Political Culture in the Reign of Henry VIII* (Aldershot: Scolar, 1996), pp. 178–203

—— *Writing Under Tyranny: English Literature and the Henrician Reformation* (Oxford: Oxford University Press, 2005)

WALZER, ARTHUR E., 'The Rhetoric of Counsel and Thomas Elyot's *Of the Knowledge Which Maketh a Wise Man*', *Philosophy and Rhetoric*, 45 (2012), 24–45

—— 'The Rhetoric of Counsel in Thomas Elyot's *Pasquil the Playne*', *Rhetorica*, 30 (2012), 1–21

WAYNE, VALERIE, 'Zenobia in Medieval and Renaissance Literature', in *Ambiguous Realities: Women in the Middle Ages and Renaissance*, ed. by Carole Levin and Jeanie Watson (Detroit, MI: Wayne State University Press, 1987), pp. 48–65

WILKINS, ELIZA GREGORY, *'Know thyself' in Greek and Latin Literature* (Chicago, IL: University of Chicago Libraries, 1917)

WILSON, KENNETH J., *Incomplete Fictions: The Formations of English Renaissance Dialogue* (Washington, DC: Catholic University of America Press, 1985)

WORTHAM, JAMES, 'Sir Thomas Elyot and the Translation of Prose', *Huntington Library Quarterly*, 11 (1948), 219–40

°<A1r>

PASQVIL
THE
PLAIN

LONDINI IN AEDIBVS

THOMAE BERTHELETI

M. D. XXXIII

° The text is from *A* = 1533 ed. (RSTC 7672 = ESTC S105473), departures from which are enclosed in angled brackets <>; collated with the unique copy of *B* = 1534 ed. (RSTC 7672.5 = ESTC S1924), which survives in defective state (missing sigs C1, C4–C5, and C8); and with *C* = 1540 ed. (RSTC 7673 = ESTC S108773), a reprint of *B*, for the pages missing from *B*.

<A1v>
<Prologue>

°To Gentle Readers.

Since plainness in speaking is of wise men commended, and diverse do abhor long proems of rhetoric, I have set out this merry treatise, wherein plainness and flattery do come in trial, in such wise as none honest man will be therewith offended. The personages that do reason be of small reputation. For Pasquillus, that speaketh most, is an image of stone, sitting in the city of Rome openly, on whom once in the year it is leeful to every man to set in verse or prose any taunt that he will, again whom he list, how great an estate so ever he be, notwithstanding in this book he useth such a temperance that he noteth not any particular person or country.[1] Gnatho was brought in by writers of comedies <A2r> for such a servant as alway affirmed what so ever was spoken of his master; but he was a Greek born, and therefore he savoureth somewhat of rhetoric.[2] Pasquil is an old Roman, but, by long sitting in the street and hearing market men chat, he is become rude and homely. Harpocrates was the prelate of the temple of Isis and Serapis, which were honoured for gods in Egypt, whose image is made holding his finger at his mouth, betokening silence.[3] These three communed together as it followeth, but where I had forgotten to ask. Albeit, because the matter is merrily brought in and therewith savoureth somewhat of wisdom, I thought it not inconvenient to participate it with you that will not interpret it but according to the best meaning and, in the reading this little treatise, distinctly will consider diligently the state <A2v> and condition of the person that speaketh, with the order and conclusion of his whole reason. And if it seem to you that Pasquil saith true, in declaring how much ye do favour truth, defend him against venomous tongues and overthwart wits, which doeth more mischief than Pasquil's babbling.

Fare ye well.

1 See Introduction, pp. 13–14 and n. 42.

2 Eras., *Adagia*, praef. (CWE 31, 27), amongst his examples of proverbial hyperboles 'from characters in comedy', lists *Gnathone adulantior*, 'fawning as Gnatho'.

3 Cf. Elyot, *Bibl.*, '*Harpocrates*, the god of silence' and '*Harpocratem reddere*, to put one to silence', from Eras., *Adagia* 4.1.52, *Reddidit Harpocratem*, 'He turned him into Harpocrates' (CWE 35, 472), using Catul. 74 to explain that 'Harpocrates was pictured in ancient times as a god who, by a finger raised to his lips, enjoined silence'; also, *Adagia* 1.5.74, *Momo satisfacere et similia*, 'To satisify Momus and the like' (CWE 31, 450), where the idiom is used.

° To Gentle Readers] Thomas Elyot knight to gentle readers *B*

<A3r>

PASQVIL

Pasquillus. Gnatho. Harpocrates.

PASQUIL It is a wonder to see the world: nowadays, the more strange, the better liked. Therefore, °with great pain a man may know an honest man from a false harlot.

But peace, who is this °gallant that standeth here harkening? What, I say, mine old fellow Gnatho! I pray thee, come forth! Yea, steal not so away. Perdie, I know your old fashion, though ye be now thus strangely disguised.

GNATHO Who speaketh to me? °Pasquillus? Sawest thou not Harpocrates late? I seek for him: he must come to my °lord.

PASQUIL I wot not whether thine eye sought for Harpocrates, but sure I am that thine ear sought for Pasquillus. But, I pray thee, turn about: thou hast the stran-<A3v>gest apparel that ever I looked on! What have we here? A cap full of eyelets and buttons! This long ostrich feather doeth wonderly well; the tyrf of the cap turned down afore like a pantile hath a marvellous good grace, but this long gown °and straight sleeves is a *non sequitur*, and it shall let you to flee, and then your feather shall stand you in no stead, and so mought ye happen to be cumbered, if ye should come into a stour where ye would shift for yourself. God avow, what dost thou with this long tippet? If it were °white, I would have said that thou camest to challenge men at wrestling; but, I ween, ye have walked late in the street and pulled it from some worshipful doctor. What, a God's name? Have ye a book in your hand? A good fellowship, whereof is it? Let me see. *Novum Testamentum*! What, thou deceivest me! <A4r> I had wend thou couldest have skilled of nothing but only of flattery. But what is this in your bosom? Another book, or else a pair of cards of vallary falsehood: did I not say at the first that it is a wonder to see this world? °Some will be in the bowels of divinity ere they know what °longeth to good humanity. °Abide, what is here? *Troilus and Criseyde*? Lord, what discord is between these two books! Yet a great deal more is there in thine apparel; and yet, most of all between the book in thy hand and thy conditions, as God help me, as much as between truth and leasing!

° with great pain] uneath *B*
° gallant] gentleman *B*
° Pasquillus] Pasquil *B*
° lord] master *B*
° and] with *B*
° white] white as it is black *B*
° Some] Lo, some *B*
° longeth] belongeth *B*
° Abide] Let see *B*

GNATHO Well, °Pasquil, thou wilt never leave thine old custom in railing, yet hast thou wit enough to perceive what damage and hindrance thou hast thereby sustained, and more art thou likely and with greater peril, if thou have not good await, what and to whom and where thou speakest. I heard the words that thou spa-<A4v>kest whilere, whereof, if I would be a reporter, it mought turn thee to no little displeasure. But I know that thou art a good fellow and wouldest that all thing were well, though thy words be all crabbed. Wherefore, notwithstanding that thou speakest rebukefully to me, I take it in jape, ne will carry hence with me the presumptuous words that thou spakest. But, by mine advice, leave now at the last thine undiscrete liberty in speech, wherein thou usest unprofitable taunts and rebukes. I may well call them unprofitable whereby nothing that thou blamest is of one jot amended, and thou losest thereby preferment which thine excellent wit doth require and, that worse is, travailest in study of mind to augment thine own detriment, and therein losest much time that mought be better employed.

I remember that once I asked a <A5r> man that was wise and very well learned, how I mought soonest come to promotion. He said, 'Using Aeschylus's counsel', which was a writer of tragedies, and I demanded what it was. And he answered, 'Holding thy tongue where it behooveth thee, and speaking in time that which is convenient'.[4] And the same lesson, Pasquillus, if thou wouldest observe, I doubt not but that thou shouldest find therein no little commodity.

PASQUIL Marry, Gnatho, I will no more wonder at thy side gown, for thou art much wiser than I supposed. I had wend all this while that by nature only thou hadest been instructed to flatter, but, by Saint John, I see now that thou joinest also thereto a shrewd wit and preparest to the helping thereof as it were a craft gathered of learning and scripture. Notwithstanding, a good fellowship, if thy tarrying shall not <A5v> be grievous or hurtful unto thee — for I know how expedient it is that thou be not long out of the sight of thy master — if thou wilt be, Gnatho, alone, tell me how thou understandest the said sentence of Aeschylus's tragedy? For I fear we two do understand him diversely, and then thy counsel in respect to thy purpose shall little profit me.

[4] Aesch., *Cho.* 581–82, 'ὑμῖν δ' ἐπαινῶ γλῶσσαν εὔφημον φέρειν, | σιγᾶν θ' ὅπου δεῖ καὶ λέγειν τὰ καίρια', 'I say 'twere well to bear a tongue | Full of fair silence and of fitting speech | As each beseems the time' (trans. by E. D. A. Morshead); though cf. Eras., *Apoph.*, 1 ded. ep. (= *Ep.* 2431; CWE 37, 12), 'Likewise the line "Keeping silent where silence needful is and in due season speaking timely words", comes from Aeschylus' *Prometheus*, but we find it in Euripides with the small change to "To keep silent [...] to speak"', where Erasmus is repeating Aul. Gell., *NA* 13.19.4.

° Pasquil] Pasquillus *B*

GNATHO Supposest thou so? In good faith, and to me it seemeth so plain that it needeth none expositor. But to the intent that my counsel to thee may take some effect, in the little time that I may now tarry, I will as compendiously as I can shew my conceit, in declaring what I think that Aeschylus meant by the said sentence.

It behooveth a man to hold his tongue when he aforeseeth, by any experience, that the thing which he would purpose or speak of to his su-<A6r>perior shall neither be pleasantly heard nor thankfully taken; and, in words, opportunity and time alway do depend on the affection and appetite of him that heareth them. How sayest thou, Pasquil, is it not so?

PASQUIL So? No, so mought I go. But one thing, hear me: I will not flatter thee, Gnatho. If thou understandest no better the New Testament — which thou carriest as solemnly with thee as thou shouldest read a privy lesson, hem, I had almost told where openly — than thou doest Aeschylus's sentence which, as if thou hadest been learned, thou toldest to me for a counsel, thy breath will be so hot shortly that thou wilt make men afeared to come within twenty foot of thee. And hark, in thine ear: by my truth, I ween it be neither better nor worse.

GNATHO Will ye not leave your overthwart fashion? I can <A6v> no more. I see it is vain to counsel a mad man to look to his profit. Farewell: I have somewhat else to do than to attend to thy prating.

PASQUIL What, be you angry for this? Look on the book in your hand: perdie, it agreeth not with your profession to be out of charity. But, gentle Gnatho, tarry so long as I may shew thee how I understand the said sentence of Aeschylus.

GNATHO Say on.

PASQUIL Where two hosts be assembled and in point to fight, if thou be among them, though thou be a great astronomer, it behooveth thee to hold thy tongue and not to talk of conjunctions and of the trine or quartile aspects, but to prepare thee to battle.

Where a good fellowship is set at dice or at cards, though thou be learned in geometry, hold thy tongue and speak not of proportions or figures.

Where men be set <A7r> at a good supper and be busily occupied in eating and drinking, though thou be deeply seen in philosophy, hold thy tongue and dispute not of temperance or moderate diet.

Where thou art among a great °company of gallants and young women at banquetings or other recreations, though thou be well learned in holy scripture, hold thy tongue; interpret not Paul's epistles, for therein is no dalliance.°

° company of gallants and young women at] company at *B*

°] *B add* When thou art sitting in council about matters of weighty importance, talk not then of pastime or dalliance but, omitting affection or dread, speak then to the purpose.

Where thou seest thy friend in a great presence honoured of all men, though thou knowest in him notable vices, yet there hold thy tongue and reproach him not of them.

Where thou seest thy lord or master in the presence of many resolved into fury or wantonness, though thou hast all ready advertisements how he shall refrain it, yet hold thy tongue then, for troubling that presence. <A7v>

On the other part, if, before battle joined, thou beholdest thy side the weaker and thine adversaries more puissant and stronger, speak then of policy, whereby thou hopest to obtain the victory.

Before that thy friend sitteth down to dice, if thou dost perceive that he shall be overmatched, discourage him betime, ere he repent him in poverty.

When thy friends be set down to supper, before the cups be twice filled, rehearse the peril and also dishonesty that happeneth by gluttony.

When young men and women have appointed a banquet, then, ere the ovens be heated and tables all covered, rehearse hardly the sentences of Saint Paul or Saint Jerome, if thou be learned.°

If thou knowest a vice in thy friend which is of a few men suspected, ere it be talked of at the ta-<A8r>vern or of his enemy reproached, warn him of the damage that may happen if it be not amended.

When thou perceivest thy master to be resolved into wrath or affections dishonest, before wrath be increased into fury, and affection into °beastly enormity, as opportunity serveth thee, reverently and with tokens of love toward him, speak such words as shall be convenient.

Opportunity consisteth in place or time, where and when the said affections or passion of wrath be some deal mitigate and out of extremity. And words be called convenient which have respect to the nature and state of the person unto whom they be spoken, and also to the detriment which mought ensue by the vice or lack that thou hast espied, °<and> it ought not to be as thou hast supposed. For opportunity and time for a counsellor to speak do not depend <A8v> of the affection and appetite of him that is counselled. Marry, then counsel were but a vain word, and every man would do as him list. For if he listed not to hear any counsel, he should never be warned of his own error, but by satiety and tediousness of his own vice, or by grace, if he were worthy to have it.

°] *B add* If thou be called to council, after thou hast either heard one reason before thee or, at the least way, in the balance of thine own reason pondered the question, spare not to shew thine advice and to speak truly, remembering that God is not so far off but that he can hear thee.

° beastly enormity] voluptuous appetite *B*

° and] *B* : *A om*

GNATHO Now, by the faith I owe to God, I would not have thought that thou hadest been so well reasoned. For men have alway reputed thee but for a babbler and °a railer.

PASQUIL Yea, what men? By God, those which ought most to have thanked me, I say; hark in thine ear: popes, emperors, kings, and cardinals! Thou hearest what I say. When they, by such as thou and Harpocrates be, were with flattery and dissimulation brought into the hate of God and the people, once in a year, I gave them warning. <B1r> Neither for menaces nor yet for beatings, I never ceased. Thou art remembered when Pope Leo sware that he would throw me into the river of Tiber?[5] And that year, I went to Saint James on pilgrimage, which I avowed if I escaped drowning. But in an unlucky hour was I a pilgrim, for since there have comen both to Saint James at Compostella and to Saint Peter at Rome every year ten thousand pilgrims fewer than there did a thousand years before that time. And men say that in other countries diverse monasteries be like to break hospitality, because their offerings be not the third part so much as they were accustomed. For indeed, nowadays, men's devotion waxeth even as cold as the monks be in the choir at midnight. That commodity had Rome by mine absence. And yet, after my pilgrimage done, I had <B1v> for my truth and plainness as much pardon of God as if I had builded one cloister in Rome and another in Paris and put into everich of them an hundred friars conventuals. And yet were that a blessed deed if the law were not again increasing of valiant beggars.

But to my purpose: if these men that we spake of had wisely and coldly expended and tried my words that they called railing, many things mought have been prevented that were after lamented. Germany should not have kicked again her mother; emperors and princes should not have been in perpetual discord and oftentimes in peril; prelates have been laughed at as dizzards, saints blasphemed, and miracles reproved for jugglings; laws and statutes contemned, and officers little regarded. What must needs follow, since my breath faileth me, I leave that to thee, Gnatho, to <B2r> conject, for thou art wise enough to consider.

[5] Giovanni de Medici (1475–1521), Pope Leo X from 1513 March. The undertaking is usually imputed to Leo's necessarily parsimonious successor, Pope Adrian VI (r. 1522–1523), e.g. in the contemporary Paolo Giovio (1483–1552), *Vita Hadriani sexti* 15, ed. by Gaspar Burmann, *Analecta historica de Hadriano Sexto* (Utrecht, 1727), pp. 133–34: 'That he had been injured with infamous verses set up upon the statue of Pasquil was a matter of the utmost gravity to him; afterwards, however, he bore it more civilly, once he had been instructed that such satiric license for freedom and malice ought be allowed to obscure persons, such that, by carping with impunity at those of eminence, they might mitigate their own misfortune with the pleasures of satire. Famously enraged with the poets, Adrian decreed it that the statue of Pasquil by the Wall should be pulled down and cast into the Tiber'.

° a railer] railer *B*

GNATHO I know what thou meanest, but, a fellowship, leave thy bourding and currish philosophy, since it is neither profitable, pleasant, nor thankful. Who would be so mad, to drive about a mill, and is sure that all the meal that he grindeth shall fall on the floor, saving a little mill-dust that shall fly into his eyen and put him to pain and perchance make him blind? And thou studyest to speak many good words, which be lost in the rushes; and, if any ill meaning may be picked out, it is cast in thy nose, to put thee in danger. Leese no more labour, Pasquil, but follow my counsel; and if, within two years, thou be not new painted and gilt and have mo men wondering at thee than at any other image in Rome, by my truth, I will stand in the rain and sun as long as thou <B2v> hast done, and yet it were an unreasonable wager.

PASQUIL Go to! Let see, what is thy counsel?

GNATHO Marry, I will tell thee. Thou hast a very sharp wit and a ready, wherefore thou art meet for the world. And pity it were that such a jewel should be neglected.

PASQUIL And pity it were that such a flatterer as thou art should long be unhanged! But pass on, a God's name.

GNATHO I wist well that in such a froward piece of timber I should lose much labour. Yet will I prove if good counsel may wark anything in thee. Now hear, Pasquil, what I say. By thy long railing, thy wit is well known. Now turn the leaf and, when thou hearest anything purposed by them whom thou hast offended, what so ever it be, affirm it to be well, and therewith advance the wit and intent of the person that spake it, which thou mayst do <B3r> excellently well. For he that can despise spitefully can, if he list, praise and commend also incomparably. And if thou canst not refrain from rebuking and taunting, practice thy natural fury and woodness again them that repugn again the said purpose. And where thou didst wonder to see me have in my hand the New Testament, if thou wouldest do the same and now in thine age lay apart the lesson of 'gentilesse',[6] called humanity, since thou mayest have good leisure, being not yet called to council, pick out here and there sentences out of holy scripture to furnish thy reason with authority. I make God avow, thou shalt be within three months able to confound the greatest divine in all Italy. And when thy conversion and good opinion is known, then shalt thou be called for. But then alway remember, how so ever the tenor <B3v> bell ringeth, he ringeth alway in tune; and though he jar somewhat, yet thou canst not hear it, his sound is so great and thine ears be so little. And if other men find it, say that it is no fault but a quaver in music and became the bell, if they had the wit to perceive it. I teach thee in

[6] The key concept in *Troilus and Criseyde*, mentioned just above, and other courtly writings of Chaucer.

parables, for this craft would not be opened to every man, for it should not be for my profit; but thy subtle wit comprehendeth all that I mean, thou art so acquainted with all our experience.

PASQUIL Now, on my faith, well said! I could not have founden a craftier knave to learn of between this and Jerusalem. But who cometh here? He seemeth a reverend personage: he is none of thy sort, I trow.

GNATHO By God! We be °cousin-germanes removed, I by the mother side and he by the father. And that caused me to speak so °much and him so little, and yet is <B4r> there small diversity between our conditions.

PASQUIL What meanest thou thereby?

GNATHO For we both have one master, and when he speaketh or doeth anything for his pleasure, I study with words to commend it; if my cousin stand by, he speaketh little or nothing but, forming his visage into a gravity with silence, looketh as if he affirmed all thing that is spoken.

PASQUIL What is his name?

GNATHO Harpocrates.

PASQUIL That is a hard name, by Jesus. But why holdeth he his finger at his mouth?[7]

GNATHO For he hath espied me talking, and, because he weeneth that I speak too much, he maketh a sign that I should cease. But I am glad that I have met with him. Cousin, Harpocrates! I have sought for you this two hours.

PASQUIL Why speaketh he not?

GNATHO Oh, that is his gravity, to pause a while ere he speak. He lear-<B4v>ned it when he was student at Bonony.[8]

HARPOCRATES What is the matter, Gnatho?

GNATHO My °lord, when he hath dined, will sit in counsel about weighty causes.

HARPOCRATES And when I have dined, I will give attendance.

PASQUIL Lo, is it not, as I said, a wonder to see this world? In old time, men used to occupy the morning in deep and subtle studies and in counsels concerning the commonweal and other matters of great importance; in likewise, then to hear controversies and give °judgment. And if they had any causes of their own, then to treat of them, and that did they not without a great consideration, proceeding both of natural reason, and also counsel of physic. And after dinner, they refreshed their wits, either with

[7] See above, p. 30 and n. 3.

[8] Bologna, where the university had long been Europe's leading centre for the study of Roman law.

° cousin-germanes removed] right cousins *B*

° much and] much as I do and *B*

° lord] master *B*

° judgment] judgments *B*

instruments of music, or with reading or hearing some pleasant story, or beholding <B5r> something delectable and honest. And after their dinner was digested, then either they exercised themselves in riding, running on foot, shooting or other like pastime, or went with their hawks to see a flight at the river, or would see their greyhounds course the hare or the deer, which they did as well to recreate their wits as also to get them good appetite. °But now all this is turned into °another fashion; God help us, the world is almost at an end! For afternoon is turned to forenoon, virtue into vice, vice into virtue, devotion into hypocrisy, and, in some places, men say, faith is turned to heresy. Did I not now say well at the beginning, that it is a wonder to see this world?

HARPOCRATES Hem, Pasquillus.

PASQUIL Well, ye think as much as I speak, for all your pointing and winking.

HARPOCRATES But in silence is surety.

PASQUIL <B5v> Perchance, nay. If I perceived one at thy back with a sword drawn, ready to strike thee, wouldest thou that I should hold my peace or else tell thee?

HARPOCRATES Nay! Silence were then out of season.

PASQUIL Now well fare you for your bald reason![9] A man may see what wisdom there is in your compendious speaking: ye will season silence. Marry, I ween my lord should have a better cook of you than a counsellor.

°GNATHO Peace, whoreson! He is also my lord's counsellor.

PASQUIL For his silence he may be. But yet I doubt me, for I °remember what thou saidest whilere that, when ye were present both with your master, if thou commendest his sayings or doings, this man would approve it with silence and countenance, which mought do more harm than all thy flattery, <B6r> then what mischief mought follow of his damnable silence, if °in the secret time of confession, wherein confessors have above all men most largest liberty to blame and reprove, he should either dissemble the vices that he knoweth in °his master, or else forebear to declare to him the enormity of such capital sins as he hath confessed.

GNATHO By my truth, thou art a busy fellow! Doest thou remember what thou saidest when thou didest espy that I had a book of the New Testament?

[9] With the previous speech, concluding a rhymed pentameter couplet.

° But now] But lo now *B*
° another] a new *B*
° GNATHO: Peace, whoreson! He is also my lord's counsellor. PASQUIL: For his silence he may be] Notwithstanding for your silence ye mought be a confessor *B*
° remember what] remember Gnatho what *B*
° in the secret] in secret *B*
° his master] him whom he hath in confession *B*

PASQUIL What said I?

GNATHO Marry, this thou saidest, that some would be in the bowels of divinity ere they know what belongeth to good humanity. Now thou takest thyself by the nose, for, without having regard to whom thou speakest, thou presumest to teach this worshipful man what he shall do in confession.

PASQUIL It is well reasoned of you, by sweet Saint <B6v> Runyon:[10] ye define teaching as well as he did season his silence! Didest thou hear me teach him what he should do? Nay, and if thou hast so much wit to remember upon the words that thou thyself spakest, I declared what inconvenience mought happen by the flattering silence of a confessor. Weenest thou that I was never confessed? Yes, I have told a tale to a friar ere this time, with a groat in my hand, and have been assoiled forthwith without any further rehearsal; where if a poor man had told half so much, he should have been made equal to the devil and have been so chid that when he had gone from confession he should have hanged down the ears, as if he had been learning of pricksong. Albeit, it is the custom of some of you that be courtiers, when ye cannot defend your matter with reason, to embraid him that spea-<B7r>keth with presumption, treason, misprision, or such other like praty morsels, to stop him of talking. But between two men full of words, truth shall never or late be espied, wherefore I will no more, Gnatho, meddle with thee, but from henceforth I will speak to Harpocrates. For if he can persuade me that his silence is better than my babbling, I will follow his doctrine rather than thine, for I have professed from my childhood never to speak in earnest to my master or friend contrary to that that I think.

GNATHO Ergo, thou hast professed to stand still in the rain, and once perchance to be thrown into Tiber, or broken in pieces.

PASQUIL And perchance, if God never lied, I may be in the palace merry, when °such as thou art shall sit without on a ladder and make all thy friends sorry. Heardest thou never that the world is round, and <B7v> therefore it is ever turning, now the wrong side upward, another time the right? But let this pass.

I pray thee, Harpocrates, teach me how thou doest season thy silence. Doest thou it with salt or with spices?

HARPOCRATES Nay, with sugar, for I use little salt.

PASQUIL And that maketh your counsel more sweet than savoury.

HARPOCRATES Ye speak like a pothecary.

10 'Saint Runyon' occurs in Chaucer, in an exchange of oaths between the Host and Pardoner, in the headlink of the *Pardoner's Tale* (*CT* 6.310, 320), where it may or may not refer to a familiar saint but almost certainly puns on the obscenity for penis, 'runnion', attested later, in Shakespeare, for example.

° such as thou art shall] thou shalt *B*

PASQUIL And I have known a wise pothecary done much more good, if he were trusted, than a foolish physician. But now to thy silence, that thou so much praisest, Harpocrates. Thou saidest that in silence was surety; and I asked, if I perceived one at thy back with a sword drawn ready to strike thee, whether should I speak or keep silence; and thou answeredest that silence was then out of season.

HARPOCRATES So said I.

PASQUIL I can thee thank; <B8r> thou abidest by thy word, although at this day that be accompted no policy. But why saidest thou that silence were then out of season?

HARPOCRATES For I mought be sore hurt or perchance killed, if I were not then warned, mine enemy being so nigh me.

PASQUIL Yea, I wist well that ye would not be slain nor yet wounded, if ye mought have room enough to run, or your long clothes did not let you. But I put case I knew that your enemy were at your chamber door or, let it be further, at Poitiers in France, who had avowed to slay you and were in his journey toward you, but, when or where he would strike you, I know not: should I forthwith warn you, or else keep silence until I saw his sword over your head, ready to kill you, that I mought keep silence alway in season?

HARPOCRATES No! That were no friendship, but rather treason, to know me to <B8v> be in such peril and to hide it from me, that there were no mean to escape but only by fortune.

PASQUIL What, no less than treason? Peace! Ye are yet no pope and, because ye be a priest, ye be exempted from being °emperor.

HARPOCRATES Hast thou any other term more proper, where a man consenteth to the destruction of his friend, which specially trusteth him?

PASQUIL By my truth, nay, if I shall not lie. But now I am glad that I have found you. Yet will I a little better assay you: if I saw your cousin Gnatho put poison into a cup of wine secretly and bring it unto you, should I hold my peace or else tell you?

GNATHO Marry, I defy thee! Thou knowest not me to be of such disposition.

PASQUIL What? Ye be of a very choleric complexion: what art thou the worse that I name thee herein for an example? If, by the way of argument <C1r> and to make the offence the more horrible, I would put for the case that Pope °Adrian the fourth were poisoned by one of his cardinals, because he would have minished their majesty and have brought them to humbleness, perdie, this were no blasphemy.[11]

[11] Adrian IV (r. 1154–1159), a reforming pope and the only English one, born Nicholas Breakspear. He died in unremarkable circumstance, and the matter of poisoning that Elyot

° emperor] emperor or king *B*
° Adrian the fourth] Adrian *C*

GNATHO There is in thy railing none harmony.

PASQUIL No, for therein is no flattery. But, Harpocrates, that with thy sober silence mockest us both, what sayest thou to my question?

HARPOCRATES Now, on my faith, thou art a merry companion.

PASQUIL Yea, good enough, when ye have nothing left to save with your honesty, then you bring forth that merry conclusion. But say on: wouldest thou then that I should keep silence or no? Admit the case to be true, though Gnatho be angry.

HARPOCRATES Keep silence then, quotha? Nay, by the faith of my body!

PASQUIL So I thought, except <C1v> ye be weary of worldly worship and be now contented to die and let other men step into your rooms and take pains for you. But ye say that silence were then out of season?

HARPOCRATES By Saint John, yea.

PASQUIL And for what cause, tell me, your reason?

HARPOCRATES Marry, for if thou didest not warn me, I mought be deceived by him that I trusted and drink poison in the stead of wine, whereof I should either be dead or fall into such sickness and breaking out that all men should abhor me.

PASQUIL I would to God that thou wouldest affirm alway truth to thy master, as thou doest now to me. But, Harpocrates, thou wouldest not die, nor yet live to be abhorred of all men; therein I can praise thee. Now, since thou art a °Christian man (as I suppose) and also learned, wouldest thou that any worse thing should happen to thy master, that trusteth <C2r> thee, than thou wouldest to thyself?

HARPOCRATES No, truly.

PASQUIL And if thou knewest any danger toward him, as I have rehearsed, thou oughtest as well to warn him of it, as I ought thee.

HARPOCRATES I cannot deny that.

PASQUIL And also thou wouldest.

HARPOCRATES Why, wherefore should I not?

PASQUIL For, peradventure, if your master mistrusteth him not that hath avowed to kill him and accompted your tale for a fantasy, or if he favoureth him much that ye know would poison him, he will suppose that ye tell it him of some suspicion or malice and will lean a deaf ear toward you. And then he on whom ye complained, being advertised, shall omit that which

introduces may refer rather to the death of Christopher Cardinal Bainbridge in 1514. Elyot's *amicus* Richard Pace promulgated the notion that Bainbridge's murder by poisoning was the doing of the Italo-English bishop Silvestro Gigli (1463–1521), a client of Wolsey: see D. S. Chambers, *Cardinal Bainbridge in the Court of Rome, 1509 to 1514* (Oxford: Oxford University Press, 1965), esp. p. 138.

° Christian] good *B*

he purposed, to prove you a liar. And then should ye both leese your thank of your °friend and be called a detractor, and also to have him whom ye accused and all his band vigilant <C2v> espials to bring you in danger. Is it not thus?

HARPOCRATES Yea, sir, by Jesus.

PASQUIL What if another man, which loveth your master no less than ye do, gave him such warning, and ye knew it to be true; but ye perceive that your master listeth not to hear of such matter, or perchance commendeth him which is complained on. Would ye also praise him, to support the trust that your master hath in him, or commend your master therein for his constancy and little mistrusting?

HARPOCRATES Nay, then were I worthy a hot mischieving, if I would help to bring my master unto his confusion.

PASQUIL What, would you hold your tongue and say nothing?

HARPOCRATES No, but I would forbear for a time and await diligently, to see if the peril would cease, or mought be by some occasion prevented, or by my master otherwise spied; but when <C3r> it were imminent, then would I give warning.

PASQUIL Imminent, what call ye that?

HARPOCRATES When his enemy is at his back, with his sword drawn, ready to strike him.

PASQUIL And what for poisoning?

HARPOCRATES When I saw my friend have the cup in his °hand, ready to drink.

PASQUIL Now, gat ye all this wit °without any learning? It is not for naught that ye be a °counsellor. Since ye have such a praty feat in °seasoning a likelihood, ye be well seen in °predestination and do know perfectly the subtle distinctions of times and moments. Ye would forbear to warn your master at the beginning of danger; and when he is at the point to fall into it, perchance or ye shall not be present, or else not able or of power to resist it. But teach me, I pray you, what ye call imminent, for it is a word taken out of Latin and not <C3v> commonly used.

HARPOCRATES Marry, the thing that is imminent is when it appeareth to be in the instant to be done or to happen, and, after some men's exposition, as it threatened to come.

PASQUIL It is well expounded, and clerkly. Then, if ye will divide the time into

° friend] master *B*
° hand ready] hand and were ready *B*
° without any] with so little *B*
° counsellor. Since] counsellor, since *B*
° seasoning a likelihood] seasoning. Of likelihood *B*
° predestination] constellations *B*

instants, because perchance ye be a good °Duns-man,[12] the instant when it appeareth that your friend shall be slain, and the instant when he is in slaying, be not one; but those instants be diverse. Nor the act is not in one point, when it is threatened, and when it is in doing. Wherefore, when there is a sword drawn at your °friend's back, ready to kill him, or your °friend hath a cup with poison in his °hand, ready to drink, the peril is not now imminent — that is to say, to be done or to happen — but it is in the instant of doing or happening. Neither it threateth, but is at the <C4r> very point of executing. Wherefore, there is repugnancy in your own reasoning, if this word imminent be truly expounded.

HARPOCRATES Yes, that may not be denied. It hath been so long by noble authors approved.

PASQUIL Then resort to your first assertion. When the peril were imminent, then would ye give warning, and it followeth that then silence were out of season.

HARPOCRATES Yea, truly.

PASQUIL Ergo, speech were then in good season: is not this your conclusion?

HARPOCRATES Thou hittest it °as just as may be devised.

PASQUIL What, before and after this instant?

HARPOCRATES Speech is unprofitable: before, to him that speaketh, as I have rehearsed; after, to him which is spoken unto. For where may be no longer defence or resistance, speech nothing availeth.

PASQUIL Ye thought all this while that in maintaining your silence ye had reproved my li-<C4v>berty of speech, which ye call babbling, and that ye had appointed a time °of silence and speaking which ye thought that I lacked. Now behold, Harpocrates, how in the time to speak ye and I have all this while agreed. And in the two instants wherewith ye season your silence, if we two disagree, see that it is because ye err so much from natural reason.

[12] i.e. a 'Dunce', in the *OED*, s.v. 'An application of the name of John *Duns* Scotus [*c*. 1265–1308], the celebrated scholastic theologian [...]. His works on theology, philosophy, and logic, were textbooks in the Universities, in which (as at Oxford) his followers, called *Scotists*, were a predominating Scholastic sect, until the 16th c., when the system was attacked with ridicule, first by the humanists, and then by the reformers, as a farrago of needless entities, and useless distinctions. The *Dunsmen* or *Dunses*, on their side, railed against the "new learning", and the name *Duns* or *Dunce*, already synonymous with "cavilling sophist" or "hair-splitter", soon passed into the sense of "dull obstinate person impervious to the new learning", and of "blockhead incapable of learning or scholarship"'.

° Duns-man the instant] Duns-man ye must remember the instant *C*
° friend's] master's *C*
° friend] master *C*
° hand ready] hand and is ready *C*
° as just as may be devised] justly in mine opinion *C*
° of] for *C*

HARPOCRATES How prove ye that?

PASQUIL Even by your own conclusion.

HARPOCRATES Nay! Ye cannot bring that to pass, for all your subtle invention.

PASQUIL Well, I will do what I can. And, I trow, ye will not deny me if ye be not of the condition of some men, which by no reason will be removed from their own opinion. But now to the matter. Thou saidest at the first that if thine enemy stood at thy back with his sword drawn to slay thee, thou wouldest then be warned, <C5r> lest thou moughtest be sore hurt or perchance killed, which, although it were foolishly spoken of so great a learned man (as who saith thine enemy could not slay thee, except he stood at thy back and had his sword drawn), yet °in the speaking have we two accorded. But to your own saying ye have repugned, where ye said that in silence was surety. But to excuse that, ye did season your silence: that is to say, putting to time, which undoubtedly is a wholesome herb and a savoury, and then ye were content to warn your friend, when the peril were imminent. And that term ye expounded thus: when the thing appeared to be in the instant to be done or to happen and, as °it were, threatened to come. And hereupon ye grounded your conclusion, that speech were then in good season. Which argument I will not deny, for I have <C5v> been alway of the same opinion. But now remember your grammar, and consider that the said definition is in the future time, that is to say, the thing which is imminent is to be done hereafter, and not in doing, which is the present time. Then, whether your master's enemy be at his back or at Poitiers in France, as I said at the first, if ye know that he purposeth to slay him, then it appeareth to you that the killing of your master is in the instant to be done and is threatened to happen; ergo, the peril is imminent, and ye are bound to give your friend warning.

HARPOCRATES Perchance I may know a thing, and yet it appeareth not to me; and then your argument availeth not an herring, as I may know by other men's telling, or by conjecture of a light suspicion.

PASQUIL Nay, then shall we have much ado with you, if ye will compel <C6r> me, of every word that I speak, to make definition. Though I have not so much learning as you, I use alway my words in their proper signification and to serve to the matter that I reason unto. I know a thing which by a cause I consider evidently; and that which is only reported, I do hear but I know not; but conjecture is by signs, resemblance, or likelihood, which may be false, and yet is it not to be neglected, as it shall appear afterward. But now return we to knowledge, which, being certain, as I have defined it,

° in the speaking] in speaking *C*
° it were, threatened] it is, were threatened *C*

as soon as thou knowest that one will kill or poison thy master, the peril is imminent; then by thine own reason, thou oughtest to warn him. If not, thou art by thine own sentence condemned of treason.

HARPOCRATES Thou sayest sore to me, Pasquil. Notwithstanding, yet me seemeth I <C6v> should not warn him so soon, for the dangers which thou rehearsedest mought happen unto me, if I lacked a thankful and secret hearer, or else the purpose were changed; but it were better to tarry until it came to such preparation that it mought not be denied.

PASQUIL So mought it be, if ye were partner of the conspiracy, for then mought ye happen to be made privy to the time when and the place where that your master should stand in such jeopardy; but else, ye mought know of such a thing purposed, and °yet be not sure of the time when it should be executed. Then if ye forbare to warn your master until the peril mought be more evident and, as ye say, mought not be denied, before that time it mought be more than imminent, and in the second instant, that is to say in the self doing, or, to speak it more cleanly, in execution. <C7r>

HARPOCRATES But then were I out of danger.

PASQUIL Yea, that is all that °ye care for! Yet mought ye happen to be deceived, and your silence, instead of surety, turn you to trouble. For seldom is the master in jeopardy, and the servants at liberty, specially they which be next about him. Or if ye happen to escape enemies, if it may be perceived that ye knew of the peril and would not discover it, ye should perchance escape hardly the halter, though ye had shaken off all your long robes and were but in a jerkin. Yet if ye warned your master at the beginning, though he took it not thankfully, yet did you your duty and cannot lack reward of God, who loveth truth, for your fidelity. And though he whom ye disappointed or his affinity shall seek how to be avenged on you, either God will defend you or, if there fall to you thereby any ad-<C7v>versity, finally falsehood long kept in will brast out at the last; and then shall repentance cause your simplicity to be had in renome and perpetual memory, which part of honour to every honest man passeth all other reward that may be given in this life that is transitory. But because we spake whilere of conjecture, if by signs and likelihoods, deeply considered without malice or other vicious affection, ye do conject that your master is in peril, although ye be not so much bounden to tell him as if ye knew it, yet if ye tell it him with your conjecture, ye fulfil more the parts of a good servant than he that hath the same conjecture and speaketh nothing. For if that thing happen not that ye mistrusted, the cause is to be referred to God; but the signs and likelihoods ought not for all that to be another time despised, and your care and love to-<C8r>ward your

° yet] ye *B*
° ye] he *B*

master are to be highly commended. If it do happen, then your diligence and study are to be extolled.

HARPOCRATES By the faith of my body, thou hast reasoned cunningly.

PASQUIL That cunning I never learned in schools, but by long observation and marking of other men's folly.

HARPOCRATES But, Pasquil, though in perils concerning man's life, speech may be preferred sometime before silence, it concludeth not that it shall be so in all other things.

PASQUIL To bring thee to this point have I made all this long babbling. Esteemest thou life more than good renome or the wealth of thy country, for the which so many puissant and noble princes, so many wise and excellent philosophers have left their lives willingly? Who gladly will leave a better thing for a worse? Except for wantonness or for the new fashion, is any death so much to be <C8v> drad as perpetual infamy, the subversion of the commonweal, or universal destruction of all the whole country, which to escape or resist many valiant knights, honourable matrons, and chaste damsels have offered themselves to the death? And who refuseth the less pain to cast himself into the greater torment? Or doest thou esteem the death of the soul to be of less importance than the death of the body? What saist thou? That judgment belongeth to thy faculty.

HARPOCRATES Indeed, there ye touch me.

PASQUIL Likewise, a knock on the head, though it be to the skull, is not so dangerous to be healed as an evil affection thrast into thy master's brains by false opinion. Nor a wipe over his face with a sword shall not blemish so much his visage, as vice shall deform his soul and deface his renome, whereby he is further known than by his <D1r> physiognomy. Is there any poison can make him to be so abhorred of man as avarice, tyranny, or beastly living shall cause him be hated of God and man universally?

HARPOCRATES No, in good faith; I think thou sayest truly.

PASQUIL Then confer all this together with that which we before reasoned and see: where in anything that thy master speaketh or doeth, if there be any of the perils imminent which I late rehearsed, whether it were better to speak or keep silence, and in which of them were most surety? And consider also that between these two perils that I have rehearsed is no little diversity, besides that the one is much more than the other. For in the bodily peril, in the time of the stroke, perchance your master would hear you and thereby escape, ere ye mought defend him. But the other peril, of soul or mind, the longer that he <D1v> continueth therein, the more gladly he receiveth the stroke, and the more he will disdain to be warned by you, and then ye put yourself in more danger of that which we spake of before. But for all that, neither in time of danger thou oughtest to leave thy master unwarned, which thou hast already granted; nor yet, when thy master is striken or poisoned, speech is unprofitable as thou hast supposed.

HARPOCRATES How prove you that? For if ye be a surgeon, ye know it must be your deeds and not your words that must help him.

PASQUIL Now, it is well remembered: ye shall have God's blessing! I never heard a more fool, by my halidom! Doeth a surgeon all his cure with plasters and instruments? Sometime he speaketh also, or, if he be dumb, one speaketh for him and telleth his patient what meats and drinks be unwholesome, which be <D2r> levitives and helpeth his medicine. Also, when he perceiveth him to be faint or discomforted, then with sweet words and fair promises he reviveth his courage. If he be disobedient or riotous, he rebuketh him and do aggravate the danger to make the sickness more grievous. °And, perdie, Gnatho named you to be your master's physician, when he said that ye were his confessor. For a confessor serveth for none other purpose but to cure man's soul of deadly sins, which be her mortal diseases: can °ye do that without speaking? Also ye said, where mought be no longer resistance, speech nothing availed: I ween ye said truer than ye were ware. For when Gnatho with his flattery and ye with your silence have once rooted in your master's heart false opinions and vicious affects, which is the poison that we so much spake of, <D2v> though ye °after repent you and perceive the danger, yet shall it perchance be impossible with speech to remove those opinions and cure those affects, except ye loved so well your master that, for his health, ye would confess your own errors.

GNATHO Nay, God's body, so mought we get for ourself a pair of terriers.

PASQUIL Well, it were better tarry[13] than run to the devil with your master, or that good renome should run away from him. But tell me, Harpocrates, as thou thinkest, were not speech now expedient? Or how mought thy master be otherwise cured? With silence, trowest thou?

HARPOCRATES It seemeth that silence should nothing profit nor speech should anything avail, if the opinions and affects be so impressed that they cannot be removed.

PASQUIL Yet again, if ye speak no wiselier to your master than ye do to me, he hath of you a <D3r> worshipful counsellor. I demand of you remedy to cure wrong opinions and vicious affects, and ye answer me that neither speech nor silence is profitable, like as if I had asked counsel of a physician what

13 The pun may be obscured by the modern spelling.

° And, perdie, Gnatho named you to be your master's physician, when he said that ye were his confessor. For] The same is the office of a good confessor, where he perceiveth man's soul to be wounded with vicious affections, since that *B*
° ye] he *B*
° after repent you and perceive the danger] perceive the danger and then sore repent you *B*

thing would heal me of my sickness, and he would say that giving to me medicine or giving me none should not avail me!

HARPOCRATES Spake I not well, where I find no remedy?

PASQUIL No, and, look ye, wisely. For and if ye remember, I did not affirm expressly that it should be impossible to remove false opinions or vicious affects where they were impressed, but I joined thereto 'peradventure' and also an exception: if ye that induced them confessed not your own error. Then if your confession mought cure them, speech were then not unprofitable. And if your own confession availed not, since I affirmed not expressly that <D3v> the said diseases were incurable, if neither silence nor speech should be profitable, what should then be the remedy?

HARPOCRATES °I cannot tell, except it were grace.

PASQUIL I heard thee never speak so wisely. But yet supposest thou that grace will so lightly enter where false opinion and vicious affects be so deeply imprinted, except they be first somewhat removed by good persuasion, unless thou thinkest that every man shall be called of God as Saint Paul was, who was elected? And yet now I remember me: at his conversion, Christ spake unto him and told him that it was hard to spurn again the prick, where, if Christ had hold his peace, Saul, which was then beaten down to the ground, mought have happened never to have been called Saint Paul; but if he had escaped, he would by likelihood have continued <D4r> still in his errour.[14]

HARPOCRATES It is not for us, Pasquil, to ensearch the impenetrable judgments of God; but the grace of God hath happened far above men's expectation, and where all other remedy lacked. For then the puissance of almighty God is specially proved.

PASQUIL But trusting only therein, to leave our own endeavour, I think it presumption. And what endeavour may be in silence? Wherefore speech is not only profitable, but also of necessity must be used in healing the diseases both of the soul and also the body.

HARPOCRATES I cannot deny that, if I say truly.

PASQUIL Then when is your silence in season?

HARPOCRATES I cannot shortly tell, I am so abashed at thy froward reason.

PASQUIL Then will I help you to know your own virtue, wherein ye have such delectation. I trow ye heard not how I did expound the sentence of Aeschylus,[15] which <D4v> Gnatho rehearsed to me for a counsel?

[14] Reference is to Act 9. 5, 26. 14: 'It is hard for thee to kick against the pricks', though the phrase may also recall Chaucer, 'Truth' 8–11: 'Tempest thee noght al croked to redresse, | In trust of her that turneth as a bal: | Grete reste stant in litel besinesse, | And eek be war to sporne ageyn an al'.

[15] Above, p. 32 and n. 4.

° I] I make God avow, I *B*

HARPOCRATES Yes, that I did, for I stood all that while at the window, hearkening of thee.

PASQUIL See how full the world is of such false images, that do hear all when they seem to hear nothing? As I trust to be saved, with such fellows it is perilous dealing. But yet that shall not cause Pasquil to leave his babbling. Now, Harpocrates, bear away the said sentence with mine exposition, and use it.

HARPOCRATES So I will, as much as pertaineth to silence.

PASQUIL Yea, God avow, and also to speaking, or else all the counsel is not worth three half-pence. Think ye to be a counsellor, and speak not? What, were the emperor the better if instead of counsellors he had set in his chamber the images of Cato, Metellus, Laelius, Cicero, and such other persons, who, living, far excelled in wit, experi-<D5r>ence and learning, them which be now about him?[16] Be men that sit and speak nothing any better than they? No, but rather much worse: for they serve for nothing, yet the images do that wherefore they be ordained, that is to say, bring to men's remembrance the wisdom and virtue of them whom they represented. But dumb counsellors do not their office wherefore they be called to counsel, but by their silence they cause many things to be brought to an unlucky conclusion.

HARPOCRATES And thou that art not called to counsel art full of babbling.

PASQUIL But once in a year. And wotest thou why that is?

HARPOCRATES Nay; tell me, I pray thee.

PASQUIL Marry, if they that be called would alway play the parts of good counsellors, and both spiritual and temporal governors would banish thee and Gnatho out of their cour-<D5v>ts, except ye amend your conditions, I would speak never a word, but sit as still as a stone, like as ye see me. But forasmuch as it happeneth all contrary and that things be so far out of frame that stones do grudge at it — rememberest thou not what a clattering they made at the last wars in Italy?[17] — and yet counsellors be speechless, I that am set in the city of Rome, which is the head of the world, once in the year shall hear of the state of all princes and regions. And because in the month of May men be all set in pleasure, and then they take merrily such words as be spoken again them, then boldly I put forth my verdict, and that openly.[18]

HARPOCRATES There thou doest foolishly, for thou shouldest do more good if thou spakest privily.

[16] The one of these figures not elsewhere much discussed by Elyot is the central figure in Cic., *Amic.* (also appearing in Cic., *Rep.*): C. Laelius (fl. 190–129 BCE), called 'Sapiens', prominent as an orator and propagator of Stoicism.

[17] Probably referring to the sack of Rome in May 1527 by mutinous imperial mercenary troops.

[18] The usual date for posting *pasquinate* was April 25.

PASQUIL Tush, man, my plainness is so well known that I shall never come unto privy chamber or gallery. <D6r>

HARPOCRATES Since thou profitest so little, why art thou so busy?

PASQUIL To the intent that men shall perceive that their vices, which they think to be wonderful secret, be known to all men. And that I hope alway that, by much clamour and open repentance, when they see the thing not succeed to their purpose, they will be ashamed.

HARPOCRATES Yet mayst thou happen to be deceived.

PASQUIL But they much more, when they know not who loveth them°.

GNATHO Harpocrates, it is time that we repair to the court, lest we be blamed. And let us leave Pasquil with his pratery.

PASQUIL And I will leave you both with your flattery.[19] Yet I trust in God to see the day that I will not set by the best of you both a butterfly. As great a wonder have I seen ere this time.

HARPOCRATES Farewell, Pasquil, and think on silence.

PASQUIL Farewell, Harpocra-<D6v>tes, and think on thy conscience.[20] I ween I mought buy as much of the costermonger for two pence!

Now, when these two fellows come to °the court, they will tell all that they have heard of me, it maketh no matter. For I have said nothing but by the way of advertisement, without reproaching of any one person, wherewith no good man hath cause to take any displeasure.° Judge what men list, my thought shall be free. And God, who shall judge all men, knoweth that I desire all things to be in good °point, so that I mought ever be speechless, as it is my very nature to be. Adieu, gentle hearers, and say well by Pasquil when he is from you.

CVM PRIVILEGIO.

19 With the previous speech, concluding a rhymed pentameter couplet.
20 Making rhyme with the ending of the previous speech.

°] *B add* truly
° the court] their master *B*
°] *B add* And he that doth, by that which is spoken he is soon spied, to what part he leaneth.
° point so] point on the condition *B*

°<A1r>

THE DOCTRINAL OF PRINCES

made by the noble orator Isocrates

and translated out of

Greek into English by

Sir Thomas Elyot,

knight.

° The text is from *B* = *c.* 1550 ed. (RSTC 14279 = ESTC S109091), departures from which are enclosed in angled brackets <>, including the standard enumeration of the periods of the Greek original embedded in the text, 1–54; collated with *A* = 1533? ed. (RSTC 14278 = ESTC S2142). The editions' marginalia, enclosed between slashes, \ /, have been removed to the textual notes.

°<A2r>

°<Prologue>

SIR THOMAS ELYOT, knight, to the reader

This little book, which, in mine opinion, is to be compared in counsel and short sentence with any book, holy scripture excepted, I have translated out of Greek, not presuming to contend with them which have done the same in Latin; but to the intent only that I would assay if our English tongue mought receive the quick and proper sentences pronounced by the Greeks. And in this experience I have found, if I be not much deceived, that the form of speaking used of the Greeks called — in Greek and also in Latin — *phrasis*[1] much nearer approacheth to that which at this day we use than the order of the Latin. I mean in the sentences and not in the words; which I doubt not shall be affirmed <A2v> by them who, sufficiently instructed in all the said three tongues, shall with a good judgment read this work. And where I have put at the beginning this words, 'vessel, plate', or, for that which is in Greek, 'brass or gold wrought', it is perceived of every wise man for what intent I did it. Finally, the chief cause of this my little exercise was to the intent that they which do not understand Greek nor Latin should not lack the commodity and pleasure which may be taken in reading thereof. Wherefore, if I shall perceive you to take this mine enterprise thankfully, I shall that little portion of life which remaineth — God sending me quietness of mind[2] — bestow in preparing for you such books, in the reading whereof ye shall find both honest pastime and also profitable counsel and learning.

Fare ye well.

[1] On the remark, see J. B. Trapp, 'Conformity of Greek and the Vernacular', in *Classical Influences on European Culture A. D. 500–1500*, ed. by R. R. Bolgar (Cambridge: Cambridge University Press, 1971), pp. 239–44 (p. 244); also, Stewart, 'The Trouble with English Humanism', p. 90, quoting Elyot, *Bibl.*, '*Phrasis*, The proper form or manner of speech, which in one country is oftentimes diverse, as Southern, Northern, Devonish, Kentish; French, Picard, Gascoigne, Walloon; some do set the negative before the affirmative, some contrary; some speech is quick, some grave, some flourishing, some temperate'.

[2] Elyot used similar phrasing elsewhere: *Gov.*, praef. (Watson, p. xxxi), 'God giving me quietness' and *Gov.* 1.2 (Watson, p. 15), 'God granting me quietness and liberty of mind'; and there is a section headed 'QUIETNESS OF MIND' in Elyot, *Banquet*, sig. F8r. The ancient notions of *ataraxia* or *apatheia* that these phrases represent were developed by others associated with Henry VIII's court and counsel, including the poet Wyatt, whose translation of the Plutarchan *De tranquillitate animi* found its way into print: *Quyete of Mynde* (London: Pynson, 1528); see David R. Carlson, 'Morley's Translations from Roman Philosophers and English Courtier Literature', in *Triumphs of English: Henry Parker, Lord Morley*, ed. by Marie Axton and James P. Carley (London: British Library, 2000), pp. 131–51 (pp. 137–40).

°] omitting sig. A1v (blank).
° <PROLOGUE> SIR THOMAS ELYOT, knight, [...] learning. Fare ye well.] *A om*

<A3r>

<THE DOCTRINAL OF PRINCES>

The Oration of Isocrates to Nicocles the King.

<1> They that be wont, Nicocles, to bring °you that be kings garments, °vessel or plate, or other like jewels, whereof they be needy and ye be rich and have plenty; they plainly seem unto me, not to present you, but to make open market, selling those things much more craftily than they that confess themself to retail. <2> For my part, I suppose that to be the best gift and most profitable, also most convenient °as for me to give as for thee to receive, if I moght prescribe unto thee by what studies desiring and from what works abstaining thou mayest best order thy realm and city. <3> For to private persons be sufficient instructions, specially that they live not delicately, but daily do labour for things con-<A3v>cerning their living; and, moreover, they have laws whereby they are governed. They have also liberty of speech, wherewith it is leeful for friends to blame each other and enemies to reproach each other of their offences. Thereto diverse ancient poets have °left sundry works instructing men how to live well, so that, by all those means, it °seemeth that diverse men have amended their living.

<4> But to great princes no such thing happeneth. For they who of all other ought to be best taught or instructed, after they be once stablished in their authority, they still persevere most ignorant and without learning, forasmuch as many men dare not approach them and they that keep them company speak alway to please them.

Moreover, being made lords of much substance and great authority and not using well such °occ<a>sions as <A4r> happen, they have caused many to doubt which life is best to be chosen, either of them that live privately and meanly or of them that be in princely dignity. <5> For when they behold their honour, richesse, and authority, they suppose that all princes be equal to gods. But when they consider the fear and perils and, revolving in their remembrances, do find some slain by them that least ought to have done it, other °doing some displeasure to their most familiar companions — to diverse happeneth both the one and the other — then contrariwise they think it better and more commodious to live in any other manner, how so ever it be, than in so many dangers to be king of all Asia.

<6> The cause of this disorder and trouble is forasmuch as they repute a kingdom as meet for every man to have as any other mean office; where, of all things pertaining to man, a king-<A4v>dom is the greatest and requireth most

° you] to you *A*
° vessel or] *A om*
° as] as well *A*
° left] loft *A*
° seemeth] is very likely *A*
° occasions] *A* : occsions *B*
° doing some displeasure to their] enforced by chance to offend his *A*

providence, touching every act whereby a man may best govern according to the manners of people; and, to observe such things as be good and eschew those that be noyful, it is expedient to take counsel and examine such acts as be in daily experience.

<7> Generally, all studies which ought to be observed most diligently and wherein a man ought to be exercised, I will assay to declare. But whether this my gift, once finished, shall accord to the purpose that I go about, it is hard to know at the beginning. For many things which have °been written, as well in verse as in prose, as long as they were in the minds of the writers, men had of them great expectation; but after they were once finished and openly published, men had of them opinion much less than they hoped. <8> Howbeit, this mine enterprise is to be commended, <A5r> wherein I seek for that which other men have committed and do prescribe rules to them that be governors.

For they that teach private persons do profit them whom they teach only. But if any man instructeth in virtue them that have rule over the multitude, he thereby profiteth the one and the other, as well them that be in authority as those that be under their governance; forasmuch as, to the first, he maketh their authority the more stable and sure, and, to the other, he causeth the rule or governance to be the more easier.

<9> First, therefore, it must be considered what is the office of them that do govern. For if we order well the head and that which is the principal of the whole matter, having our respect thereunto, the better shall we treat of the residue.

I suppose all men will °grant that it pertaineth to princes, their country by any adversity being troubled, to set <A5v> it in quietness, and, if it be wealthy, so to preserve it; and to make also great of that that is little, since therefore all other things, which daily happen, ought to be done and experienced. <10> And verily, it is apparent to all men that it behooveth them that are and shall be of power to do the premises, and also those which shall thereof consult not to be ignorant, but to consider how they may use them more prudently than other in their ministration.

<11> For it is °very certain that such shall °princes have their realms and governance as they themselves have prepared their own minds and opinions. And therefore, no wrestler or champion ought so much to travail his body in exercise as kings ought their minds in study. For all the prizes that ever were given in common games or jousts[3] are in no part to be °compared to that prize, wherefore ye that be kin-<A6r>gs daily do labour.

[3] ἆθλοι 'public festivals'.

° been] be *A*
° grant] confess *A*
° very] *A om*
° princes] they *A*
° compared] conferred *A*

<12> Which things considered, it is expedient to take good heed that, as much as thou excellest other °men in honour, so much more thou mayest exceed them in virtues. And think not care and diligence, in all other things profitable and in making us better, to be of none importance; ne °condemn not man's infelicity, that, concerning beasts, we have found crafts to make them tame and to be of more value, and °little do advance ourselves to the attaining of virtue. But rather, as learning and industry may be in any thing beneficial unto our °souls, so order thy wit and opinion. <13> Be also most familiar with them which, being about thee, be wisest; and get other such as thou mayest come by most like unto them.

Think not that it shall become thee to lack the knowledge of any famous poets and other great learned men; <A6v> but be thou of the one the hearer, of the other the disciple or scholar.

Prepare thyself so that in virtue thou mayest be judge of °them which therein be thine inferiors and °a contender with them that be thy superiors. <14> By such manner of exercise thou shalt soon attain to be such one as we determined °he ought to be that ruleth aright and governeth well his country or city.

Thou shalt be °counselled best by thyself in thinking it inconvenient that the better be ruled by the worse or that fools before wise men should be preferred.

The more vehemently thou abhorrest other men's madness or folly, the better shalt thou °practice thy wit. <15> For thereat must they begin that purpose to do any of those things which be convenient and necessary, and therewith love well their people and country. <A7r> For no man shall rule well, either horse or hounds, nor men, or anything else, if he delight not and take pleasure in those things which be under his governance.

<16> Take care of the multitude, and °esteem above all things to °rule graciously over them whom thou governest, remembering that, as well where few persons governeth, as also in other commonweals, they longest do continue that for the multitude do take most care and study.

° men] *A om*
° condemn not man's infelicity] reprove that infelicity of man *A*
° little do advance ourselves to the attaining of virtue] as for ourselves in acquiring virtue we little may do *A*
° souls so order thy wit and opinion] wits so order thine opinion or sentence and *A*
° them which therein be] *A om*
° a contender with] follower of *A*
° he] that he *A*
° counselled best by thyself in thinking] advertised and exhorted best by thyself if thou wilt think *A*
° practice] exercise *A*
° esteem] esteem this *A*
° rule graciously over them whom] be beloved of them while *A*

°Thou shalt truly rule well thy people if thou neither °doest suffer any man to do wrong nor despiseth any that suffereth wrong. And takest good heed that good men be rewarded with honour and authority and that other by any injury be not endamaged. These be the principles and chief introduction into the right and commendable governance of a public weal. <A7v>

<17> °Repeal or change such laws and ordinances as be not well constitute. Specially be thou the author of those that be good, or at °least the follower of them that were well made by other.

°Seek for such laws that on all parts be good, and do profit to all universally, and in themselves be of one accord and consent; moreover, those that among the people make fewest contentions. And such controversies as be, determine them shortly. All these things ought to be in laws that be well and substantially ordained.

<18> Provide for thy people such occupation as whereby may grow great advantage and lucre; and that °contention and suit may bring to them detriment; to the intent that they may eschew the one, to the other they may °be well disposed and ready.

In controversies, give always such sentence as °is not repugnant; and pro-<A8r>nounce thy judgments without favour to any man and without discordance; so that they be ever all one and like in semblable causes.

It becometh — and is also expedient — to princes, in matter of justice, to have the mind immoveable, like °to the laws that be well provided.

<19> °Order thy city or country °like thy house left by thy father — in stuff, gay and royally decked; in occupation, busy and diligent — that thou mayest have both honour and abundance of richesse.

Albeit, declare thy magnificence not in °such sumptuous expenses that shortly do °vanish, but only in the things before expressed; that is to say, in the adorning or garnishing of thy possessions and in beneficence and liberality toward thy friends. For that which is so employed shall remain with thee still, and thou shalt leave to thy <A8v> children more commodity thereby than they should °have of superfluous expenses.

° \Injuries to be avoided/
° doest] *A om*
° \Hurtful traditions to be avoided./
° at least the follower of] at the least follow *A*
° \What the laws should be./
° contention] all other business *A*
° be well disposed and ready] apply them diligently *A*
° is] be *A*
° to the laws] as the laws ought to be *A*
° \To govern a city./
° like] like as *A*
° such] *A om*
° vanish] vanish away and be soon forgotten *A*
° have of superfluous expenses] have had of the money that thou hast bestowed *A*

<20> In the honour due unto God, observe diligently that which is left unto thee by thy progenitors; and suppose verily that sacrifice to be most °acceptable and service most °thankful to God if thou endeavour thyself to excel all other men in virtue and justice. For undoubtedly, thereby shalt thou obtain more reasonable petitions than if thou didst give unto him great treasure or offerings.

Reward thy familiar counsellors with principal dignities, and to them whom thou knowest benevolent and trusty, give perpetual and stable promotions.

<21> °Think that the best and most sure guard of thy person be friends virtuous and honest, loving and benevolent subjects, and thine own will stable <B1r> and circumspect. For by those things authority is obtained and longest preserved.

°Have good await on the households and expenses of thy subjects, thinking that they, dispending unprofitably, do consume thine own proper treasure. And that which they get by their good husbandry augmenteth thy °substance and honour, considering that all the goods of them that be subjects be at the commandment of the prince that ruleth °well and honourably.

<22> Let men perceive thee to have alway truth in such reverence that to thy words they may sooner give credence than to other men's oaths.

Make thy country safe and sure abiding to all them that be strangers, and in their contracts just and indifferent.

Of such as do repair unto thee, <B1v> set more by them that for some merit do look to have something of thee than of those that do bring presents to thee. For honouring °men for their merits, thou shalt much more be of other commended.

<23> Take away fear fro thy subjects; and be not terrible to them that have not offended but, like as thou wouldest have them disposed toward °thee, so be thou toward them.

Do thou nothing in °fury, since other men know what time and occasion are meetest for thee.

Be thou seen to have such wisdom and gravity that nothing that is done can be hid from thee; notwithstanding, be thou easy and merciful in punishing offences under their merits.

° acceptable] acceptable to God *A*
° thankful to God] thankful *A*
° \A prince's sure guard/
° \A prince's right over his subjects/
° substance and honour] treasure and maketh thee rich *A*
° well and] for the public weal *A*
° men for their merits] them *A*
° thee] thee in love or fear *A*
° fury since other men know what time and occasion are meetest for] anger for it appeareth to other when opportunity serveth *A*

<24> Shew thyself princely, not in sturdiness or punishing cruelly, but in surmounting all other in wisdom, °that they may suppose that thou canst <B2r> counsel them better for their weal than °they can themselves.

Be also warlike and valiant in feats of arms and provision for wars; but yet notwithstanding embrace °then peace and do nothing injustly.

Deal thou with inferior countries, in all intercourses and mutual contracts, according as thou wouldest that they that be to thy country superiors should do unto thee.

<25> Strive not for everything, but for that only which, if thou °obtainest, may be to thy profit.

Blame not them that be vanquished to their commodity, but accompt them to be fools that do vanquish other to their own detriment.

Suppose not them to be °men of great wisdom that do take greater things in hand than they can order, but those which in mean things do bring well to pass that that they pur-<B2v>posed.

<26> Follow not them that do obtain greatest authority, but them that best °use things that be present.

Finally, do not think thyself happy if thou rulest over all men terribly and in great danger. But if, being such as thou oughtest to be and doing as °the time present requireth, thou desirest moderate things and thereof thou lackest nothing, then art thou happy.

<27> Get thee friends, not all them that do seek friendship of thee, but such as be most agreeable unto thy nature; neither those with whom thou shalt live pleasantly, but with whom thou mayest govern thy country most surely.

Make diligent espial and proof of thy most familiar servants, remembering that such as be not with thee so conversant do suppose that thou art like in conditions to them whom thou usest familiarly. <B3r>

<28> Matters wherewith thou thyself wilt not meddle commit to such persons as, whatsoever they do, the blame shall be imputed °chiefly unto thee.

Think not them to be loyal or faithful that do praise all thing that thou doest, but them that do blame the thing wherein thou errest.

Give to wise men liberty to speak to thee freely, that, °in things whereof thou doubtest, thou mayest have them with whom thou mayest try °out the certainty.

° that they may suppose that thou canst] and how to *A*
° they can] *A om*
° then] thou *A*
° obtainest] doest vanquish *A*
° men of great wisdom] valiant or of great courage *A*
° use things that be present] order those things that do happen unto them *A*
° the time present requireth] opportunity serveth *A*
° chiefly unto] to *A*
° in] *A om*
° out] *A om*

°Discern crafty flatterers from them that do serve thee with true heart and benevolence, lest the evil men receive more profit by thee than they that be honest and virtuous.[4]

<29> Hear diligently what men speak mutually one of another, and assay to know as well what manner of persons those be that have spoken, as also they of whom they reported. <B3v>

°Accordingly as thou correctest offenders, semblably and with the same punishment correct false detractors and accusers of innocents.

Have no less dominion or rule over thyself than over other.

Think it most incident unto a king and most royal never to be subject to pleasant affections[5] but to rule more over thine appetites than over thy people and subjects.

Admit no recreation without good advisement; but delight in such exercise whereby thou mayest receive some commodity, and that other may perceive that thou art thereby the better.

<30> Glory not in such things which are possible to be done by that be unthrifts; but rejoice in virtue, wherein evil men cannot participate with thee.

°Suppose not honour to be that which is published abroad with fear, but very honour to be where men by them-<B4r>selves wonder more at thy wisdom than at thy fortune.

If it chance thee to take any pleasure in anything that is not honest or virtuous, do it very secretly; but, going about things of great weight and importance, shew thyself abroad unto all men.

<31> Require not that all other men should live in good order and princes to be in their living remiss and negligent; but order thy temperance in living to be an example to other, considering that the manners of all the whole city or country do ensue and resemble their prince's conditions.

It shall be to thee a token that thou hast well governed, if thou perceive them that °be under thy governance to be by thy diligence wealthy and more temperate in living.

<32> °Set more by leaving to thy children honest fame or renome than great possessions or richesse. For these be tran-<B4v>sitory, the other immortal. Also, goods may be gotten by fame, but good fame can be bought with no

4 Cf. Elyot, *Banquet*, sig. F7r (with attribution to 'Socrates'), 'Separate them that do craftily flatter thee from those that do faithfully love thee, lest ill men have most profit by thee'.

5 ἂν μηδεμιᾷ δουλεύῃς τῶν ἡδονῶν, 'when you are a slave to no pleasure'. The key term, ἡδοναί, here 'pleasant affections', recurs below, pp. 63 and 64.

° \Crafty flatterers/

° \False detractors/

° \Very honour./

° be] been *A*

° \Honest fame./] *A* : *B om*

money. Also, goods happen to men that be of evil disposition; but so doth not good estimation, but cometh only to them that endeavour themself with virtue to get it.

Be delicate[6] in thine apparel and garments that serve for thy body; in all other parts of thy living, be continent; as it beseemeth all princes of honour, °to the intent that they that behold thee, for thine honourable presence may deem thee worthy to be a governor, and thy familiars and servants for thy noble courage may have of thee a like good opinion.

<33> Consider diligently both thine own words and thy deeds, to the intent thou mayest fall in very few errors.

Of all things, it is best to happen on the right point of all things that <B5r> are to be done; but, forasmuch as that is very hard to be knowen, better is to leave somewhat than to exceed. °For that wherein somewhat doth lack is nearer to temperance than that wherein is too much abundance.

<34> °Endeavour thee to be both courteous and of a reverend gravity. For the one beseemeth a prince; the other is expedient and more agreeable to every company; albeit to use both, it is of all other things the most difficile. For thou shalt find for the more part them that use a reverent gravity to be unpleasant; them that be courteous, to be of base courage and simple. Therefore, the one and the other is to be used, °but then eschew that thing which in any of them is ill or seemeth °inconvenient.

<35> °If thou wouldest perfectly know that which belongeth to kings to perceive, give thee to experience and study of philosophy. For philosophy shall declare un-<B5v>to thee the means or ways how to bring to pass thine affairs; experience in semblable business shall make thee able to do or sustain them.

Behold diligently °that which as well princes as private persons do daily and what of their acts doth succeed °in conclusion.

Surely, if thou remember well things that are past, thou shalt the better consult of things coming.

<36> Think where private persons have died with good will, to the intent that after their death they mought be commended, that it were great shame to

[6] τρύφα, usually with a more negative connotation than Elyot gives: 'be licentious, run riot, wax wanton', 'be extravagant', 'live softly, luxuriously, fare sumptuously'.

° to the intent] *A om*
° For that wherein somewhat doth lack is nearer to temperance than that wherein is too much abundance] For moderation shall prevail more where somewhat doth lack than where that anything is superfluous *A*
° \Courtesy and gravity./
° but then] than *A*
° inconvenient] not convenient *A*
° \Experience and philosophy./
° that which] what *A*
° in conclusion] or happen *A*

princes not to travail in such study or business whereby in their lives they may be worthily praised.

Desire to leave when thou diest rather monuments or images of thy virtues than of thy personage.[7]

Endeavour thee specially to keep alway thyself and thy country in surety. <B6r>

If necessity constrain thee to jeopard thy person, chose rather to die with honour than to live in reproach.

<37> In all thine acts, remember that thou art a prince, and therefore do nothing unworthy to so °high a dignity.

°Set not so little by thy nature that thou suffer thyself all wholly to perish; but, inasmuch as thy body is mortal and thy soul immortal, assay to leave to thy soul an immortal remembrance.

<38> Use thee to speak of honest affairs and studies, that, by such custom, thou mayest think on like things as thou speakest of.

Things that in °counselling seem to be best, those execute thou in thy proper acts.

°At whose good renome thou hast most envy, his deeds do thou follow.

Look what thou counsellest thy children or servants to do, think it convenient that thyself do the °same. <B6v>

Either use that which I have advised thee to do, or inquire for better than that is.

<39> Suppose not them to be wise men that sharply can talk of small things and trifles, but those that can substantially °reason in matters of weighty importance.

Nor think not them wise that promise to other men wealth and good fortune, they themself being in great necessity; but rather those that, speaking of themselves moderately, can with other men and in their affairs use themself well and discretely and, being not troubled with any change of their living, know how to bear honestly and temperately as well adversity as also prosperity.

<40> And marvel thou not that I have now rehearsed many things that thou knewest before; nor that forgot I not, but knew well enough that, being <B7r>

[7] Cf. Elyot, *Gov.* 1.11 (Watson, p. 45), 'Moreover, the sweet Isocrates exhorteth the King Nicocles, whom he instructeth, to leave behind him statues and images that shall represent rather the figure and similitude of his mind than the features of his body, signifying thereby the remembrance of his acts written in histories'.

° high a dignity] noble estate *A*
° Set not so little by] Do not despise so *A*
° counselling] consultation *A*
° At whose good renome thou hast most envy] Whose opinions thou envyest *A*
° same] semblable *A*
° reason] speak *A*

such a multitude as well of princes as of private persons, some of them have spoken the same that I did, and many have heard it, and diverse have seen other men done it, and some there be that by themselves have experienced it.

<41> Notwithstanding, in matter concerning instruction, novelty is not to be sought for; for therein ought not to be founden either singular opinion, or thing impossible, or contrary to men's °conjecture. But suppose that to be in hearing most gracious or pleasant which, being sown in the minds of other, may assemble most matter to the purpose; and the same declare best and most aptly.

<42> For this know I well, that the counsels and wise sentences of poets and other good authors are thought of all men to be very profitable; yet will not they °very gladly give ear unto them, but be therewith in the same case as they be with °those that do <B7v> give them good counsel. For they praise them all, but they care not how seldom they come in their company, desiring to be rather with offenders than with them that of sin be the rebukers. <43> Example we may take of the poems or works of Hesiodus, Theognes, and Phocylides.[8] For every man affirmeth them to be excellent counsels concerning man's life; but although they say so, yet had they lever use that whereto their own madness induceth them than follow that whereto the others' precepts doeth advise them.

<44> Moreover, if one should gather out of the said authors that which men call sentences, wherein they perchance have been studious; in semblable wise, toward them should they be disposed. For they should with more pleasure hear a lying fable or °a fantasy[9] than the said precepts, made by much cunning and diligence.

8 Hesiod (fl. *c.* 700 BCE) is mentioned elsewhere in Elyot, including brief characterisation in *Bibl.*, below; Theognis (fl. *c.* 550 BCE), the Sicilian moral elegist, was widely quoted in antiquity, and Elyot translated some of his verse from Greek in *Knowledge*, below, p. 130; the gnomic poet Phocylides (fl. *c.* 560–520 BCE) is not mentioned elsewhere in Elyot's writings, however. Nonetheless, writings of all three of these poets were printed together — along with other aphoristic verse like the *Carmen aureum* of Pythagoras that Elyot also knew (see below, *Knowledge*, p. 90) — in the Greek textbook, *Scriptores aliquot gnomici, iis, qui Graecarum literarum candidati sunt, utilissimi* (Basel: Froben, 1521): see Paul Botley, *Learning Greek in Western Europe, 1396–1529* (Philadelphia, PA: American Philosophical Society, 2010), pp. 77–79. Also cf. Eras., *Apoph.*, 1 ded. ep. (= *Ep.* 2431; CWE 37, 4–5), 'Learned men have endeavoured to use their skills to lighten the prince's burden of care. Some, like Theognis and Isocrates, wrote books of maxims; others collected the stratagems and apophthegms of distinguished men, writers such as Valerius Maximus and Sextus Iulius Frontinus. Frontinus tells us that several other people had done the same thing'.

9 κωμῳδίας τῆς φαυλοτάτης: 'the cheapest comedy'.

° conjecture] expectation *A*
° very] *A om*
° those] these *A*
° a fantasy] fantasy *A*

<45> But what needeth it to tarry long upon every mat-<B8r>ter? Generally, if we will consider the natures of men, we shall perceive that many of them delight neither in meats that been most wholesome, nor in studies that been most honest, nor in deeds that °be most convenient, nor yet in doctrine that is most commodious; but, embracing pleasant appetites which be repugnant to profit, would seem to be painful and laborious °although they do nothing expedient or necessary.[10]

<46> How may any man content any such persons — either by preaching, or teaching, or telling of anything that is profitable — that for the words that be spoken do envy and have indignation at them that speak truly, and do take them for plain men or simple in whom lacketh wisdom? So much they abhor truth in all things that they know not what is theirs or do belong to their office; but, consulting or reasoning of that which doth pertain unto them, <B8v> they be sad and unpleasant; when they talk of other men's affairs they be merry and joyous.

<47> Moreover, they had leaver suffer some grief in their bodies than, in revolving what should be most necessary, travail anything in their minds. And if a man take good heed, he shall find in their mutual assemblies and companies that either they reprove other men or else that they of other be in some thing reproved; and when they be by themselves, they be ever wishing and never consulting. I have not spoken this again all men but only again them that be guilty in that which I have rehearsed.

<48> Finally, this is apparent and certain: whosoever will make or write anything pleasant and thankful to the multitude, he may not seek for words or matters most profitable, but for them that contain most fables and leasings.[11] For in °<h>earing such things they rejoice. <C1r> But when they perceive to be labours and contentions in their affairs, then be they pensive. Wherefore, Homer and they that found first tragedies may be well marvelled at, who in their works used both the said forms in writing. <49> For Homer expressed in °his works the contentions and battles of them which for their virtues were

[10] Elyot's translation, 'men [...] embracing pleasant appetites which be repugnant to profit, would seem to be painful and laborious', is improved somewhat by the *B* revision; though long, the Greek is clearer: 'ἀλλὰ παντάπασιν ἐναντίας τῷ συμφέροντι τὰς ἡδονὰς ἔχοντας, καὶ δοκοῦντας καρτερικοὺς καὶ φιλοπόνους εἶναι τοὺς τῶν δεόντων τι ποιοῦντας', 'but they have tastes which are in every way contrary to their best interests, while they view those who have some regard for their duty as men of austere and laborious lives'. The key term, ἡδοναί, here 'pleasant appetites', recurs above, p. 59 and below, p. 64.

[11] τῶν λόγων [...] τοὺς μυθωδεστάτους, 'discourses [...] which most abound in fictions', or 'in the legendary' or 'fabulous'.

° be] is *A*
° although they do nothing expedient or necessary] *A om*
° hearing] *A* : bearing *B*
° his works] *A om*

named half-gods; the other brought those fables into actual appearance, in so much as we not only may hear them but also may presently behold them. By such example °is it declared to them that be studious to please their hearers that they must abstain from exhorting and counselling them, and that they apply them to write and speak that only wherein they perceive the multitude to have most delectation.

<50> This before written have I declared, thinking that it beseemeth not thee, that °art not one of the people, to be of like <C1v> opinion with the multitude; °or to judge things to be honest or men to be pleasant according to thy sensual appetite;[12] but to try and esteem them by their good and profitable acts.

<51> Moreover, forasmuch as they that labour in the study of philosophy, concerning the exercise of the minds, be of sundry opinions — some saying that men become wiser by much disputing and reasoning; other affirm that it happeneth by exercise in politic governance or civil causes; diverse suppose it to come of other doctrines — but finally, they all do confess that he which is well brought up may by every of the said studies gather matter sufficient to give good counsel.

<52> Therefore, he that will leave the doubtful opinions and will apply to that which is certain, he must examine the reasons thereof; and specially, they that be counsellors ought to have con-<C2r>sideration of the occasion, time, and opportunity; if they cannot bring that to pass, then to reject and put away as well them which speak in all matters generally, as also those that °perceive nothing that is expedient or necessary. For it is apparent and certain that he which cannot be to himself profitable, he shall in other men's business do nothing wisely.

<53> Make much of them that be wise and do perceive more than other men; and have good regard toward them, °remembering that a good counsellor is of all other treasure the most royal and profitable; and think verily that they which can most aid and profit to thy wit or reason shall make thy kingdom most ample and honourable.

<54> Wherefore, for my part, as much as I can, I have exhorted thee and honoured thee with such presents as be in my power to give thee. And desire thou not <C2v> that other men should bring unto thee, as I said at the beginning, their accustomed presents, which ye should buy much dearer of the

[12] ταῖς ἡδοναῖς κρίνειν, 'to judge by the standard of pleasure'. The key term, ἡδοναί, here 'sensual appetite', recurs above, pp. 59 and 63.

° is it] it is *A*
° art] are *A*
° or] nor *A*
° perceive] know *A*
° \A good counsellor/

givers than of the sellers. But covet thou such presents which, if thou do use well and diligently, omitting no time, thou not only shalt not consume them, but thou shalt also increase them and make them of more estimation and value.

Finis.

°ADDITION, TO FILL UP vacant pages.

Full truly writeth Salomon, 'The heart of the king is in the hand of God; and which way so ever he willeth, he shall incline it'.[13] But the very laud of a good king is if he again incline his heart to God, the king of all kings, alway bending to his will, without whose fa-<C3r>vourable aid man's endeavour can nothing do; and so frameth all his acts as knowledging and minding that, whatsoever he doeth, he doeth it before his eyes, who is no less judge over kings than over common people.

Nothing is truly prosperous, nothing can be called wealthy, that the author of all felicity will not vouchsafe to make fortunate. Most luckily, most happily is it done, whatsoever is done according to his will, who sayeth: 'By me, kings do reign, and the law-makers discern just things; by me, princes rule, and mighty men judge just things'.[14] This said the eternal wisdom, which is the son of God.

What prescribeth Sapience to kings? 'Mercy', sayeth she, 'and Truth do keep the king, and his throne is made strong with clemency'.[15] He sheweth mercy in succouring the oppressed, truth in judging <C3v> truly, clemency in tempering the severity of the laws with lenity.

The special duty, and whereunto kings were wont to be sworn when they

[13] Prov. 21. 1, 'ita cor regis in manu Domini; quocumque voluerit inclinabit illud'; cf. Elyot, *Gov.* 1.2 (Watson, p. 14), 'I do well perceive that to write of the office or duty of a sovereign governor or prince far exceedeth the compass of my learning, holy scripture affirming that the hearts of princes be in God's own hands and disposition'.

[14] Prov. 8. 15–16, 'per me reges regnant, et legum conditores iusta decernunt; per me principes imperant, et potentes decernunt iustitiam'; cf. Elyot, *Gov.* 3.23 (Watson, p. 270), 'The authority of sapience is well declared by Salomon in his proverbs. By me (saith Sapience) kings do reign, and makers of laws discern things that be just. By me princes do govern, and men having power and authority do determine justice. I love all them that love me, and who that watcheth to have me shall find me. With me is both riches and honour, stately possessions, and justice. Better is the fruit that commeth of me than gold and stones that be precious'; and *Banquet*, sig. A4v, 'To me do belong counsel and equity; mine is prudence, and mine also fortitude. By me kings do reign, and makers of laws do determine those things that be righteous. By me princes do govern, and men in authority do give sentence according to justice'.

[15] Prov. 20. 28, 'misericordia et veritas custodiunt regem et roboratur clementia thronus eius'; cf. Elyot, *Banquet*, sig. E2r (with attribution to Salomon), 'Truth and compassion keepeth a king, and his place of estate with mercy is stablished'.

° ADDITION, TO FILL UP [...] trusty counsellor. Finis.] *A om*

began their reign, was this: to help widows, to succour the fatherless, and to deliver and defend all that are oppressed from injury.[16]

Truth hath two companions, Sapience and Constance. Sapience giveth light unto the eyes, whereby is perceived what is right and what not, what is profitable for the weal public, and what is contrary to it. Constancy causeth that the mind, overcoming all covetous desires, neither with ire, nor with love, nor with hatred is moved from honesty.

Clemency tempereth with lenity necessary severity. Clemency is not forthwith to go in hand with war, when cause of war is given, but to leave no reasonable mean unassayed to see whether the <C4r> matter may be determined without war. And otherwise it is better to dissemble the injury, than to revenge it by force of arms. It is clemency, if by no means it may be eschewed, so to make war that as little human blood be spilt as can be and that the wars be ended as shortly as may be.

For this wisdom that bringeth all good things with it, Salomon prayed for, that she should alway be assistant to his throne, as a most faithful and trusty counsellor.

Finis.

IMPRINTED AT
London in Fleet Street, in the
house of Thomas
Berthelet°.
Cum priuilegio
°ad imprimendum solum.

16 Cf. Prov. 31. 8–10, 26, 'Aperi os tuum muto, et causis omnium filiorum qui pertranseunt. Aperi os tuum, decerne quod justum est, et judica inopem et pauperem. Mulierem fortem quis inveniet? procul et de ultimis finibus pretium ejus [...]. Os suum aperuit sapientiae, et lex clementiae in lingua eius', 'Open thy mouth for the dumb in the cause of all such as are appointed to destruction. Open thy mouth, judge righteously, and plead the cause of the poor and needy. Who can find a virtuous woman? for her price is far above rubies [...]. She openeth her mouth with wisdom; and in her tongue is the law of kindness'.

° near to the conduit at the sign of Lucrece] *A add*
° ad imprimendum solum] *A om*

°<A1r>

OF °THE

Knowledge

which maketh a wise

man

LONDINI IN AEDIBVS

THOMAE BERTHELETI.

M. D. XXXIII.

CVM PRIVILEGIO.

° The text is from *A* = 1533 ed. (RSTC 7668 = ESTC S100565), including the *errata* listed on sig. A7v, designated *eA* in the apparatus, departures from which are enclosed in angled brackets <>; collated with *B* = *c.* 1550 ed. (RSTC 7670 = ESTC S100568).
° the] that *B*

°<A2r>

°THE PROEM

The proem of Sir Thomas Elyot knight.

God — unto whom all men's hearts be opened and the will of man speaketh[1] — is my witness that, to the desire of knowledge, whereunto I have hitherto been ever of my nature disposed, I have joined a constant intent to profit thereby my natural country, whereunto, according to the sentence of Tully, we be most specially bounden.[2] Wherefore, °after that I had applied the more part of my life in perusing diligently every ancient work that I mought come by, either Greek or Latin, containing any part of philosophy necessary to the institution of man's life in virtue, I have endeavoured myself to set forth such part of my study as I thought mought be profitable to them whi-<A2v>ch should happen to read or hear it. But diverse men, rather scorning °my benefit than receiving it thankfully, do shew themselves offended, as they say, with my strange terms. Other, finding in my books the thing dispraised which they do commend in using it, like a galled horse abiding no plasters, be alway gnapping and kicking at such examples and sentences as they do feel sharp or do bite them, accompting to be in me no little presumption that I will, in noting other men's vices, correct *Magnificat*,[3] since other much wiser men and better learned than I do forbear to write anything; and, which is worse than all this, some will maliciously divine or conject that I write to the intent to rebuke some particular person, coveting to bring my works, and afterward me, into the indignation of some man in authority.<A3r> Thus unthankfully is my benefit received, my good will consumed, and all my labours devoured. Such is of some men the nature serpentine, that, lapping sweet milk, they convert it forthwith into poison, to destroy him of whose liberality they late had received it.

How incomparably be these men unlike to the most excellent prince, our

[1] The Sarum Rite Missal 'Collect for Purity', 'Deus, cui omne cor patet et omnis voluntas loquitur, et quem nullum latet secretum', was translated (probably by Elyot's putative rival Cranmer) in the 1549 *Book of Common Prayer*, 'Almighty God, unto whom all hearts be open and all desires knowen, and from whom no secrets are hid', in *The First and Second Prayer Books of Edward VI*, ed. by E. C. S. Gibson (London: Dent, 1910), p. 212.

[2] Cf. Cic., *Rep.* 6.16 (*Somnium Scipionis*), 'But rather, my Scipio — like your grandfather here, like me your sire — follow justice and natural affection, which though great in the case of parents and kinsfolk, is greatest of all in relation to our fatherland. Such is the life that leads to heaven and to this company of those who have now lived their lives and released from their bodies dwell in that place which you can see'.

[3] A proverbial phrase for misapplied, ignorant criticism, with reference to the 'Canticle of Mary', from Lc. 1.46–55 (inc. 'Magnificat anima mea dominum').

°] omitting sig A1v (blank).
° THE PROEM] *B om*
° after that] after *B*
° my] the *B*

most dear sovereign lord?[4] Whose most royal person I heartily beseech God to preserve in long life and honour. His highness, benignly receiving my book which I named *The Governour*, in the reading thereof soon perceived that I intended to augment our English tongue, whereby men should as well express more abundantly the thing that they conceived in their hearts — wherefore language was ordained — having words apt for the purpose, as also interpret out of Greek, Latin, or any <A3v> other tongue into English, as sufficiently as out of any one of the said tongues into another. His grace also perceived that, throughout the book, there was no term new made by me, of a Latin or French word, but it is there declared so plainly, by one mean or other, to a diligent reader, that no sentence is thereby made dark or hard to be understand. Ne the sharp and quick sentences, or the round and plain examples set out in the verses of Claudian the poet in the second book,[5] or in the chapters of 'Affability', 'Benevolence', 'Beneficence', and 'Of the Diversity of Flatterers',[6] and in diverse other places, in any part offended his highness; but, as it was by credible persons reported unto me, his grace not only took it in the better part, but also, with princely words full of majesty, commended my diligence, simplicity, and courage, in that I spared none estate in <A4r> the rebuking of vice.

Which words, full of very nobility, brought unto my remembrance the virtuous Emperor Antonine, called for his wisdom Antonine the philosopher, who, on a time hearing that there was in the city of Rome a plain and rude person, which alway spake in the rebuke of all men and never praised any man, he sent to him, requiring that he would come and speak with him. And when he was come, the Emperor had these words unto him: 'My friend, wherein have I ever offended thee?' The fellow, therewith sore abashed, answered in this wise: 'Sir, your highness never offended me that I am ware of'. 'Then art thou', said the Emperor, 'an uncourteous subject, that thou hast so long dissembled with me, not telling unto me my faults'. And after, the Emperor retained him still, giving unto him double <A4v> wages, commanding him to use his old liberty. And when diverse men marvelled thereat, he affirmed openly that princes' vices were sooner espied by other men than by themselves and that there was much more difficulty in remembering them of their vice or lack than in extolling and commending their virtues. So well did this most noble Emperor consider that his example mought be more profitable unto the public weal of the city than any other thing in his person or dignity.

4 sc. Henry VIII (r. 1509–1547).

5 Elyot, *Gov.* 2.1 (Watson, p. 120), translating (more and less closely) Claud., *Panegyricus de quarto consulatu Honorii Augusti*, 257–268, 276–277, 296–302.

6 Elyot, *Gov.* 2.5, 'Of affability and the utility thereof in every estate' (Watson, pp. 130–36), 2.9, 'Of what excellence benevolence is' (Watson, pp. 149–58), 2.10 'Of beneficence and liberality' (Watson, pp. 158–61), and 2.14 'The election of friends and the diversity of flatterers' (Watson, pp. 189–94).

In likewise, our most dear sovereign lord perfectly knew that no writer ought to be blamed which writeth, neither for hope of temporal reward, nor for any private disdain or malice, but only of fervent zeal toward good occupation and virtue. Perdie, man is °not so yet conformed in grace that he °cannot do sin. <A5r> And I suppose no prince thinketh himself to be exempt from mortality. And forasmuch as he shall have mo occasions to fall, he ought to have the mo friends, or the more instruction to warn him. And, as for my part, I eftsoons do protest that in no book of my making I have intended to touch more one man than another. For there be Gnathos in Spain as well as in Greece; Pasquils in England as well as in Rome; Dionises in Germany as well as in Sicily; Harpocrates in France as well °as in Egypt; Aristippuses in Scotland as well as in Cyrene. Platos be few, and them I doubt where to find.[7] And if men will seek for them in England which I set in other places, I cannot let them. I know well enough, diverse do delight to have their garments of the fashion of other countries, and that which is most <A5v> plain is unpleasant; but yet it doth happen sometime that, one man being in authority or favour of his prince, being seen to wear something of the old fashion, for the strangeness thereof it is taken up again with many good fellows. What I do mean every wise man perceiveth.

Touching the title of my book, I considered that wisdom is spoken of much more than used. For wherein it resteth, few men be sure.[8] The common opinion is into three parts divided. One sayeth it is in much learning and knowledge. Another affirmeth that they which do conduct the affairs of great princes or countries be only wise men. Nay, saith the third; he is wisest that least doth meddle, and can sit quietly at home and turn a crab, and look only unto his own business. Now, they which be of the first opinion be al-<A6r>way at variance. For some do chiefly extol the study of holy scripture, as it is reason; but while they do wrest it to agree with their wills, ambition, or vainglory of the most noble and devout learning, they do endeavour them to make it servile and full of contention. Some do prefer the study of the laws of this realm, calling it the only study of the public weal. But a great number of persons, which have

[7] The references are to Elyot's previously published dialogue *Pasquil*, as well as to the present one.

[8] Though Elyot does not mention it in the remarks following, his title probably comes from the discussion of counsel in Pl., *Resp.* 4 (428b–429a), concluding with Socrates's summary statement (429a), 'So it is by virtue of this smallest class and sector of it [i.e. the 'guardians'], and in the knowledge that is in it — the leading and governing part — that a state that has been constructed by natural principles would be wise as a whole; and it looks as if this group is naturally the smallest, the group which is entitled to have a share in that knowledge which alone of all sorts of knowledge should be called wisdom'.

° not so yet conformed] not yet so confirmed *B*
° cannot do sin] cannot sin *B*
° as in Egypt] as Egypt *B*

consumed in suit more than the value of that that they sued for, in their anger do call it a common detriment, although undoubtedly the very self law, truly practised, passeth the laws of all other countries.

In thinking on these sundry opinions, I happened for my recreation to read in the book of Laertius the life of Plato, and, beholding the answer that he made to King Dionise,[9] <A6v> at the first sight it seemed to me to be very dissolute and lacking the modesty that belonged to a philosopher; but when I had better examined it, therein appeared that which is best worthy to be called wisdom. Wherefore, to exercise my wit and to avoid idleness, I took my pen and assayed how, in expressing my conceit, I mought profit to them which without disdain or envy would oftentimes read it. If any man will think the book to be very long, let him consider that knowledge of wisdom cannot be shortly declared, albeit of them which be well willing it is soon learned, in good faith, sooner than 'Primero' or 'Gleek'.[10] Such is the strange property of that excellent cunning that it is sooner learned than taught, and better by a man's reason than by an instructor.

Finally, if the readers of my works, <A7r> by the noble example of our most dear sovereign lord, do justly and lovingly interpret my labours, I, during the residue of my life, will now and then set forth such fruits of my study, profitable, as I trust, unto this my country. And, leaving malicious readers with their incurable fury, I will say unto God the words of the Catholic Church in the °book of Sapience: °'To know the good lord is perfect justice, and to know thy justice and virtue is the very root of immortality'.[11] And therein is the knowledge that is very wisdom.

[9] For particulars, see below, pp. 73–4 and n. 17.
[10] Both contemporary gambling games at cards.
[11] Sap. 15.3, 'nosse enim te consummata iustitia est et scire iustitiam et virtutem tuam radix est inmortalitatis'.

° book] kook *B*
° \Sap. 15./

°<B1r>

<OF THE KNOWLEDGE WHICH MAKETH A WISE MAN>

THE FIRST DIALOGUE

ARISTIPPUS. PLATO.

ARISTIPPUS Who is this man, whom I perceive coming hitherward? It seemeth to be Plato. Let me see. It is, verily, Plato himself! What meaneth it that he is in this wise apparelled? His garments be very short and more simple than he was accustomed to wear. Well, though there were some debate between us in Sicily,[12] yet will I salute him and desire him to shew to me the state of all his affairs; for in wise men resteth no malice, although diversity in opinions or form of living causeth sometime contention between them.

Plato, thou art well founden again in this country!

PLATO Gramercy, Aristippus. But yet thou hast said truer than I ween thou art ware of. <B1v>

ARISTIPPUS Why, I know thee to be Plato, though thou be in this single apparel.

PLATO Yea, that I suppose. But thou saidest that I was well founden, and indeed thou saidst true after the common opinion. For since thou departedest from Sicily, I have been twice in the point to have died, and also twice sold for a bondman or slave,[13] wherefore thou mayst with good reason say that I am well founden, that have been so often in peril to be lost. For commonly men do call him lost which despaireth of his life, or of a free man is made a slave. But whether that opinion be true or no, we shall speak more thereof hereafter. Finally, Aristippus, God be thanked, I am well escaped.

ARISTIPPUS I do not a little marvel of this that thou tellest me. For when I

[12] Aristippus (*c.* 435–350 BCE) is subject of another biography in Diog. Laert. 2.8.65–85: 'He was capable of adapting himself to place, time and person, and of playing his part appropriately under whatever circumstances. Hence he found more favour than anybody else with Dionysius, because he could always turn the situation to good account. He derived pleasure from what was present, and did not toil to procure the enjoyment of something not present' (2.8.66); 'He laid down as the end the smooth motion resulting in sensation' (2.8.85). Diog. Laert. 2.8 establishes that, with Plato and others, Aristippus was a disciple of Socrates, as Elyot's 'Plato' often reminds; the Plato biography in Diog. Laert. 3.36 points out that 'Plato was also [i.e. in addition to Xenophon] on bad terms with Aristippus'. Erasmus, *Apoph.* 3.102–63 (CWE 37, 252–71) has a substantial collection of anecdotes of Aristippus, likewise drawn (though more widely) from Diogenes Laertius. But cf. Elyot, *Gov.* 1.2 (Watson, p. 15), where Elyot claims that governors can learn 'to be alway virtuously occupied, and not without pleasure, if they be not of the schools of Aristippus or Apicius, of whom the one supposed felicity to be only in lechery, the other in delicate feeding and gluttony'; also, Elyot, *Bibl.*, s.v. '*Aristippus*', below.

[13] For particulars, see below, pp. 74–5 and nn.

°] omitting sigs A7v (*errata*) and A8r–A8v (blank).

went from King Dionise,[14] he mought not suffer that thou °moughtest be one hour from him. <B2r> Moreover, he regarded nothing that was spoken except it were by thy sentence approved. In the morning, as soon as he was out of his bed, Plato was sent for. Uneath Dion and Aristomenes[15] could get of him one hour in the day, that thou moughtest teach them and other towardly gentlemen such part of philosophy as they desired to learn. Finally, for the incomparable favour that the King bare to thee, thou were had in the court almost in as much reverence as the King's own person. And when thou passedest by, noble men and other of the King's household would rise quickly and, as a storm had fallen in their necks, duck to thee with their heads uncovered. Yet diverse in their minds grudged at thy fortune, thinking that the great pleasure that the King had in communing with thee withdrew him from hearing <B2v> of other men, of whom there was a great number which had, some common, some private causes to treat of with him, if they mought by thine absence have found opportunity.

PLATO Thou sayest truth, Aristippus, and that perceive I more clearly now than I did before those things happened unto me. But now will I recite thee my story.

Soon after that thou hadest obtained licence of the King to go unto Athens, he became wonderful sturdy, in so much as no man mought blame anything wherein he delighted, nor praise anything which was contrary to that that he used. And that sober and gentle manner in hearing sundry opinions reasoned before him, whereto of a custom he was wont to provoke thee and me, was laid apart, and, supposing that by hearing of sundry philosophers dispute and reason he himself had at-<B3r>tained to a more perfect knowledge than any other that spake unto °him, he began to have all other men in contempt; and, as it were Jupiter, who, as Homer saith, with a wink made all heaven to shake,[16] he would with a terrible countenance so visage them whom he knew would speak their opinions freely that they should dread to say anything which they knew should be contrary unto his appetite.

14 Dionysius I of Syracuse (*c.* 430–367 BCE).

15 Dion (*c.* 408–353), son-in-law of Dionysius I; with Dion, 'Aristomenes', is mentioned in Diog. Laert. 3.19, below.

16 Reference is to Hom., *Il.* 1.523–30, in Eras., *Adagia* 3.8.5, *Pollicentis se promissa re praestiturum*, 'Of one who promises to stand by what has been promised' (CWE 35, 284). Elyot translated the same Homeric passage into iambic pentameters, 'as well as my poor wit can express it in English', in *Gov.* 1.8 (Watson, p. 31): 'Then Jupiter the father of them all | Thereto assented with his browes black, | Shaking his hair, and therewith did let fall | A countenance that made al heaven to quake'.

° moughtest] mightest *B*

° him he began] *eA B* : him began *A*

Notwithstanding, on a time he willed me to declare in his presence the majesty of a king and how much he excelled and was above the estate of any other person. Which request I gladly heard, thinking to have had good opportunity to warn him of his blindness and folly. Therefore, I began to commend the perfect image or figure of God, which was manifest in the estate of a king who ruled himself and his people for <B3v> the universal weal of them all. And when I had described his authority and pre-eminence °by the excellency of his virtues, proving that nothing mought be amended but by that which surmounted or was better than it which was to be corrected — as vice by virtue, falsehood by truth, wrong by justice, folly by wisdom, ignorance by learning, and such other like — afterward, I studiously did set out a tyrant in his proper colours, who attendeth to his own private commodity.

Hereat, King Dionise frowned and became angry and, interrupting my words, said unto me: 'This is a tale of old fools that cannot be otherwise occupied'.

And I answered again that those words of his savoured of tyranny.[17]

ARISTIPPUS I marvel, Plato, that thou spakest so unadvisedly. I do mean, since thou knewest well enough King <B4v> Dionise's nature and disposition, that thou, perceiving him to be moved, wouldest so suddenly embraid him of his words, so despitefully.

PLATO Well, as for that, we shall reason thereof hereafter; finally, I was well advised what I would speak. But now will I tell forth my tale, what happened afterward to me.

Sir, the King, being inflamed with fury, forthwith would have slain me. But being entreated importunately by Dion and Aristomenes, he withdrew his sentence, notwithstanding to the intent that he would be avenged. He gave me to Polidis, who was then ambassador sent to him from the Lacedaemonians, who had me with him to Aegina, and there sold me.[18]

Now, a little before there was an ordinance made in that country that, if any man of Athens came into that isle, he should immediately <B4v> lose his head; which ordinance was made by Charmander, then being captain

[17] The episode is developed from Diog. Laert. 3.18, esp. 'But when Plato held forth on tyranny and maintained that the interest of the ruler alone was not the best end, unless he were also pre-eminent in virtue, he offended Dionysius, who in his anger exclaimed, "You talk like an old dotard". "And you like a tyrant", rejoined Plato'.

[18] Cf. Diog. Laert. 3.19, 'At this the tyrant grew furious and at first was bent on putting him to death; then, when he had been dissuaded from this by Dion and Aristomenes, he did not indeed go so far but handed him over to Pollis the Lacedaemonian, who had just then arrived on an embassy, with orders to sell him into slavery. And Pollis took him to Aegina and there offered him for sale'.

° by the excellency] by excellency *B*

of that country, who, espying me and knowing who I was, caused me to be apprehended and brought unto the place of judgment, requiring that on me his said ordinance mought be put in execution. Whereunto I made no defence, but, taking mine adventure patiently and contemning death, as it became me, I abode my judgment. At the last, one, either in despite or of purpose to save thereby my life, speaking openly and with a loud voice, said to Charmander and the judges: 'The ordinance, if it be well perceived, is made again men of Athens; but Plato that is here is a philosopher'. Which words, as it happened, were well taken and laughed at of all them that were present; and therewith, they discharged me of the said penalty, <B5r> albeit, for the hostility that was then between them and Athens, they would not let me freely depart but decreed that I should eftsoons be sold.[19]

There happened to be at that time Aniceris, which dwelleth at Cyrenas,[20] a man well learned, who paid for me twenty pounds, and, forthwith delivering to me his servant, whom thou beholdest here, hath sent me as thou seest home to my country.[21] The garments that I wear, he that bought me °of Polidis took from one of his slaves and gave them unto me, when he had taken from me mine apparel that I brought out of Sicily, which, as thou knowest, was right honest and competent. Notwithstanding, neither the cruelty of King Dionise nor the malicious decree of the Aeginites mought remove my courage from virtue and truth, no more than the twice selling of me, nor this vile habit of a <B5v> slave or bondman may change mine estate or condition.

19 Cf. Diog. Laert. 3.19, 'And then Charmandrus, the son of Charmandrides, indicted him on a capital charge according to the law in force among the Aeginetans, to the effect that the first Athenian who set foot upon the island should be put to death without a trial. This law had been passed by the prosecutor himself, according to Favorinus in his *Miscellaneous History*. But when some one urged, though in jest, that the offender was a philosopher, the court acquitted him. There is another version to the effect that he was brought before the assembly and, being kept under close scrutiny, he maintained an absolute silence and awaited the issue with confidence. The assembly decided not to put him to death but to sell him just as if he were a prisoner of war'.

20 Cyrene, seat of the 'Cyrenaics', the philosophical school with which Aristippus was associated; near Modern Shahhat, Jabal al Akhdar region, Libya.

21 Cf. Diog. Laert. 3.20, 'Anniceris the Cyrenaic happened to be present and ransomed him for twenty *minae* — according to others the sum was thirty *minae* — and dispatched him to Athens to his friends, who immediately remitted the money. But Anniceris declined it, saying that the Athenians were not the only people worthy of the privilege of providing for Plato. Others assert that Dion sent the money and that Anniceris would not take it, but bought for Plato the little garden which is in the Academy. Pollis, however, is stated to have been defeated by Chabrias and afterwards to have been drowned at Helice, his treatment of the philosopher having provoked the wrath of heaven, as Favorinus says in the first book of his *Memorabilia*'; also, Diog. Laert. 2.86, 'Anniceris, who ransomed Plato', was a student of a student of a student of Aristippus.

° of] and *B*

But now, Aristippus, I will answer thee to that wherein thou seemest to blame me of imprudence or lightness, saying thou marvellest that I would speak so unadvisedly, since I knew the nature of King Dionise and his disposition. Remembrest thou not that my coming into Sicily was to behold the wonderful mountains, which do send out of the tops of them great flames of fire and smoke, and to ensearch out the natural causes thereof? And that although the King sent often times for me, yet would I not come unto him, forasmuch as, through all Greece, he was named a tyrant?[22] At the last, he sent unto me Dion, which is a man, as thou knowest, of honour and °gravity almost incomparable, who said unto me that the King was incredibly moved with <B6r> desire to see me, for the great fame (as he affirmed) of wisdom and knowledge, although I myself know no such thing to be in me. And moreover, the same Dion shewed me that he supposed much profit should happen to the realm of Sicily by our meeting and communication, the King presently beholding and hearing in me that whereof he hath so great expectation, that is to say, as I mought use Dion's word, virtue and wisdom.

ARISTIPPUS Indeed, I heard not only Dion but also diverse other report everything as thou hast spoken.

PLATO Then thou knowest that the King fervently desired to see me?

ARISTIPPUS That is truth.

PLATO And moreover, to speak also with me?

ARISTIPPUS Yea, verily.

PLATO Because he heard good report of me?

ARISTIPPUS So it appeareth.

PLATO Supposest thou, Aristippus, that the <B6v> report of wisdom and virtue is good in a tyrant's opinion?

ARISTIPPUS Yea, as long as he thinketh that nothing that is spoken or done repugneth against his affections.

PLATO What afterward?

ARISTIPPUS He accompteth it but a vanity, judging, as sick men, nothing to be good that agreeth not with the scent of his appetite.

PLATO Now, in good faith, though thou thyself hast a delicate mouth and thy taste distempered, yet I can thee thank; for now thou sayest truly. But it seemeth to thee that, when Dionise sent for me, he then thought that wisdom and virtue were good and that I, having them, as it was reported, was a good man; and therefore, he desired to see me.

[22] Cf. Diog. Laert. 3.18: Plato 'made three voyages to Sicily, the first time to see the island and the craters of Etna: on this occasion Dionysius, the son of Hermocrates, being on the throne, forced him to become intimate with him'.

° gravity] dignity *B*

ARISTIPPUS Yea, so it seemeth.

PLATO And men do desire to see a thing either for the beauty thereof, which causeth them to love it; or for the strangeness thereof, whereby they be mo-<B7r>ved to wonder at it; or for commodity that they before have received by it?

ARISTIPPUS I think thou sayest truly.

PLATO But, except I be deceived by false mirrors, or, like to changeable lovers which do mislike the beauty whereof they have daily fruition, perchance I contemn that in myself which I would praise in another. I am neither in beauty nor personage to be compared to an infinite number of young men which be in Greece and also in this realm of Sicily. Besides that, I am now above the age of forty years and have also travelled into divers countries to seek for wisdom,[23] whereby the form and strength of my body is not a little appaired. Moreover (thanks be to God), I suppose there is neither stature nor form in my personage so far out of just measure or fashion whereat any man can find occasion <B7v> to wonder or marvel. And as for any commodity that King Dionise hath received of me before my coming unto him, I cannot perceive what it should be, since I never wrote unto him nor never before was in his company. What thinkest thou was then the cause that he desired to see me?

ARISTIPPUS What else, but to the intent that, having thee in his presence, he mought, in demanding of thee, hear that declared by thy mouth wherefore thou were called a wise man, and if thou didest express the same in thy demeanour and countenance which helpeth much (as I mought say) to the ratifying of good opinion.

PLATO What sayest thou? Doeth demeanour and countenance ratify the opinion of wisdom?

ARISTIPPUS Yea, verily, so think I.

PLATO What meanest thou thereby?

ARISTIPPUS For according to the profession or quality wherein men have opinion that <B8r> wisdom doeth rest, so ought to be the form of living, countenance, and gesture; which, joined all together, maketh one whole and perfect harmony which sendeth into the hearts of the beholders and hearers a volupty or fervent delectation.

PLATO I can thee thank, Aristippus: thou hast now declared to have been, as I was, the disciple of Socrates. And if thou wouldest extend volupty no further — which thou so much praisest — than thou hast done now, there should never be contention between us but, following directly the doctrine and steps of our master Socrates, not only we two should agree in our opinions and form of living, which should make that harmony whereof thou

[23] Cf. Diog. Laert. 3.6.

speakest; °but, moreover, all men that know us both, by the unity of our doctrine, should be brought to ensue one conformity of living or at the least co-<B8v>vet to follow it, wherein should be a perfect harmony, the whole choir singing in one tune; °where, by the discord of our two doctrines, men doubting which of us two speaketh most truly — I commending the volupty or perfect delectation which is in knowledge, thou preferring the volupty of the body and senses — they be divided into sundry opinions: some extolling mine admonitions as more pure and separate from the nature of beasts, and therefore approaching near unto divinity; other, more sensual and having less reason, do embrace thy persuasions as more illecebrous or delectable, calling thy doctrine more natural and of less arrogance.

Many there be which do covet learning and wisdom but, having not their minds sufficiently purged of affects but, either by nature or by ill bringing up, inclining alway to plea-<C1r>sant motions or appetites of the body, they admit them gladly. But while they study to follow both our doctrines, they of all other do make the greatest discord and imperfect music. For when they would seem to extol the delectation in knowledge, they advance it marvellously in their disputations and reasonings; but in pursuing their affects and wanton appetites, they destroy their first opinion and vainly do enforce them to make a concord between that which of their own nature be most repugnant, which discord dissolveth that harmony whereof thou spakest. For men, beholding in one person such instability, they semblably do wander in sundry opinions, now praising one and using another, as occasion happeneth. But here will I leave to dispute any more in this matter, lest I mought happen to refricate the <C1v> late variance between thee and me, and now will I return again where I was.

I trow thou saidest that, according to the profession or quality wherein men have opinion that wisdom doeth rest, so ought to be the form of living, countenance, and gesture. In good faith, I suppose thou sayest truly. For if Lais the harlot, in whom thou takest pleasure in fulfilling thy carnal appetite,[24] should shew herself to thee in sluttish and vile apparel, her head

24 The historical *hetaira* (fl. end of the fifth century BCE) — subject of a painting by Hans Holbein (*c.* 1497–1453), who also portrayed Elyot and his wife — is said to have had significant relations with Aristippus, Diogenes the Cynic, and Demosthenes, among others; cf. Plut., *Amat.* (*Mor.* 767F), 'You have, of course, heard of Lais, the theme of song, the essence of loveliness — how she threw all Greece into a fever of longing or was, rather, the object of contention from sea to sea'. Along with the titles of the books he wrote for her, her relations with Aristippus are mentioned in Diog. Laert. 2.8.75: Aristippus 'enjoyed the favours of Lais, as Sotion states in the second book of his *Successions of Philosophers*. To those who censured him his defence was, "I have Lais, not she me; and it is not abstinence from pleasures that is best, but mastery over them without ever being worsted"', quoted

° but moreover] *eA B* : For *A*
° \Discord in doctrines./] *B* : *A om*

unkempt, her face and hands soiled and imbrued with grease of the potage that she had eaten, and her legs and feet spotted with mire, beholding thee with a sturdy countenance, thou shouldest not be much moved to embrace and kiss her, although she spake to thee words wanton and amorous and, after the custom of harlots, praise thee with <C2r> rebukes and rebuke thee with praises.

°In likewise, if Diogenes, who (as thou knowest) contemneth all thing save only poverty,[25] would °stond in the marketplace with his beard clean shaven, and his hair trussed up in a caul of gold, and having on his fingers rings with diamonds and rubies, and on his legs fine hosen well guarded and shoen of the trimmest fashion, and, because perchance it is winter and therefore the weather is cold, having a pan with hot coals standing at his elbow; if he would rebuke the people of too much curiosity and delicate living, and praise wilful poverty and apparel that only serven for necessity, also would exhort them to contemn or despise all riches and honour and to embrace painfulness; thinkest not thou that they would laugh him to scorn, and accompt him for a dizzard, or with <C2v> too much study fallen into a frenzy?

ARISTIPPUS Yes, by my troth; for it were a marvellous folly.

PLATO And why supposest thou?

ARISTIPPUS For the fresh apparel and riches that he sheweth openly declareth to all men that he therein delighteth and taketh pleasure; and that wherein a man doth delight, in delighting therein, he praiseth it. Then is it not a great foolishness to praise and dispraise, as it were, in one instant? That is to say, in use to commend a thing openly and in words to dispraise it expressly? And it should seem to the beholders that he exhorteth men to contemn

in Eras., *Apoph.* 3.132 (CWE 37, 261). Cf. Eras., *Adagia* 1.4.1, *Non est cuiuslibet Corinthum appellere*, 'It is not given to everyone to land at Corinth' (CWE 31, 318), also mentioning Lais's relations with Aristippus; and *Apoph.* 6.572–73 in Erasmus's section on the *hetairai*, 6.561–83 (CWE 38, 752–59).

[25] The contemporary Cynic philosopher (*c.* 404–323 BCE) is represented as often at odds with Plato in Diog. Laert. 6.2. Cf. Elyot, *Bibl.*: '*Cynici*, were a sect of philosophers, which do signify doggish for the similitude of their conditions with dogs: for they barked at all men, and occupied women openly, and lived without any provision; the first author thereof was Antisthenes; next him followed Diogenes', as well as '*Diogenes*, a famous philosopher's name', possibly drawing from Eras., *Adagia* 1.8.61, *Vita doliaris*, 'Life in a tub' (CWE 32, 160); more likely, from Eras., *Apoph.*, esp. 3.268 (CWE 37, 302), 'Diogenes used to say that love of money was "the stronghold", "the metropolis" of all evils, a turn of phrase not far from the saying of Solomon, who said, "love of money was the root of all evils"'; and 3.388 (CWE 37, 334), 'Diogenes called poverty "self-taught" virtue. For rich men need many rules to make them live decently, exercise their bodies by hard work, not delight in showy adornment of the person, and countless other things, all of which poverty teaches of itself'.

° \Diogenes./] *B* : *A om*
° stond] stand *B*

riches that he mought be rich only; and that he persuadeth them to sustain cold and other pains that he mought take his ease and sit by the fire whiles other men laboured; wherefore, if they regarded little his counsel, they were not to be blamed.

PLATO Yes, his counsel perchance were <C3r> to be considered, whether it were expedient or no; but, surely, his person and discretion were to be little esteemed.

Now, Aristippus, thou thinkest that King Dionise desired to see me to the intent that he mought behold if, in my countenance and form of living, I did express that thing wherefore he heard me commended. And it seemeth that therein the King declared himself to be a very wise man, that he trusted more to the act than to words or opinion.

ARISTIPPUS Yea, truly, he hath a sharp wit, and in that a man mought well praise his imagination.

PLATO Then what thinkest thou, Aristippus? If I should have laid apart mine own apparel and have bought such as thou wearest, guarded and decked with golden buttons, supposest thou not that, when I came to his presence and that he saw me in such wise apparelled, he would think <C3v> that I would speak of the delectation that is felt in meddling with fair women and pleasant, or in the sundry diversities of sweet savours and tastes of meats that the cook hath well seasoned, and in other like things, in whose effects thou determinest to be perfect felicity? Then, because he hath before heard thee dispute as abundantly thereof as any man's wit mought imagine, he would little esteem my coming and think the report which was made of me to be false. But if he would vouchsafe to tarry, then if I disputed of fortitude, temperance, and other like virtues and therewith exhorted him and other princes to abstain and be continent, blaming their avarice, lechery, and other dissolute manners with their curiosity and superfluous apparel; supposest thou not that he would laugh at me and, in mockage, bid <C4r> me change mine apparel?

ARISTIPPUS Nay, peradventure; he would command one to fetch for you a furred hood to save with your honesty.

PLATO Ah, King Dionise is beholding unto thee! For thou wouldest that men should think that he were of great modesty. But what if, before that he heard me speak, he had caused me to sit with him at supper and there beheld me feed errantly, perusing all the delicate dishes; and thereto drank stoutly of every cup that was offered me; and, after supper, with such wenches as were present, devise wantonly, and also play and dally, exceeding the terms of honesty; but when I beheld him do the semblable, I would then commend soberness and dispraise gluttony, commend exceedingly continence and dispraise vehemently wanton dalliance and lechery. How much, trowest thou, <C4v> would he then set by me?

ARISTIPPUS As much as of a good fool that should make him merry. For he would take all thy words but for japery.

PLATO I ween thou sayest truly. Now let us ensearch somewhat on the other part. When Dion brought me until him and that he beheld me clad in apparel convenient and seemly to my profession — neither scant nor superfluous, neither most rude nor yet sumptuous — my countenance thereto equivalent, which, be it spoken without any boast, with great study and diligence I have prepared to have alway in such a temperance that it shall never be founden dissolute or light, nor yet froward or sturdy; thinkest thou that he had then good opinion of me and thought that the wisdom and virtue was in me which men had reported?

ARISTIPPUS Ye undoubtedly, and therefore he rejoiced much at <C5r> thy coming.

PLATO For any other thing, trowest thou, than because I was wise and virtuous, as he judged by mine apparel and countenance? And that he hoped to hear of me some wisdom declared?

ARISTIPPUS No, truly, but even for that cause only.

PLATO On my faith, Aristippus, thou well doest deserve the great gifts and benefits that thou hast received of King Dionise, since thou so diligently hast affirmed him to be the lover of wisdom. For in that that he coveted to hear it declared, he desired it, and no man would desire that thing that he loveth not.

ARISTIPPUS So I suppose.

PLATO But yet hereafter it shall appear contrary; but for this time, admit thy persuasion of King Dionise to be true, that he favoured wisdom and virtue and that he hoped to hear it declared better by me than by other.

If now he, sit-<C5v>ting and studiously applying his ears to give me good audience, should hear me commend the pleasure that is in sumptuous and pleasant houses, in rich apparel and tapestries, in plenty of goodly and fair concubines, in abundance of delicate meats and drinks, and heaping up great treasure of money and jewels; thinkest not thou that I spake contrary to his expectation, which he had of me by the report of my living, confirmed by mine apparel and countenance, as thou late affirmedest? Thinkest thou that he would not have thought that either I had mocked or flattered him, if he hath so sharp a wit and quick invention as thou doest suppose him to have, and therefore have caused me to be expelled out of his palace as a counterfeit dizzard or spy? Or answering me that, of such things as I commen-<C6r>ded, he had more knowledge and experience than I; and therefore in vain I laboured to declare that to him which I knew much less than he himself did, saying that he coveted to hear of me what wisdom was, whereof he had heard so many diverse opinions and wherein, as the report was made unto him, I was instructed sufficiently; wherefore he would require me to declare that only unto him which he supposed I knew better than he did?

ARISTIPPUS It is very likely that he would have done so.

PLATO If thou hadest then been there, Aristippus, wouldest thou have counselled me to have resisted that gentle prince's request, who, with such humanity as thou hast heard of, so much desired to see me and to hear me speak?

ARISTIPPUS Nay, that would I not.

PLATO Then thou wouldest that I should satisfy his desire?

ARISTIPPUS Yea, truly.

PLATO <C6v> After that he had seen me, what remained?

ARISTIPPUS To hear thee speak.

PLATO Any otherwise than he had opinion of me?

ARISTIPPUS No, verily.

PLATO And according as mine apparel and countenance pretended, so I should do?

ARISTIPPUS According.

PLATO Not usurping thy profession, in persuading to him things that were delectable or praising the dissolute form of his living, not only contrary to mine apparel and countenance, but also which I myself do abhor and have alway reproved openly?

ARISTIPPUS No. That dissimulation were too foul and apparent and should have set him, as thou saidest whilere, in great displeasure with thee, supposing that thou hadest mocked him.

PLATO Then wouldest thou not that I should have used any dissimulation? For thou supposest that King Dionise would have been therewith displeased. It <C7r> seemeth therefore that thou concludest that I should tell him truth and according to my profession.

ARISTIPPUS Yea, so God help me.

°PLATO Thou knowest well, Aristippus, that my profession hath ever been that no man is happy, except he be wise and also good, °and that felicity is in wisdom and goodness. °And, contrariwise, that they which be ignorant and ill be unhappy, and that ignorance and sin is °infelicity and misery.[26]

ARISTIPPUS I know well thou hast been in that tale yet continually.

PLATO What sayest thou, Aristippus, is not wisdom knowledge? Or what thing is it else?

[26] Cf. Pl., *Alc.* 1 (134a), 'he who is not wise and good cannot be happy [...]. The bad are miserable'.

° \Alcib. 1./
° \Happy. Felicity/] *B* : *A om*
° \Ignorance./] *B* : *A om*
° infelicity] in felicity *B*

ARISTIPPUS Why doest thou ask me that question whereof no man maketh any doubt?

PLATO For I feared lest thou wouldest have said that the using of things delectable had been wisdom only.

ARISTIPPUS But not without knowledge, whereof proceedeth electi-<C7v>on. For then should I have affirmed that a horse, which delighteth in eating — a dog, in hunting; a goat, in lechery — did it by wisdom, whereby I should prove myself to be foolish and ignorant. Moreover, I am of that opinion that a wise man liveth not alway in volupty or pleasant delectation, but that for the more part he is so affectioned; also, without knowledge, the troubles and impediments whereby delectation is letted may not be comprehend to be eschewed.

PLATO Well, then, although in the affect of delectation we two disagree — thou preferring the delectations of the flesh before the delectations of the soul; I, condemning all such affection, do utterly sever it from wisdom — yet we do agree that knowledge is ever in a wise man.

But what knowledge meanest thou? The knowledge of a good horse from a bad, a whole sheep from a cothed, or <C8r> such other like? Or else the knowledge how to build a fair house, or how to set trees that in a little space of time thou maist have a fair orchard?

ARISTIPPUS That knowledge is good.

PLATO Yea, and proceedeth of a sharp wit; but yet it is not that knowledge that maketh him that hath it to be a wise man.

ARISTIPPUS I suppose not.

PLATO What sayest thou by him that findeth the means to gather great sums of money, offices, or great possessions with little labour? Thinkest thou not him to have that knowledge which we call wisdom?

ARISTIPPUS It approacheth very nigh, but I dare not affirm it to be so, because I see daily that the most part of those persons happeneth to such things more by fortune than by their own merits or industry.

PLATO On my faith I love thee, Aristippus, for now thou sayest truly. What, they, which <C8v> from a poor estate do come to great rule and authority, shall I name them all wise men?

ARISTIPPUS Much less than the other. For, besides that that fortune hath also there no little portion, it moreover dependeth not on the power, wit, or diligence of him that cometh to authority, but wholly on the will of a second person, that is to say, of him that promoteth him to it; wherefore, have he much wit or none, as he shall like or content the person that may advance him, so shall he come to authority. Wherefore, since it happeneth not only of his own study, I see no cause why to call him a wise man.

PLATO Thou speakest very well and reasonably. But what supposest thou them to be, which in every matter that is moved can reason featly, making men that do hear them wonder at their conveyance though it be sometime far from the purpose? Be not <D1r> they wise men? And, that thing that they have, is it not the very knowledge that maketh wisdom?

ARISTIPPUS No, but it is a good part of invention, which cometh of wit; albeit, because that which they do reason is never certain, it is rather opinion than wisdom; and also, that manner of prompt reasoning happeneth more of nature than study; and therefore, it is more commended of vulgar persons or ignorant than of them which be of a ripe and perfect judgment.

PLATO Perchance thou saist truly. Yet may it also be in them that be wise, not as wisdom itself, but as a setter forth of wisdom to him that heareth, like as the painter hath the very image in his mind, but, when he would that other men should perceive it, he on a table with sundry colours painteth it and setteth it forth? And yet, if the painter do not, before <D1v> he worketh and °in the painting, conceive in his mind the whole proportion of the image, when it is painted, it shall lack his perfection; and although the fresh colours and varnish maketh it pleasant to the eyen of the common people and them that be ignorant, yet, to good workmen and to them that have beholden many perfect pieces and delighted therein, the imperfection of the work is shortly perceived.

Even so knowledge, wherein is wisdom, being once truly had, if it be well set forth with eloquence and reason, it shall the better please and profit the hearers. But if he that speaketh do lack that knowledge, howsoever the beauty of his words and reason shall content the ears of them that be ignorant, yet thereof shall come to them but little profit; and to them that have tasted something of that knowledge, the error or lack shall <D2r> soon be espied.

But now, what supposest thou is the knowledge which we have all this while talked of? And that wherein that wisdom is, for the which King Dionise desired to see me and to hear me speak? And the which, according to my profession, apparel, and countenance, and to the expectation that he had of me, I declared unto him?

ARISTIPPUS I wot not, Plato. Therefore, I pray thee, tell me, to shorten our communication.

PLATO I am content, but yet with a condition; that is to say, when I demand of thee any question, thou shalt speak even as thou thinkest, without enforcing any reason to maintain therewith thine old opinion.

ARISTIPPUS Thereto I assent for this time, since there be no mo here but we two; for °our servants be now out of hearing.

° in the painting] in painting *B*
° our] onr *B*

PLATO Thou rememberest that it is agreed by us both that neither the knowing <D2v> of good cattle °from bad, or how to plant well and to make a fair orchard, ne the devising of fair houses and buildings, nor the °increasing of goods or possessions, or the obtaining of great offices or dignities, or the sharp wit and quickness in reasoning, is that knowledge wherein is wisdom? What sayest thou to other sciences or crafts which are not rehearsed?

ARISTIPPUS I suppose the same of them all, generally. For of everich of them, I have knowen some men to be little better than natural fools and, out of the feat which they daily exercised, uneath perceiving that which we call common reason.

PLATO Yea, and that worse is, living beastly and out of all order, which is the greatest and most evident token of ignorance, which is contrary and enemy to knowledge.

But now, Aristippus, forasmuch as long disputation <D3r> provoketh tediousness, me seemeth if we brought in some variety or change in the order of our communication, it should refresh both our wits.

ARISTIPPUS What meanest thou thereby? Take heed that we run not out of our matter.

PLATO No; doubt thou not thereof I shall provide well enough therefore. But hark, I will tell thee now what I mean.

We have hitherto spoken of knowledge wherein is sapience; but what or wherein it is we yet perceive not, but be now in seeking.

What and if we now used the way of a cunning painter? Which, in making an image of a very fair woman naked, to the intent that he will set out the figure perfectly and, as I mought speak like a workman, by prospective — that it may seem to the beholders thereof most lively, and therefore the body and members should shew to them as round <D3v> and full as it were embossed and wrought in timber, metal, or stone — he maketh the ground of his work of the deepest black colour that he may come by; which, the more intentively that a man doeth behold it, the more lively or quick shall the °fleshly colour of the image appear to the eye and the proportion seem more round and in the form of a body living.

In semblable-wise, I intending to set out a perfect figure of knowledge, if I treat first of ignorance and making that to be well perceived, I suppose it shall not be inconvenient; but the true proportion of knowledge afterward, when I shall go about to declare it, shall be more apparent and easy to be understand, and the variety in our communication shall make the matter more pleasant.

° from] or *B*
° increasing] in creasing *B*
° fleshly] *eA B* : freshly *A*

ARISTIPPUS In good faith, Plato, thy device liketh me wonderful well. Wherefore, say on, a Go-<D4r>d's name.

PLATO Is °ignorance any other thing, Aristippus, than lack of knowledge?

ARISTIPPUS No, surely.

PLATO Then nothing is so contrary to knowledge as ignorance?

ARISTIPPUS Nothing.

PLATO Is a brute beast inferior to mankind by anything so much as by ignorance? For in bodily strength, long life, agility, and swiftness, there be diverse beasts which far do exceed him. Only by ignorance, they be all inferiors unto him.

ARISTIPPUS Thou were wont also to say that beasts lacked the soul that man hath, which is immortal.

PLATO That is true. But thou must remember that the soul with the body maketh the man. For if the body lacked a soul, though it had life, yet were it no man, but a beast. And that the figure maketh not a man, it appeareth by those beasts which be called *satyri, fauni, hippocentauri*, and diverse other, which be founden in Afric, having some the visage, some the whole figure of man's body. And in <D4v> the same soul, which maketh the man and without it man is not nor may be, hath nothing less in him than ignorance. And if a man seem to be ignorant, it happeneth never a whit of the soul, but of the grossness of the body, which is bestial, as of the same matter and substance that brute beasts be of, which will not let the soul, that is of a divine substance, to shew the effects and disposition of her nature, which is only knowledge, the lack whereof, being caused by the object or let of the body, is nothing but ignorance, likewise as a thick and great cloud covering the sun will not let him to send forth his beams on the earth, whereby the earth lacketh light, and that lack is called darkness.

Now lay apart all arts and sciences, which, as thou knowest well enough, were founden by man's invention and experience long <D5r> after that man was created; and set man in the same estate that he was in before the said arts and sciences were invented; yet were he then a man, as he is now, and lacketh not anything whereby he is named a man. Wherein now doth appear the diversity between him and a brute beast? Tell me now, as thou thinkest.

ARISTIPPUS What else but in the same thing, for the which beasts be surnamed brute.

PLATO Thou sayest truth. But yet, lest I be deceived by the diversity of our two understandings, I pray thee tell me, in few words, what by the said word, 'brute', is signified.

° \Ignorance./] *B* : *A om*

ARISTIPPUS Marry, agreed. I take °that <it> signifieth gross, insensate, lacking capacity of knowledge; finally, it amounteth to as much as ignorant.

PLATO By the faith of my body, thou hast made an exposition very compendious and elegant. Then be we both <D5v> agreed that ignorance maketh the diversity between a beast and a man. But what ignorance, I pray thee? Ignorance in building of houses, making of cloth, or working of metal? Or, peradventure, ignorance in grammar, or logic, or making of verses, or else playing on the shawms or the lute? Doth ignorance in any of these cause the diversity?

ARISTIPPUS It seemeth nay. For thou didest presuppose that a man were in the same estate that all men were in °ere ever any arts or sciences were founden; and then, of that thing that is not, it were folly to suppose any ignorance.

PLATO Thou speakest not much amiss. But yet for another cause, ignorance in any of the said arts or sciences doeth not make the diversity that we now speak of. For if it should so do, then, whosoever lacked any of the said arts or sciences, it should follow that he were ignorant and therefore he were no man <D6r> but a beast. And also bees, silkworms, and spiders should not compare with us only but should seem also to exceed us in knowledge; forasmuch as, without any instructor or teacher, they at the first, without loss of anything, can perfectly make wax, honey, silk, and cobwebs; which no man can do like, nor by none invention can attain to the knowledge how it ought to be done. And as for the bee and the spider, whosoever studiously do behold their work, he shall see therein such order that, beside the office of nature, he shall wonder at the equality or justness of proportion, so exactly observed, that none artificer can amend it.

But now, Aristippus, since this is not the ignorance that any of us both have meant hitherto, I pray thee, what ignorance supposest thou it is that maketh this diversity?

ARISTIPPUS I suppose it be this, that a beast <D6v> hath not the knowledge of himself and of other, in the diversity of their kinds. For my horse knoweth not that he is a horse; no more he doeth that he is a beast and I a man. Neither the bee, at whose industry thou hast so much wondered; when the hive is broken, he knoweth not whether it be a man or a beast that taketh his honeycombs and putteth him out of his lodging, whereon he hath bestowed so much labour. Nor the spaniel, that is so jealous over his master, hath not the knowledge whether his master be a man or else a beast as he is. Contrariwise, a man knoweth that he is a man and knoweth also every other beast in his kind.

° that it signifieth] *eA B* : that signifieth *A*
° ere] or *B*

PLATO Thou comest nigh °to the point, Aristippus. But beware that thou be not deceived, if, after Pythagoras's doctrine, when men be dead, their souls enter into horses, lions, and swine, <D7r> and, after many years travailing, they return again to be men.[27] Then there mought be in thy horse the soul of King Sardanapalus, whereby thy horse mought know what thou art and himself too.

ARISTIPPUS Thou advancest me highly, Plato, when thou supposest me to ride on a king, and on so great a king as Sardanapalus was, which reigned over Assyria and Babylon.

PLATO Thou art worthy to have no worse horse, Aristippus, since by thy profession thou art deemed prelate of all volupty or wanton appetites, unto whom much greater princes than Sardanapalus was have been known to be servants.[28]

ARISTIPPUS Mo, peradventure, than of thy sour and unpleasant virtues would gladly be followers.

PLATO But now that I remember me, thou needest not to be afeared, Aristippus, for thou art never the more deceived. In good faith, <D7v> thy horse hath yet no more knowledge than a very horse hath indeed.

ARISTIPPUS What meanest thou thereby?

PLATO For when Sardanapalus lived and was king of Assyria, he then knew not himself. For abandoning not only the majesty of a king but also the office of a man, he left the company of men and sat continually with his concubines, attired in the form of a woman, spinning °in the rock, and cared for nothing but how he mought excel all his wenches in wantonness.[29]

[27] Cf. Diog. Laert. 8.1.14, 'He was the first, they say, to declare that the soul, bound now in this creature, now in that, thus goes on a round ordained of necessity'.

[28] Sardanapalus (Ashurbanipal, 668–627 BCE), the quasi-legendary last Assyrian monarch, was imputed an Aristippus-like devotion to hedonism in Western sources; cf. Arist., *Eth. Nic.* 1.5.2–3, 'On the one hand the generality of men and the most vulgar identify the Good with pleasure, and accordingly are content with the Life of Enjoyment [...]. The generality of mankind then show themselves to be utterly slavish, by preferring what is only a life for cattle; but they get a hearing for their view as reasonable because many persons of high position share the feelings of Sardanapalus'; also, Elyot, *Bibl.*, '*Sardanapalus*, a king of Assyria, monstrous in all kinds of lechery, and therefore was slain of one of his lords as he sat spinning among harlots'.

[29] Cf. Diod. Sic. 2.23.1–2, 'Sardanapalus, the thirtieth in succession from Ninus, who founded the empire, and the last king of the Assyrians, outdid all his predecessors in luxury and sluggishness. For not to mention the fact that he was not seen by any man residing outside the palace, he lived the life of a woman, and spending his days in the company of his concubines and spinning purple garments and working the softest of wool, he had assumed the feminine garb and so covered his face and indeed his entire body with whitening cosmetics and the other unguents used by courtesans, that he rendered it more delicate

° to the point] *A eA B*
° in] on *B*

Now, since he, then being in the form of a man, so much forgot what he was, thinkest thou that there be in him less ignorance now that he is in the form of a horse?

ARISTIPPUS Nay, in good faith, but much more. And because thou sayest so, Plato, I have even the fondest horse that ever man rode on. For when he was young, he was so mare-wood that no man <D8r> mought ride him. And now that he is old and that I, pitying him, do use to ride on him some small journeys, by my troth, when we be in the broad highway, if he see four miles off a race of mares, he will in spite of my teeth leave the way and go to them when he is not able to run. Nor bridle nor spur may hold him. And yet when he cometh thither, saving only neighing and kicking, he can do nothing. And therefore, it may well be, if Pythagoras's doctrine be true, that the soul of Sardanapalus is in Sorrel my horse.[30] But if I knew it for certain, by God, I would have the fairest mares that anywhere mought be gotten for him.

PLATO Now, on my faith, that is merrily spoken. But indeed, Aristippus, the said sentence of Pythagoras ought not to be taken as it is written without any other exposition, no more than his mystical counsels, called 'symbola', as: 'cut not the fire with a sword'; 'leap not over the balance'; <D8v> 'taste nothing which hath a black tail'; and such other like, which thou hast oftentimes heard of.[31] But therein is a more secret meaning, and

than that of any luxury-loving woman. He also took care to make even his voice to be like a woman's, and at his carousals not only to indulge regularly in those drinks and viands which could offer the greatest pleasure, but also to pursue the delights of love with men as well as with women; for he practised sexual indulgence of both kinds without restraint, showing not the least concern for the disgrace attending such conduct'; whence derives Elyot, *Gov.* 1.26 (Watson, p. 108), 'But who abhorreth not the history of Sardanapalus, king of the same realm? which, having in detestation all princely affaires and leaving all company of men, enclosed himself in a chamber with a great multitude of concubines? And for that he would seem to be some time occupied or else that wanton pleasures and quietness became to him tedious, he was found by one of his lords in a woman's attire spinning in a distaff among persons defamed, which, knowen abroad, was to the people so odious that finally by them he was burned with all the place whereto he fled for his refuge'.

[30] The Pythagorean doctrine of the transmigration of souls is mentioned in Eras., *Adagia* 1.9.1, *Amyclas perdidit silentium*, 'Silence destroyed Amyclae' (CWE 32, 179), mockingly, as justification for vegetarianism.

[31] Elyot's Plutarch translation, *Education* 12 (London: Berthelet, [1532?]), sigs F1v–F2r, has a section 'Of the reverent precepts of Pythagoras': 'To this purpose [i.e. removing children 'from the company of riotous and flagitious persons'] were left by Pythagoras, the noble philosopher, wonderful and good precepts in dark sentences, which I purpose now to expound. For they be right necessary for the obtaining of virtue'. Amongst them are the three *symbola* Elyot mentions here: 'Cut not the fire with weapon: do not irritate a man in his fury but rather, when he rageth, give place to his anger'; 'Leap not over the balance: esteem justice, and skip not over it'; and 'Taste nothing that hath a black tail: that is to say, company with no person whose manners be spotted with vice'. The same three occur also in the lengthy section *Pythagorae Symbola*, 'The Precepts of Pythagoras', in Eras., *Adagia* 1.1.2 (CWE 31, 31–50); and see also *Adagia* 2.1.43 (CWE 33, 40–41), mentioning *Ne gustaris quibus*

approaching near unto reason, as, in mine opinion, by the translation of man's soul, whereof we have spoken, from a man to a beast and finally eftsoons unto a man again.

It may be well understand in this wise, that men, being in the state of innocency, have then the figure of man, the soul having the whole pre-eminence over the body. But after, if it happen that the appetites and desires of the body so much do increase that they have the whole possession of the body; and that the affections of the soul, that is to say, virtues, be suppressed or put to silence; then the life becometh beastly.

Then look in what beasts the said appetites be most vehement. He in whom is the semblable appetite <E1r> may be said hath his soul in that beast enclosed; as he that is lecherous and wanton, in such a horse as thou spakest of whilere; a cruel man or tyrant, into a tiger or lion; a glutton or drunkard, into a wolf or a swine; and so forth of other. And if one man happen to be possessed of many vices, then is his transformation more diverse and, as I mought say, more monstrous. Also, being in that beastly estate and the soul with her affects being hid and not shewing her puissance, what any other thing is more in them than ignorance? Which, being a thing beastly, is as proper to them as beastly appetite.[32]

But if, God so willing, after long travailing in ill affections, the soul recovereth her might and, vanquished ignorance, making the body to know his misery, then the beasts, hid, by little and little falleth away, as knowledge increaseth; <E1v> and finally man resumeth his very figure and proportion, living after the rule of the soul, and so continueth perpetually.

How sayest thou, Aristippus, to this exposition?

ARISTIPPUS It seemeth to me to stand with good reason; for ever me thought that Pythagoras's sentence, which was a man of incomparable wisdom, had such a meaning.

PLATO Also, it appeareth by the said sentence that ignorance maketh a man beastly and that knowledge putteth away beastliness and restoreth a man to his dignity.

ARISTIPPUS Yea, verily.

PLATO And it seemeth by that which is rehearsed that ignorance, that we call beastly, is in that, that beasts do not know what they themselves be

nigra est cauda, 'Taste not of anything with a black tail', and *Adagia* 1.4.55 (CWE 31, 358–59), *Ignem dissecare*, 'To cleave fire'. There was extensive ancient doxography that Elyot would have encountered: e.g. Diog. Laert. 8.1.17–19; Plut., *Quaest. conv.* 8.7 (*Mor.* 727C–728C); etc. Moreover, Elyot no doubt knew something of the tradition directly, by means of the Greek textbook that he used otherwise, *Scriptores aliquot gnomici* (Basel: Froben, 1521), which included the Pythagorean *Carmen aureum*: see above, p. 62.

32 The allegory is Homeric, possibly deriving from the version in Boethius's 'Circe' metrum and its explication, *Phil. cons.* 4p3–4m3, or Claud., *In Rufinum* 2.480–93.

nor between them and men what is the diversity. Also, that men know the diversity between them and brute beasts, it happeneth of the soul having pre-eminence over the body; <E2r> that is to say, while the soul doeth hold the senses of the body under due rule and obedience.

ARISTIPPUS I wot not how to answer thee. For I have affirmed so much before that I cannot reply now, with mine honesty.

PLATO For thy keeping of °touch, Aristippus, I can well praise thee. But how sayest thou? Have we not of ignorance spoken for this time sufficiently?

ARISTIPPUS Yes, I suppose, and we have now passed two miles in our journey. Therefore, return where thou leftest to speak of knowledge. For thou hast laid a good ground on thy table to set out thine image.

PLATO I see thou forgettest nothing that I have spoken. Therefore, let us assay to express that image; that is to say, °declare what is that knowledge wherein lieth very wisdom, which peradventure King Dionise hoped to find in me, when he first desired to see me.

° touch] touhe *B*
° declare] to declare *B*

<E2v>

THE SECOND DIALOGUE.

PLATO Thou °dost remember, Aristippus, that we be agreed that knowledge is contrary to ignorance? And I suppose also they be so contrary that they may never accord or in any part be mingled together; but alway where the one is, the other lacketh?

ARISTIPPUS Yea, surely, it must needs follow.

PLATO Then, when ignorance is once put away, clearly knowledge only remaineth?

ARISTIPPUS Yea, so I trow; or else I wot not what it is that abideth, except I would call it nothing. And yet, now I am advised, that same no-<E3r>thing is ignorance, for of nothing can be no knowledge.

PLATO Thou speakest truly, and as it beseemeth the scholar of Socrates. Now thou knowest that ignorance is of beasts, which therefore be named brute, and that knowledge is only pertaining to man; and that the ignorance whereby beasts be most unlike unto man is ignorance of themselves, in as much as they know not that they be beasts. Then it followeth that the knowledge which maketh the greatest diversity between man and beast and whereby man hath pre-eminence in dignity over beasts is the knowledge of himself, whereby also he knoweth other.

ARISTIPPUS Yea, supposest thou so? Doeth a man by knowing himself know other also?

PLATO No doubt thereof, and that shalt thou see proved in the order of our communication by the same reason that shall make him to know him-<E3v>self. But yet, lest thou be deceived, I will by the way demand one question of thee. Thou saidest whilere, Aristippus, that a beast hath not the knowledge of himself and of other in the diversity of their kinds; I pray thee, what understoodest thou thereby? Any other than thou didest declare by the example of the bee and the spaniel?

ARISTIPPUS None other. Why, thinkest thou, Plato, that I said not well?

PLATO Thou camest, as I said, nigh to the point; but yet thou hittest it not. For peradventure thy supposal may be in some part false, although thou hast not espied it.

Dost thou not behold that beasts which be savage, as they be diverse in kind, so do they covet to be together and will sever themselves from other? And in the act of generation will accompany with none other beast but such as is of his own proper kind, not-<E4r>withstanding that there be diverse of them one so like an other that uneath a man can discern the diversity, as wolves and mastiffs, foxes and curs, hares and conies, and many other beasts which were tedious to be rehearsed? And, as touching the bee that

° dost remember] doest remembrest *B*

we spake of, be there not divers flies like unto him? And for all that, he will company with none of them, nor yet suffer them — if he be of power to resist — entry into his hive, but at the first sight will withstand him. Moreover, all the said beasts, when they perceive a man coming toward them, they will not abide but flee sooner from him than from any beast.

°<Further>, among an infinite number of people, a dog will know his master although there were a thousand men, in personage, fashion, and colour of garments very like unto him. And if thou wouldest say that the <E4v> dog doeth discern that by scent of smelling, yet would I demand of thee again how it happeneth that a dog, taken up at Olinthum[33] and brought unto Athens — which be distant forty miles, one place from the other, and is a very diffuse way to keep and little travelled — yet after that the dog have been retained at Athens by the space of six months, when he hath been at liberty, he hath returned again home to his master's house. How wouldest thou answer me, Aristippus?

ARISTIPPUS How else, but even as thou thyself didest suppose that I would say? That the dog found the way by scent specially, adding too, peradventure, some part of his sight?

PLATO But perchance, ere he come to Olinthum, his master hath forsaken the house that he dwelled in when he was with him and is removed into another house. <E5r> Doest thou not think that the dog will go to the house where he left his master and not to the house where he dwelleth?

ARISTIPPUS Yes, in good faith.

PLATO And yet percase he shall find his master's steps in the street toward his new house, and, notwithstanding, as soon as he espieth the other house, he passeth forth and goeth straight to it; but when he cometh in and findeth not his master there, yet he layeth him down as he were at home, trusting that his master will shortly come in. Doeth he this by sight or by smelling?

ARISTIPPUS Thou makest me doubt, Plato, whether he doeth it by any of them.

PLATO What if it happen that his master, not knowing him to be there, standing nigh to the window, talketh loud with his neighbour, so that the dog heareth him? Thinkest thou not that he will rise suddenly and with great haste come joyfully until <E5v> his master?

ARISTIPPUS Yes I have seen that in experience.

PLATO Doth he that by savour or by sight?

ARISTIPPUS By neither of them, but only by hearing.

PLATO And when he cometh to him, he straight leapeth upon him without any smelling?

[33] Olynthos, on the Calcidice peninsula, central Macedonia.

° Further] *B* : Moreover *A*

ARISTIPPUS I am yet in doubt what I may say.

PLATO Only because thou wilt not grant, contrary to thine assertion, that a beast hath knowledge of himself and other in the diversity of their kinds. But what wilt thou say if it shall appear unto thee that beasts have yet another knowledge among themselves than by their senses?

Hast not thou seen, when men have prepared themselves to go on hunting and to that intent have brought forth their leashes, collars, and lyams, or else their hays and purse nets, that the hounds, espying these things, have rejoiced <E6r> and leapt about the house, as if they knew that they should go on hunting? Likewise, when they hear the hunter blow his horn, they do all rise and with one voice do make a great noise, as if they consented to go to that solace; and if they heard one blow in a shawm or a trumpet, they would not do so.

The courser, which is used to battle, as soon as he heareth the trumpets blowen, he snorteth and brayeth, and, °taking to him his courage, he treadeth high and pranceth and, with such brags, declareth himself ready to set forth in battle.

Supposest thou that these beasts have this knowledge only by the senses whereof we have spoken?

ARISTIPPUS No. It seemeth to me now that they have another knowledge than only by senses; but what it is or whereof it proceedeth, I cannot <E6v> discuss, except I should name it natural influence, diversely disposed, more or less, after the grossness or capacity of the body whereunto it floweth.

PLATO By the faith of my body! And that definition is not to be dispraised, if thou add thereunto the senses.

But by this that thou and I have now spoken, it seemeth that beasts have knowledge of themselves and other, in the diversity of their kinds, contrary to thy first division; and, if it be so, then be they equal to men, and without cause we do call them ignorant or brute.

ARISTIPPUS I wot not what to say to thee.

PLATO Abide, Aristippus; despair not. Thou hast spoken more wiselier than thou art ware of.

ARISTIPPUS Trowest thou so, Plato?

PLATO Yea, and that shalt thou perceive, if thou wilt hear me.

ARISTIPPUS Go to, then, I pray thee.

PLATO Let it not be tedious unto thee to have some things repea-<E7r>ted, which thou hast spoken.

First, if thou remember thyself, thou wouldest not deny but that wisdom was knowledge. Afterward, thou grantedest also that ignorance was none other thing but lack of knowledge, which concluded that ignorance could

° taking] taketh *B*

be no wisdom. And then didest thou reason that the diversity between man and beast was only ignorance, and that ignorance didest thou suppose to be the lack of knowledge of themselves and other in the diversity of their kinds. This was very well gathered of thee, in mine opinion. And the reason that followed, by the example that thou didest put, of thy horse, the bee, and the spaniel, was not unfit to the purpose, if thou wouldest have abiden well by it. But by our merry digression into Pythagoras's regenerations, thou were brought from that argu-<E7v>ment sooner than thou shouldest have been, which happened unto thee as it doeth ever to them which, like unto thee, do follow the concupiscence and pleasant affects of the body.

For like as they be unstable, so the followers and lovers of them be ever inconstant, as well in their opinions as in their acts. But if thou, being sometime the hearer of Socrates as well as I was, hadest followed directly his doctrine according as he spake it, and also practiced it by his example of living, and hadest not, as a truant, picked out of his arguments such matter as thou supposedest mought only maintain thy sensual appetite, thou shouldest have perceived what thou thyself hadest meant, which thou doest not now, it varieth so much from thy profession; and, peradventure, the knowledge that we now seek for should never have comen between us <E8r> two in question; but it should have sufficed to have told to thee what I said to King Dionise and how he dealt with me, and thou shouldest soon have judged if he had according to my merits entreated me.

But now, Aristippus — to the intent thou mayest take some comfort of the seeds of Socrates' doctrine which remain in thee, but they will not spring in such wise as thou mayst see them, except I do water them with my declaration — first remember that, of all that which beareth the name of a thing, there be two kinds. One hath no body and is ever steadfast and permanent; the other hath a body, but it is ever moveable and uncertain. The first, because it may be understood only, it is called intelligible; the second, because it may be felt by senses, it is called sensible. The way to know the first is called reason, and the knowledge thereof is named under-<E8v>standing; the way to know the second is called sense or feeling, °<and> the knowledge thereof is named perceiving.

Moreover, of that which is called intelligible, there is the first and the second: in the first is that portion of divinity which is in man, whereby he is made to the image and similitude of God; in the other be numbers and figures. Of this, beasts have no part, neither of the first nor yet of the second. Of the first, I suppose thou wilt grant me; and as for the second, experience will prove it. For I dare say thou never heardest of beasts that could skill of numbering.

° and] *A om B om*

ARISTIPPUS I wot nere. I never called any yet to a reckoning.

PLATO And though an ape or other like beast seem, in taking of things, to observe an order as it were in numbering, yet, if it be well considered, it shall appear that it is by an imagination engendered of custom <F1r> and not by numbering.

I have seen a man, which was born blind and used to be led to three or four houses in the city, which hath been a great distance asunder, at the last, by custom hath knowen so well where they stood that, without any man or dog leading or any man telling him, he hath gone directly unto them, whereat first I marvelled with many other; and when I communed with him, I have perceived that he never observed number but that only custom had set the distance of the places in his imagination.

Like may be spoken of figures, for that whereby beasts do discern one thing from another is not understanding. That is to say, though they discern in quantity the more from the less, yet they understand it not as round, quadrant, or triangle, or in other like figure; but the simulacre or image whereby <F1v> they perceive the said diversity is only by custom formed and imprinted in the principal sense, which is the heart. And when the thing self is removed out of sight, that impression that remaineth is called imagination, who committeth it forthwith unto memory, which °undoubted is not only in men but also in beasts. For they discern the time present and that which is passed; but the time to come they know not, and memory is only of the time passed.

And therefore, the beasts that thou spakest of do perceive the diversity of things by imagination and memory, conceiving and retaining in the heart — which is the principal sense or fountain of senses — the image of the thing that is sensible. And thereby, the dog perceiveth his master and fetcheth his glove, which he hath been before taught for to do, and goeth to the places where he hath seen his master been a little before. <F2r>

But that he knoweth not whether his master be a man or a horse, Plato or Demosthenes, a philosopher or an orator, it is evident enough. For although my dog had abiden ten years continually with me and had heard me every day speak of Demosthenes and name him an orator and heard thee call me every day Plato and name me a philosopher, yet if thou wouldest deliver unto him anything and bid him carry it to the orator, he would straight bring it unto me and not to Demosthenes. Also, if I would cast a loaf unto my spaniel and bid him carry it to my horse, I suppose he would forthwith eat it himself and lie down when he had done, without seeking for my horse, though he stood by him. Is it not so?

ARISTIPPUS Yea, in good faith; me thinketh thou saist truly.

° undoubted] undoubtedly *B*

PLATO And likewise may be reasoned of all other beasts, be they never so wily, if their acts be deeply considered.

ARISTIPPUS <F2v> It appeareth so.

PLATO Then thy saying is °not to be reproved, that a beast lacked knowledge of himself and of other?

ARISTIPPUS No, as it seemeth.

PLATO And that lack of knowledge is ignorance?

ARISTIPPUS Yea, truly, and so said I also.

PLATO And that ignorance made the diversity between man and beast?

ARISTIPPUS Yea, and the same too.

PLATO Then thou wilt conclude that man hath knowledge?

ARISTIPPUS Yea, that I must needs, thou knowest well enough.

PLATO And what callest thou that knowledge? Supposest thou it is where a man knoweth himself and other?

ARISTIPPUS Yea, so I said, and thou hast also affirmed it.

PLATO So I did indeed. But yet, good Aristippus, suffer me to demand of thee a few questions. We shall the sooner find out the knowledge that we seek for. Is it in figure and number that knowledge resteth?

ARISTIPPUS Yea, so <F3r> it appeareth.

PLATO Nay, if thou remember thee. Perdie, thou saidest thyself that thy horse knew not that thou were a man or that he was a horse.

ARISTIPPUS So said I indeed.

PLATO Thou considerst also that it was agreed by us both that the figure made not the man; but it was the soul with the body that caused the man to be so named; and that without the soul, notwithstanding the figure of man, yet were he no man but a brute beast.

ARISTIPPUS It must needs be so; I cannot deny it.

PLATO Then is there somewhat more that maketh the said knowledge, besides the figure, which is contained in the second part of that which we called intelligible?

ARISTIPPUS So me thinketh. But what it is, I cannot remember.

PLATO It is no marvel. Thy wits be so involved in carnal affections that this clean and pure doctrine cannot enter into <F3v> them without great difficulty, and, when they be once in, they cannot long abide, thy memory is so occupied about wanton and beastly fantasy. But yet will I once again rehearse unto thee that which thou hast so shortly forgotten. Did not I say that in the first part of that which is named intelligible is that portion of divinity in man, whereby he is made to the image and similitude of God?

ARISTIPPUS Yes, I remember well that.

° not to be reproved] not reproved *B*

PLATO And is that form printed in any other thing than in man's soul, which is immutable and of one proportion and figure, although it lieth bounden in the body as it were in a prison, considering things diversely as the substance and qualities of the body suffereth him to take light, being deceived by the judgment of the senses or wits, esteeming things as they be sensible and visible, where that <F4r> which the soul by himself doeth consider is intelligible and also invisible?

ARISTIPPUS I doubt me what I shall say. But supposest thou, Plato, that the image and similitude of God is not in the body of man, as well as in the soul?

PLATO Hast thou so soon forgotten that which I have so often rehearsed? That if the body of man were without a soul, he were then but in the number of brute beasts, which have senses as well as he and some, more sharp and quicker? And no man that will affirm that God is will presume, as I trow, to say expressly that the image of God is in satyrs and other beasts and fishes, which have form and shape like unto man. And to speak to thee merrily, without reproach unto God's majesty, if that which is in every man's body were the image of God, certes then the image of God were <F4v> not only diverse, but also horrible, monstrous and in some part ridiculous; that is to say, to be laughed at. For every man hath not in visage and personage one proportion or figure: some have a plain and equal visage; some look as they laughed; other as they wept; diverse as they were ever angry; many have in the quantity of their bodies or members excess or lack. Wherefore, to think that all these be like unto God — which, as he is the creator of them all and may make and do what he listeth, so it agreeth with all reason that he incomparably excelleth them all in every perfection and, consequently, in beauty — it were of all other the greatest madness.

ARISTIPPUS Thou answerest me reasonably. But now, I pray thee, declare to me as plainly how the image of God is in the soul, as thou supposest.

PLATO Thou wilt not deny that <F5r> God is, without any body, invisible and immortal, whose form cannot be deprehended with the eyen of mortal men, nor described by any sensible knowledge?

ARISTIPPUS No, truly.

PLATO And the same, I trow, thou wilt confess of the soul?

ARISTIPPUS Yea, verily.

PLATO Also, God is in power in all and every part of the world, and by his providence all thing is governed and moved; and he himself is of none other moved nor governed, but is the first incomprehensible mover?

ARISTIPPUS I can by no reason deny it, except I would deny that God is, and that I may not, since that the order of all thing that is visible declareth that there must needs be one principal cause and beginning, which we call

God; and also, that order cannot be without providence and one perpetual governance.

PLATO Yet thou sayest well, and as it beseemeth Socrates' scholar.

<F5v> But now, Aristippus, forasmuch as God is the first and principal cause; and, as he is one in beginning, so is he ever one in governance; and therefore having in him all sufficiency and power, wilt thou not grant me that he is of an absolute and full perfection?

ARISTIPPUS Yes, that must I needs.

PLATO And is not perfection, in that it is perfect, good also?

ARISTIPPUS No man will deny it.

PLATO Yea, peradventure, the same perfection is goodness, since goodness is alway complete, profitable, and without any lack. And goodness and evil: the one is contrary and ever repugnant unto the other. How sayest thou? Is it not so?

ARISTIPPUS Yea, that is true.

PLATO Then is there ever variance between them?

ARISTIPPUS So it appeareth.

PLATO But in God can never be variance, which of his nature is ever one and may never suffer division.

ARISTIPPUS I grant thee.

PLATO Then in <F6r> God nor about God can be none evil; therefore, all evil is far from God. But yet me seemeth we have spoken somewhat less of God than we should do.

ARISTIPPUS What meanest thou thereby?

PLATO For since we both have agreed that he is the first beginning and cause, we should have also concluded that all goodness proceeded of him and that he was the fountain and principal goodness.

ARISTIPPUS I admit all to be true that thou sayest.

PLATO Then thou grantest that evil is contrary to God?

ARISTIPPUS Yea, verily.

PLATO And all thing that is ill is contrary to that thing which is good?

ARISTIPPUS Yea, surely.

PLATO Those things that be contrary one to another, be they like in that wherein they be contrary?

ARISTIPPUS No, truly.

PLATO Then it seemeth that they be unlike?

ARISTIPPUS So it appeareth.

PLATO That wherein things be like or unlike one to another, do we not <F6v> call it an image or similitude?

ARISTIPPUS Yes, undoubtedly.

PLATO Hitherto, we have well agreed. Now, let see, Aristippus: since thou hast confessed that the soul is invisible and immortal, how sayest thou? Shall it suffice that therein only he be like unto God, and in all other thing unlike or contrary?

ARISTIPPUS No. For then should he be in part like and in part unlike, and then were it not well spoken to say that man was made to the image and similitude of God, without joining thereto distinctly and particularly in what thing he was made to the said image and similitude. As if one would say that in thy son were thy proper image and similitude; if thou thyself didest perceive that he were like to thee in favour, proportion of body, and conditions, thou wouldest hold thee pleased and say nothing; but if thou beheldest <F7r> that in his personage he were like thee; but in some part of the visage, as in the nose, the eyen, or the mouth, he were unlike thee; also in liberality, he followed thee; but in lechery, he did degenerate from thee; shouldest thou not then be constrained to demand of him that spake wherein thy son is like to thee, or in what part of him thine image should appear to be most?

PLATO Now on my faith, Aristippus, thou speakest very well and wisely. Lo, see how, by our long communing, thou art drawen from thy wanton affections and fantasies, whereby the sparks of wisdom that thou gatest of Socrates's lessons, like as fire hid under askes and dead coals, when they be removed, is found cindering in little embers. So, thine affections being withdrawen, wisdom doth begin to glitter and shew; which, if it would abide kind-<F7v>ling and not, like unto embers, remove and flee away with every puff of wind, I doubt not but, for the sharpness of thy wit, of all Socrates's scholars thou shouldest be at the last one of the most wisest and excellent. But I will speak thereof no more, lest thou shouldest suppose I did to thee that I would not do to King Dionise; I mean, flatter thee.

ARISTIPPUS No, no; I perceive whereabout thou goest. Thou wouldest, with persuasion, wherein I know thou art marvellous, withdraw me, if thou moughtest, from my professed opinion; but that is now no part of our matter.

PLATO Yet I suppose thou art deceived, for thou shalt find it otherwise ere we be at an end of our communication. But where left we? Thou didest affirm (as I remember) that, forasmuch as man was made to the image and similitude of God, he ought to be like unto God, not in part, but in all universally.

ARISTIPPUS In all such likeness as that <F8r> which is created may be most like unto his creator, without comparison of equality; for God, that is alway one, may suffer no peer or like in equality of substance.

PLATO That is verily well said, Aristippus, although that was ever meant in our reasoning; for I never supposed that thou hadest so little learning to think that God made men equal unto him, or so ignorant that thou knewest not what an image or similitude is in respect of that whereunto it is wrought. By that which we before have affirmed, that God is the first cause and principal goodness, it argueth that all thing which is not the self God is inferior unto him; wherefore, the image or similitude of God, although it be an imitation or following in likeness of that whereunto it is made and resembled, yet is it inferior to God, who, by the virtue of his unity, hath ever a pre-eminence and sovereignty.

Therefore, we will stick no more thereupon; <F8v> but now I will assay to declare how we may understand that the similitude of God is imprinted in man, wherein the knowledge that we began to treat of perchance shall appear unto us. Wherefore, Aristippus, I pray thee, as thou hast done hitherto, hear me patiently; and when I shall demand of thee any question, answer me simply without cavillation.

ARISTIPPUS Contented; but be short, then, I pray thee, for me thinketh it long ere we come to an end of our matter.

PLATO Yea, so I suppose. For as I said, the little sparks of wisdom that appeared in thee will never be brought to be a good fire, they be so mingled with askes of affection, whereby they be made so inconstant that they will not abide the end of my reason whereby, perchance, they mought be caused to kindle and wax more. But since thou hast promised to hear me patiently, I will go forth with this mat-<G1r>ter; and doubt not but that I will make an end ere we come to the city.

ARISTIPPUS Go to, then, for I am now prepared to hear thee.

THE THIRD DIALOGUE

PLATO Since we have treated somewhat of God and of man's soul — but not sufficiently, for that would require a much longer time and also that both thou and I had our minds more clean purged with prayer and pure sacrifice — now let us see, as much as we may be suffered, what it is wherein they most do resemble.

First, all that is in God is perpetual and immutable, and by <G1v> none occasion or for any cause may be appaired, minished, or corrupted; that which is in the soul, part is perpetual and immutable, part is not perpetual and is also mutable. For that the soul is immortal and invisible, that is perpetual and may never be changed. But understanding, which I did put for the knowledge of that which was intelligible and named it a portion of divinity, is not perpetual in the soul, as it is in God, nor always immutable; but, during the time that it is conserved by contemplation of the divine majesty, it is perfect and maketh man's soul like unto God. And when it is joined unto corporal affects, it is made then unperfect, and the form of the soul is in a part decayed from the right simili-<G2r>tude of God. But if the soul, being dedicate to vices, be once fallen from the possession of reason, then understanding is vanished away, and the soul remaineth with the body transformed, as we spake of before. And then that immortality which, being joined to understanding, made the soul like unto God, being now separate from it, shall be to the soul confusion and torment.

The majesty of God, in beholding whereof the said understanding or knowledge is conserved and kept in perfection, is all his goodness, whereof I have spoken, and his providence, which proceedeth of the same goodness. In beholding the goodness of God, man doth perceive that thereof procedeeth virtue. In considering his providence, he findeth that <G2v> nothing is made without cause or (as I mought say) °at a venture, but that all things be made for a purpose, profitable and also necessary; and so, to the respect thereof, all things be good.

Now I will demand of thee, Aristippus, one question. Doest thou not remember that thou thyself saidest late that it were not well spoken to say that man was made to the image and similitude of God, if he had in him no mo things like unto God but only that he were invisible and immortal? And that didest thou ratify with a good and familiar example.

ARISTIPPUS It is not so long passed since I spake it but that I may well remember it.

PLATO And thou didst not deny but that the part intelligible of man is a divine substance wherein is understanding?

° at a venture] at venture *B*

ARISTIPPUS No, nor yet will I.

PLATO Then it seemeth that, in understan-<G3r>ding, man is like unto God, and the same understanding is knowledge. But is man like to God in any other knowledge, trowest thou, than in contemplation of the divine majesty?

ARISTIPPUS I pray thee rehearse that more plainly unto me.

PLATO By my truth, thou art very dull in perceiving. I say, in beholding perfectly the providence and goodness of God, did I not declare to thee, but even now, that therein was God's majesty?

ARISTIPPUS Well, now I perceive thee. It seemeth verily, Plato, that therein is the knowledge wherein, as thou hast affirmed, is a portion of divinity.

PLATO By that same knowledge, also he knoweth that virtue is good, because it proceedeth of goodness?

ARISTIPPUS Yea.

PLATO Doth he not also know that evil is contrary to good?

ARISTIPPUS Why not?

PLATO And he knoweth that vice is contrary to virtue?

ARISTIPPUS <G3v> Yea, that is true.

PLATO Then knoweth he that vice is ill, because it is contrary to that which is good?

ARISTIPPUS I agree also thereto.

PLATO By the same reason doth he know that he which is vicious — that is to say, he which is possessed with vice — is ill, and he that is virtuous is good?

ARISTIPPUS Yea, truly.

PLATO Then he that is vicious is contrary and unlike unto him that is virtuous?

ARISTIPPUS It must needs be so.

PLATO In any other thing but that he is ill?

ARISTIPPUS In none other thing.

PLATO And he that is virtuous, is he like unto God, which is all goodness, for any other thing but for that he is good?

ARISTIPPUS No, I suppose.

PLATO Then see how he that is virtuous is <G4r> like unto God, and that he which is possessed with vice is contrary and unlike unto him.

ARISTIPPUS I must needs agree to thy reason.

PLATO Now, in considering the providence of God, which also belongeth to understanding, order in everything is perceived to be. °Which order, like a straight line, issueth out of providence and passeth directly through all things that be created. And therein be degrees, wherein, those things being set, one hath pre-eminence over another in goodness?

° \Order./] *B* : *A om*

ARISTIPPUS So it appeareth.

PLATO Did not we call that goodness whilere necessary and profitable?

ARISTIPPUS Yes; that I remember.

PLATO Unto whom, supposest thou, be things profitable?

ARISTIPPUS Unto whom else but to them which do use them?

PLATO <G4v> And to them that do use them most, be they most profitable?

ARISTIPPUS Yea; so it followeth.

PLATO But if they fall from the degrees of the said line, wherein they were ordained and set by the said providence, and change their order, then those things do cease to be necessary one to another, because they be out of their right places where God had once set them for to be necessary?

ARISTIPPUS Indeed; so it seemeth.

PLATO And where order lacketh, there is disorder?

ARISTIPPUS Yea; that is true.

PLATO Also, either order is good and disorder ill, or else contrary?

ARISTIPPUS No, but as thou saidest first.

PLATO And that which is good is also profitable, and, contrariwise, that which is ill is also unprofitable?

ARISTIPPUS Yea, verily.

PLATO Then thou wilt grant me that order is good and profitable, and disorder is ill and unprofitable?

ARISTIPPUS That must I <G5r> needs do.

PLATO Then what saist thou? Be not all things wherein is order or disorder either good and profitable or ill and unprofitable, in using one another?

ARISTIPPUS Yes, doubtless.

PLATO And to them that do use them?

ARISTIPPUS So it appeareth.

PLATO More or less, as they be much or little used?

ARISTIPPUS I cannot deny it.

PLATO I am very glad, Aristippus, to see how seriously and truly thou keepest tack with me, since thou didest promise me that thou wouldest answer according as thou thoughtest, without leaning to any particular opinion; and in that appeareth in thee a token of more wisdom than is in all the residue of thy profession.

But now, remember well what thou hast spoken and shew me if thou thinkest that any other creature hath so much use of all things that be created as man hath. <G5v> Revolve them well in thy mind ere thou speakest, considering what commodity one thing may have by using another and of how many things one thing may receive any commodity.

How sayest thou? Hast thou now well advised thee?

ARISTIPPUS Me seemeth, Plato, that only man hath the use of all things that be created and may receive of everich of them a commodity. Other things do use sometime one another, but not so generally.

PLATO Then it seemeth also that all things were created for him specially?

ARISTIPPUS What meanest thou thereby?

PLATO For man doeth use or may use all thing that is, but not contrary; for the horse, the ox, or the sheep — likewise, other things living or growing — cannot use man nor receive of him anything but for man's proper commodity.

ARISTIPPUS Me <G6r> thinketh thou sayest truly.

PLATO Ergo, we be agreed that man useth things most of all other?

ARISTIPPUS Yea, surely.

PLATO Then be they to him either best and most profitable or else worst and most unprofitable?

ARISTIPPUS Thou speakest marvellously.

PLATO Why saist thou so, since this is but common reason, and, except I be deceived, to every man easy? But that the said things be to man best and most profitable, it happeneth of order; that they be worst and most unprofitable, it cometh of disorder.

ARISTIPPUS So verily, it seemeth.

PLATO Moreover, the pre-eminence that man hath, being in the highest degree of the line that we spake of, augmenteth also the quality; that is to say, maketh the thing that he useth better or worse. As by example, a fat sheep, having much wool on his back, forasmuch as a man <G6v> may be fed with his carcass and clothed with his wool, is better than a lean and poor sheep, whose wool being torn all off with the brambles, the carcass will only feed dogs, which, gnawing on the bones and bowels, will therewith be nourished. Likewise, herbs, in that they be medicinable and wholesome in preserving or restoring health unto man, be much better than for that they feed cattle or beasts. So that for the benefit that every creature bringeth unto man, it is the better in his kind and more profitable.

But, since it seemeth that for man specially all things were created and that unto him they be either best and most profitable or else worst and most unprofitable, I would now know wherein they be unto man good and profitable or ill and unprofitable?

ARISTIPPUS What meanest thou? Didest not thou declare it even now thyself, <G7r> when thou saidest that it happened by order and disorder?

PLATO I can thee thank: thou art now of a good remembrance. But doest thou perceive, Aristippus, what I meant thereby?

ARISTIPPUS Didest thou not mean that some beasts were ordained for man to eat, some to clad him with, some to till his land for corn, other to ride on? Likewise, herbs and fruits: some serve for meat and nourishing, diverse for medicine; stone and timber, to build with. And whiles they be used in this wise, as they be ordained, there alway is order; but if they be used for any other purpose, or one in the place of another, there is disorder.

PLATO Abide, Aristippus. Thou hast forgotten something behind thee that will make much of the matter. Perdie, there be some beasts, fowls, and fishes which will serve to none of the purposes which thou hast re-<G7v>hearsed, as serpents, scorpions, and such other like; of birds, the eagle, the dun kite, the osprey, and the cormorant, which do ravine and devour that which is necessary for man's living; also, crows and rooks may be brought into the same company. And of fishes, that which in Latin is called 'torpedo', ere ever he cometh out of the water, mortifieth the hands of the fisher whiles he is drawing up of his net. Another fish, called 'remora', although he be very little in body, yet will he stay and retain a great ship, being under sail, and let him that he shall not pass forth in his voyage.[34] And diverse other both fishes and birds there be of semblable malice: how wilt thou bring them into the order that thou hast spoken of?

ARISTIPPUS Marry, as thou saist, Plato, I cannot well tell what to say thereto.

PLATO I <G8r> believe that well enough, for thou art so nuzzled in carnal affections that thou keepest nothing in remembrance but only that which is commodious and pleasant. But I will help thee forth, as well as I can, albeit I know well enough I shall not bring these things in order sufficiently: the providence of God is so inscrutable that it cannot all be comprehended by man's imagination, notwithstanding, by my demanding and thine answering, I trust we shall find therein matter competent enough to help us to that thing that we go about; that is to say, to find out knowledge, wherein wisdom lieth hid.

First, Aristippus, thou wilt agree that all creatures, in the final cause of their creation, be good; that is to say, having respect to that they be made for?

ARISTIPPUS Yea, that have I granted already. <G8v>

PLATO Therefore to that respect they cannot be ill?

ARISTIPPUS That is truth.

°PLATO But malice is contrary to good and also taketh his denomination of evil?

ARISTIPPUS That I know well enough.

PLATO Then spake I not well, when I said that diverse beasts, fishes, and birds were of semblable malice, as they were of whom I had spoken?

ARISTIPPUS It seemeth so.

[34] The description is repeated below, p. 118; it occurs twice also in Eras., *Parabolae* (CWE 23, 231, and 253), and twice also in Plin., *NH* 9.79 and 32.2.

° \Malice./] *B* : *A om*

PLATO Forasmuch as, by their creation, they be all good?

ARISTIPPUS Yea, for the same cause.

PLATO Of the said beasts, birds, and fishes, there be some parts which by physicians and them that seek for the natural properties of things be founden remedies against diverse sicknesses.

ARISTIPPUS So it hath been affirmed by Democritus and his disciple Hippocrates;[35] and I myself have seen marvels, when such things have been practiced.

PLATO And forasmuch as goodness came of them, thou di-<H1r>dest judge all such things to be good?

ARISTIPPUS Yea, in good faith.

PLATO Thou didest therein judge truly and as it was. But when thou knewest any man to be stungen with a serpent or scorpion, whereby the man perished, didest thou suppose then that the scorpion or serpent was ill, or good still as he was when he served for a medicine and preserved man from the death?

ARISTIPPUS I am not so mad to suppose that to be good whereby man is destroyed.

PLATO I suppose thou art not. But since we have affirmed all thing to be good in his creation, having respect to the end wherefore it was created — forasmuch as the said beasts, birds, and fishes received in their creation the dispositions before touched, which thou supposest to be ill because thereby man may perish and die — let us consider the cause final where-<H1v>fore those dispositions were put by God of nature into the said creatures. Wherein, I will as briefly as I can declare to thee mine opinion or sentence, foreseen alway, that thou remember, that the providence of God is above man's capacity to comprehend wholly. But I doubt not some part of it shall serve, as I said, to the sufficient declaration of that thing that we purpose.

[35] Democritus (*c.* 460–*c.* 370 BCE), the 'laughing philosopher', and Hippocrates (*c.* 460–*c.* 370 BCE), who is said to have treated him, are mentioned together in Diog. Laert. 9.7.42; also, in Elyot, *Bibl.*, s.v. '*Democritus*': 'When he beheld the City of Athens, he continually laughed at the foolish diligence of them, which spared for no pains to get authority and riches, which they were not sure to keep, other which laboured to get their children great possessions, who either died before the fathers, or else overliving their fathers, shortly spent all that their fathers left unto them. But the *Athenienses*, not perceiving the cause of his laughter, thinking him to be mad, caused Hippocrates the physician to go unto him. Who perceiving the occasion of his laughter, said, Democritus is not mad, but the *Athenienses* be mad, at whom he doth laugh'.

THE FOURTH DIALOGUE

PLATO Shall we need, Aristippus, to make any plainer declaration what thing it is, for the which all other things, lacking the use of reason, were created?

ARISTIPPUS No. For it appeareth to me sufficiently that it is man, as thou hast already declared.

PLATO And we <H2r> be agreed, long agone, that man is of body and soul?

ARISTIPPUS Yea; no fail thereof.

PLATO And to the body, the senses or wits be joined, as understanding is joined to the soul?

ARISTIPPUS According.

PLATO Also, the body is sensual and mortal; the soul is intellectual and immortal?

ARISTIPPUS So it seemeth.

PLATO The first is in common with beasts, and therefore it is beastly; the other is a portion of divinity, and therefore it is divine and godly.

ARISTIPPUS That hast thou long agone proved, wherefore I will not now reply therein again thee.

PLATO I am glad that I find thee so reasonable. But dost thou also remember that I said that the divine portion, during the time that it is conserved by contemplation of the divine majesty, °it is perfect and like unto God; and when it is joined unto corporal affects, it is unperfect and vanisheth away?

ARISTIPPUS Yea, I remember it well.

PLATO Now hear me out patiently, <H2v> and we shall come shortly to an end of this matter. Thou knowest well enough, Aristippus, that the body, and consequently the senses or wits that do pertain thereunto, is the habitation or vessel which receiveth the soul. Also, affects or affections, although whilere I named them corporal, yet in very deed they be first in the soul, as intentions be in the workman before he doeth work; and when the soul doeth exercise them, having his chief respect to understanding, whereof we have so much spoken, then be they virtues. But if they, being mixed with the senses, be all ruled by them, in having only respect to the body, then be they vices, and, the soul by the excluding of understanding being made subject unto the body, they may then be well called corporal, as that ought to be called the goods of the vanqui-<H3r>sher which were the prisoner's before he was taken, or the goods of the bondman be called the lord's.

Now so it is that God, of whose majesty we have spoken and be yet in speaking, when he hath put the soul — accompanied with affects as her perpetual servants and ministers — into the body as into her proper habitation, he giveth to her the senses to be as her slaves or drudges; and,

° it is] is *B* (*fortasse recte*)

committing to her, for a chief counsellor, understanding, he leaveth with her also free will to be her secretary.

Now, if she mought alway keep her habitation and company in that estate as they were left °unto her, then should men be as gods and those things which brought any annoyance to men should alway be ill and be made by nature in vain; and also God should seem to do ill in the ordaining of them, or else <H3v> that in things there were no providence. But, since of so many men as now we be, have been, and shall be in the world the bodies in the principal humours whereof they be compact — which, as thou knowest, is blood, red choler, phlegm, and black choler, called melancholy — be of diverse temperatures, therefore be they in sundry wise inclined in the operation of their senses or wits: as some to acts venereal and highness of courage; other, more to get possessions and richesse; diverse for every little displeasure to be cruelly revenged; many to employ all their study and labour in ill craft and deceit; other do abhor all travail, as well of mind as of body, desiring only — as the block which Jupiter did send down into the water to have rule over the paddocks — to lie still and do nothing.

As soon as any of the said incli-<H4r>nations be conceived in the senses, the mind beginneth to have delectation therein and offereth it to us, as it were good, pleasant, and profitable. Then, if our affects, by whom we be moved to do anything, do consent to the said delectation and then immediately will is corrupted, so that she, as false and disloyal, writeth in the heart of man — which is the soul's book, wherein all thoughts be written — that the said inclination, moved and set forth by the said affects, is profitable and good; if the soul hastily, without asking counsel of understanding, do approve the said persuasion, believing will without any other investigation or search, then she, being abandoned of understanding, loseth her dignity and becometh minister unto the senses which before were her slaves, who, usurping the pre-eminence and having the affects and will wholly at their commandment, <H4v> do possede the body as their proper mansion, leaving nothing to the soul but to use only her powers after their sensual appetites. And so man, bereft of that portion wherein he was like unto God, is become equal, or rather inferior, to brute beasts for such causes as I before have rehearsed.

Now, Aristippus, when man is once brought unto this estate, doest not thou suppose that he forgetteth now or knoweth not what he is? Or, to express more plainly to thee what I mean, is he not ignorant that he is transformed from a man to a beast and supposeth still that he is like unto God and, in the order that we spake of, superior unto all other creatures and dominator over them all?

° unto] with *B*

ARISTIPPUS Yea, that is true: he believeth so, verily.

PLATO But yet it is not so. For when understanding was excluded by the soul and that she was subdued or <H5r> mastered by the senses, then the similitude of God which was in understanding vanished from him. And when he left his own place of pre-eminence and did participate in carnal affects with creatures which were to him inferiors, he brake the line of order, and lost his superiority, and consequently brought himself and other into disorder, which, as we have agreed, is evil and contrary unto good and by the same reason is enemy unto God, which is only goodness. For no man will deny but °that <the> thing which is so contrary unto another that in no part they may accord but be alway repugnant, they be mutually enemies one to another.

ARISTIPPUS I suppose it be even as thou saist.

PLATO Now call to thy remembrance that we were agreed that all creatures were made for man <H5v> and that he had the most use of them all; also, they all were good in the order of their creation and that to man they were best and most profitable, as long as they continued in the said order; and, being in disorder, they were also to man worst and most unprofitable. Moreover, although some beasts, fowls, and fishes seem to have in them a malice whereby man may be hurt or annoyed, yet, having respect to the cause final wherefore they were made, they were (notwithstanding) necessary unto man specially.

ARISTIPPUS I thank thee heartily, Plato, for this repetition, whereby thou hast well revived my remembrance, which was well nigh oppressed with the abundance of matter wherewith thou hast, as I mought say, enfarced this communication!

PLATO I know well enough, Aristippus, that, in matter of great <H6r> importance, to men that be sensual, having their minds engrossed with carnal affections, there is required a plain and sensible form of reasoning, broken now and then with often repetitions; which, although to froward hearers it seemeth to make the matter tedious, yet if they can abide it, they shall thereby retain some seeds of knowledge, like as, in a land that was never well husbanded, corn will grow and spring in ear when men little looked for to have gotten such fruit by their ill husbandry.

But now set up thine ears, Aristippus, and diligently hear the mystery of the wonderful goodness and providence of God, which shall be declared in the said cause final, which I intend now to express and open unto thee without further delay.

ARISTIPPUS Go to, now, Plato; I have all my whole mind settled and prepared to hear thee, and I shall not <H6v> willingly let one word that passeth from thy mouth escape me.

° that the thing] that thing *A B*

PLATO Thou hast already granted that a cunning artificer foreseeth in his imagination the figure of the thing that he warketh and to what effect it is wrought, which is properly called the cause final. And when it is made, he delighteth in the beholding it. And the more perfect and excellent that the work is, the more he therein rejoiceth and prepareth some mean to preserve it from breaking or other destruction.

But there is °none artificer to be compared unto God, either in foresight or in care to preserve that which he himself wrought, nor there is any man's workmanship like to his in perfection. Wherefore, he most excellently rejoiceth in his creatures; and because he considereth that man is the most wonderful of all his works, he rejoiceth therein most, <H7r> and incomparably. Also, because he made him to his own similitude, he loveth him, according to the common proverb, all thing loveth that which is most like to himself.[36] And therefore he is most circumspect in the preservation thereof. Wherefore, considering that, by will perchance corrupted, as I late declared, man mought decline from that perfection wherein he was made and by the part sensible °<be> induced to rebel °again his own creator, thinking that of his own power he hath all other creatures under his subjection and that all that he willeth is good, not as understanding would instruct him but as his affections deceived by his senses do falsely persuade him.

This eternal and incomprehensible goodness which we call God, loving man as his image incomparably, hath provided to sit in the <H7v> way whereby will shall pass many sundry obstacles and lets to cause him to tarry, that in his course he fall not headling in the bottomless pit of ignorance, while he is in the way to rebel °again his maker and most merciful lord. These necessary lets be diseases and sicknesses, whereby bodily strength is abated and therewith carnal affects oppressed or minished; adversity, vexation, and trouble, whereby sturdy courage, pride, and ambition, and other like mallenders of the mind, may be cured or at the least ways reformed. And besides these be other obstacles whereby man shall be warned of his arrogance, when he too much presumeth on his proper power, knowledge, and industry, and therefore he will freely use all things at his pleasure, wherein his senses have delectation and his appetite moveth him.

36 Cic., *Sen.* 3.7, 'pares autem vetere proverbio cum paribus facillime congregantur', possibly from Eras., *Adagia* 1.2.20, *Aequalis aequalem delectat*, 'Everyone loves his own age' (CWE 31, 166); cf. *Adagia* 1.2.21, *Simile gaudet simili*, 'Like rejoices in like' and 1.2.22, *Semper similem ducit Deus ad similem*, 'God always leads like to like' (CWE 31, 167–69).

° none] no *B*
° be] *A om B om*
° again] against *B*
° again] against *B*

These things God foreseeing (as I said before), most <H8r> lovingly and wisely providing for his most dearest creature against the said peril of forgetfulness, like as he made man of soul and body, so with things necessary and profitable to the body he ordained things °also necessary and profitable unto the soul, sowing among the herbs that be wholesome or pleasant other noisome and venomous. In the green bank lieth the serpent hid, ready with his trembling tongue to strike mortally them which do approach him. The scorpion wounden in the green grass lieth watching with his forked tail in a readiness to sting them which look not down to their feet. The body infected or wounded findeth in pain and anguish his own proper ignorance, in that that he so much esteemed delectation and pleasure, which in so short a moment vanished away. Also, since a little herb, which is inani-<H8v>mate, may change pleasure into pain and health into sickness; or a little vile worm at one stroke may bereave him of all delectation and pleasure and fill him with so much anguish and dolour that the life, which he °desired ever to continue, becometh to him tedious and loathsome; he shall thereby not only remember that he is passable and therefore no God, but also perceive and consider of how little importance or valour is then his strength, authority, or puissance, were he never so mighty a champion or so puissant a king or emperor.

And, with that remembrance, the part sensible being rebuked, understanding eftsoons resorteth unto the soul and helpeth her to reform all her whole household, setting eftsoons everything in his proper place and office, as it was before free will was corrupted. And if then the soul be cir-<J1r>cumspect and do restrain will of her liberty, compelling her to be subject and so obedient to reason that, without her consent, she shall dare to do nothing, then the crafty persuasions of the senses shall nothing avail; but they themselves — will they or no — shall be constrained to be still drudges unto the soul, as they were ordained.

But if man do forget to set will under the governance of reason and, with a circumspect deliberation, to appoint unto her limits and bonds, which she shall not be so hardy to pass or exceed; after the body is escaped from adversity or is delivered of vehement pain and anguish, forthwith the senses do prepare themselves eftsoons to rebel; and affects, which, as wanton girls, be flexible or ready to incline to every motion, do prepare them with wanton countenance and pleasant promises to <J1v> allure eftsoons will to their appetite, whereby the soul shall be again in danger to perish; unless she, retaining still with her understanding, in considering her proper state and condition, and revolving what she before had suffered, do put will

° also] *B om*
° desired] dsired *B*

into the prison of dread, under the straight custody of remembrance and reason.

And in this wise as I have rehearsed, not only he that suffereth receiveth commodity of this wonderful providence; but also other, which do behold him that suffereth or heareth it sufficiently reported, may and ought thereby examine the state of his own person and, as mortal and passable — and no god, but the image of God by understanding — endeavour °themsel<ves> to keep that in perfection; having in good await that they let not affects become too malapert, but that the soul have understanding alway <J2r> at her elbow, which shall bid reason correct will, if °he be conversant with these affects. And then shall man still remain, without any of the said transformations that we before spake of; and use everything according to the effect that they were first ordained for him, which is the cause final; whereof I have spoken and promised to declare unto thee, wherein shineth the wonderful providence, whereby God is best knowen.

How saist thou, Aristippus? Doest thou bear away and perceive what I have all this while spoken?

ARISTIPPUS Yea, that I do, Plato, although it be marvellous. But yet me seemeth thou hast omitted somewhat which should make of all that which thou spakest a perfect conclusion.

PLATO Trowest thou so? Marry, I pray thee, tell me what lacketh as thou doest suppose, and I will a-<J2v>mend that gladly; for I would be loath that in that which we go about should be found imperfection.

ARISTIPPUS I remember thou hast affirmed, through all thy reasoning, that all things, in respect of their creation, be good and that all was created for man. Moreover, that some things which do seem to be ill in very deed be not so, but be all good in their order of their creation. And for proof of that, thou didest induce by example that adversity and sickness did cure or mitigate affects and vanities of the mind. Also, that venomous herbs, serpents, and worms, which seemed to have in them nothing but malice only, by annoying of men that were sensual, following their affects and forgetting their state, with pain and anguish bereft them their pleasure, wherein they delighted, and made them remember that <J3r> they were passable and, by that consideration, to reform themselves, according to their first perfection, wherein they were ordained. And so didest thou conclude that adversity, sickness, venomous herbs, and beasts were good to that respect and therefore necessarily provided of God to the use of man.

Now, forasmuch as all men be not sensual nor led with carnal affects or vanities, but some men, keeping the senses in their proper office or

° themselves] them self *A* : him self *B*
° he] she *B*

duty, also keeping will (as I mought use thy words) within the precinct prescribed to her by understanding, need not so sharp a monition as thou hast spoken of, where adversity, sickness, venomous matter, or beasts do as soon and grievously annoy or hurt those good men as them that be vicious, how darest thou affirm them to be good or declare them to be a part of providence, <J3v> whereby the goodness of God is expressed? These things considered, me thinketh, Plato, thy conclusion, as I said, is yet insufficient.

PLATO Indeed, Aristippus, it seemeth that thou hast diligently heard me; but I fear me that, for the old controversies between us, thou markest more what I say to take me with some lack than to bear away and observe anything that may profit thee to know, in as much as my conclusion, which thou reprovest, is not so insufficient as thou doest suppose.

Thou knowest that °Scammony, given where need is and in a due and convenient proportion, healeth them which be vexed with melancholy but, exceeding his measure or taken where that humour doeth not abound, in the stead of health bringeth mortal sickness, almost incurable. The same doth Thapsia, Agaricus, and diverse other, which <J4r> do purge the body of superfluous humours. The fruits named Millones and Cocombres assuageth the inordinate heat that proceedeth of choler; yet in them which, either by nature or occasion, have their bellies cold, they procure intolerable torments or frettings. Mandragora and the juice of Poppy called Opium, to them which, by some °innatural cause, be let from sleep, do profit much if they be measurably taken; contrariwise, if they be taken by him that is much phlegmatic and of nature disposed to sleep very soundly — and also the medicine exceedeth his portion — °he bringeth the patient into so deep a sleep that he never awaketh. But, although these things which I have rehearsed, if they have not joined unto them opportunity and measure, do bring either damage or death to them which receive them, yet no <J4v> man °do accompt them for ill; but, being put in the number of medicines whereby man's body is cured, they be called good.

°Is there anything among men better or reputed more profitable than laws? And yet was there never law made by any man so perfect but that diverse have thereby sustained detriment, yea, some that willingly never offended. Also, some laws, by adding to sundry opinions, be so involved or wrapped in doubts that they, which once were and ought to be open and plain to the people which liveth under them and be bound to obey them, may not without long debating and great charges be declared sufficiently.

° Scammony] Scammonia *B*
° innatural] unnatural *B*
° he] it *B*
° do] doth *B*
° \Laws/

And yet who is so much displeased with any law but that he will affirm that laws be good? Yea, and although it happen sometime that they be ill executed? <J5r> Likewise the venomous herbs, beasts, and fishes, to that end and purpose which I have declared, whereunto they be ordained, be good, which thou doest not deny me. And then, by the examples that I have rehearsed, my conclusion in declaration of providence is good and sufficient.

For if thou thinkest that I should have proved those things to have been so absolutely good that they mought not be to any respect ill, then thou lackest that natural wit which all this while I supposed had been in thee. For I would have thought that thou hadest known that nothing is in this world so good but that it may bring damage to some man; finally that, under the region of the moon, is nothing so good that it is not mixed with some ill; but, remaining in their proper degrees of order, whereof I have spoken, one is better than another <J5v> and be never ill but by disorder; and there also one is worse than another, by the degrees. I do mean the causes wherefore they were ordained.

As by example to declare it more plainly: doest thou remember, Aristippus, when we were speaking of order and disorder, that thou saidest that some beasts were ordained for man to eat, some to clad him with, some to till his land, other to ride on? Likewise herbs, fruits, and trees, some to serve for nourishing, diverse for medicine, and other to build with?

ARISTIPPUS Yea, I do remember that well.

PLATO Now mark well, Aristippus.

The ox, which tilleth the land, beareth beef wherewith man is nourished, and his hide serveth to make °shoen to save men's feet from cold and other annoyance. The sheep beareth wool to clad with the body of man commodiously, and his flesh is good to be eaten; and, where <J6r> he lacketh puissance to draw the plough or the wain, instead thereof he, going and lying on the land with his ordure and piss, compasseth the ground and maketh it fertile and able to bear plenty of corn. Wherefore, these two be set in one degree in the line of order.

The horse — and all other beasts which be like to that kind — will draw or carry, and also their hides will serve to that purpose that the ox-hide doeth; but their flesh is not apt to be eaten of men, wherefore they be a degree under the other. And so consequently, all things, as they be profitable more or less unto man, if he do use them, so be they higher or lower in degree, in the said line of order.

And if an ox or a sheep have much flesh on him and sweet, he is named therefore a good ox or a good sheep. If a horse or a mule will <J6v> bear a

° shoen] shoes *B*

great weight and go far journeys, he is named a good horse or a good mule. And although a man, advisedly or unadvisedly, do eat more beef or mutton than his stomach will bear and therewith is sick, the ox or the sheep ought not therefore to be called ill. Nor if a man take away thy money or garments, and lay it on thine own horse or mule, and carry it away with him: this letteth not but that thy horse or mule shall be called still good.

But if thou wilt ride by post on thine ox or thy sheep, or roast thy horse or thy mule to banquet with thy friends, to those purposes thou canst not call any of them good; for they be out of their proper degrees or places in the line of order, and therefore they be now ill.

Semblably, if into thy potage, wherewith thou intendest to be nourished, thou doest cause to be put <J7r> such herbs as do serve for violent purgations; or into thy salad, chips of oak or of maple; or buildest thy house with stalks of fennel or mallows; or coverest it with the leaves of lettuce or beets: these herbs or trees so used do cease to be good and may to these purposes be now called ill.

So there is nothing that is perfectly good but God only; and all other things, the nearer they approach toward his similitude, the more do they draw to that perfection, and the higher be they in the line of order whereof I spake at the beginning.

This that I have now said, Aristippus, if thou dost well revolve in thy mind and consider, thou shalt not find that lack in my conclusion that thou hast objected. But yet to satisfy thee thoroughly, that in no part thou shalt think my reason vain or unprofitable, wilt thou see that <J7v> I shall sufficiently prove that sickness, adversity, matter or beasts venomous, being in their degrees in the line of order, be never ill, but, to that end and purpose that they were made for, they be alway good?

ARISTIPPUS I think, to prove that, it shall be impossible.

PLATO Perchance, nay. But forget not that I protested that the whole providence and judgments of God be to man (while he is mortal) inscrutable and far above his imagination or knowledge. Yet of his infinite goodness, he holdeth him contented that, with due reverence, we shall measurably search for them only to the intent thereby the more to know him, honour him, and love him. And after that manner do I now endeavour me, with the help of his spirit, to prove that his providence is excellent and most to be wondered at in that thing wherein thou and many other do suppose that provi-<J8r>dence lacketh.

ARISTIPPUS If thou canst bring that well to pass, I will then say that the fame and renome of thy wisdom, that is sprung throughout Greece, is well employed; and I will affirm also that King Dionise, when he gave thee to Polidis, was more liberal than wise, for he had been better to have given to him six the best cities in Sicily than to have departed from such a counsellor.

PLATO Well, I trust to verify thy good opinion. But now a little while answer to such questions as I will demand thee.

Be not we agreed that man is of soul and body, and that the soul is immortal and intelligible, but the body is mortal and sensible?

ARISTIPPUS Yes; no doubt thereof.

PLATO We be also accorded that all other things in this world were made chiefly for man? <J8v>

ARISTIPPUS Yea, so God help me.

PLATO And I trow thou wilt not deny that God is all goodness and that he made man unto his own image and similitude?

ARISTIPPUS No, verily.

PLATO If God made anything to the intent that it should be ill unto man, which is his proper similitude, it should then seem that there should be some malice in God, which were not only untrue, but also to affirm horrible and unleeful. Wherefore, the contrary must needs be true, that God made everything to the intent that it should be good unto man. But how that may appear in such things as thou hast rehearsed, which seem to be ill, thereon resteth our question.

Now take heed, Aristippus. The soul of man, being immortal, never dieth or ceaseth to be; but, after that it is joined with the body, °the body living, it liveth also, showing thereby her operati-<K1r>ons. And when life departeth from the body, the soul also departeth immediately, notwithstanding she afterward liveth. Then, if when she was joined to the body, she retained the senses and affects in due obedience, not suffering them to exceed their duty or offices, and have, until the separation of her from the body, ensued alway the counsel of understanding and reason, and so have continued in the form of a man; surely, after her departing from the body, according as by her operation the body abounded in virtues, so is she then immediately with God, whose similitude she so well hath kept, and there is promoted to joy and pleasure perpetual, more or less, after her merits. And that pleasure, being intellectual, shall more exceed the delectations of the body, which only be sensual, than perfect health doeth <K1v> exceed sickness, or the greatest rejoicing of the mind that man mought possibly have of a sensual motion mought surmount the greatest discomfort or heaviness.

God desiring that all souls mought come to this joy, to warn them of their office whom he seeth negligent, he suffereth the body wherewith they be joined (as I said before) to be touched with sundry afflictions, to the intent that they, perceiving how unable they be, the lecher to execute

° the] ethe *B*

his beastly pleasure in the fever double tertian or ethic; the proud man to advance himself above other, being infected with lepry, or the lousy sickness called phthiriasis, or stungen with the little and feeble scorpion; he that is cruel and fierce, how little he may prevail again the cholic passion, the stone, or the gout, or the falsehood of the adder, which as soon <K2r> as he hath stung the man, he glideth forthwith into the hedge and escapeth the fury of him, which, being hurt, is not able to follow him.

The covetous merchant, with his ship, cutteth the seas and, with his sails and stern, presumeth to enforce the winds to bring him into those coasts, from whence he may bring home that miserable traffic, whereon he will consume all his study and wit and, at the last, leave it to be consumed by other; while he is in the midst of his journey, under all his sails, the wind blowing a good cool, and having therewith a fair water, cometh the fish called 'remora' — little more than a gurnard — and, cleaving fast to the keel of the ship, maketh her tarry and holdeth her still, without moving;[37] until some time riseth a pirrie and breaketh all the tackling, so that the merchant is fain, if he will save his life, to flee away in a boat <K2v> and return home again without money or merchandise.

Among those things, adversity — or, as it is more commonly called, froward or contrarious fortune — countervaileth as much as all this whereof we have spoken and proceedeth to the same effect.

ARISTIPPUS But what sayest thou if he that is sick, hurt with venom, or vexed with fortune, do in nothing reform his living, but, in his pains or trouble, do blaspheme God; and when they be withdrawen from him, he is as ill or (perchance) worse than he was before? Shall we then suppose that thing to be good or profitable, whereby he not only is not reformed but also made worse than he was erst?

PLATO I marvel that thou wilt demand any such question! I pray thee, is the art of a surgeon good and profitable, or ill and unprofitable? Answer me thereto.

ARISTIPPUS Good and <K3r> profitable; who will deny it?

PLATO And he which in that art is cunning and perfect is to that respect good and therefore is called a good surgeon?

ARISTIPPUS Yea, that is true.

PLATO Then thou doest admit that a surgeon is good and that his art is good and profitable. But is his art declared by anything else but by his medicines or instruments, wherewith he doth cut, pierce, or °cauterize, as necessity of the wound or sore doeth require?

[37] Cf. above, p. 106 and n. 34.

° cauterize] *eA B* : cantherize *A*

ARISTIPPUS Yes. There requireth also that he know the nature and cause of the wound or sore, and that he can well order his plasters and ointments and also use handsomely the said instruments.

PLATO O, Aristippus! Thou art now importunate and wouldest put me to more business than needeth. Since I rehearsed 'that surgeon which in his art is cunning and perfect', what moveth thee to put to this ad-<K3v>dition, which is vain and superfluous? As if that in him which is perfect mought anything lack, or that in 'perfect' thou wouldest set degrees of comparison!

But admit for the case that our surgeon have all thing that in that art may be required, and also that he be thy natural father, which above all other and with great affection loveth thee. Suppose also now for this time that in everich of thine eyen grew a fistula, whereby thou art in jeopardy to lose thy sight and also to have thy visage thereby deformed. If thy father, desiring to have thee healed, and knowing (as thou spakest) the nature and cause of the said fistula, would prepare such remedies as were most expedient to cure thee, wouldest thou refuse him for thy good father and accompt him thine enemy?

ARISTIPPUS Nay, I trow! Then were it alms to hang me.

PLATO That <K4r> is heartily spoken, Aristippus, I make God a vow; therefore, I commend thee. Then wilt thou love him better than thou didest before?

ARISTIPPUS So ought I. For to that natural benefit that I received of him by my generation, he addeth too much humanity and kindness, in helping that I lose not my sight, whereby I should be deprived from all worldly comfort and be also deformed in my visage, which blemish should cause men that were honourable to abhor my presence.

PLATO Thou speakest reasonably. And therefore see that thou change not hereafter this good opinion.

Now, thy father doeth perceive by his cunning that this disease requireth sharp medicines, as those which be mordicative or biting, abstersive or cleansing, or perchance °cauterization, that is to say, that the place corrupted be scorched with a hot burning iron; which if thou wilt <K4v> patiently suffer and use ever after such order in diet as thy father appointeth thee, thou shalt alway have thy sight sound and thy visage safe and undeformed; which shall be, not to thyself only but also to thy father and surgeon, that cureth thee, great joy and comfort.

But, contrariwise, when thou feelest the medicine wark sharply, fretting and gnawing in the flesh that is putrefied, or else art touched with the fire which is in the hot glowing iron, wherewith he doeth cauterize the sore; if then thou doeth strive °again thy surgeon and father that goeth about

° cauterization] *eA B* : cantherization *A*

° again] against *B*

to heal thee, murmuring against him with all disobedience and words of villainy, despising his humanity and kindness, and refusing to be cured by the said remedies — either thou rubbest thine eyen and removest the medicine from the sore into all the sight of thine <K5r> eyen, or else struggling contemptuously again the wholesome hand of thy father doest wilfully °thrast the burning iron into thine eyen — then what marvel is it, if that which thy father ordained to cure thee now by thine impatience and disobedience turn to thy damage? That is to say, as well put clean out thy sight as also deform thy visage for ever? Which thing happening, mayst thou, Aristippus, by any reason, blame therefore thy surgeon?

ARISTIPPUS Nay, in good faith, to say truly.

PLATO What? The medicine or instrument? Which, by thine impatience and folly, thou didest convert from the place where they should have wrought for thy health and didest thrast them into thine eyen, whereby ensued to thee more grief and peril: shall we judge the medicine or instrument therefore to be ill? And here remember well, Aristippus, the cause final and the <K5v> degree and place in the line of order, which I have before sufficiently declared.

ARISTIPPUS In good faith, I will not dissemble: I see nothing here that ought to be called ill but I myself, if I were in the case that thou hast now purposed.

PLATO If thou hold thee there, we shall soon be agreed!

Also, if now — thou being blind, and the fistula growing every day greater and greater, the deformity of thy visage more and more — thou not only refusest to receive any medicine but also doest murmur against thy good father, cursing him for his medicine giving, which, through thine own folly and wilfulness, is converted from remedy unto thy damage; if then thy father — beholding thee to be incurable, and also malicious toward him, without hope of amendment — did exclude thee out of his company, refusing thee for his son, supposest <K6r> thou that, for this, he should be called an ill father or surgeon?

ARISTIPPUS No, in good faith, seeing that everything that he doth is with good justice and reason.

PLATO But he is still good as he was before? And also, that which he doth now, for the due punishing of a disobedient and unnatural son, is as well good as that which he did before, to the intent to cure him of his malady, if he would have been patient and suffer those medicines, which were prepared to heal him?

ARISTIPPUS Ye, in good faith.

PLATO Well said, Aristippus. Now wilt thou see what I mean hereby? Is any so properly thy father as God, which is the first, the chief and immediate cause of thy generation? Or is any surgeon so cunning as he, which seeth

° thrast] thrust *B*

more plainly the original motion and cause of every disease of the soul, that is to say, of vicious affects, than any man can see the outward sore or scurf <K6v> of the fistula? And more perfectly knoweth the best remedy therefore than any surgeon knoweth how to heal a small whelk in a child's finger?

ARISTIPPUS No, surely; in that, thou saist truly.

PLATO Now, since once thou hast granted to me that vice is ill because it is contrary to virtue, which thou affirmedest to be good, suppose vice to be the sickness of the soul, as it is indeed. And forasmuch as it bringeth in ignorance, which is enemy to reason and knowledge, who be as the eyen of the soul, and if it grow much it deformeth the soul and putteth clean away understanding, which is the visage wherein (as I said) is the similitude of God; therefore, resemble it unto the fistula. Which foul and dangerous disease, God as a loving father and good surgeon, espying in thee and desiring to heal thee thereof, doth his cure more speedily and quickly. He <K7r> useth sharp medicines, touching thee with sickness — wherein I reckon as well diseases growing in the body, as also hurt or griefs by outward occasion or chance — or with adversity: by wrongful imprisonment; death of assured friends, towardly children, or of a wife, constant and patient; loss of thy prince's favour, or great authority, possessions, or moveable richesse, or other like temporal benefit.

If thou, suffering this patiently, doest thankfully receive thy father's kindness and industry in curing of thee and exactly observe the diet whereto he doeth appoint thee — that is to say, doest live in the custom of virtue, eschewing vicious communication, ill counsel, and flattery, which be the unwholesome and queasy meats of the soul, whereby is engendered the venomous humour of ill opinion, whereof commeth vice, which I have resembled <K7v> unto the fistula — thou shalt be cured and have the sight and visage of thy soul preserved pure and clean.

Contrariwise, if thou murmur or grudge at the said remedies, esteeming them as griefs and no medicines, blaming or reproving God as undiscrete or cruel in the ministration of them, and striving there against with the power of thy senses, using them dishonestly in some pleasure voluptuous, thou turnest them from the sore, whereon they should wark, and with them doest thou put out reason and knowledge, the eyen of the soul. And then, for thy foolishnesses, impatience, and blasphemy — God suffering the soul to be both blind with ignorance and deformed with vice, since thou hast utterly lost his glorious similitude — he will from thenceforth abject thee; and for thine unkindness, commit thee to perpetual <K8r> prison, there to be punished in darkness, where thy foul deformed visage shall never be seen, to the reproach of him unto whose similitude thou were created.

Now, Aristippus, since thou didest approve that which was done by the carnal father and surgeon to be good, because he did it with justice and reason, what saist thou to that which God ordaineth and doth? Who so far excelleth in those two qualities that the justice executed among men that be mortal, in comparison of his justice, is wrong, and that which we take for reason, in regard of his wisdom, is foolishness and fantasy; not because it is not justice and reason that we have, but because that which is in God is ever one and perfect, without any division or mixture.

ARISTIPPUS In good faith, Plato, I wot not well what to say to thee. Finally, I am compelled by that argument that thou hast made to agree that such things <K8v> which before seemed to me to be ill be to that respect which thou hast rehearsed good and profitable — that is to say, in the reforming of man's soul, where it is curable; and in the declaration of the justice of God, where man is incurable.

But what sayest thou to that which thou hast so lightly passed over? I mean, where the said diseases and afflictions °happeneth to him which is already good and needeth not so sharp reformation?

PLATO Why, Aristippus! Supposest thou that ever any man was so good that in him were never vicious affection? Perdie, our master Socrates, when he was young and wrought in a masons' shop with his father, was not so pure from affects as he was after that he had been the hearer of Anaxagoras;[38] by whose doctrine, and also being continually vexed with poverty, sundry reproaches, and sometime <L1r> stripes of malicious and quarrelling persons — also, with the continual and never ceasing brawling and chiding of his most cursed wife Xanthippe, which he called his domestical exercise[39] — he by the gentle virtue of patience became a good man, as he was called and taken.

But to the intent that thy mind may be satisfied, let us now admit that men which be good, or at the least have such abundance of virtue and so little do incline to vicious affects, that it requireth not, that they be purged with such sharp afflictions as we have spoken of: how sayest thou? Supposest thou that unto them the said afflictions be ill and unprofitable?

ARISTIPPUS Yea, verily. And also, if it were leeful to speak it, me seemeth that therein God dealeth not with all men indifferently.

PLATO Surely, Aristippus, that is not only unleeful to speak, but also, to °think it, it is great <L1v> presumption and folly. And that shall I well prove, if

[38] Cf. Diog. Laert. 2.5.19.

[39] Cf. esp. Xen., *Symp.* 2.10; also, Diog. Laert. 2.5.36–37; and Eras., *Apoph.* 3.59–64 and 82 (CWE 37, 239–40, and 246).

° happeneth] happen *B*

° think it it is] think it is *B*

thou wilt attentively hear me.

ARISTIPPUS Speak on hardily.

PLATO In all the train of our communication hitherto, since we began to speak of providence, it hath alway appeared that God is father to man by creation and loveth man above all his creatures. But what sayest thou? Is there any more token of love than when the father, with all his study and power, endeavoureth himself to bring his son to great honour, which, if he may bring to good pass, there is nothing may cause him so much to rejoice?

ARISTIPPUS Surely, nothing.

PLATO And to the intent that his son may be deemed of all men worthy to be promoted to honour, he accustometh him to travail, either in learning and study or else in corporal exercise, the one to make him wise, the other to make him strong and valiant in body, <L2r> whereby he may declare himself worthy to have promotion. And wise fathers, the better that they love their sons, the more diligent be they; and, as I mought say, the more importune in keeping them in continual exercise, thinking that thereby the strength and deliverness of the body increaseth and, if it be in study of mind, wit is augmented; like as contrariwise, by sluggardy and idleness, the said activity is appalled and the wits consumed, whereby men be made unapt for the life which is active or politic.

ARISTIPPUS I suppose that hitherto thou hast said truly.

PLATO If the son be of gentle disposition and like to his father, perceiving his father's honest desire and purpose and therewith being inflamed with desire of glory, he will not only content him with labour, but also, if his father do bring him unto any great tourna-<L2v>ment or wrestling, he will prepare himself to refuse no man which will offer to assail him. And when he beholdeth one come again him which is of such puissance that in his sight hath vanquished or overthrowen men mo than °a hundred, although nature somewhat toucheth him with fear, yet remembering that his father beholdeth him, who hath so taught him and given him comfort that he shall not be vanquished, except he will and that his heart fail him; considering also the prize of the battle or wrestling, which is honour, less or more after the estimation of his prowess in vanquishing the most strong and dangerous champions; will he not, trowest thou, abide sternly his adversary and receive his assaults joyously, without any shrinking? And await, when his adversary's strength doth de-<L3r>crease or his breath faileth, that he, then enforcing his might, joining thereunto policy, may overthrow him? And so, with much gladness and commendation of all the beholders, of whom some peradventure at the beginning judged him foolhardy, he shall receive the honour that he hath deserved, to his own comfort and to the

° a] an *B*

incredible joy of his good father, who above all things wished to see this conclusion.

ARISTIPPUS This accordeth well and standeth with good reason.

PLATO Now hath he that thing wherefore his father brought him up, so diligently, and the which he himself, being like to his father, of his natural inclination desired.

ARISTIPPUS Yea, verily.

PLATO Had he it given to him for anything else but because he approved himself to be valiant and hardy, whereof honour was the prize and reward?

ARISTIPPUS No, I sup-<L3v>pose.

PLATO Wherewith did he approve himself in such wise, to have won that honour? By any other thing than by overthrowing or vanquishing his puissant adversary?

ARISTIPPUS No, truly.

PLATO Then it seemeth that, without a puissant adversary, his hardiness and prowess could never have been proved?

ARISTIPPUS No; that well appeareth.

PLATO And without proof, hardiness or strength is a voice vain and of none effect or profit?

ARISTIPPUS That is very true.

PLATO Forasmuch as proof is the operation whereby the said qualities — hardiness and strength — be expressed: is it not so?

ARISTIPPUS Yes, verily.

PLATO Yet am I glad that thou art so reasonable; it may perchance turn thee to some commodity.

But, Aristippus, as we remembered whilere, in those exercises which be commonly called games be diverse prizes, one more than an other; and they be gi-<L4r>ven to men according to the strength that they have employed, which is judged by the comparison of their strength whom they have excelled: to some, the first game or prize; to another, the second; and so in order.

ARISTIPPUS And that is but reason.

PLATO And doest thou not think these exercises to be good and profitable, whereby thou shalt win a reward and also worship, with comfort also unto thy father and increase of his love and favour toward thee?

ARISTIPPUS Yes, in good faith.

PLATO And also, thou wouldest love him better than ever thou didest, if often times he brought thee to that whereby thou shouldest receive such profit and worship?

ARISTIPPUS Yea; I were bound so to do.

PLATO Aristippus, wottest thou where we be now?

ARISTIPPUS What is that, Plato?

PLATO We be now at °that conclusion, the which thou hast so long gaped <L4v> and looked for; that is to say, it shall plainly appear unto thee that the sundry afflictions that do happen to good men come not without providence and the goodness of God, ne be ill and unprofitable to them that do patiently suffer them.

Therefore, I pray thee, Aristippus, while I declare to thee patience, do thou patiently hear me, and I shall — sooner than thou weenest — set out to thine eye that we two have sought for: I mean that knowledge, wherein wisdom is hid. And then, like as the miner which, after he hath found the place where the vein of gold lieth, laboureth busily to dig up the ore; and after, ceaseth not to try it from the stones and with continual travail to find out the pure gold; so shalt thou, once having the said knowledge, never cease to travail in the exercise of thy life, to find out wisdom.

ARISTIPPUS I am very <L5r> well content and desirous to hear how thou wilt bring to pass that marvellous conclusion.

PLATO Thou rememberest, Aristippus, that we were agreed long agone that, forasmuch as God is perfectly good and the fountain from whence all goodness proceedeth, all that is ill is contrary and enemy to God?

ARISTIPPUS Yea. I am not so short witted but that I remember all that thou hast spoken, if thou in this wise doest eftsoons rehearse it.

PLATO That is well said. And thou hast not denied but that he is the first mover and, without him, nothing is moved or done?

ARISTIPPUS No; I will not deny it.

PLATO Since good and ill cannot proceed from one fountain, God never moveth to ill nor doeth anything that is ill: what saist thou thereto?

ARISTIPPUS I must needs grant that, except I will repugn unto reason.

PLATO We were also agreed <L5v> that God created the serpent, the scorpion, the venomous fishes and herbs, as well as them which were commodious and wholesome; and that he made all thing for man, whom he loved above all his creatures?

ARISTIPPUS Yea; that is °truth.

PLATO Also, nothing happeneth without him which is the first and principal mover — either health or sickness, prosperity or adversity, richesse or poverty — and he beareth the keys of life and death; for he that made and did put the soul into the body hath the power to pluck it out. Supposest thou that any other hath with him equal authorities?

° that] the *B*
° truth] true *B*

ARISTIPPUS No: I granted long agone that, as he is one in beginning, so is he ever one in governance and may suffer no peer or like in equality.

PLATO That is remembered very well of thee, Aristippus.

Now, by that we two have gathered, it appeareth — and if thou look <L6r> well — that nothing is made ill of God; and then need we no further argument.

But since God made all things for man, whom he loveth, what exterior thing so ever happeneth to any good man, it is good; and therefore, sickness, adversity, and death, if they happen to a good man, be good; and therefore, it should suffice to a good man, if he suffer any of the said afflictions, to think and say to himself: God, which sent to me this, is all good and hath in him none ill, nor any ill proceedeth of him; and I am one of the number of those creatures whom he loveth best; °wherefore, since this that he hath sent me is good and not ill, it is necessary that I be therewith contented, and take heed that with mine opinion I make not that ill which is good.

But although this were sufficient to satisfy a good man, who would <L6v> not labour to seek any further in the providence of God; yet to thee, Aristippus, who, being long nuzzled in worldly pleasures, wilt not admit that anything which is thereunto contrary may be expedient or necessary unto a man that is virtuous and lacketh such vice which requireth sharp admonition, and therefore thou requirest a more ample and large declaration; I will set out a more plain proof, in applying my reasons to the examples and similitudes which I have already induced.

God, who made man unto his image and loveth him with more fervent affection than any carnal father loveth his child, bringeth us up in the exercise of the common imbecility or feebleness of our nature, as hunger, thirst, cold; weariness after labour; annoyance; displeasures which do happen in the society or living of men <L7r> together; diseases wherein is no jeopardy; and such other little incommodities, incident to mortality. Of all the which no man may be quit, declaring unto us, by understanding, that in this life we must of necessity travail and suffer; therewith giving us comfort, that who so ever by this exercise waxeth strong and hardy, hereafter being brought where he shall prove his strength against puissant and mighty adversaries — that is to say, anguish and pain; sharp and perilous sickness; cruel adversity in anything that Fortune seemeth to rule; loss of children, friends, or favour of princes; prisonment or exile; and °like other torments and vexations, of body and mind — if he valiantly do resist and, with fortitude, which is the strength of the mind, do subdue and

° wherefore since this that he hath sent me is good and not ill it is necessary] *eA* : wherefore this that he hath sent me is good and not ill since it is necessary *A* : wherefore since that he hath sent me is good and not ill it is necessary *B*

° like other] other like *B*

vanquish those adversaries, he shall have the reward that belongeth to good men, which <L7v> no time can consume, no power can minish, none evil can deface.

And to whet the courage of man to desire this enterprise, God giveth to him this comfort; that these things which shall so sharply assail him be ordained only to prove his strength; and that they be inferiors unto him, if he put out his strength to the uttermost; since God, which loveth him above all his creatures, hath ordained nothing to the intent to destroy him, but to his benefit, if he do employ his power and will thereunto, according as he hath received them.

Now, if the soul have in the body entire dominion and rule; and that man be in his right fashion, as I said long ago — that is to say, like to his father — of his noble nature, he desireth to win that incomparable prize which is promised to them that shall be so happy to <L8r> get the victory.

Wherefore, in this wise, he armeth thereto his courage.

First, he considereth that his father is good and that he most tenderly loveth him. Also, that he brought him not up, from the first time that he lived, in those little exercises of natural infirmity in vain or without any purpose; but to the intent that thereby he shall feel (as it were) the scent of more grievous afflictions, whereof they be but the shadows; and by a little labour and sufferance, he shall prepare himself to sustain and contemn a more greater travail and patience.

He revolveth also in his mind that every man which in his heart desireth honour coveteth some honest occupation or labour and is prompt and alway forward to do his office or duty in every peril or danger. For to what wise and diligent man is it not a pain to be idle? And <L8v> yet where idleness is not needs must be labour; and where an adversary lacketh, prowess lieth hid and unknowen. What a man may or may not, patience declareth.

The fathers °bideth their children to apply them earnestly to study or labour and will not let them be idle, although it be holy day, and do constrain them to sweat and often times to weep, where the mothers would set them on their laps and keep them at home all the day in the shadow for burning their white. God hath toward good men and women the mind of a father and best doeth love them; and therefore, he vexeth them with sundry business, griefs, and damages, that they may thereby gather a substantial strength, since they which be franked up in idleness do become unlusty and with their own burden be shortly suffocate.

It is to men no little pleasure to behold a young man <M1r> that, with a good courage, receiveth on his spear a wild boar or a great hart coming upon him; or without fear abideth with his sword in his hand the fierce

° bideth] bid *B*

lion, which cometh to assail him. But these are not the things whereto God deigneth to turn once his look, being but trifles and only pleasures of man's vanity and lightness. For the sight which is worthy to have God the beholder thereof is to see the creature which he loveth best to try his strength, with fortune or anguish, if he be challenged. For thereby strength, which is a virtue and part of that divine portion whereby man is like unto God, is proved.

The other strength, as it is of the body, so is it, as the body is, common with beasts; and as it is more frail and uncertain than the self body, in likewise the prize or reward that it deserveth, or rather looketh for, <M1v> is uncertain and also inconstant. But look to the other fortitude or strength, which is patient resistance of such things which opinion doth set forth with a terrible visage of damage or grief. If thou be sick, the humours whereof thy body is made do but their nature. Choler contendeth with phlegm, blood with melancholy; the one coveteth to vanquish the other; that which is hot refuseth to be cold; moisture and drouth will not abide in one place. By this variance, they haste them to their dissolution. If this contention be curable, hope maketh it tolerable; and if the worst fall, death shall dissolve it, for it is not for aye or perpetual.

Adversity is not grievous, because it is out of the body; and nothing compelleth us to suffer but our own wills. For if we were content with that which only our <M2r> nature hath given us, we should not be constrained to know what that word 'adversity' meant. But since we contemn her as needy and miserable and sue to come into the service of Fortune, whose nature is to be alway mutable and ever inconstant, nor giveth anything, but lendeth it only; if we receive anything of her mockish hand, what shall it grieve us to pay that again which we have borrowed? Why should we either be ungentle creditors, or be angry that we cannot turn the nature of her that will not obey or follow any man's commandment or counsel, but may be subdued with patience, where she can never be vanquished with reason?

Moreover, God is content that we shall excel him in that, that he may not suffer ill and we may by sufferance subdue it. For he is in more estimation that hath overcome <M2v> a puissant and valiant enemy than he which hath none enemy at all. Thou receivest of thy father this comfort, that no man liveth so poorly in the world as he came into it. And he hath need of a little that measureth abundance by nature's necessity, and not by superfluity of ambitious desire.

Grief shall dissolve, or else be dissolved. Fortune hath not so sharp a weapon that it may bite on the soul. And whom she longest supporteth and with most abundance of all thing, them for a general rule God little favoureth, since there is no reward where lacketh merit. Contrariwise, the end of travail is ease; and the father which beholdeth his son labour mightily rejoiceth thereat and prepareth that after his labour he may live pleasantly.

Who, knowing a great heap of gold to be hid on the top of a rough hill, would <M3r> not creep up through thorns and brambles to fetch it? And although his visage and hands were scratched, and his body and legs grievously pricked, yet would he not cease until he came to the top. And if any man which beheld him thus travailing would call him wretched and foolish, he, saying nothing, would think how happy and wealthy he shall be, when he hath obtained that thing wherefore he laboureth, and doeth laugh at the ignorance or folly of them which, for a pain that dureth not long, will forbear to go with him and to be partners of that whereby they shall ever after be wealthy.

Gold is a corruptible matter and shall once be consumed. But that treasure, wherefore man's soul ought to labour, may never be wasted, or in any quality or quantity appaired or minished; that is to say, it shall <M3v> ever be like good and like much. Wherefore, what pain so ever be taken about the getting thereof, it is not grievous, having respect to the gain; nor he that travaileth therefore may be named miserable or wretched, since misery is the privation or lack of all manner of comfort. For in hope of victory, if thou fail not thyself, comfort is ready, if thou doest not refuse it; in so much as nothing is miserable, but if thou doest so think it.

For all Fortune is good to him that constantly suffereth. And who was ever so fortunate that, when he was subdued with impatience, did not desire to change his estate? Sufficeth it not to thee that he that vanquisheth is deemed honourable and he that is recreant is wretched and miserable? How shall it be knowen on what part thou standest, without an experience? If thou have alway good <M4r> will, strength never faileth thee. But if, by the puissance of fortune, thou be set on thy knee, have a good heart; for God standeth at thine elbow, and, if thou think on him, he will set thee up and make thy strength double as much as it was.

Wilt thou learn one good point of defence, which may perchance do thee ease again some dangerous assaults? Fortune hath taken from thee that which she had lent to thee.

Revolve then °<in> thy mind that either those things were not good indeed, as they were supposed to be; or else man is in better estate than God is himself. For them which we have, God useth not, as carnal delectation, pleasant and dainty meats, orient jewels, or great treasure of money: these pertain not to God. Then is it to be thought that either God lacketh those things that be good, and then lacketh in him beatitude <M4v> or perfection of joy; or else it is a good argument that those things be not good that God will not use but is contented to lack.

° in] *B* : in in *A*

Finally, those be very goods that be within us, given by reason. For they be sure and during, nor cannot decay or minish for any occasion. They that be without us, lent only by Fortune, they be good by opinion only; and though they participate their name with the other, yet is there not in them the property or nature of goodness; for they be not durable, and also they be oftentimes the occasion of evil. Wherefore, they be for the more part with ill men, as most apt for their nature; and few good men have them, or they do continue but a little time with them, by the just ordinance of God, lest the much using of them should bring delectation into the senses, whereby they mought be provoked to rebel <M5r> and understanding, which is occupied in contemplation of the divine majesty, mought be suddenly expelled and, the soul lacking counsel, should give place to carnal affections and appetites. Thou rememberest Theognides' verses:[40]

God giveth to ill men good fortune and substance,
Which be not the better to themself nor their friend.
There is aye lack where is inconstance,
But honour of virtue doeth endure without end.

Finally, there is no greater comfort to him that is good than to be seen in the company of good men. If thou seekest for a good carpenter or a good smith, as thou goest through the city thou harkenest where is most hewing or beating with hammers; and there thou goest in and supposest to find him that thou lookest for. Semblably, if thou wilt have a good man, go look him <M5v> out where thou hearest that sharp sickness reigneth, or where injustice governeth, will ruleth, great power oppresseth. There shalt thou find him that thy heart desireth.

Thou mayst well accompt him for a great fool that, to live double his natural life, would not abide to be once or twice lanced in the most tender part of his body, or would not beg his bread for one twelve month, to be a king afterward during his life.

Stand boldly again sickness and fortune. The one is natural; the other is casual. In the first is necessity which, will thou or no, thou must suffer. If thou doest it willingly, thou knowest the prize. If thou addest to anger, thou doublest thy pain. In the second is no necessity, for thou moughtest alway refuse it, as well when it was prosperous, knowing it to be unstable and burdenous, as al-<M6r>so when it is adverse or contrarious, considering that it was never so much thine own that thou hadest any right to retain it,

[40] Theognis (fl. *c.* 550 BCE) is mentioned above, in *Doctrinal*, where Elyot is translating Isoc., *Nicocl.* 42–43, on the 'wise sentences of poets': see p. 62 and n. 8. As with Elyot's other verse translations, this one appears to be free, possibly from something like Theognis, 161–164, in *Greek Elegiac Poetry*, ed. and trans. by D. E. Gerber (Cambridge, MA: Harvard University Press, 1999).

since it was ordained for other as well as for thee. And Fortune, which is the disposer thereof, never made bargain with thee that thou shouldest still keep it; and if she did, bring forth thy records: she lacketh not witnesses innumerable to prove that she hath been ever inconstant.

Defy her malice! For when she hath done her worst, yet shalt thou have more than thou broughtest with thee; and that which aboundeth shall come of thine industry, and not of her false liberality. And if thou doest boldly resist her, thou shalt have that advancement and richesse given thee of God, wherein she shall have no power or authority, <M6v> which shall be such as the hundred thousand part thereof shall surmount all that ever she gave, since she was first called Fortune.

Now how saist thou, Aristippus? Be those things which thou didest suppose to be annoyances and incommodities, injustly sent unto good men; or having respect to order and the cause final, that is to say, to the end whereunto they were ordained, which I have declared: be they unto them necessary and most expedient?

ARISTIPPUS Now, in good faith, thou hast brought me to that point that I wot not what to say to thee!

PLATO But yet keep thy promise, and tell to me what thou thinkest in this matter.

ARISTIPPUS Me seemeth by thy reason that pain and adversity be as expedient to them which be good, as labour and business °are to them which be industrious.

PLATO And wherefore? Go to, Aristippus; be not <M7r> ashamed to confess the truth, though it be contrary to thy profession.

ARISTIPPUS Indeed, thou hast almost made me change mine old opinion. But since thou hast gotten me into such a strait that I cannot stert from that I have promised, I will now confess that the cause why the said afflictions be expedient for good men is forasmuch as, thereby, they be not only preserved still in their right image or figure; but also, for their constance in travail, they shall receive that inestimable reward, which thou saidest was ordained for good men.

PLATO Ah, good, Aristippus. Now I perceive that the seeds, which Socrates had sowen in thy mind, do begin now to spring with this little watering; whereunto, if thou wilt add to thy diligence, in plucking up the weeds of wanton affections as soon as they begin to appear in thy <M7v> mind, thou shalt shortly perceive the fruits of wisdom — for the which we do seek — spring abundantly, with whose most delectable fruition thou shalt never be satiate.

° are] *B om*

But now, since we have treated of sundry matters sith we first entered into communication, lest hereafter thou mayst repute me for one of them which do speak of many things and conclude upon none, and so accompt me but for a babbler; let us examine if our matter have hitherto hanged well together, or if there have been any vain digression which served nothing to the purpose that we first intended, or what thing lacketh now which may make to our communication a sufficient end or conclusion; and, I pray thee, think not the time tedious that is saved from idleness. And we have now little more than two miles to ride, and I trust so to <M8r> moderate myself that we shall at one time arrive both at the city and at the conclusion of our matter that we have purposed.

ARISTIPPUS Shall I tell °the truth, Plato, it is less grief to me to abide the residue, although thou wouldest talk two days continually, than it was at the beginning to abide hearing one hour, such sweetness I feel now in thy reasoning. Therefore, do what thou wilt; for I have both mine ears and my mind wide open to receive all that thou speakest.

PLATO I am glad thereof. Therefore, prepare now thy memory ready! Or if thou hast anything forgotten, call it again with thy remembrance.

ARISTIPPUS I will do as thou biddest me; therefore, say on, Plato, and spare not.

° the] *A B* (*fortasse* MnE 'thee')

<M8v>

THE FIFTH DIALOGUE

PLATO The first entry into our disputation, Aristippus, if I be not forgetful and unlike to that I was wont to be, was that thou beheldest me in this poor estate and apparel, the occasion whereof I declared to thee in the form of a story; which, although it seemed to thee to be more than in the answer of a philosopher was expedient — which should use in few words much matter and quick to the purpose — yet examining diligently everything therein included, it shall well appear unto thee that nothing thereof mought have been omitted, the words which we spake before, with my profession being well pondered. <N1r>

ARISTIPPUS Me thinketh thou sayest truly, now that I have considered everything deeply.

PLATO But yet, Aristippus, as I do consider, me seemeth to that purpose that we go about, the argument which I have made, lacketh yet somewhat to make it perfect.

ARISTIPPUS Trowest thou so? In good faith, I do not perceive it; for, as me seemeth, thou hast touched everything handsomely.

PLATO I am glad that it doeth so well please thee. But, Aristippus, thou doest remember that we were both agreed that wisdom is knowledge?

ARISTIPPUS Yea, that is truth, and so have I heard it alway defined.

PLATO But see whether that knowledge only maketh one to be called a wise man. Is not wisdom good? What saist thou thereto?

ARISTIPPUS Why, thinkest thou that I am such a fool that I will deny it?

PLATO No, so I trow. Now admit that a man knew all that we have hitherto <N1v> talked of, concerning the goodness and providence of God; but in deed he letteth his senses and affects have the rule over his soul and in his acts abuseth the said goodness and providence. If thou perceivedest him to do this, wouldest thou suppose him to be a good man?

ARISTIPPUS No, verily.

PLATO Thou wouldest say, perchance, that he were ill, because that his acts were contrary to good; but to his knowledge, thou wouldest take little regard.

ARISTIPPUS In good faith, thou saist truly.

PLATO If a man named to be a tiler would tell thee that thy house were ill tiled, and that the mortar was ill tempered by reason that the lime was too hot, and the holes of the tiles were made too wide for the pins, and that the laths were rent in the nailing, and thou foundest all that he said to be true, thou wouldest suppose him to be a good tiler. But if, coming to his own house, thou shouldest find it <N2r> negligently covered by him — his tiles and lath so set out of order that the rain and snow did beat into every place, whereby the beams and rafters of the house were decayed and rotten, and thereby all the house in jeopardy to fall down every hour — wouldest thou call him then a good tiler, or no?

ARISTIPPUS Nay, in good faith! I would call him but a prater.

PLATO Because that, where he ought most, he did not practice his cunning, which he had often avaunted?

ARISTIPPUS Yea, in good faith.

PLATO And that were but reason; then it seemeth that knowledge is indifferent to good and to ill. But, although goodness, being in knowledge, maketh that knowledge to be good, yet he which hath that goodness is never the more a good man, except, by the exercise of the same goodness, the thing that is good appeareth in his act; for that is manifest and declareth what the man is. Knowledge is secret and bringeth <N2v> forth no fruit but by operation; and thou art agreed that wisdom is good; wherefore, no more than knowledge of goodness maketh one to be named a good man, no more doth knowledge of wisdom only cause any person to be named a wise man. And that was affirmed by thee in the beginning of our communication, where it was agreed that King Dionise desired to see me to the intent that he mought behold if, in my countenance, speech, °or form of living, I did express that thing wherefore he heard me commended, which was nothing but wisdom.

Then, if I were a wise man, it ought to be declared by operation, which is not in man without knowledge preceding or going before, whereof proceedeth election, which lacketh naturally in other beasts; wherefore, although wisdom be knowledge, yet by knowledge only none <N3r> may be called a wise man; but operation of that which is in knowledge called wisdom, expressing the wisdom, maketh the user or exerciser thereof to be justly named a wise man.

ARISTIPPUS Now on my faith, Plato, thou art a wonderful fellow! For by the subtle persuasions, brought in by induction, which form of arguing I know is most natural, thou compellest me to assent alway to thy reason. For now me thinketh that none may be called a wise man, except unto that knowledge wherein is wisdom he joineth operation. But for what purpose, I pray thee, hast thou brought in now this last conclusion?

PLATO Art thou so dull witted, Aristippus, that all this while thou doest not perceive it? Perdie, the occasion of all our long reasoning did rise of that, that I assayed to prove that, if I were a wise man indeed, mine answer to King Dio-<N3v>nise declared me to be so, according to his expectation. And therefore, first, as reason was, I sought for wisdom; and in our communication, it appeared to be in man only and not in beasts; and that

° or] and *B*

it was in knowledge of himself and other. And that knowledge was in this wise declared.

First, to know his own pre-eminence and dignity over all other creatures, it was remembered that he was of body and soul, whereby he was man, and was made to the image and similitude of God; and that all other creatures were made only for him and to his use principally. The said similitude was expressed to be in the soul as well, for that it is °<in>visible and immortal, as also in understanding, whereby she hath sovereignty and rule in the body, as God hath over all universally; moreover, that the senses, affects, and will be °<t>he servants and ministers, which, <N4r> if she do keep in such obedience and order as she received them, she shall ever remain in authority. But if she let them to have more liberty than pertaineth to them — that is to say, to delight in things which be corruptible — they will then conspire and rebel again understanding and drive him from the soul; and then should man be transformed from the image of God until a brute beast, being governed and ruled only by senses.

The second part of the said knowledge was opened by the description of the goodness and providence of God. In describing his goodness was declared his power, his perfection, and love that he hath unto man, as unto his child more than natural. In setting out his providence appeared his inscrutable wisdom, magnificence, prudence, and policy in his wonderful order, wherein were his creatures in their sundry <N4v> degrees, higher or lower, as they did participate in goodness, more or less; in the top whereof, above all other, man was set next unto God, from whom order proceeded. Moreover, by the said providence it was declared that nothing keeping his place in order, shewed to man by understanding, mought be ill unto him but alway profitable, although to the senses some things did seem to be ill and unprofitable.

And last of all it was proved, in a few sentences, that adversity was sent by God unto a good man, not injustly or cruelly, but for a good consideration and lovingly, as of a good father, which, with an incomparable charity, desiring to advance his son to perpetual honours and dignity, by such manner of exercise proveth his virtue.

Now, Aristippus, revolving all this in thy mind, which in a short <N5r> epilogation I have endeavoured myself to reduce unto thy remembrance, consider well both me and King Dionise, as we were at that time, when we were together. Thou knowest well that, from the time that I was twenty years old, I alway continued disciple of Socrates, until that he died, who, as thou knowest, the answer of God determined to be of all mortal men the

° invisible] visible *A B*
° the] *eA B* : he *A*

wisest.[41] And that which I learned of him was wisdom, which, as he ever affirmed, was included in these two words: know thyself.[42] And by that doctrine, as thou mayst remember, he abated the presumption of diverse which supposed themself to be excellent wise men; also, revoked many that were dissolute and resolved into vice, and made them to ensue virtue. And by his example of living, he provoked men to contemn fortune and to have only virtue in <N5v> reverence. And also thereby, last of all, when he was injustly condemned to death, he constantly and joyfully sustained to have the mortal body dissolved, that the soul mought be at rest and have °her immortal reward. Which example given of him was the corroboration of all his doctrine, and no less part of learning unto his scholars, but rather much more than his often disputations or lessons.

Imagine, Aristippus, that I was so studious and industrious about the said learning that I most curiously and, as I mought say, superstitiously observed every point of the said doctrine; and that, therefore, all men in Greece and also King Dionise had conceived of me an opinion that I was a wise man; and that the same king sent for me only to that intent, as I said at the beginning, to see and hear whether I were according to his expectation. <N6r>

Consider also, on the other part, that my coming into Sicily was not to serve King Dionise or to receive by him any commodity, but only to augment wisdom by addition of knowledge; and that he desired to have me with him for the cause that I before have rehearsed; wherefore, it seemeth that he had need of that which, by seeing and hearing of me, he trusted to know; that is to say, wisdom. For no man coveteth that thing which he already hath or whereof, in his own opinion, he hath no need.

[41] Elyot, *Bibl.* s.v. '*Socrates*', below; also e.g. *Gov.* 1.25 (Watson, p. 105), 'The philosopher Socrates had not been named of Apollo the wisest man of all Graecia if he had not daily practiced the virtues which he in his lessons commended'; possibly from Eras., *Moria* (CWE 27, 99), or *Adagia* 1.6.95, *Nosce teipsum*, 'Know thyself' (CWE 32, 63), or *Apoph.* 3.36 (CWE 37, 232–33); from Diog. Laert. 2.37, from Pl., *Ap.* 21A.

[42] The Delphic inscription γνῶθι σεαυτόν; cf. Elyot, *Gov.* 3.3 (Watson, p. 202), 'Knowledge also, as a perfect instructress and mistress, in a more brief sentence than yet hath been spoken, declareth by what mean the said precepts of reason and society may be well understand and thereby justice finally executed. The words be these in Latin: *Nosce te ipsum*, which is in English: Know thyself. This sentence is of old writers supposed for to be first spoken by Chilo or some other of the seven ancient Greeks called in Latin *Sapientes*, in English sages or wise men. Other do accommodate it to Apollo, whom the paynims honoured for god of wisdom. But to say the truth, were it Apollo that spake it or Chilo or any other, surely it proceeded of God, as an excellent and wonderful sentence'; probably from Eras., *Adagia* 1.6.95, *Nosce teipsum*, 'Know thyself' (CWE 32, 62–63), naming the same possible originators as does Elyot, *Gov.* Ancient propagations of the inscription are listed in Eliza Gregory Wilkins, *'Know Thyself' in Greek and Latin Literature* (Chicago, IL: University of Chicago Libraries, 1917), pp. 100–04.

° her] it *B*

Now, I knew, partly by common report, partly by the information of Dion, which is a just man and an honest, that King Dionise was a tyrant; that is to say, comen to that dignity by usurpation and violence, and not by just succession or leeful election; also, that he was a man of quick and subtle wit, but therewith he was wonderful sensual, unstable, and wandering in <N6v> sundry affections; delighting sometime in voluptuous pleasures, another time in gathering of great treasure and richesse; oftentimes, resolved into a beastly rage and vengeable cruelty; about the public weal of his country, alway remiss; in his own desires, studious and diligent. And all this I perceived very well ere I spake to him anything.

Only I exercised myself with thee, Aristippus, Dion, and other, in such part of philosophy as mought induce you unto the said knowledge, whereof I have spoken; approving alway my doctrine with the form of living by the example of my master Socrates; abiding opportunity to speak, which mought rise of some special demand of King Dionise. In the mean time, to such light questions and problems as he did purpose — concerning natural causes, rhetoric, or poetry, or of the <N7r> duties and manners of private persons — I resolved them so as he held him contented and delighted not a little in the form of my reasoning.

At the last — as I have told to thee at the beginning — he required me to declare openly the state and pre-eminence of a king which ruled over other. Thereat I rejoiced, weening to have found the opportunity to speak that I so long looked for. And then forthwith, I considered that the sentence which I should pronounce should either commend and approve me for a wise man, as I was supposed to be, or else condemn that opinion that King Dionise and other had of me as false and untrue, I declaring myself unworthy to have it. I remembered also that, like as ignorance and knowledge or ill and good may never accord, no more may falsehood and truth be joined in one; and whatsoever ap-<N7v>peareth otherwise than it is in deed, it is other than truth; and that which is not truth must needs be falsehood. Moreover, as truth is good, so falsehood is ill; wherefore, whatsoever is other than truth cannot be in a wise man, who by the consent of all men is good.

Having still in my mind this consideration, I described a king, not perchance as he would have had me, but as truth and the trust that he had in me compelled me.

Therefore, by the said knowledge of the which we so long have disputed, I set out and expressed such a man in whom the soul had entire and full authority over the senses and alway kept the affects in due rule and obedience, following only the counsel of understanding, and by that governance was most like unto God. This man I called a king, although he had no more in his possession than had Crates the Theban;[43] and if that such one were by the free consent of <N8r> the people chosen or received to be a principal ruler and governor, governing them in like manner as he doth himself, then is he a great king or emperor and to be had in reverence and honour above any mortal man — saving to God that excellent honour that is due to the creator and first cause of all thing — not only for the pre-eminence given unto him by a common consent, but also forasmuch as, by his knowledge, example, and authority, the people shall daily receive of him an incomparable profit and benefit, being allured and provoked by him to set their souls in the said estate and authority as they may also be kings and be ever like unto God.

Moreover, this king, by that knowledge that he hath of himself, he also knoweth other men. For by the operation which proceedeth of their affects, he perceiveth how far they be removed from their right place in the line of order. That is to say, leaving <N8v> knowledge and reason whereby they were in the highest top of the line, they descend to the places of brute beasts by participating with them in sensual appetites. And then will he endeavour himself by all good means to restore them again, if he may, to their proper place in order.

Also, such a king, stablished in the said knowledge, can never be deceived by his most pernicious or mischievous enemies, which be flatterers and glozers, by whom princes be devoured alive and their souls utterly consumed with most mortal pestilence, wherewith their countries and people be also in peril to be lost and destroyed. For as soon as either in their counsels, or in their praises and dispraises, or in their own order of living, he, by the said knowledge, perceiveth and noteth to what affects they be inclined, he awaiteth <O1r> them and, by avoiding their company, escapeth their snares.

Finally, to the intent that the excellency of such a king should be more evident, like as I did set out whilere knowledge by ignorance — for everything sheweth most perfectly and, after the common proverb of merchants, best to the sale, when it is joined or compared with his contrary — I began to describe a tyrant, which in everything and, as I might say, by rule, repugneth and is most unlike unto the said king; whose soul ruleth not but, excluding from her knowledge and reason, suffreth herself to be governed by the senses and, obeying to the foolish affects, letteth them lead

[43] On this figure (*c.* 365–*c.* 285 BCE), see Elyot, *Bibl.* s.v. '*Crates*', 'The name of a philosopher, which to the intent he mought the more quietly study philosophy, he being rich, threw all his goods into the sea, saying: "Hence with a mischief, ye ungracious appetites; I had lever drown you, than ye should drown me", supposing that he mought not have virtue and riches together', probably from Diog. Laert. 6.5.87; though cf. Eras., *Apoph.* 7.266, 268, 280, etc. (CWE 38, 831, 832, 835).

her out of her high place in the line of order, into a more base degree, and to be made equal or inferior to beasts, and to lose the figure or image of God wherein she was created; and by that transformation, <O1v> she loseth also understanding, so that a tyrant is willingly taken in the said snares which a king doeth escape and perceiveth not that he is deceived until he sensibly feeleth some grievous damage.

And if any man expert in the said knowledge, of a sincere love that he beareth toward him, would warn him of the said snares and, perchance, shew them unto him, as they be laid; yet — knowledge and reason, the two eyen of the soul, being put out with affections, and understanding, her chief counsellor, being excluded — the man giveth no credence; but, rebuking perchance his most assured friend that warned him, suffreth gladly himself to be taken in the snare of hypocrisy or dissimulation; where, for lack of liberty, he shall be constrained to abide all dangers which mought happen unto him.

And he that is such <O2r> one — how poor so ever he be — he is a tyrant; and if he have rule over other, the more is he unlike unto God, since by God man is made and preserved: by cruelty and ill example, man both in body and soul is destroyed.

This description King Dionise mought not abide to hear but, thinking the time lost that I had spent for his profit, said that these were but words of idle dotards, whereby it seemeth that he understood not my words. For if he had, he would have thanked me for declaring that thing so plainly unto him which he had so long desired to hear — that is to say, wisdom, which, as we two be agreed, consisteth in knowledge — or else he required some act of me to be shewed which, agreeing with my words, should approve me to be a wise man, according to his first opinion. <O2v>

How saist thou? Was it not for one of these causes that he spake those words unto me?

ARISTIPPUS Yes, in good faith, I suppose that, verily.

PLATO We were agreed whilere that he had need of me when he sent for me, and therefore he desired to see me and to speak with me; but when I was with him, although I endeavoured myself to satisfy him of that which he had need of and so much desired, yet, if he did not understand what I said, indeed my words were in idle. I put case, Aristippus, that one of the philosophers of °Inde or of other countries speaking no Greek had come unto him, whom he would have required by an interpreter to have taught him wisdom, how should he have instructed King Dionise to have satisfied his gentle desire?

ARISTIPPUS How else but by an interpreter?

° Inde] Indee *B*

PLATO What if Zeno Eleates, after that he had bit off his <O3r> own tongue and spit it in the face of the tyrant that tormented him,[44] had been sent for to King Dionise, whom he would have desired to teach him wisdom? How should Zeno, which lacked his tongue, satisfy the request of so good a prince and so well disposed?

ARISTIPPUS I know not how, except it should be by signs and tokens, which were a diffuse way to instruct a man in so high a learning.

PLATO Yes. He mought do it sooner by writing.

ARISTIPPUS Yea that is truth; but I meant the answering his demand without any tarrying.

PLATO Yet then, perchance, he should also have need of an interpreter that knew his tokens, lest King Dionise, which had not been used unto them, should not understand what he meant by them. But supposest thou, Aristippus, that any man can better interpret another man's sentence, either spoken in a strange language <O3v> or signified by tokens, than I could expound mine own intent or meaning?

ARISTIPPUS Nay, surely. For every wise man is of his own sentence the best expositor.

PLATO And if it be °expound sufficiently in a few words, it is the more commendable?

ARISTIPPUS Yea, that is sure.

PLATO Mought I have used any plainer and shorter way, °th<e>n, in fewer words than King Dionise reproved me with, to remember him that in his own words he mought deprehend that thing that he sought for, since that which I spake before was in his own language and therefore he understood the words sufficiently? And if there were anything which he understood not, it was in the sentence.

ARISTIPPUS What meanest thou thereby?

PLATO Marry, I will tell thee. In the definition of a king, I instructed him how he mought be in the highest dignity next unto God and also in <O4r>

[44] Zeno of Elea (fl. early fifth century BCE); Elyot's anecdote probably from Plut., *De garr.* 8 (*Moralia* 505D), 'Zeno the philosopher, in order that even against his will no secret should be betrayed by his body when under torture, bit his tongue through and spat it out at the despot'; though cf. Eras., *Apoph.* 7.379 (CWE 38, 861), 'Zeno was accused of conspiring to assassinate the tyrant Nearchus, and when he was being tortured to make him reveal the names of the conspirators, he named a lot of close associates of Nearchus. When the tyrant had executed them and asked if there was anyone else, Zeno replied, "Only you, you curse of the state". Finally, he bit off his tongue and spat it into the tyrant's face, all unguarded as he was through fury', abbreviated from Diog. Laert. 9.5.26–27. Different versions of the same tale are in Elyot, *Gov.* 3.11 (Watson, p. 233), and in Eras., *Apoph.* 7.377 (CWE 38, 860), from Val. Max. 3.3ext4 or Diog. Laert. 9.10.59.

° expound] expounded *B*
° then] than *A* : and *B*

most perfect surety; which was no small benefit, of so poor a person as I am, to give to a prince; wherefore, if the eyen of King Dionise's soul — knowledge and reason — had not been out, he should soon have perceived the said benefit and, like a noble man, have given to me thanks, which I well deserved. And in the description of a tyrant, I warned him of all dangers whereby he mought lose the said dignity. In the which two declarations was wholly comprehended all that for the which he so much desired to see me; and all this while I knew not but that he had been a good man, because he desired to know that which thou hast granted is good, that is to say, wisdom.

Now, when he gave not to me condign thanks as my benefit deserved but accompted me to have been idle whiles I instructed him, then it seemed that <O4v> understanding was absent and fled from the soul; and that he ruled not as a king; but that he was ruled by his affections. Wherefore, his ingratitude declared his words to savour of tyranny; which I rehearsed unto him, to the intent that he, perceiving by my words °in what peril he was in, mought, by the remembering of my first instruction concerning a king, revoke again understanding and, subduing the affects, be eftsoons restored unto his dignities.

How saist thou? Considering well all that which is before said, were my words ill as they were spoken?

ARISTIPPUS Nay, as thou hast declared them; but yet me seemeth they were very sharp.

PLATO Wotest thou what maketh thee to think so? Because they were short. But thou must consider that he that lacketh, in that which he doeth lack, he is inferior to him of whom he desireth it; where-<O5r>fore, in as much as King Dionise to have benefit of me became my hearer, he was inferior unto me. And therefore respect ought to be alway had to that whereunto the reason extendeth and not to the estate of the person that heareth, and that I alway considered. And therefore spake I as I did to King Dionise; yet did I it with such a temperance that, if he had not been a tyrant indeed, he would never have been discontented. For I did not call him a tyrant or reproached him of any tyranny, but only said that his words savoured of tyranny.

I put thee case thou gavest to me wine out of a vessel and, when I had drunk of it, I would say that it had a scent of mustiness. It argueth not that the vessel is musty. For perchance within five or six days that scent will be gone and the wine will drink clean and gently. And there-<O5v>fore, I suppose, for my words thou wouldest not be angry. What if that King Dionise had desired me to teach him rhetoric and, when I heard him declaim or saw his writing, if I, finding any fault in his words, would warn

° in what peril he was in] in what peril he was *B*

him in this wise: 'Sir, your words do savour of too much arrogance', or that they savoured of suet °and painting, or be like unto apples of °the Dead Sea — which be delicate in colour without but, within, there is nothing but coals and powder unsavoury[45] — revoking him thereby to such rules as I had before read unto him, whereby, if he would be diligent, he should bring the form of speaking and writing into a perfection. Supposest thou that this manner of instruction should provoke King Dionise to be angry with me?

ARISTIPPUS No, for it were no reason.

PLATO Then hath he not so sharp a wit <O6r> as thou hast supposed, since he perceiveth not how much the learning of wisdom exceedeth the learning of rhetoric, and therefore he that teacheth wisdom ought to be of a greater authority than he which teacheth rhetoric. And therefore, since thou doest confess that King Dionise in learning rhetoric would take in good worth what so ever I would say in correcting his words concerning eloquence, how much more ought he then to take in good part °those words that I spake in correcting his words whereby he seemed to refuse wisdom, which a little before he so much coveted to hear declared? And one thing mought have contented him, that all that I had spoken was at his desire and for his commodity where, if I had purposed to have gotten anything by him, my wit was not so single but that I knew how to speak words, as <O6v> well as thou, which should delight him; but when he deemed me to be a wise man, he with that opinion bound me that I could not deceive him.

ARISTIPPUS In good faith, and that is very well spoken. But, peradventure, thou spakest too soon; and if thou hadest forborne a day, two, or three, until his fume had been passed and that he had used eftsoons with thee some familiarity, peradventure thy words would have been more easily taken, and thereunto thou shouldest have founden more opportunity.

PLATO But take one thing with thee, Aristippus: in the office of a wise man, that word, °'Peradventure', is never heard spoken, no more than, in the end of his works, these words, 'Had I wist'. For he hath alway the three times in remembrance — time present, time past, and time to come — and, referring all thing to necessary causes or (as I said long agone) <O7r> unto

[45] Also known as 'Sodom Apples'; cf. Joseph., *BJ* 4.484, 'Still, too, one may see ashes reproduced in the fruits, which from their outward appearance would be thought edible, but on being plucked with the hand dissolve into smoke and ashes'; and Tac., *Hist.* 5.7.1, 'In fact, all the plants there, whether wild or cultivated, turn black, become sterile, and seem to wither into dust, either in leaf or in flower or after they have reached their usual mature form'.

° and] or *B*
° the Dead Sea] the deed se *eA* : the deed so *A* : the dead so *B*
° those] these *B*
° \Peradventure, Had I wiste/] *A om*

providence, reputeth nothing to fortune. Therefore, the deferring of time should have nothing availed but rather should have been the cause of much damage.

ARISTIPPUS How so, I pray thee?

PLATO Take heed, and I shall tell thee. Thou hast granted already that King Dionise desired to see me to the intent that, in beholding and hearing me, he mought perceive whether I were a wise man or no; and then, desiring me to describe unto him the excellency of a king, supposest not thou that he made that request unto me for some laudable purpose?

ARISTIPPUS Yes, doubtless.

PLATO Thinking that by no question he mought either prove me more sooner to be a wise man, or else that he might learn more wisdom?

ARISTIPPUS I think both for the one and the other.

PLATO Thou hast not denied hitherto but that wisdom which King Dionise supposed to be in me is in the <O7v> knowledge that I have declared. What remained then to prove me to be a wise man? Doest not thou remember that we were agreed whilere that it was operation?

ARISTIPPUS Yes, marry, do I.

PLATO And that operation was part of that which King Dionise desired to know; and not only part, but also the principal portion?

ARISTIPPUS It hath hitherto agreed so with reason.

PLATO If I had hold my peace and said nothing after that King Dionise had spoken, what should have ensued of all my instruction?

ARISTIPPUS I suppose nothing. For he would have let thee depart without thank or damage, and that which thou hadest spoken should have been lightly forgotten.

PLATO And then his words had been verified that my words had been idly spoken. But how saist thou? Supposest thou that he said <O8r> truly?

ARISTIPPUS Nay, in good faith. For me seemeth that thy description of a king was wonderful true and necessary, and also therein was the knowledge whereof thou hast treated, compendiously and plainly declared; and me thinketh that the words that King Dionise spake beseemed not a king, but were much rather the words of one that lacked that knowledge wherein is wisdom.

PLATO Now I am glad, Aristippus, that I find in thee so much conformity in reason!

Then, since these ungentle words of King Dionise beseemed not a king to speak, it appeareth that they beseemed him that was contrary unto a king, which is a tyrant; and, being the words of one that lacked knowledge, it accordeth also that they were the words of one that was ignorant; and ignorance is most contrary to wisdom and, as I have <O8v> said, transformeth a man into a beast or a monster.

But what ignorance is it that thou supposest by the said words was declared to be in King Dionise?

ARISTIPPUS What other but that ignorance whereby he knew not himself?

PLATO And what supposest thou that he was, when he spake (as thou hast granted) words that beseemed a tyrant?

ARISTIPPUS What else, but as thou hast rehearsed?

PLATO What, a tyrant? Aristippus! Thou speakest now more plainly than I did. God forbid that I should suffer so gentle a prince to be transformed into such a monster, if I could help him.

But, I pray thee, which benefit wouldest thou prefer? Either that which is given or employed forthwith, or that which is longer deferred?

ARISTIPPUS What question is that? That kindness or benefit that is most prompt or soonest employed is to be chiefly esteemed.

PLATO Then if, forthwith and <P1r> as soon as I perceived the transformation of gentle King Dionise, I endeavoured myself to make him to know by his own words what he was, whereby, if he would, he mought by the expelling of ignorance have been not only restored unto the form of a man but also have been made a great emperor by the well-using of his dignity, supposest not thou that I did as it became me? And for that benefit so soon offered, was I not worthy a great gramercy?

ARISTIPPUS Yes, if he would have so taken it. But ere thou camest to him, thou knewest by credible report that he was obstinately inclined to all vicious affections and therewith impatient and cruel; wherefore, when thou didst perceive that he contemned thy doctrine, thou shouldest then have ceased and not have offered thyself to peril without hope of benefit.

PLATO That ad-<P1v>vantage only thou hast of me, Aristippus, for thou that doest profess pleasure moughtest have done so leefully; but I that have professed wisdom and virtue mought by no means have done it. For if I had not replied unto him, I had left that undeclared which he required to know, which, by his own words, as by an example in other arts or sciences, was plainly set out and expressed. And likewise, as I knew that he was impatient and cruel, so more certainly I knew that he had no power to endamage my soul, by whose operation I was called a wise man. And if I should have holden my peace then, it should have been for fear of damage which mought happen by his impatience and cruelty toward my body. Then should I have proved myself to have been a fool and no wise man, that I had not holden my peace at <P2r> the beginning; and then should King Dionise have found no cause to have taken displeasure.

But since he desired to know if I were a wise man; and for that opinion that he had in me, he favoured me; and also, thou doest confess that my description of a king, by his definition and also by comparing him to his contrary, contained that knowledge wherein is wisdom; now remained nothing but operation to prove me to be a wise man. Wherefore, contemning or little regarding that vain fear, to bring King Dionise to knowledge which he desired declared that my mind was not subject to corporal passions and, consequently, not to sensual affections, which mought have incensed or °stirred me to speak that thing that mought have pleased King Dionise's appetite, which was corrupt and vicious, hoping to have had thereby <P2v> preferment and singular favour. And herein began the operation, which agreed with my said knowledge.

And afterward, by taking liberty from me and making me a slave, he more declared my words to be true and thereby had the larger example whereby he mought the better have knowen himself. And after when he heard — as I doubt not but that he hath — how constantly I contemned the peril that I was in of my life at Aegina, he mought well perceive that operation in patience to agree with my knowledge.

And thereby he had fully all that knowledge of me wherefore he desired to see me; where, contrary-wise, if I should have holden my peace, as well my coming to King Dionise had been frustate and vain, and his gentle desire had been unsatisfied; as also by my silence, being thought (as reason was that I should be) to be subdued either <P3r> with fear or affection, I should seem to condemn mine own doctrine; wherefore I should be deemed unworthy that good opinion that King Dionise had of me.

ARISTIPPUS Well, Plato, in such experience of wisdom I will not follow thee.

PLATO Therefore, when any adversity shall happen unto thee, as I suppose thou hast not fortune locked fast in a coffer, no more than had Croesus the rich king of Lydia, for all that he thought that all gods and men were his friends, and yet was he openly bourned by Cyrus, whom he little feared;[46] thou shalt feel both adversity and grief, and also make thy soul subject unto thy senses, whereof what doeth follow thou dost yet remember what we have already discussed. Where I or any other, by the said knowledge and operation thereunto joined, shall be so armed again adversity that, whatsoever the body feeleth, yet the very man — which is <P3v> the soul — feeleth no disease or, as I mought say, is never inquieted, but is ever entire and in his true proportion and figure (that is to say, like unto God); and also shall have the prize that he hath deserved by vanquishing of his adversary (that is to say, corporal disease or adversity).

[46] Cf. Hdt. 1.86–87, or Xen., *Cyr.* 7.2.20–7.3.1, where the tale is made to hang by another version of the Delphic γνῶθι σεαυτόν (above, n. 42). Cf. Elyot, *Bibl.* s.v. '*Croesus*', 'Much more Herodotus the noble historian writeth hereof in *Clio*, which I would God were read oftentimes of kings and their counsellors', below; also, *Gov.* 2.9 (Watson, pp. 154–55), 'Lord God, what a notable history is this, and worthy to be graven in tables of gold'.

° stirred] stered *A B* (*fortasse* MnE 'steered')

But now, Aristippus, since by anything that hath happened I never fell from that place in the line of order wherein God had set me; but my mind was ever in one state and condition; and there as it was at my coming into Sicile, there it hath hitherto ever continued; mayest thou reasonably say that I was ever lost, in so much as I was never transformed or out of that estate wherein a wise man ought alway to be?

ARISTIPPUS No, in good faith, as it now seemeth.

PLATO What saist thou then by King Dionise? Whom instructing to know himself I thus much displeased and, <P4r> instead of thank and preferment, hath rewarded me with danger and bondage?

ARISTIPPUS On my faith, I think that he hath both lost himself, by refusing the said knowledge whereby he should have been delivered from the said transformation; and also he hath most foolishly lost thee, Plato, in putting thee from him, which by thy counsel shouldest have been to him so royal a treasure; and the same do I think also of Polides the ambassador and of the Aegenites.

PLATO Gramercy, Aristippus, for thy gentle audience! Now be we come to the town and have made a good end, both of our journey and also of our communication.

ARISTIPPUS Farewell, Plato, and for my part I would not have lacked it for the horse that I ride on! And, to say the truth, it hath made me to change somewhat of mine old opinion.

PLATO The next time that we <P4v> meet, I will make thee to change all, if thou wilt hear and abide reason.

°FINIS.

°] Imprinted at London in Fletestrete in the house of Thomas Berthelet. Cum priuilegio ad imprimendum solum. *B*

°<A1r>

THE DEFENCE OF GOOD WOMEN,

devised and made by Sir Thomas Elyot Knight

Anno. M.D.XL.

° The text is from *A* = 1540 ed. (RSTC 7657.5 = ESTC S366), departures from which are enclosed in angled brackets <>; collated with *B* = 1545 ed. (RSTC 7658 = ESTC S105492); the editions' marginalia, enclosed between slashes, \ /, have been removed to the textual notes.

°<A2r>

<PROLOGUE>

°To the most noble and most virtuous princess Queen Anne, wife unto the most excellent prince, our most gracious sovereign lord, King Henry the eighth,[1] Thomas Elyot, knight, desireth all honour.

After that I had diligently read and considered the life and history of Queen Zenobia,[2] a lady of most famous renome for her excellent virtues and most noble courage, I was right desirous that it should be read in our own language, whereby women specially mought be provoked to embrace virtue more gladly and to be circumspect in the bringing up of their children. But with that ima-<A2v>gination, there came also to my remembrance the ungentle custom of many men, which do set their delight in rebuking of women, although they never received displeasure but oftentimes benefit by them; °ye<t>, when their wanton appetite stirreth them, they offer to serve them and do extol them with praises far above reason. Which thing, I, of my nature abhorring, determined, for the reverence that all honest men ought to bear to the virtuous and gentle sort of good women, to prepare for them a sufficient defence against ill-mouthed reporters.

Then forthwith entered into my fantasy the device of this little treatise, wherein I did imagine that the time were now when Zenobia lived, which was about the year after the incar-<A3r>nation of Christ two hundred and seventy-four, when also the noble Aurelian was Emperor of Rome.[3] And to induce that noble princess to declare her own life, I devised a contention between two gentlemen, the one named Caninius, the other Candidus. Caninius, like

[1] Anne of Cleves (1515–1557), fourth wife of Henry VIII, though the marriage formalized January 6 1540 was formally annulled so soon as July 9 1540, and Henry married Katherine Howard (d.1542) three weeks later, July 28 1540. Reference to Anne was expunged from the subsequent edition.

[2] The historical figure Iulia Aurelia Septimia Zenobia (Aramaic *Bath Zabbai*, Arabic *al-Zabbā*, late third century), Queen of Palmyra and Emperor *c.* 270–272. Cf. Elyot, *Bibl.*, '*Zenobia*, a queen of Syria, which in Greek and Latin was very well learned, and was also valiant in arms'.

[3] L. Domitius Aurelianus (imp. 270–275).

°] omitting sig A1v (blank).

° To the most noble and [...] Causeth good understanding] *A* : The argument A contention between two gentlemen, the one named Caninius, the other Candidus. Caninius, like a cur, at women's conditions is alway barking; but Candidus, which may be interpreted benign or gentle, judgeth ever well and reproveth but seldom; between them two, the estimation of womankind cometh in question. After long disputation, wherein Candidus (as reason is) hath the pre-eminence, at the last, for a perfect conclusion, Queen Zenobia, which lived about the year after the incarnation of Christ two hundred seventy four, the noble Aurelian being Emperor of Rome, by the example of her life, confirmeth his arguments and also vanquisheth the obstinate mind of froward Caninius, and so endeth the matter. *B*

° yet] ye *A*

a cur, at women's conditions is alway barking;[4] but Candidus, which may be interpreted 'benign' or 'gentle', judgeth ever well and reproveth but seldom;[5] between them two, the estimation of womankind cometh in question. And after long disputation, wherein Candidus (as reason is) hath the pre-eminence, at the last, for a perfect conclusion, Queen Zenobia, by the example of her life, confirmeth his arguments and also vanquisheth the obstinate mind of froward <A3v> Caninius, and so endeth the matter, which I do dedicate unto your highness's most noble princess, humbly desiring your highness in such wise to accept my good will and service and this little work as your own, that under your grace's protection and favour it may safely pass through the dangerous race of disdain and envy and be received thankfully and joyously of all good women in this your noble realm, who by the only example of your excellent majesty, may be alway desirous to embrace virtue and gentleness, wherein consisteth very nobility.

Often reading
Causeth good understanding

4 Cf. Elyot, *Bibl.*, '*Caninus*, doggyshe, or of a dogge'.

5 Cf. Elyot, *Bibl.*, '*Candidus*, *a*, *um*, whyte, more than *Albus*, orient white. It is sometimes taken for fortunate, gentle, or easy'.

°<B1r>

<THE DEFENCE OF GOOD WOMEN>

CANINIUS, CANDIDUS, ZENOBIA

CANINIUS Such is the condition of Venus' darlings, so long as they be stirred with pleasant affections, they be still insensible in the feeling of sapience. Ye all do know Candidus, kinsman to Aurelian the Emperor that now is, an honest young gentlemen, well learned and courteous, so that his nobleness doth appear in his manners. Yesterday did I see him devising with ladies, whereby I conjected that he was a lover, and therefore I lamented. And as he happened to come by me, I rounded him in the ear and <B1v> said to him softly, 'Beware, noble young man. I perceive ye be gyved: pluck out your legs ere the bolts be riveted'. Thereat he smiled and, laying his hand upon mine, he said to me privily, 'I wot what ye mean. I pray you, be tomorrow with me at Tiburtum, which is but a little out of the city, where I have a fair and commodious lodging; there shall we sup with some other gentlemen, and there will I vanquish your wilful opinion conceived against women, or else, I being vanquished with sufficient reason, will from henceforth leave all mine affection'. And so departed he from me. This is Tiburtum, for yonder is the palace of Hadrian.[6] Well, Candidus will not be long. His noble nature will not let him break <B2r> promise, for lack of faith defaceth all virtues.

CANDIDUS Ye spake never a more true sentence, nor a more honest, for undoubtedly faith, which some do call trust, is of justice so great a portion that without it neither God may be pleased, nor any weal public may be surely stablished. And they which do lack it themselves, with a little touch broken, be not a little offended.

CANINIUS It is truly spoken! And now to talk of the matter, for the which ye willed me to meet with you: here is now happened a right good occasion.

CANDIDUS Ye mean the matter concerning women, which we two now have taken upon us?

CANINIUS Even the same, Master Candidus.

CANDIDUS Go to, on God's name. What have ye to <B2v> charge with all women?

CANINIUS Nay, first, I pray you, tell me one thing that I will ask of you. Be not

6 Modern Italian *Tivoli*, Latin *Tibur*, site of the villa of P. Aelius Hadrianus (imp. 117–138); for longer also residence of the truth-telling female *Sibylla Tiburtina*, prophecies by whom (probably written *c.* 378–390) survived in wide circulation. Cf. SHA, *Tyr. Trig.* 30.27, '[Zenobia's] life was granted her by Aurelian, and they say that thereafter she lived with her children in the manner of a Roman matron on an estate that had been presented to her at Tibur, which even to this day is still called Zenobia, not far from the palace of Hadrian or from that place which bears the name of Concha'; also, Boccaccio, *De mul. clar.* 100.22.

°] omitting sigs A4r (woodcut) and A4v (blank).

ye of that sect of philosophers called *Pyrrhonici*?[7]

CANDIDUS What mean ye thereby? I know not that sect, yet have I seen a good part of philosophy.

CANINIUS It is the sect which affirmeth that nothing is indeed as it seemeth to be, saying that snow is black and not white, the earth is not stable but ever moving, and many another froward affection, contrary to truth and all common reason.

CANDIDUS No, no, Caninius. I never favoured such vain opinion.

CANINIUS Yet many one doth, changing only the terms. For, since snow is so oftentimes seen, they fear to say it is black lest they should therefore be laughed to scorn. But <B3r> virtue, who is not so commonly seen and of so many men looked on, is now of diverse men so perversely esteemed that it is of some called folly, of many men fantasy, and of some curiosity. Also, the favourers thereof are little set by, as persons unprofitable and nothing worldly. But to our purpose: I asked of you, if ye were of the sect called *Pyrrhonici*, for if ye so were, I would think it vain to reason then with you. But ye say ye be not of that sect; then is it as I said at my first coming hither.

CANDIDUS What is that, I pray you?

CANINIUS Ye that be lovers be dull and insensible in feeling of sapience. For although ye be informed by daily experience that in womankind faith never rested, yet be you still as <B3v> blind as your little god Cupid; for the childish affections which ye bear to your ladies causeth you to think the things which ye see to be nothing but vanities.

CANDIDUS Now, in good faith, that is merrily spoken.

CANINIUS Well, yet, some have repented them bitterly, finding the link suddenly broken, and, in the stead of faith, falsehood and treachery.

CANDIDUS Nay, ye now do but rail, I promise you, truly. Indeed, both by reading and hearsay, I have found women much blamed for their inconstancy; but, for mine own knowledge, I never perceived any such lack to be in them, but rather the contrary.

CANINIUS Sir, by the consent of all authors my words be confirmed, and your experience in comparison thereof is to be little esteemed.

CANDIDUS I perceive ye be of <B4r> the company which, disappointed some time of your purpose, are fallen in a frenzy and, for the displeasure of one, do spring on all women the poison of infamy. But now, Caninius, since ye be wise and well learned, subdue your passion, for unpatient hearing,

7 Sceptics, in other words, called so here after the ancient philosophical school ostensibly deriving from the work of Pyrrho of Ionian Elis (*c.* 365–*c.* 275 BCE), though transmitted in large part through the widely circulating work of Sextus Empiricus (*c.* 160–*c.* 210 CE). Cf. Elyot, *Bibl.*, '*Sceptici*, were a sect of philosophers, which affirmed nothing; the chief of that sect was Pyrrhus and Herillus'; Diog. Laert., esp. 9.11.69–70, 74, 7.1.37, and 7.3.165–166.

with words hastily and unadvisedly spoken, is a sign of folly and little discretion. Wherefore, now hear me speak, though it shall not favour to your opinion.

The authors whom ye so much do set by for the more part were poets, which sort of persons among the Latins and Greeks were never had but in small reputation. For I could never read that, in any weal public of notable memory, poets were called to any honourable place, office, or dignity. Plato, out of the public weal which he had devised, <B4v> would have all poets utterly excluded; Tully, who next unto Plato excelled all other in virtue and eloquence, would not have in his public weal any poets admitted.[8] The cause why they were so little esteemed was forasmuch as the more part of their inventions consisted in leasings, or in stirring up of wanton appetites, or in pouring out in railing their poison of malice.

For with their own gods and goddesses were they so malapert that, with their advoutries, they filled great volumes. Jupiter, whom they call king of gods and of men, they bring him out of heaven to his harlots transformed sometime into a bull, another time like a ram, a stinking goat, or a serpent; his queen Juno, like a <B5r> cow; Mercurius, like a wolf. Ne they left heaven unpolluted, saying that the god Mars made Vulcan cuckold, committing advoutry with Venus, wife to Vulcanus. But Vulcan was a wily pye and said nothing; but, being a smith, he made such subtle manacles that, ere the two lovers were ware, he tied them so fast together that they mought not be severed; and then called he the whole rout of gods and goddesses and made them to see Mars and Venus where they lay naked, whereat they all laughed; but Mars was angry, and Venus, almost ashamed.

Other poets there be which, in their most lamentable and woeful ditties, so do humble themselves to their mistresses as they would lick the dust from <B5v> their slippers; and, as soon as either by age or with haunting of brothels, the flame of carnality is thoroughly quenched, or else if women do constantly refuse their unhonest desires, anon arm they their pens and tongues with serpentine malice, objecting against all women most beastly conditions, whereby they more detect their proper inconstancy than women's unfaithfulness.

CANINIUS Now, in good faith, ye have well circumscribed your masters' properties.

CANDIDUS Whom call ye my masters?

CANINIUS Marry, poets, for in their works is the only study of you that be lovers. For that book which lacketh complaints, with weepings and sighings, is to you men that be amorous wonderful tedious.

[8] Pl., *Resp.* 2 (377b–383c), esp. 3 (386a–394d), and 10 (595a–608b); also, the derivative Cic., *Rep.*, largely lost to the sixteenth century and still known only in fragmented state.

CANDIDUS Tru-<B6r>ly, Caninius, ye are much abused, taking me to be of that sort of wantons; nay, truly. True lovers, of which company I confess myself to be one, are in no part of their conditions. For only delighting in the honest behaviour, wisdom, and gentleness of ladies or other matrons or damsels, we therefore desire to be in their companies and, by mutual devising, to use honest solace. But show me, Caninius, what other authority have ye to prove that in women lacketh fidelity?

CANINIUS Why set ye so little by poets and poetry?

CANDIDUS Yea, when they exceed the terms of honesty. But if they make verses containing quick sentences, void of ribaldry, or in the commendation of virtue some pretty allegory, or do set forth any °<B6v> notable story, then do I set by them as they be well worthy.

CANINIUS If ye will give no credence to poets, what say ye to philosophers and writers of stories? With whom ye may find such abundance of examples and sentences of the falsehood of women and their unhappiness that, if they should be rehearsed, I trow ye would not abide it, I know so your shamefastness.

CANDIDUS Truly, none of them which were themselves honest and continent have written in dispraise of the whole kind of women. What hath Plato, Xenophon, Plotinus, and Plutarch[9] or other philosophers like unto them written in that matter, whereby they have made them inferior to men? Or if they have in women anything blamed, it may appear to be but in <B7r> some and not in the more part, if it be well and sincerely considered. And also, in stories where one woman perchance is for some fault dispraised, that is counterpoised with a great number for their virtue commended.

Now, I pray you, was Helen, for whom Troy was destroyed (being ravished by Paris), so much to be blamed, as Hercenia, the wife of Romulus, and more than a thousand of her companions are to be praised, which, in the rage of battle joined between their husbands and parents, so reconciled them that, with one consent, they inhabited one city and lived together in perpetual unity?[10]

Ought the unchastity of any woman to be remembered as the continence of Queen Penelope ought to be honoured? Who, in <B8r> the absence of Ulysses her husband, the space of twenty years kept her honour and fame

[9] The Neoplatonist philosopher and theurgist Plotinus (205–269) is not mentioned elsewhere in Elyot. Neither Xenophon (*c.* 430–354), a follower of Socrates, nor Plutarch, the Roman citizen L. Mestrius Plutarchus (fl. 50–120), a priest of Delphi and local magistrate, both of whose extensive and varied writings were very often sources for Elyot, attracted any biographical attention in *Bibl.*

[10] Romulus's wife is ordinarily called 'Hersilia', as in Elyot, *Bibl.*, '*Hersilia*, the wife of Romulus king of Romans'. For her contribution, see Liv. 1.11.2; Plut., *Rom.* 14.7–8.

° <beginning B6v> notable story [...] with a knife which <end B8v>] *B om*

uncorrupted, notwithstanding that with many diverse wooers she was daily assaulted, but by no manner of mean mought she be founden, by deed, word, nor countenance, in her chaste purpose unconstant; and, to resist carnal affections, she was alway seen, although she were a queen and a king's daughter, virtuously occupied.

What cause found Paris to forsake his first lady, Oenone, but only that the beauty of Helen was much more famous? And yet his cruel unkindness mought not exclude love from her gentle heart; but, she remaining still continent after that Paris was slain by Achilles, she with exclamations and effusions of tears <B8r> entered into the chariot where his carcass lay; and when she had bained her fair lips in his putrefied wounds and had satiate herself with mortal solace, finally she there died, oppressed with heaviness.[11]

But because these be of some men taken for fables, I will briefly declare the faithfulness of diverse women rehearsed in stories. In the host of the noble King Cyrus was a great prince (as Xenophon writeth) whose name was Abratades, who had to his wife a fair lady, named Panthea, of excellent beauty.[12] This prince being slain in battle, she attaining his body, and with her own hands washing the wounds, and embalming it after the fashion of her own country, she in the presence of Cyrus, with a knife which <B8v> she had privily hid, seeming in words and countenance desirous to be with her husband, whom she most tenderly loved, she pierced her own heart and with him was buried, notwithstanding that of King Cyrus, whom her husband had much praised a little before, she was in marriage desired.

Portia, daughter to the wise Cato and wife unto Brutus, when she had heard of the death of her husband, finding occasion to be alone from her servants, she taking the hot burning coals out of a chimney devoured them hastily and forthwith died.[13]

Also when Seneca, by the sentence of the cruel Nero the Emperor, was condemned to die, his wife, called Paulina, desirous to be continual companion with her old husband, caused also her <C1r> veins to be pierced and so would have died, had not Nero commanded her veins to be bound and the blood to be stopped. She notwithstanding afterward lived in sorrow continual, more painful than death; and, during her life, her deadly pale colour declared to all men which before knew her the bitter sorrows which for her husband she alway sustained.[14]

[11] Cf. Elyot, *Bibl.*, '*Oenone*, the concubine of Paris before that he ravished Helen'. Oenone is the subject of an Ovid poem, *Her.* 5 (Oenone Paridi), as is Penelope, mentioned just above, *Her.* 1 (Penelope Vlixi).

[12] Xen., *Cyr.* 7.3.4–16.

[13] Porcia Catonis (*c.* 70–42 BCE), as in Val. Max. 4.6.5, and cf. 3.2.15; also, Plut., *Brut.* 53.5–7 and *Cat. min.* 73.4. Cf. Boccaccio, *De mul. clar.* 82.11.

[14] Pompeia Paulina (d. *c.* 68), as in Tac., *Ann.* 15.62–64; cf. Boccaccio, *De mul. clar.* 94.5–6.

In the time of the cruel confederacy of Lepidus, Octavian, and Anthony, a gentleman called Ligarius was by his wife and a maiden servant kept at Rome in his house, privily; but, what for fear of punishment and hope of reward, he at the last was discovered. Whom being led to be beheaded, his loving wife continually followed, desiring the ministers to put her <C1v> also to death with her husband, alleging that also to die she had well deserved, forasmuch as she had kept her husband at home, after that she knew that he was attainted. But seeing that no man did take regard to her hearty request, she returned home to her house; and, shutting fast all the doors and abstaining from all meats and drinks, finally with sorrow and famine she ended her life and departed to her husband, whom she so much loved.[15]

But lest we should be too long from our supper, I will cease to recite any mo stories, whereof there be no little number, declaring the constance of ladies and damsels. And if ye would say that there hath been and is a much greater number of them that are ill and full of unfaithfulness, yet <C2r> if that were true, then must ye consider that in all kinds of things are commonly found more worse than better, or else should good things lack their estimation, as it shall appear by this conclusion. For he that never hath seen any other metal than gold marveleth not at it, nor in his estimation setteth much by it. And where there be none other stones found but diamonds, sapphires, emeralds and rubies, there men do tread on them and sell them for trifles. But if one should come to a country, which seemed barren, covered with an infinite number of stones ragged, of ill colour and fashion, if he chance to find here and there a pointed diamond, well proportioned and orient, I dare say, he will lay up <C2v> those few diamonds as a great treasure and, not remembering the ragged stones, in the beholding of them take no little pleasure. Semblably, although a great number of women perchance were vicious, yet ought not a man reproach therefore the whole kind of women, since of them undoubtedly many be virtuous.

CANINIUS Ye have well assembled things for your purpose. But what say you to Aristotle, whom ye have skipped over, in the naming of philosophers? He saith that a woman is a work of nature unperfect. And, moreover, that her property is to delight in rebuking and to be alway complaining and

[15] App., *B. civ.* 4.23, 'Ligarius was concealed by his wife, who communicated the secret to only one female slave. Having been betrayed by the slave, the wife followed her husband's head as it was carried away, crying out, "I sheltered him; those who give shelter are to share the punishment". But since no one killed her or informed on her, she came to the triumvirs and accused herself before them. Being moved by her love for her husband, they pretended not to see her; so she starved herself to death. I have mentioned her in this place, because she failed to save her husband and would not survive him'.

never contented.[16] Now take heed, Master Candidus. Perfection is ever constant and never changeth, but a <C3r> woman is a creature unperfect; she, therefore, may never be stable or constant. Ye know this form of argument, for I espy by your talking ye are learned in logic. Moreover, rebuking is a misliking, and no man misliketh the thing that he loveth, but all that he loveth he favoureth and liketh. But women of their nature do delight in rebuking; and the thing, wherein any person delighteth, he coveteth, and, coveting it, he will at the last (if it be in his power) execute it. Women, therefore, lacking some other on whom they may practice their property, will rebuke some time their husbands, whom perchance they loved, and then misliketh she the thing that she erst loved; wherefore, ye must grant that she is unconstant. Also, who <C3v> that is never content may never be constant. The cause why is to all men apparent; wherefore, there needeth not any more argument. Women, for these reasons that I have rehearsed, be of their nature alway unconstant: is it not thus? Now knack me that nut, Master Candidus. I trow it be too hard for your teeth, although ye were as well toothed as Curius Dentatus, which, as men say, held fast a ship with his teeth until it was taken.[17]

CANDIDUS In good faith, Caninius, ye are a merry companion. But although my teeth be not so strong, yet that I so use my tongue in the stead of my teeth that I will therewith open your cob-nut that, to all them that will be contented with reason, it shall appear well that it is pipped.

CANINIUS In faith, ye be a <C4r> meet advocate for women, since ye have teeth in your tongue; for likewise have they all, if they be toothless.

CANDIDUS And it seemeth that ye lack teeth to hold in your tongue, that it go not too lavish. But now will I assay to knack your nut, Master Caninius. Where ye said that, of a purpose, I skipped over Aristotle, there ye said truly; in good faith, so did I. And here have at your blockhouse, out of the which is shot against women all this artillery.

Sir, when I affirmed that none of the philosophers which were honest and continent wrote any thing in dispraise of womankind, I remembered

[16] Cf. Arist., *Hist. an.* 9.1 (608a–608b).

[17] Manius Curius Dentatus (d.270 BCE), a military hero of the early republic, elsewhere called 'Curius' by Elyot, was said to have earned the cognomen ('Toothy') by virtue of his having had teeth from a remarkably early age: see Plin., *NH* 7.16, and cf. Elyot, *Bibl.*, '*Dentatus*, he that hath great teeth, strong teeth or many teeth'. This anecdote about him, not used elsewhere by Elyot, may have been borrowed from some version of the story of the Athenian hero Cynegirus (d.490 BCE), i.e. Just., *Epit.* 2.9.16–18, 'Likewise, the merit of Cynegirus, an Athenian soldier, has met with great commendation from historians; for, after having slain a great number in a battle and having chased the fleeing enemy to their ships, he laid hold of a crowded vessel with his right hand, and would not let it go till he had lost his hand; and even then, when his right hand was cut off, he took hold of the ship with his left, and, having lost this hand also, he at last seized the ship with his teeth'.

even then your master Aristotle and judged him not worthy to be of that number, but his report much less to be regarded than the feignings <C4v> of poets whom I have rehearsed, and for this intent. For poets wrote against women in wanton ditties, to content men with newfangled devices. But the reproach to women given by Aristotle was in treating of matter weighty and serious, whereby it appeareth that the said words, so spitefully spoken, proceeded only of cankered malice, whereunto he was of his own nature disposed, which may be of them shortly perceived that beholdeth in his works none other philosopher escape unrebuked.

Ne truly he was ashamed to rent with rebukes the immortal fame of Plato, his master, of whose divine mouth he had twenty years sucked the most sweet honey of noble philosophy, which malice grew of this occasion, as anci-<C5r>ent authors have made thereof mention. Forasmuch as where he was more curious in his apparel and decking than was convenient to his profession, also more light in countenance and dissolute in living than became an instructor of virtue and wisdom, Plato therefore preferred other his scholars before him; which he very displeasantly taking sought occasion to rebuke his master when he was dead, which he never darest while he was living.

That Aristotle was dissolute and also inconstant, it may appear by this which is written of him. For to Hermia, which was his concubine, he did sacrifice and made solemn hymns while she was living.[18] Can ye compare any madness or folly to this man's abuse and unconstancy? <C5v> May there be so great an abuse as to give divine honours to a mortal creature, also to an harlot and common sinner? What unconstancy was in him which calleth that a creature unperfect to whom he did solemn sacrifice, sang devout hymns, and often times kneeled? To blaspheme so his goddess, ought not this great philosopher be foul ashamed? Wherefore, Caninius, by mine advice, do ye not lean more to his authority than unto truth, virtue, and honesty, but consider his nature, inclined to malice, his fond error and vain curiosity, and, that which ye dispraise in women, apparent inconstancy.

CANINIUS Ye have a great affection to Plato, I perceive verily. But will ye deny that a woman is of her nature un-<C6r>perfect?

CANDIDUS Yea, marry, will I. For wherein do you note her to be unperfect? Is it in the soul or in the body?

CANINIUS In both of them, truly. For they be weaker than men and have their flesh softer, less hair on their visages, and their voice sharper, and, as I

[18] This and the remarks in the previous paragraph derive from Diog. Laert. 5.1.1–4; cf. also Eras., *Apoph.* 7.221 (CWE 38, 821), 'Aristotle was prosecuted for writing a hymn in honour of Hermia, a woman he loved, extolling her like a goddess'.

have read, they have in some parts of their bodies their bones fewer. And as concerning the soul, they lack hardiness, and in perils are timorous, more delicate than men, unapt to painfulness, except they be thereto constrained or °steered by wilfulness. And the wit that they have is not substantial but apish, never flourishing but in ungraciousness, or in trimming themselves with pretty devices, or excusing their faults with unstudied answers, <C6v> or in pretty mocks or scornful dalliance, or to invent mischiefs to satiate their malice. In other things, it is unapt unto knowledge, except one or two which I have read of who in Rome hath pleaded as orators.[19] But that is not to be marvelled at, since, they being instructed in eloquence, their domestical exercise — I will not say chiding — maketh them bold to contend in pleading. In the parts of wisdom and civil policy, they be founden unapt and to have little capacity. But their most unperfection is their inconstancy, which proceedeth of their said natural debility. For whereas the affection of much dread or much love aboundeth, stability lacketh, and wit little prevaileth. Contrary to this, I dare say, ye can <C7r> make none evasion.

CANDIDUS Yes, and disprove all your malicious conclusion. But, I pray you, Caninius, let me ask you a question. Be all the books of your master Aristotle of equal authority?

CANINIUS Yea, that be they, verily.

CANDIDUS In the institution of household-keeping called *Oeconomicae*, Aristotle writeth in this wise: 'The company most according to nature is that which is ordained of man and woman, which was constitute, not to the intent only to bring forth their semblable, as other beasts participators of nature and without reason, but for love specially and mutual assistance'. And he saith also, in the same book and not far from thence: 'This company is not because that each of them hath in every thing and the same all their <C7v> virtues like profitable; but some of their virtues seem to be contrary one to another; and yet, in conclusion, they agree to one purpose. For nature made man more strong and courageous, the woman more weak, fearful, and scrupulous, to the intent that she, for her feebleness, should be more circumspect, the man for his strength much more adventurous'.[20] Be not these the words of your master? How say you?

[19] Best known was probably Hortensia (fl. 42 BCE), daughter of Cicero's great rival Q. Hortensius Hortalus (cf. Boccaccio, *De mul. clar.* 84). Her crucial oratorical intervention is reported at length in App., *B. civ.* 4.32–34; and she and other women orators of Rome are listed in Val. Max. 8.3.init.–8.3.3, for example, and Quint., *Inst.* 1.1.6, including Laelia, 'said to have reproduced the elegance of her father's language in her own speech', the daughter of the C. Laelius mentioned in *Pasquil*, p. 49.

[20] Arist., *Oec.* 1 (1343b–1344a).

° steered] steryd *A* : stered *B* (*fortasse* MnE 'stirred')

CANINIUS Where ye say truth, I will not deny you. It is of his sentence the very pith and effect. For he wrote in Greek, ye know well enough; wherefore, they be not in the same words as ye do speak them.

CANDIDUS It maketh no matter, if I do truly interpret them. But now to our purpose. Is perfection and unperfection in thin-<C8r>gs anything else than abundance and lack of that which is expedient to the end whereunto nature hath ordained them?

CANINIUS Nay, in good sooth, for I think that a true definition.

°CANDIDUS But let me see: where I called it abundance, I mought better have named it sufficience, for abundance doth properly signify more than is necessary. Sufficience descriveth the thing, with bounds and limits, the excess whereof is called superfluity and the lack may be named necessity.

CANINIUS In faith, ye be too curious. Perdie, the word neither made nor marred any thing of °our purpose. For abundance and sufficience is commonly taken for one thing.

CANDIDUS Yea, and that hath subverted the order of all thing. For, truly, words <C8v> used in their proper signification do bring things to a plain understanding; and where they be much abused and wrested from their true meaning, they cause sundry errors and perpetual contention. But let us now return to our question.

Clay is a kind of earth soft and clammy, and for those qualities serveth to make walls for houses and to that end hath his perfection, although a stone be a matter hard and consolidate, and serveth also for walls, and maketh them stronger to serve for munition. The horse hath much strength and therefore is apt for journeys and burdens; the sheep is feeble and fearful and may therefore easily be shorn. And yet each of these in his kind hath his perfections.

To men, nature hath gi-<D1r>ven puissance in members, braveness, hard and consolidate, the skin thick, perchance mo bones, as ye say, to sustain outward labours, and, to seem the more terrible, much hair on their visage. To women, she hath given the contrary, to the end and intent, which your master rehearsed, that her debility should make her more circumspect, in the keeping (°saith he) at home such things as her husband by °his puissance hath gotten, for those words also he added to them which are before spoken.

°Is not that a company according to nature, where the one diligently keepeth that which the other by labour prepareth? For what profiteth it

° \Abundance Sufficience/

° our] your *B*

° saith] sayeth *B*

° his] this *B*

° \Getting and keeping./

to prepare where safe keeping lacketh? In preparing is labour or study; of keeping cometh use <D1v> and commodity; and therefore, to speak indifferently, it deserveth much more praise than the getting.

But now tell me one thing: wherein, suppose you, doth a man excel all other creatures? Is it in greatness or puissance of body?

CANINIUS No, verily.

CANDIDUS Then wherein, suppose ye?

CANINIUS In that that his soul is adorned with reason.

CANDIDUS Stop there, I pray you, a little season. What call ye reason?

CANINIUS Why, be ye now to learn what thing is reason?

CANDIDUS Yea, by my halidom. And this is the cause. For many men lean to their singular opinion, judging all that is contrary to stand with no reason. Wherefore, I pray you, make me thereof a true definition.

CANINIUS I will, to content with your fantasy, although that ye can do it, I know <D2r> well, much better than I.

°Reason is the principal part of the soul, divine and immortal, whereby man doth discern good from ill. °This thing, whiles it discerneth or severeth the one from the other, it is called discretion. °When it taketh the one and leaveth the other, it is named election; judgment, of some men. °The exercise thereof is called prudence; of some, circumspection. And yet is everich of these things nothing but reason, which to man is so proper that, lacking it, he loseth his denomination.

CANDIDUS In good faith, ye have made of reason a right good description. And now I perceive that the thing whereby man excelleth all other creatures is reason only.

CANINIUS Yea, verily.

CANDIDUS What think you, is reason only in men? Is it <D2v> not also in women, suppose you?

CANINIUS Yes, that is it naturally; for the word 'man', which I named, includeth as well woman as man when it is written or spoken so generally.

CANDIDUS I am glad that I have found you so reasonable in talking of reason. °But what say you by sharpness of wit? Doth it not, between man and beast, make like diversity?

CANINIUS No, surely. For wit is of the part of man that is mortal, and that is founden by daily experience. For where the vapours in the body be pure and subtle which do ascend into the brain, the wit becometh sharp and delicate. And where they be gross, ponderous, and smoky, the wit is dull

° \Reason/
° \Discretion/
° \Election/
° \Prudence Circumspection/
° \Wit/

and nothing pleasant. And therefore physicians have experienced, by clarifying and <D3r> temperating the corporal humours to correct the wit, which is either with gross matter oppressed or with adust vapours smouldered or choked. But reason mought never be brought into a beast, which by nature lacketh it; and yet in diverse of them have been perceived so subtle wits that therein men have seemed to be of them vanquished.

CANDIDUS I think it to be true that ye say. Then in whom reason most doth appear, ye will affirm, doth most excel a beast in his nature?

CANINIUS Yea, Master Candidus, that may ye be sure.

CANDIDUS And ye were agreed whilere, that to keep diligently that which is gotten is worthy more praise than in the getting?

CANINIUS Yea, for there cometh more effect of the keeping.

CANDIDUS <D3v> And so ye conclude that the power of reason is more in the prudent and diligent keeping than in the valiant or politic getting; and that discretion, election, and prudence, which is all and in every part reason, do excel strength, wit, and hardiness; and, consequently, they in whom be those virtues, in that they have them, do excel in just estimation them that be strong, hardy, or politic in getting of anything?

CANINIUS Ye have well gathered together all that conclusion.

CANDIDUS Behold, Caninius, where ye be now. Ye have so much extolled reason that in the respect thereof bodily strength remaineth as nothing, forasmuch as the corporal powers with powers of the soul can make no comparison. And <D4v> ye have not denied but that this word, 'man', unto whom reason pertaineth, doth imply in it both man and woman. And, agreeing unto Aristotle's saying, ye have confirmed that prudence, which in effect is nothing but reason, is more aptly applied to the woman, whereby she is more circumspect in keeping, as strength is to the man, that he may be more valiant in getting. And likewise, ye have preferred the prudence in keeping, for the utility thereof, before the valiantness in getting; and, semblably, them which be prudent in keeping before them that be only strong and hardy in getting. And so ye have concluded that women, which are prudent in keeping, be more excellent than men in reason, which be only strong and <D4v> valiant in getting. And where excellency is, there is most perfection. Wherefore, a woman is not a creature unperfect but, as it seemeth, is more perfect than man.

CANINIUS Why have ye dallied herefore with me all this long season?

CANDIDUS Surely I have used neither dalliance nor sophistry; but, if ye consider it well, ye shall find it but a natural induction and plain to all them that have any capacity. But yet have I somewhat more to say to you. Ye said, moreover, Caninius, that the wits of women were apt only to trifles and shrewdness and not to wisdom and civil policy. I will be plain to you. I am sorry to find in your words such manner of lewdness. I cry you mercy. I would have said so much ungentleness and, <D5v> in your own words, so much forgetfulness.

CANINIUS What mean ye thereby?

CANDIDUS Ye have twice granted that natural reason is in women as well as in men.

CANINIUS Yea, and what then?

CANDIDUS Then have women also discretion, election, and prudence, which do make that wisdom which pertaineth to governance. And, perdie, many arts and necessary occupations have been invented by women, as I will bring now some unto your remembrance. Latin letters were first founden by Nicostrata, called also Carmentis;[21] the seven liberal arts and poetry, by the nine maidens called the Muses. Why was Minerva honoured for a goddess but because she found first in Graecia planting or setting of trees; also, the use of armour, and, <D5v> as some do testify, she invented making of fortresses and many necessary and notable sciences?

Also, that the wits of women be not unapt to laudable studies it appeareth by Diotima and Aspasia, two honest maidens, which in all parts of philosophy were so well learned that Socrates, master to Plato, nothing disdained to come to their lessons, and called Diotima alway his mistress.[22] Cleobulina, the daughter of Cleobulus, one of the seven wise men of Greece, wrote diffuse and mystical questions in heroical verses.[23] Also Leontium, a woman, excelled all men of her time in wisdom and eloquence, in so much as she wrote against Theophrast, the most eloquent disciple of Aristotle, in women's defence, which book, if it now had <D6r> remained, should have been sufficient to have put you to silence.[24] If the learning and wisdom of the lady Cassandra, daughter to King Priamus, had been regarded more than the counsel of flatterers, the city of Troy

21 Cf. Boccaccio, *De mul. clar.* 27.5–6, 12–13.

22 Diotima features in Pl., *Symp.* 201d–207b; Aspasia, in Pl., *Menex.* 235e–249e, and also in Plut., *Per.* 24. Cf. Elyot, *Bibl.*, '*Aspasia,* a woman of Miletum in Greece, of notable learning in rhetoric, and taught the eloquent Pericles duke of Athens, and loved him. Wherefore notwithstanding that she was a captive, he took her to his wife. It is written, that she was one of the concubines of Cyrus King of Persia, after whose death Pericles took her, and afterward by her procurement, for displeasure that she bare to the Peloponnesians, he was the cause that the *Athenienses* made war against them. Wherein is to be noted, that in a fair woman eloquence is of such puissance, that if she will abuse it unto ill affections, she may pervert the wisdom of men, and be occasion of much unhappiness'.

23 Diog. Laert. 1.6.89; she features in the same capacity as a riddler in Plut., *Conv. sept. sap.* (*Mor.* 148c–148e and 154b) by the name 'Eumetis'. Cf. Elyot, *Bibl.*, '*Cleobulus,* was one of the seven sages of Greece, who had a daughter called *Cleobulina,* which was an excellent poet, and made a book of riddles contained in three thousand verses'.

24 Cic., *Nat. D.* 1.33.93; also, Eras., *Adagia* 1.10.21, *Suspendio deligenda arbor,* 'Choose your tree and hang yourself' (CWE 32, 242); and cf. Boccaccio, *De mul. clar.* 60.

and kingdom of Phrygia had longer remained, and Priamus with his noble succession had many years reigned.[25] Behold our progenitors, the ancient Romans, in all extreme dangers, when other counsel utterly failed, did not they resort to the books of *Sibylla Cumana*, called also Amalthea, and, pursuing her advice, which she had there declared, did they not escape the perils which then were imminent?[26]

Hundreds of such women are in stories remembered, but, for speed of time, I will pass them over since <D6v> I trust that these be sufficient to prove that the whole kind of women be not unapt unto wisdom, as ye have supposed. As concerning strength and valiant courage, which ye surmise to lack in them, I could make to you no less replication, and, by old stories and late experience, prove that in arms women have been found of no little reputation. But I will omit that for this time, forasmuch as to the more part of wise men it shall not sound much to their commendation — saving that we now have one example among us, as well of fortitude as of all other virtues, which, in mine opinion, shall not be inconvenient to have at this time declared, and so of this matter to make a conclusion.

CANINIUS And I have mine <D7r> ears thereto prepared.

CANDIDUS The best matter is ever good to be spared until the tale be almost at an end, and then shall the hearers with the length thereof be little offended.

Sir, there dwelleth here by me a lady, late a great queen and wife to Odenatus King of Palmyry, which is a city and country in Syrey. Her name is Zenobia. She hath had of our host victory twice, and now late was taken prisoner by Aurelian the Emperor, albeit for her nobility, virtue, and courage, she was pardoned of her life, and a fair house is appointed to her in this village.[27] She is well learned in Greek, and doth competently understand Latin, but excellently the Egyptian language. She herself teacheth her children good letters and, being now vacant <D7v> from

[25] Cf. Boccaccio, *De mul. clar.* 35.

[26] Cf. Elyot, *Bibl.*, '*Amalthea*, a woman, which with her sister called Melissa, nourished Jupiter with the milk of a goat. Also, the name of a prophetess'; probably deriving (somewhat confusedly) from Eras., *Adagia* 1.6.2, *Copiae cornu*, 'A horn of plenty' (CWE 32, 4), 'The image is taken from a very early myth, told by our authorities in various forms. In some it runs like this. Rhea, having given birth to Jupiter, hid her baby in Crete for fear of his father, to be nursed by two nymphs, Adrastea and Ida, daughters of Melisseus. They fed him on the milk of a she-goat called Amalthea; and Jupiter, when he was grown up, set this goat among the stars, where it is called in Greek the Heavenly She-goat'. Elyot elsewhere manifests a knowledge of other sources of information about the sibyls, esp. Lactant., *Div. Inst.* 1.6.

[27] SHA, *Tyr. Trig.* 30.27, 'Huic vita ab Aureliano concessa est, ferturque vixisse cum liberis matronae iam more Romanae data sibi possessione in Tiburti'; and cf. 30.23, 'When Aurelian had taken her prisoner, he caused her to be led into his presence and then addressed her thus: "Why is it, Zenobia, that you dared to show insolence to the emperors of Rome?"'.

other business, writeth, as they say, of Alexandria and the Orient eloquent stories.[28] I have boden her to supper. It will not now be long ere she come hither. And when ye do hear her, I dare well say ye will be changed from your opinion and confess that in women is both courage, constance, and reason.

CANINIUS But, I pray you, of this matter say to her nothing.

CANDIDUS Ah, I see well ye be loath to come to a reckoning. Thus do they all that be of your fashion: in wise women's absence, speak reproachfully and, when they be present, flatter them pleasantly.

But lo! where she cometh. Let us meet with her.

Your ladyship is very heartily welcome.

ZENOBIA Ye have caused me to do that I have used very seldom. <D8r>

CANDIDUS What is that, madam?

ZENOBIA To be out of mine own house at this time of the night.

CANDIDUS I thank therefore your ladyship, for I think the same; but I will promise you nothing shall come to your hearing or sight, but that both to hear and see may stand with your worship.

ZENOBIA That I heartily pray you, for the remembrance of my princely estate may not sustain words of dishonesty. And because I am now as a private person, I fear the common success of familiarity.

CANDIDUS What is that, madam, I pray you heartily?

ZENOBIA For I dread infamy, I tell you plainly, more than ever I did the loss of my liberty.

CANDIDUS No such thing shall happen, madam, I promise you, truly. For here ye shall find <D8v> no men but of honest condition.

ZENOBIA Yet some, in devising with ladies, rejoicing to be therefore had in a certain suspicion, will by the way of dalliance convey from them some thing which, being shewed, do engender in the beholders some dishonest opinion. Diverse be not ashamed to make their avaunt that they have received which, of her that they speak of, was never once proffered. These things, Master Candidus, have made me afraid to come to suppers and banquets.

[28] Cf. SHA, *Tyr. Trig.* 30.20–22, 'She ordered her sons to talk Latin, so that, in fact, they spoke Greek but rarely and with difficulty. She herself was not wholly conversant with the Latin tongue, but nevertheless, mastering her timidity she would speak it; Egyptian, on the other hand, she spoke very well. In the history of Alexandria and the Orient she was so well versed that she even composed an epitome, so it is said; Roman history, however, she read in Greek'; also, Boccaccio, *De mul. clar.* 100.14, 'She spent most of her time in hunting and fighting, but these pursuits did not prevent her from learning Egyptian, and she also learned Greek from the philosopher Longinus. Zenobia's knowledge of these languages enabled her to read voraciously and commit to memory all the Latin, Greek, and barbarian histories. Moreover she is believed to have composed epitomes of these works. Besides her own language, she knew Egyptian and spoke it although she also knew Syriac', but not mentioning the children's education nor 'Alexandria and the Orient'.

CANINIUS Marry, that is well said. And yet some time such things have been seen offered.

CANDIDUS Perchance of some young maidens, which did it of courtesy; yet much more hath been asked that have been denied. I have known it myself, I pro-<E1r>mise you faithfully.

ZENOBIA Truly, I like not such manner of folly. I have been brought up in other study.

CANDIDUS I pray you, madam, let me ask you a question. But first pleaseth it you to sit down and rest you, for I trow your supper is not yet ready.

ZENOBIA Now, what is your demand? Speak on hardily.

CANDIDUS Of what age was your ladyship, when first ye were married?

ZENOBIA Twenty years and above.

CANDIDUS It was great pity that you so long tarried.

ZENOBIA But it was the more for my commodity. For I knew the better what longed to my duty.

CANDIDUS Your duty, madam? What mean ye thereby?

ZENOBIA For by my study in moral philosophy, wherein I spent the years between sixteen and twen-<E1v>ty, I perceived that, without prudence and constancy, women mought be brought lightly into error and folly and made therefore unmeet for that company whereunto they were ordained — I mean, to be assistance and comfort to man through their fidelity, which other beasts are not, except they be by the force of man thereto constrained.

°I found also that justice teacheth us women to honour our husbands next after God, which honour resteth in due obedience, whereby mutual love betwixt them is in a more fervence; for, undoubtedly, no woman him loveth whose hate or displeasure she nothing feareth. Also, justice restraineth us to do anything which is not seemly.

°By fortitude are we still kept in a virtuous constancy, as well in re-<E2r>sisting affections and wanton persuasion, as also to sustain (when they do happen) afflictions patiently.

°But in a woman, no virtue is equal to temperance, whereby in her words and deeds she alway useth a just moderation, knowing when time is to speak and when to keep silence, when to be occupied and when to be merry. And if she measure it to the will of her husband, she doeth the more wisely, except it may turn them both to loss or dishonesty; yet then should she seem rather to give him wise counsel than to appear disobedient or sturdy. In every of these things consisted my duty, which I should not so well have known if to my husband I had sooner be wedded.

° \Justice/

° \Fortitude/

° \Temperance in women/

CANINIUS Indeed, ye had been past learning thereof <E2v> when ye had once been bedded.[29]

ZENOBIA In good faith, ye say truly! For when I had been out of the dread of my father, who kept me in this study continually, and had once tasted the pleasant devices which are provided for queens and other great ladies, ye may well suppose I should soon have lost that delectation which I had in study.

CANDIDUS Ye say even truth, by the faith of my body! But, madam, after that ye were married, what profit was to you the knowledge of letters?

ZENOBIA Much, Master Candidus, I promise you verily. For during the life of my noble husband, of famous memory, I was never heard or seen say or do anything which mought not content him, or omit anything which should delight him. <E3r> Such circumspection good learning ministered unto me that, in hunting and other pastimes, I retained alway such gravity that, of any dissolute appetite, none could conceive of me any suspicion; and yet, my learning was had of none honest man in any derision.

But after the death of my husband, I found of learning a marvellous treasure. For when I considered the state of things which then happened together — what danger was to the realm imminent for lack of a governor, and that my children for their tender youth should be little regarded, and I being a woman should nothing be feared; also, what tutors my children should have — it was very uncertain.

°Ambition alway reigning <E3v> in every country, which cannot gladly suffer in any one person such manner of sovereignty that, under the name of protection, he should have in subjection all the nobility; and, although that such one mought happen to be, yet having in remembrance as well ancient histories as late examples, I drad lest in so great authority, ambition and avarice mought cause men to forget their obedience, trust, and fidelity.

I considered also that the realm of Palmyry was environed with enemies. For on the one side was the host of the Romans, which alway °awaited to find opportunity to invade my realm and to subdue it under their empire. The thieves of Araby were on the other side, which already were entered <E4r> the marches and spoiled the country. The King of Media, to be discharged of his tribute, joined with our enemies, willing to bring my realm in perpetual captivity. Was it any marvel if all these things did exceedingly trouble me?

CANDIDUS But finally, madam, what remedy found ye?

29 The speech-ending rhymes with the previous one.

° \Ambition Avarice/
° awaited] waited *B*

ZENOBIA After that I had a little bethought me, I determined to prepare remedies quickly and to sustain fortune at all times patiently; and, to the intent that the name of a woman should not among the people be had in contempt, I used so my proceedings that none of them mought be said to be done womanly.

Wherefore, I sat alway abroad among my nobles and councillors and said mine opinion, so that it seemed to <E4v> them all that it stood with good reason. I came oftentimes among the people, and remembered unto them the liberty and honour which they had received by the excellent prowess of my noble husband, shewing to them my children, which for tender age then were but feeble, exhorting them with sundry orations to retain their fidelity. I visited all the whole realm and the marches, re-edified fortresses, and new made also sundry munitions.

Moreover, I caused good laws to be published, observing them first in mine own household, and caused them in all other places to be well executed. I made justice chief ruler of mine affection, and in all consultations would I be present, where I heard all other speak first, that I would <E5r> not be ignorant, and then shewed mine advice, wherein I seemed not to be negligent. Touching my servants, I used such a diligent scrutiny that they were alway persons of singular honesty.

By this manner industry, I quietly governed the realm of Palmyry and also added much more to mine empire, not so much by force as by renome of just and politic governance, which all men had in such admiration that diverse of our said enemies, which against the realm erst did conspire and had invaded my jurisdiction, chose rather to leave their hostility and to remain in our subjection than to return to their own country.

To the which wisdom and policy, I attained by the study of noble philosophy. <E5v> Also, thereby I acquired such magnanimity that now I keep in as straight subjection all affections and passions as the Romans do now me and my children.

All this considered, my study was to me much more commodious because it was so long ere I were married. Wherefore, I may conclude that I had well tarried.

CANDIDUS Ye have said very well, by the faith of my body. And all that ye have spoken, I have before heard as well of your friends as of your enemies confessed.

How say you, Caninius? Be you anything changed in your opinion?

CANINIUS I would never have looked for such a conclusion. I see well enough that women, being well and virtuously brought up, do not only with men participate in reason, but some <E6r> also in fidelity and constancy be equal unto them.

CANDIDUS Madam, your supper is ready. May it like you to enter in toward it?

ZENOBIA With right good will. But yet, if this gentleman hath aught to say against women, I am not unprovided for to defend them.

CANINIUS No, madam. I am by your ladyship already satisfied. He is wise that with reason is shortly contented. And where reason serveth not, silence is praised.

ZENOBIA Yet a good mind in silence is ever well occupied.

CANDIDUS And he that thinketh well and speaketh truth is most to be loved.
Madam, I will lead you the way into my house.

ZENOBIA With good will, I follow you.

CANINIUS The conclusion is good, where both parts <E6v> are pleased. And if they both be wise, it maketh no matter though fools be offended.

Thus endeth the defence of good women.

L O N D I N I in ædibus Tho-
mæ Bertheleti typis
impress.
C U M P R I V I L E G I O
Ad imprimendum
solum .·.
°A N N O. M. D. XL.

° A N N O. M. D. XL.] *B om*

°<a1r>

THE IMAGE

OF GOVERNANCE

COMPILED OF THE ACTS

AND SENTENCES

notable of the most noble

Emperor Alexander

Severus,

late translated

out

of

Greek into English, by Sir

Thomas Elyot, knight,

in the favour of

nobility.

ANNO. °M.D.XLI.

° The text is from *A* = 1541 ed. [colophon '1540'] (RSTC 7664 = ESTC S100472), departures from which are enclosed in angled brackets <>; collated with *B* = 1544 ed. (RSTC 7665 = ESTC S100505); the editions' marginalia, enclosed between slashes, \ /, have been removed into the text column, with slightest relocation, sometimes, or have been removed to the textual notes.

° M.D.XLI.] M.D.XLIIII *B*

FIG. 1. Armorial woodcut, *Image of Governance* (London: Berthelet, 1541), sig. a1v, in the copy Washington, D. C., USA, Folger Shakespeare Library, shelfmark STC 7664 copy 2. By permission of the Folger Shakespeare Library

<a2r>

THE PREFACE TO ALL THE NOBILITY OF THIS FLOURISHING REALM OF ENGLAND, THOMAS ELYOT, KNIGHT, DESIRETH INCREASE OF VIRTUE AND HONOUR.

As I late was searching among my books to find some argument in the reading whereof I mought recreate my spirits, being almost fatigate with the long study about the correcting and ampliating of my *Dictionary* of Latin and English, I happened to find certain quires of paper, which I had written about nine years past, wherein were contained the acts and sentences notable of the most noble Emperor Alexander, for his wisdom and gravity called Severus; which book was first written in the Greek tongue by his secretary, named Eucolpius, and by good chance was lent unto me by a gentleman of Naples, called Pudericus.[1]

In reading whereof, I was marvellously ravished, and, as it hath been ever mine appetite, I wished that it had been published in such a tongue as mo men mought understand it. Wherefore, with all diligence I endeavoured myself, whiles I had leisure, to translate it into English; albeit I could not so exactly perform mine enterprise as I mought have done, if the owner had not importunately called for his book, whereby I was constrained to leave some part of the work untranslated; which <a2v> I made up as well as I could, with some other authors, as well Latins as Greeks.

Having this book in my hand, I remembered that in my book named *The Governour* I promised to write a book of the form of good governance; and forasmuch as in this book was expressed of governance so perfect an image, I supposed that I should sufficiently discharge myself of my promise if I did now publish this book; which, except I be much deceived, shall minister to the wise readers both pleasure and profit. Then did I eftsoons peruse it and with more exact diligence conform the style thereof with the phrase of our English, desiring more to make it plain to all readers than to flourish it with over much

[1] Both the ancient Greek secretary 'Eucolpius' and the contemporary Neapolitan gentleman 'Pudericus' appear to be Elyot's inventions. Pudericus is not mentioned again. Eucolpius reappears in the concluding post-script, where his writing is said to end (below, p. 309); otherwise, only in the invented chap. 25, below pp. 244, 246, 249, and 250, as a direct witness, to warrant the veracity of events that did not happen, like the notorious Chaucerian source 'myn auctour called Lollius' (*Tr.* 1.394); and again in chap. 26 as a negative witness, p. 253. Elyot may also cite 'Encolpius', below p. 309 — an imputed source of the SHA, *Alex. Sev.* — but only in an instance where Elyot must be following the SHA. On possible meanings of the names, see Greg Walker, *Writing Under Tyranny* (Oxford: Oxford University Press, 2005), p. 241.

eloquence; which book I do dedicate unto you noble lords, gentle knights, and other in the state of honour or worship, as being most ready to be advanced to governance under your prince, so that your virtues be correspondent unto your fortunes.

Yet am I not ignorant that diverse there be which do not thankfully esteem my labours, dispraising my studies as vain and unprofitable, saying in derision that I have nothing won thereby but the name only of a maker of books, and that I set the trees, but the printer eateth the fruits. Indeed, although disdain and envy do cause them to speak it, yet will I not deny but that they say truly. For if I would have employed my study about the increase of my private commodity which I have spent in writing of books for others' necessity, few men doubt (I suppose) that do know me but that I should have attained ere this time to have been much more wealthy and, in respect of the world, in a more estimation.

But to <a3r> excuse me of folly, I will profess, without arrogance, that when I considered that cunning continueth when fortune flitteth; having also ringing alway in mine ear the terrible check that the good master in the gospel gave to his idle servant, for hiding his money in a clout and not disposing it for his master's °advantage; those two words, *serve nequam*,[2] so stirred my spirits that it caused me to take more regard to my last reckoning than to any riches or worldly promotion.

And although I do neither dispute nor expound holy scripture, yet in such works as I have and intend to set forth my poor talent shall be, God willing, in such wise bestowed, that no man's conscience shall be therewith offended:

My book called *The Governour*, instructing men in such virtues as shall be expedient for them which shall have authority in a weal public.

The *Doctrinal of Princes*, which are but the counsels of wise Isocrates, inducing into noble men's wits honest opinions.

The *Education of Children*, which also I translated out of the wise Plutarch, making men and women which will follow those rules to be well worthy to be fathers and mothers.

The little *Pasquil*, although he be merry and plain, teaching as well servants how to be faithful unto their masters, as also masters how to be circumspect in espying of flatterers.

Semblably, the office of a good counsellor, with magnanimity or good courage in time of adversity, may be apparently founden in my book called *Of the Knowledge Belonging to a Wise Man*.

In reading the sermon of saint Cyprian by me translated, the devout reader

[2] Mt 18. 32, 'tunc vocavit illum dominus suus et ait illi serve nequam omne debitum dimisi tibi quoniam rogasti me': 'Then his lord, after that he had called him, said unto him, O thou wicked servant, I forgave thee all that debt, because thou desiredst me'.

° \Matt. 18./

shall find no little comfort in plagues or calamities.

The *Banquet of Sapience* is not fasti-<a3v>dious, and in little room sheweth out of holy scripture many wise sentences.

The *Castle of Health*, being truly read, shall long preserve men — being some physicians never so angry — from perilous sickness.

My little book called *The Defence of Good Women* not only confoundeth villainous report but also teacheth good wives to know well their duties.

My *Dictionary*, declaring Latin by English, by that time that I have performed it, shall not only serve for children, as men have accepted it, but also shall be commodious for them which perchance be well learned.

And this present book, which I have named *The Image of Governance*, shall be to all them which will read it sincerely a very true pattern, whereby they may shape all their proceedings.

And in none of these works, I dare undertake, a man shall find any sentence against the commandments of God, the true catholic faith, or occasion to stir men to wanton devices. Wherefore, I trust unto God, mine accompt shall of him be favourably accepted, although some ingrate persons with ill report or mocks requite ill my labours; to whom I will only recite this merry fable of Aesop, written by Maximus Planudes.[3]

A good woman had an husband, who would be oftentimes drunken; wherewith she being ashamed and devising by what mean she might cause him to leave that horrible vice, at the last when he was asleep, she carried him unto the charnel house, wherein were put the bones of dead men; and leaving him lying there, she made fast the door and departed. And when she thought that he was waking, she, taking with her bread and meat, returned to the charnel house and knocked at the door. Her husband faintly asked who <a4r> knocked there; the good woman answered, 'I, which have brought meat with me for the dead men'.

'Peace!', said her husband; 'thou increasest my pain in speaking of meat! Bring me some drink, I beseech thee!'

That hearing the good woman, 'Alas', said she, 'that ever I was born! For this vice, gotten by custom, my husband hath made it a natural habit, which will never forsake him'.

This fable needeth no declaration, for every man may perceive what it meaneth.

Moreover, many, being ignorant of good letters, do universally reprove all them that be studious in learning, alleging this common proverb, 'the greatest

3 The fable following is no. 246 in Ben Edwin Perry, 'Appendix: An Analytical Survey of Greek and Latin Fables in the Aesopic Tradition', in *Babrius and Phaedrus* (Cambridge, MA: Harvard University Press, 1965), pp. 470–71; evidently, since there was no Latin or other translation by the date, Elyot's version is from Greek directly, i.e. no. 108 in *Fabulae Aesopicae Collectae*, ed. by Karl Felix Halm (Leipzig: Teubner, 1889), pp. 55–56.

clerks be not the wisest men',[4] affirming that they be founden negligent about their own profit and consequently unapt to the ministration of things of weighty importance.

How untrue their allegations be and on how feeble a foundation they are builded, it shall in this wise appear unto wise men. First, the said proverb seemeth by him which lacked learning to be devised, since that he preferreth ignorance before cunning; which arrogance declared him to be a very fool and unwitty, considering that by knowledge most chiefly a man excelleth all other mortal creatures and thereby is most like unto God; and learning is none other thing but an aggregation of many men's sentences and acts, to the augmentation of knowledge.

And if some learned men do neglect their temporal commodities, it is for one of these causes: either because they have been so desirous of knowledge and in respect thereof esteemed so little all other pleasures, that they thought the time all too little which they did spend in it, holding themselves with that which ser-<a4v>ved for nature's necessity right well contented; or else like as the greyhound that was sent to great Alexander by the King of Albania.[5] When there were shewed unto him severally a great hart, a boar, and a bear, he vouched not safe to look on them, but lay still wagging his tail. Then was there brought forth a great lion, to whom he did arise softly and, setting up his bristles and shewing his teeth, fleeing to the lion, lightly strangled him. Afterward, a puissant oliphant being brought to the place, the greyhound, seeming to rejoice at the greatness of the beast, roused him; and after two or three questings, he leapt to the great oliphant and after a long fight overthrew him and killed him.

So I doubt not but that some men there be living, in whom is such courage, that, in things of little importance, may seem to be negligent, disdaining as it were to spend their wits or labours about the pelfry of riches; which, being once called to authority joined with liberty, will enforce themselves to make their ministrations noble and excellent. Such were Solon, Aristides, and Phocion in Athens; Publicola, Fabritius, Curius, and Cato Uticensis at Rome, whose lives I would to God were in English;[6] and the like be now living, if they were sought for.

And for the confutation of that pestiferous opinion that great learned men be unapt to the ministration of things of weighty importance, this shall be sufficient. First, as I late said, learning is the augmentation of knowledge; which, the more that it is, the more may be perceived what shall be most necessary in

4 Chaucer, *RvT* 4054, 'The gretteste clerkes been noght wisest men'; cf. Richard Pace, *De fructu qui ex doctrina percipitur*, ed. by Manley and Sylvester, p. 14, 'Est enim multis in ore doctiores uiros non esse sapientiores'.

5 Plin., *NH* 8.149–50. The tale is reused below, p. 285.

6 Much the same list recurs below, p. 271.

things which happen in consultation; and the more that it is perceived, the better and more aptly may it be ministered and executed.

Ex-<b1r>amples we have of Moses, who, being excellently learned in the most diffuse doctrines of the Egyptians and Ethiopians, was by almighty God chosen to guide and rule his people, which were innumerable and most froward of nature. And with what wonderful wisdom and patience did he govern them, by the space of forty years, being without any cities, towns, or any certain possessions? Who were better leaders of armies than great Alexander, Scipio, Lucullus, and Caesar, which were men all of great learning?[7] Who better handled matters of weighty importance than Octavian (called Augustus),[8] Hadrian, Marcus Antoninus,[9] Alexander Severus, and, of late years, Carolus Magnus,[10] all emperors of Rome, and men very studious in all noble sciences? When was there a better consul than Tully, or a better senator than Cato (called Uticensis)?

And to return home to our own country and whereof we ourselves may be witnesses, how much hath it profited unto this realm that it now hath a king, our sovereign lord King HENRY the eighth, exactly well learned? Hath not he thereby only sifted out detestable heresies, late mingled among the corn of his faithful subjects, and caused much of the chaff to be throwen in the fire? Also, hypocrisy and vain superstition to be clean banished? Whereof I doubt not but that there shall be, ere it be long, a more ample remembrance to his most noble and immortal renome.

This well considered, let men cease their said foolish opinion and hold them content with their own ignorance; and for my part, say what they list, I will, during my life, be in this wise occupied in bestowing my talent, being satisfied with the contenting of such <b1v> men as ye be, adorned with virtue, the most precious garment of very nobility.

But now, to the intent that ye, if ye list, may attain inestimable profit by the reading of this little work, I do exhort you that, reading it distinctly and studiously, first, ye mark diligently how, by the lascivious and remiss education of Varius Heliogabalus, he grew to be a person most monstrous in living; also how, notwithstanding that he not only suffered but also provoked the people to live in a most beastly license, yet horrible sin at the last became to all men fastidious and loathsome; wherefore, they slew in most miserable fashion him that consumed infinite treasure in supporting their lewdness.

7 As also twice in *Gov.*, Elyot makes a similar list of emperors, kings, consuls, and generals 'all of great learning' again below, pp. 282–84.

8 Cf. Elyot, *Bibl.*, '*Octauianus*, the name of Augustus before that he took on him the monarchy'.

9 i.e. M. Aurelius Antoninus (imp. 161–180), subsequently also called 'Marcus Antoninus' and 'Marcus Aurelius'.

10 i.e. Charlemagne (*c.* 742–814), King of the Franks, Emperor from 800.

Then shall ye note diligently how much it profited to Alexander, who next did succeed him, that he had so wise and virtuous a mother, and that he was brought up among so wise counsellors; also, the manner of his marvellous proceedings in reforming a public weal left unto him corrupted so shamefully, wherein was more difficulty than to begin it where never was any.

Mark also his most noble qualities, and how they were tempered; moreover, the form of his speaking, and how, as he grew in years, so waxed it more mature and serious, sometime abundant, otherwhiles short and compendious, as opportunity served; in his acts and decrees, what justice and prudence were in them contained; what severity he used, sparing neither himself nor his friends or ministers.

Finally, all his life is a wonderful mirror, if it be truly read and justly considered; which, if ye do often look on, ye may thereby attire yourself in <b2r> such fashion as men shall therefore have you in more favour and honour than if ye had on you as rich a garment as the great Turk hath any. Only, for my good will in translating it for you, I desire your gentle report and assistance against them which do hate all things which please not their fantasies.

°<A1r>

<THE IMAGE OF GOVERNANCE>

1. Of what lineage the Emperor Alexander was, and the signs betokening his empire.

Aurelius Alexander, sometime Emperor of Rome, was born in the realm of Syria, in the City of Arcene;[11] whose father had to name Varius, which was lineally descended from the noble house of Metellus the Roman, called Metellus the virtuous.[12] Albeit, some writers suppose that Severus, before he was emperor, was amorous of a woman in Syria, and, by the art of astronomy finding in her nativity that she should be an emperor's mother, he took her to wife and had issue by her, Varius, the father of Alexander.[13] But finally, the progeny of this Emperor is very uncertain; wherefore, in mine opinion, his life and acts be the more to be honoured and marvelled at, considering that, being come of so uncertain a linage, and born so far from the city of Rome and in so barbarous a country, he could so well govern the empire of Rome, which before his time was with pride and other detestable vices extremely corrupted.

The mother of Alexander was called Mammea,[14] a woman of notable wisdom, as it shall hereafter appear by the bringing up of her son and preserving of him, as well from the vices whereunto he was not only provoked, but also well nigh constrained by that most beastly Emperor Varius Helio-<A1v>gabalus, his cousin germane and predecessor.[15] Notwithstanding, there was in that noble woman Mammea a great spice of avarice, in gathering and keeping of treasure,[16] which finally was the only cause of the death both of her and her son.

The said Mammea was daughter of a woman called Mesa,[17] which was born in Phoenicia, in a town called Emesa,[18] and was sister of Julia, wife of the

[11] Modern Arqa, Akkar District, Lebanon.

[12] Cf. SHA, *Alex. Sev.* 1.2 and, for the Metellan derivation, below, p. 197 and n. 92.

[13] SHA, *Alex. Sev.* 5.4, 'si quidem, ut Marius Maximus dixit in Vita Severi, nobilem orientis mulierem Severus, cuius hanc genituram esse compererat ut uxor imperatoris esset, adhuc privatus et non magni satis loci, duxit uxorem. ex qua adfinitate hic Alexander fuit, cui vere per matrem suam consobrinus Varius Heliogabalus fuit'.

[14] Iulia Avita Mamaea (*c.* 180–235), *Augusta* after the accession of her son Alexander in 222.

[15] Elagabalus (imp. 218–222), officially M. Aurelius Antoninus Augustus, born Varius Avitus Bassianus; son of Iulia Soaemias Bassiana, the sister of Alexander's mother Iulia Mamaea.

[16] SHA, *Alex. Sev.* 14.7, 'mulier sancta sed avara et auri atque argenti cupida'.

[17] Iulia Maesa (d.224), sister of Iulia Domna, and grandmother of Elagabalus and Alexander Severus.

[18] Modern Homs, Syria.

°] omitting sigs b2v–b4r, 'THE TABLE', and b4v (woodcut).

Emperor Severus.[19] This Mesa — living Severus and Bassianus, his son[20] — was continually abiding in the courts of those emperors; and, after the decease of Bassianus, she was commanded by Macrinus, then emperor,[21] to depart to her country, albeit the Emperor granted that she should take with her such treasure as she had gathered, which was abundant. She had also two daughters, the one called Semiamira,[22] the other Mammea. Semiamira had a son named Bassianus,[23] which was of excellent beauty. And because he was prelate in the temple of the sun,[24] whom the Phoenices do call Heliogabalus, he was semblably called by that name, having added thereto the name of Varius (which is, in English, 'diverse'), forasmuch as some men suppose that he was conceived of the seed of diverse men, his mother Semiamira being incontinent and, as it were, common to many men during the time that she abode in the Emperor's court with her mother.[25]

Notwithstanding, her son Heliogabalus, by the crafty means of his granddame Mesa, was declared to be the son of the Emperor Bassianus;[26] and, by the favour of the men of war of the Romans, who then murmured and had in hatred the pride and cruelty of Macrinus (who was empe-<A2r>ror after Bassianus) and his son Diadumenus,[27] the said Varius Heliogabalus was advanced unto the empire,[28] who, with voluptuous and monstrous living, in such wise corrupted the city of Rome that therein uneath remained any step of virtue or honesty.

Contrariwise, the other daughter of Mesa, called Mammea, of whom I intend now to write, induced rather by nature and reason than by the example of her vicious mother, so nourished and trained her said son Alexander in virtue and

[19] Iulia Domna (d.217), sister of Iulia Maesa; wife of L. Septimius Severus (imp. 193–211).

[20] Caracalla (imp. 198–217), officially M. Aurelius Severus Antoninus Augustus, born L. Septimius Bassianus.

[21] M. Opellius Macrinus (imp. 217–218).

[22] Iulia Soaemias Bassiana (d.222), in the SHA, 'Symiamira'.

[23] i.e. Elagabalus.

[24] SHA, *Macrinus* 9.1–3, 'Fuit aliqua mulier Maesa sive Varia ex Emesena urbe, soror Iuliae uxoris Severi Pertinacis Afri, quae post mortem Antonini Bassiani ex aulica domo fuerat expulsa per Macrini superbiam; cui quidem omnia concessit Macrinus, quae diu illa collegerat. huic erant duae filiae, Symiamira et Mamaea, quarum maiori filius erat Heliogabalus, qui et Bassiani et Antonini nomen accepit, nam Heliogabalum Phoenices vocant solem. sed Heliogabalus pulchritudine ac statura et sacerdotio conspicuus erat'.

[25] Cf. SHA, *Heliogab.* 2.1–2, 'Hic [sc. Elagabalus] tantum Symiamirae matri deditus fuit, ut sine illius voluntate nihil in re publica faceret, cum ipsa meretricio more vivens in aula omnia turpia exerceret, Antonino autem Caracallo stupro cognita, ita ut hic vel Varius vel Heliogabalus vulgo conceptus putaretur; et aiunt quidam Varii etiam nomen idcirco eidem inditum a condiscipulis, quod vario semine, de meretrice utpote, conceptus videretur.'

[26] i.e. Caracalla.

[27] M. Opellius Antoninus Diadumenianus (imp. 218), in the SHA, 'Diadumenus'.

[28] Cf. SHA, *Heliogab.* 1.4, 'Igitur occiso Macrino eiusque filio Diadumeno, qui pari potestate imperii Antonini etiam nomen acceperat, in Varium Heliogabalum imperium conlatum est, idcirco quod Bassiani filius diceretur'.

learning, that, partly by her education but much more by his own inclination natural, he became one of the most perfect princes that ever governed.

2. The education of Alexander, and how he profited in virtue and doctrine.

Touching the education in childhood of Alexander, his noble mother Mammea failed not to provide, with all diligence and circumspection, that her son mought be nourished in virtue and among honest company; and that, fro the time that he issued out of his infancy, he were continually instructed in all manner of doctrine, both civil and martial; so that, afterward, he of his own courage never suffered any day to pass without exercising himself either in letters or in feats martial.[29]

In the first part of his childhood, he had instructors:[30] Valerius Cordius, Titus Veturius, and Aurelius Phillippus, which afterward wrote his life.[31] Also, in his country, he was taught in Greek by Nebo the <A2v> grammarian, and the rhetorician Serapio, and Stilio the philosopher. At Rome, he had teachers in the Latin tongue: first, in grammar, Scaurinus, a famous master. In rhetoric, he was instructed by Julius Frontinus,[32] Bebius Macrinus,[33] and Julianus Gravianus, albeit he did not so much delight in Latin eloquence as in the Greek, ne did

[29] SHA, *Alex. Sev.* 3.1, 'Alexander igitur, cui Mamaea mater fuit — nam et ita dicitur a plerisque — a prima pueritia artibus bonis inbutus tam civilibus quam militaribus ne unum quidem diem sponte sua transire passus est, quo se non et ad litteras et ad militiam exerceret'.

[30] The list of teachers and comments on them that follow are repeated verbatim from SHA, *Alex. Sev.* 3.2–3, 'nam in prima pueritia', etc., with some variants of spelling. None of the figures named are otherwise known; nonetheless, Elyot reuses some of them below, as indicated, for inventions of his own.

[31] This biographer, 'Aurelius Phillippus', reappears below, pp. 207 and 250.

[32] 'Julius Frontinus' occurs only here in the SHA, as a rhetor. Nonetheless, Elyot uses the figure repeatedly below, inconsistently. 'Frontine' appears as one of Alexander's counsellors, amongst 'the wisest men of the Senate', pp. 202 and 284; in this capacity he serves as the chief interlocutor in the dialogue of public health in chap. 23, p. 234. It may be that Elyot's characterisation in these instances was influenced by his knowledge of the historical figure Sextus Iulius Frontinus (d.104), a public official and writer: of *De aqueductu* (having to do with public health) and of the apophthegmatic *Strategmata*, an English translation of which had just been published (London: Berthelet, 1539) by Richard Morison (*c.* 1510–1556), with a dedication to Henry VIII. A remark elsewhere suggests that Elyot may have confused SHA, 'Iulius Frontinus', with M. Cornelius Fronto (*c.* 95–*c.* 166), the African grammarian and orator, tutor of Marcus Aurelius, who, amongst other honours, held a suffect consulship in 142: *Gov.* 1.9 (Watson, p. 34): 'Alexander the Emperor caused his master Julius Fronto to be consul, which was the highest office and in estate next the Emperor, and also obtained of the Senate that the statue or image of Fronto was set up among the noble princes'. On the other hand, Elyot's 'Frontine' also appears in another inset dialogue as a reprehensible patron, p. 274, provoking Alexander's '*virtus non sanguis*' oration in chap. 33.

[33] Marginalia below, p. 203, appears to attribute the substance of chap. 9 to the same 'Baebius Macrianus' mentioned only here in the SHA.

therein profit so much. But he loved all men that were learned and feared them also, lest they should write of him any thing sharply or to his rebuke. Moreover, he sent oftentimes for those excellent personages, communicating with them things which were done as well privily as also openly, willing them that all that they found to be true they should put it in writing, suffering also them to reprove him when they seemed convenient.[34]

Oftentimes, he made verses in Greek, very pleasant, and was much inclined to music. In the mathematical sciences, that is to say, arithmetic, geometry, and astronomy, he was very well learned; and therefore, diverse times by his commandment, the professors of those sciences purposed openly questions. In divination, he was so excellent that he therein surmounted the diviners of Gascony, Spain, and Hungary. He painted also excellently. Also, he did sing very pleasantly but never in the presence of any other, but only of his servants and pages of his privy chamber. He wrote the lives of good princes in verses, eloquently, and sang them unto the harp and organs, right sweetly;[35] but that did he only for recreating his spirits, when they were troubled with vehement study, as it oftentimes happened by incomparable labour a-<A3r>bout the great affairs of the weal public.

He was of visage fair, and well proportioned in body; large and goodly of personage, and therewith was strong and durable to sustain pains, as he that knew his own strength and in the preserving thereof was not found negligent. Thereto he was amiable, and toward every man gentle,[36] and easy to be spoken unto.

Also, there was in him so much humanity and benevolence that he would oftentimes visit not only the best and the second of his friends and servants, being sick, but also them that were inferiors and of base haviour, desiring them to tell to him freely what they thought of him; whom he would attentively hear. And when he had heard them thoroughly, then, as the thing which was spoken

34 SHA, *Alex. Sev.* 3.4–5, 'nec valde amavit Latinam facundiam, sed amavit litteratos homines vehementer, eos etiam reformidans, ne quid de se asperum scriberent. denique eos, quos dignos ad discendum videbat, singula quaeque, quae publicae privatim agebat, se ipso docente volebat addiscere, si forte ipsi non adfuissent, eaque petebat ut, si vera essent, in litteras mitterent'.

35 SHA, *Alex. Sev.* 27.5–9, 'Facundiae Graecae magis quam Latinae nec versu invenustus et ad musicam pronus, matheseos peritus, et ita quidem ut ex eius iussu mathematici publice proposuerint Romae ac sint professi, ut docerent. haruspicinae quoque peritissimus fuit, orneoscopos magnus, ut et Vascones Hispanorum et Pannoniorum augures vicerit. geometriam fecit. pinxit mire, cantavit nobiliter, sed numquam alio conscio nisi pueris suis testibus. vitas principum bonorum versibus scripsit. lyra, tibia, organo cecinit, tuba etiam, quod quidem imperator numquam ostendit. palaestes primus fuit'.

36 SHA, *Alex. Sev.* 4.4–5, 'Et erat eius corporis, ut praeter venustatem ac virilem, quem hodieque et in pictura et in statuis videmus, decorem inesset staturae militaris robur militis, valitudo eius, qui vim sui corporis sciret ac semper curaret. erat praeterea cunctis hominibus amabilis'.

of did require, he would diligently amend and correct it.[37] And when his mother would say oftentimes to him, 'Sir, ye be too familiar and easy, and therefore ye shall cause the imperial estate to be the less set by', he answered thus: 'But yet shall it be more sure, and continue the longer'.[38]

This was his disposition, proceeding as well of the perfection of his most gentle nature, as of the education of his good and circumspect mother.

Now will I precede to write of his excellent wisdom and virtue, experienced in his authority imperial, wherein was declared the most perfect form of governance that ever was practised by any prince, as I suppose; which shall appear the more manifestly if first I treat somewhat of the most miserable estate of the weal public and, as it seemed, incorrigible at the time that he received the governance thereof, he then being but of the age of sixteen years; which <A3v> being considered and kept in remembrance, this history shall be to the readers thereof (except I be deceived) both pleasant and marvellous, and no less profitable to governors that do prefer their public weal before wilful appetite and particular pleasures.

3. Of the monstrous living of the Emperor Varius Heliogabalus, whereby the city of Rome was corrupted.

°Macrinus the Emperor for his avarice and tyranny being abandoned (or rather, betrayed) of his own people and slain with his son Diadumenus, who in beauty and goodly stature excelled all men of his time, Varius Heliogabalus, of whom I late spake, was advanced unto the empire by the whole consent of the Senate and people of Rome, who gave hasty credence to all reports that were made to the honour and praise of their new princes. Such is the appetites of men, which be moved anon with credulity. For such things as they desire, they covet to hear of and do delight in new tidings, though it be falsely reported.

But Heliogabalus, as soon as he was come unto Rome out of the country of Syria, he immediately declared his beastly nature by ensuing vices most

[37] SHA, *Alex. Sev.* 20.1, 'Moderationis tantae fuit, [...] ut amicos non solum primi aut secundi loci sed etiam inferiores aegrotantes viseret, ut sibi ab omnibus libere quod sentiebant, dici cuperet et, cum dictum esset, audiret et, cum audisset, ita ut res poscebat, emendaret atque corrigeret'.

[38] SHA, *Alex. Sev.* 20.3, 'denique cum ei ob nimiam civilitatem et Mammaea mater et uxor Memmia, Sulpicii consularis viri filia, Catuli neptis, saepe dicerent, "molliorem tibi potestatem et contemptibiliorem imperii fecisti", ille respondit, "sed securiorem atque diuturniorem"', quoted in Eras., *Apoph.* 6.158 (CWE 38, 640). Cf. Elyot, *Gov.* 3.21 (Watson, p. 260), 'And when, for the honour that he did to the Senate and laws, his wife and his mother rebuked him, saying that he should bring the imperial majesty into too low an estate, he answered that it should be the surer and continue the longer'.

° \Tyranny and avarice./

abominable, and advancing the favourers and haunters of the same vices, and enforcing with all his study and puissance to exterminate out of the city of Rome all virtue and honesty, from whence a little before all the world received doctrine and example of honour, concerning as well virtuous manners as martial prowess.

First, in lechery, this Heliogabalus was so insati-<A4r>able that not only he exercised that vice openly, in common bains and bordel houses, with sundry women of diverse degrees and countries; but also, he ordained a senate of common harlots, among whom were diverse noble matrons and damsels of Rome, their husbands or parents not being so hardy to let or rebuke them, unto whom, oftentimes, after he and his ribalds had satiate with them their lecherous appetites, he made a solemn contion or proposition, calling them his companions and exhorting them to set all their study and wit to induce all other women unto the form of their living, declaring expressly that he above all other things most desired that all men and women of the city of Rome should be semblably disposed as he was.

I hold it not convenient to be written in any vulgar tongue how he transformed and abused his proper kind, in such wise as I suppose the most vicious man now living would be ashamed, not only to behold it but also to hear it; and that did he not only secretly or in his house, but also openly, all men that would beholding and looking on him. I omit the residue, which in mine opinion ought never to have been written, for abomination thereof, much more never to have been of any man knowen.

He also promoted to the greatest dignities of the public weal common bawds, notable ribalds, solicitors and furtherers of dishonest appetites, oftentimes cooks and devisers of lecherous confections and sauces. Semblably, by such persons he sold dignities, authorities, and offices in the public weal. He also elected into the Senate, and to the rooms of <A4v> great captains, dukes, and governors of countries, most vile personages, not having regard to any age, gentleness of blood, merit, possessions, or substance. He had of his privy council, in all his acts, two carters, the one named Protogenes, and the other Cordius.[39] His gluttony was almost equal unto his lechery, in so much as he therein vanquished Vitellius, of whom it is written that at one supper he was served with seven thousand fishes and five thousand fowls.[40] Heliogabalus,

[39] Cf. SHA, *Heliogab.* 6.1–3, 'Vendidit et honores et dignitates et potestates tam per se quam per omnes servos ac libidinum ministros. In senatum legit sine discrimine aetatis, census, generis pecuniae merito, militaribus etiam praepositurís et tribunatibus et legationibus et ducatibus venditis, etiam procurationibus et Palatinis officiis. Aurigas Protogenen et Cordium primo in certamine curruli socios, post in omni vita et actu participes habuit'.

[40] Aulus Vitellius (imp. 69), one of the emperors of 'the year of four emperors'. The remark is translated from Suet., *Vit.* 13.2, 'Famosissima super ceteras fuit cena data ei adventicia a fratre, in qua duo milia lectissimorum piscium, septem avium apposita traduntur'; cf.

when he sojourned nigh to the sea, he would never be served with sea-fish; but, being in places far distant from the sea, he caused all his household to be served with most delicate sea-fish.[41]

It abhorreth me to express his beastly living; but, to the intent that the excellent virtues of his most noble successor shall be more apparent and commendable — like as all thing that is vile or coarse doth set forth more pleasantly that thing which is precious and fine — it is requisite that I describe this monster in some part as he was, albeit I do not tell everything that I have read of him, as well for that it shall be to good men odious to hear, as also it mought happen to incend the wanton and lewd courages of some readers, inclined to semblable qualities, which (God knoweth) is much contrary unto my purpose.

But to return to this monstrous Emperor, which consumed days and nights in lechery and gluttony, having some day all his company served with the brains of ostriches and a strange fowl called *phenocopteri*; another day, with the tongues of popinjays, nightingales, and other sweet sin-<B1r>ging birds; oftentimes, with the milts of most delicate fishes.[42] I omit other light fantasies, whereof I have written in my book called *The Governour*, where I treat of sobriety.[43]

Finally, it is remembered that he was never two days together served with one meat, nor ware twice one garment, nor companied twice with one woman, except his wife. As often as he removed in progress, there followed him six hundred chariots laded only with bawds, common harlots, and ribalds.[44] This company had he instead of counsellors, and so delighted in this form of living, that he said oftentimes that, if he had a son, he would ordain for him masters that should compel him to live in semblable fashion.[45]

Elyot, *Gov.* 3.22 (Watson, p. 265), 'In like manner, who will not have in extreme detestation the insatiable gluttony of Vitellius, Fabius Gurges, Apicius, and diverse other, to which cormorants neither land, water, ne air, mought be sufficient?'

[41] SHA, *Heliogab.* 23.8, 'Ad mare piscem numquam comedit, in longissimis a mari locis omnia marina semper exhibuit', translated also in Elyot, *Gov.* 3.22 (Watson, p. 266), 'Who, being at Rome or far from the sea, would eat only sea fish, and, when he sojourned nigh to the sea, he would touch no fish but which was taken out of the river of Tiber or other places of equal or of more distance'. SHA, *Heliogab.* 29.8–30.6, likewise concerned with the same Emperor's 'beastly living' but not used verbatim by Elyot, is quoted in full in Eras., *Adagia* 2.2.65, *Sybaritica mensa*, 'A Sybaritic table' (CWE 33, 108).

[42] *Phenocopteri* are flamingos, the term being taken from SHA, *Heliogab.* 20.6, 'foenicopterum'; cf. Suet., *Calig.* 22.3; Plin., *NH* 10.133. Cf. Elyot, *Gov.* 3.22 (Watson, p. 266), 'Also, he would have dishes of meat made of camels' heels, the combs of cocks newly cut, the tongues of peacocks and nightingales, partridges' eggs, and other things hard for to come by, whereto be no English names founden, as I suppose, apt to the true signification'.

[43] Elyot, *Gov.* 3.22, 'Of Sobriety in Diet' (Watson, pp. 265–66).

[44] SHA, *Heliogab.* 31.5–6, 'imperator vero etiam sescenta vehicula dicitur duxisse [...]. Causa vehiculorum erat lenonum, lenarum, meretricum, exoletorum, subactorum etiam bene vasatorum multitudo'.

[45] SHA, *Heliogab.* 32.3, 'Idem dixisse fertur, Si habuero heredem, dabo illi tutorem, qui illum haec facere cogat, quae ipse feci facturusque sum'.

To these monstrous vices he added to cruelty, in putting to death diverse noble senators. Also, using the counsel of witches and enchanters, he made his sacrifice with young children, and, violently ravishing from the noble men and women of Italy their young infants, he caused in his presence their bodies to be opened, they living, and most cruelly searched in their tender bowels[46] for his most damnable destiny.

He had in special favour one named Zoticus, who, for familiarity used between them, was taken of all the chief officers for the Emperor's husband. This Zoticus, under the colour of the said familiarity, sold all the sayings and doings of the Emperor, intending to accumulate abundance of riches, by promising fair to many men, but finally deceiving all men. For coming out of the Emperor's privy chamber, after that he had heard every man speak that sued unto him, to some he would say, 'Thus said I to the Emperor of you'; unto another, <B1v> 'Of you I heard the Emperor say thus today'; to diverse he would say, 'Your matter or request shall come °th<u>s to pass', as is the fashion of such manner of persons, which, being from a base condition admitted of princes into overmuch familiarity, they sell the fame and renome of their masters.[47]

Such as I have rehearsed were the counsellors of Heliogabalus, for all wise and virtuous men he deadly hated. Wherefore, he banished the noble man Sabinus, unto whom Ulpianus the great lawyer wrate his books;[48] and semblably, he put out of the city the said Ulpian, only because he was named a good man, and caused Silvinus, the noble orator, whom he had made master to Alexander, to be put to death.[49] And he ordained a tumbler to be great master of his household;

[46] Cf. SHA, *Heliogab.* 8.1–2, 'Caedit et humanas hostias lectis ad hoc pueris nobilibus et decoris per omnem Italiam patrimis et matrimis [...]. Omne denique magorum genus aderat illi operabaturque cottidie hortante illo [...] cum inspiceret exta puerilia'.

[47] SHA, *Heliogab.* 10.2–4, 'Zoticus sub eo tantum valuit ut ab omnibus officiorum principibus sic haberetur quasi domini maritus. erat praeterea idem Zoticus qui hoc familiaritatis genere abutens omnia Heliogabali dicta et facta venderet fumis, quam maxime divitias enormes parans, cum aliis minaretur, aliis polliceretur, omnes falleret egrediensque ab illo singulos adiret dicens, "de te hoc locutus sum", "de te hoc audivi", "de te hoc futurum est". ut sunt homines huiusmodi, qui, si admissi fuerint ad nimiam familiaritatem principum, famam non solum malorum sed et bonorum principum vendunt et qui stultitia vel innocentia imperatorum, qui hoc non perspiciunt, infami rumigeratione pascuntur'. Eras., *Adagia* 1.3.41, *Fumos vendere*, 'To sell smoke' (CWE 31, 270–71) quotes the same 'Zoticus' episode likewise in full.

[48] Cf. SHA, *Heliogab.* 16.2–3, including 'Sabinum consularem virum, ad quem libros Ulpianus scripsit'. 'Sabinus', evidently an invention of the SHA, reappears repeatedly but only as a minor figure: see below, pp. 202, 206, 285, and 301. 'Ulpian', who figures more prominently in the work of the SHA and in what follows of Elyot, represents the historical jurist and state-official Domitius Ulpianus (*c.* 170–223).

[49] SHA, *Heliogab.* 16.4, 'Removit et Ulpianum iuris consultum ut bonum virum et Silvinum rhetorem, quem magistrum Caesaris fecerat. Et Silvinus quidem occisus est, Ulpianus vero

° thus] this *A B*

a carter named Gordius he made captain of his guard.[50] °Another tumbler he made chief captain of an army. The greatest rooms and affairs of the empire he committed to minstrels, players of interludes, and dizzards. To his bondmen and most vile servants, as they excelled in abomination, so preferred he them to the governance of realms and provinces.[51] Also, of his rabble of brothels, to some he gave the rule and governance of the youth of the city, some he made rulers of the Senate, to other he gave pre-eminence and sovereignty over all them that were gentlemen.

Finally, he intended to destroy all virtue and to constrain all men to live beastly as he did; and for that cause, he commanded that the noble Alexander, his aunt's son, should be slain either violently or by some poison,[52] forasmuch as he perceived him to decline from his appetite. But Alexander was alway preserved by the <B2r> providence of God, who inclined the minds of the Senate and people to his preservation. For nothing availeth the malice of tyrants against innocents[53] and good men, where almighty God will not have them to perish.

Wherefore, this monstrous Emperor, desiring the destruction of Alexander, procured his own death, agreeable with his abominable living. For his own servants and soldiers, which were prepared for the guard of his person, dreading lest the people making insurrection, that they should be partners of his mischievous end, being also tedious of his abominations, conspired to deliver the commonweal of him[54] and suddenly apprehended his adherents and familiars and, with sundry torments, did put them to death. Finally, pursuing Heliogabalus to a privy or draught whereunto he fled, there they slew him[55] and his mother Semiamira. And afterward, his horrible carrain, being drawn throughout the city with hooks, was of all the people defiled with ordure and other matter foul and stinking, and at the last was brought with all kinds of reproach to the common draughts of the city, whereinto they would have

reservatus'. 'Silvinus' the orator occurs here only in both the SHA and Elyot.

50 SHA, *Heliogab.* 12.1, 'Ad praefecturam praetorii saltorem, qui histrionicam Romae fecerat, adscivit, praefectum vigilum Cordium aurigam fecit'.

51 Cf. Hdn. 5.7.7, 'A man, who in his youth had been a dancer in public in the theatre at Rome, was appointed military prefect [...]. He assigned positions of the highest responsibility in the empire to charioteers and comedy actors and mimers. His slaves and freedmen, who perhaps excelled in some foul activity, he appointed as governors of consular provinces'.

52 SHA, *Heliogab.* 13.8, 'misit et ad nutritores eius, quibus imperavit sub praemiorum spe atque honorum, ut eum occiderent quo vellent modo, vel in balneis vel veneno vel ferro'.

53 SHA, *Heliogab.* 14.1, 'Sed nihil agunt improbi contra innocentes'.

54 SHA, *Heliogab.* 16.5, 'Sed milites et maxime praetorianus [...] facta conspiratione ad liberandam rem publicam'.

55 SHA, *Heliogab.* 17.1, 'Post hoc in eum impetus factus est atque in latrina, ad quam confugerat, occisus'.

° \Herodi. 5./] *B* : *A om*

thrown him. But forasmuch as the hole of the draught could not receive him, they tied him to a stone of great weight and threw him into the river of Tiber, to the intent that he should never be buried.[56]

This was the worthy and convenient end of this most beastly and unclean monster, who, with the emperors Nero, Caligula, Domitian, and Commodus, his predecessors,[57] was a notable and commodious example to all princes succeeding to declare that, notwithstanding their majesty and puissance, they for their vices abominable <B2v> were first hated and afterward slain and dishonoured by their proper subjects. And in this history it is to be specially noted that, notwithstanding that he not only permitted but also willed his subjects to live in a licence and without correction for sin; moreover, used toward them such liberality that he fed them with most delicate and exquisite meats, gave unto them money in abundance, and also, to them which dined or supped with him, he gave all the vessel and plate, were it of gold or silver, wherewith he was served, and made many other distributions to the whole people wonderful sumptuous — yet the Romans, notwithstanding, abhorring in him their own proper vices or, rather, being therewith satiate or tedious, they finally slew him, as is before written, after that he had reigned six years and being then but in the twenty-first year of his age.

4. How Alexander was made emperor, and of his wonderful temperance in refusing diverse great honours.

Immediately after the death of Heliogabalus, the Senate and people of Rome, being surprised with °incredib<l>e joy, used all diligence and speed that Aurelius Alexander, whom they had defended from death, mought forthwith as very emperor receive all authority and honour that pertained to the imperial majesty. Wherefore, they contended among themselves which of them mought apply to him most titles and names of dignity. Wherefore, he was the first that received at one time all ornaments and tokens of honour, °a<d>ding thereto the name of <B3r> Caesar which, a few years before, he had received, but much rather °<of> his honest life and virtuous manners; whereby he obtained such favour of all men that, when Heliogabalus would have slain him, he could not

[56] Cf. SHA, *Heliogab.* 17.1–2, 'tractus deinde per publicum; addita iniuria cadaveri est, ut id in cloacam milites mitterent. sed cum non cepisset cloaca fortuito, per pontem Aemilium, adnexo pondere ne fluitaret, in Tiberim abiectum est, ne umquam sepeliri posset'.

[57] The 'slain and dishonoured' emperors listed here but not given biographies in Elyot, *Bibl.*, are Tit. Flavius Domitianus (imp. 81–96) and L. Aurelius Commodus (imp. 180–192); below, p. 252, both are used again as examples of bad successor-sons.

° incredible] *B* : incredibie *A*
° adding] addynge *B* : aydynge *A*
° of] *A om B om*

bring it to pass, the men of arms resisting and the Senate obstinately refusing. But all °these were but trifles in regard that he approved himself worthy, whom the Senate ought to save harmless, whom the men of war desired to be in safeguard, and, generally by the sentence and opinion of all good men, was elect to be emperor,[58] being then but of the age of sixteen years.

Notwithstanding, he was then of such a wonderful soberness that, where the Senate would have given to him the surname of Antonine — which name, for the incomparable virtues that were in Antoninus Pius and Antoninus the philosopher, late emperors, was usurped of other emperors following, for a principal title of honour — he humbly refused it;[59] semblably did he the name of great Alexander, saying openly unto the Senate, 'I beseech you, honourable fathers, do not call me unto this necessity, that I should be compelled to satisfy you in the merits of so high a name as Antonine is. For if ye seek for goodness in a prince, who was better or more virtuous than Antoninus Pius? If ye seek learning, who was more wise or cunning than Marcus Antoninus? And who was more harmless than Verus Antoninus?[60] Noble fathers, these high names of honour be burdenous and too grievous for my youth to sustain. For who will gladly hear a dumb man called Tully, an idiot Varro, a tyrant Metellus?[61] And as touching the name of great A-<B3v>lexander, it is much more incongruent, considering that with better reason I mought have taken the name of Antonine, induced by colour either of affinity or else of equal estate in the imperial majesty. But the name of great Alexander, wherefore should I have it? What

[58] SHA, *Alex. Sev.* 2.3–5, 'certatim denique omnia decreta sunt et nominum genera et potestatum. primus denique et omnium cuncta insignia et honorificentiae genera simul recepit suffragante sibimet Caesaris nomine, quod iam ante aliquot annos meruerat, et magis suffragante vita et moribus, cum illi magnum conciliasset favorem, quod Heliogabalus occidere conatus est nec potuit et militibus repugnantibus et senatu refragante. atque haec parva sunt, nisi quod dignum se exhibuit, quem senatus servaret, quem salvum milites cuperent, quem omnium bonorum sententia principem diceret'.

[59] This episode of Alexander's oration derives from SHA, *Alex. Sev.* 6.1–12.1, beginning 'Interest relegere orationem, qua nomen Antonini et Magni delatum sibi a senatu recusavit', with much abbreviation and very loosely, except as indicated. Cf. Elyot, *Gov.* 3.21 (Watson, p. 259), 'Alexander, Emperor of Rome, so in this virtue excelled that, being elect and made emperor at sixteen years of his age, when the Senate and people for his virtue, wherein he passed all other, would have him called the great Alexander and father of the country, which of all names was highest, he with a wonderful gravity refused it, saying that it behooved that those names were obtained by merits and ripeness of years'.

[60] SHA, *Alex. Sev.* 8.4, 'ne, quaeso, patres conscripti, ne me ad hanc certaminis necessitatem vocetis, ut ego cogar tanto nomini satis facere', and 9.1, 'Antoninorum nomen vel iam numen potius quantum fuerit, meminit vestra clementia: si pietatem, quid Pio sanctius? si doctrinam, quid Marco prudentius? si innocentiam, quid Vero simplicius?'

[61] SHA, *Alex. Sev.* 9.4–5, 'haec enim nomina insignia onerosa sunt. quis enim Ciceronem dic erat mutum? quis indoctum Varronem? quis impium Metellum?'

° these] those *B*

great things have I yet done to deserve that name, which Alexander the Greek after great enterprises, Pompey the Roman after many triumphs, had given unto them? Cease therefore, honourable fathers, to confer to me honours above my merits.[62] And since ye will have me called great, suffer me to be one of you, who in very deed be great in honour and perfect magnificence.'

This moderate and sober answer, of so young a prince, inflamed immediately the hearts of the Senate and people much more to honour him than if he had received those strange names, and from that time he had the renome of constance and gravity. Moreover, for his great austerity again the presumption and lightness of his soldiers and servants, he was named of them Severus, which betokeneth constant or sharp in punishment; which name in his time got him much reverence and afterward great fame and renome among his successors.[63]

Finally, this most towardly prince, with incredible joy, was triumphantly conveyed by all the Senate and people, to the imperial palace,[64] where, being left, he prepared himself to the reformation of the whole empire, then being in ruin. <B4r>

5. The example of virtue given by Alexander in the form of his living and daily customs.

Immediately after that Alexander, by the consent of the Senate and people, was stablished in the imperial authority and for his excellent goodness was most ardently beloved of the multitude — also, the remembrance of Heliogabalus and his adherents for their detestable vices being everywhere hated and with detestation abhorred — this noble young Emperor, taking then opportunity to restore the public weal to her pristinate form, with the majesty imperial late violated and well-nigh perished through the negligence of the said monster;

[62] SHA, *Alex. Sev.* 11.3–4, 'facilius fuit, patres conscripti, ut Antoninorum nomen acciperem, aliquid enim vel adfinitati deferrem vel consortioni nominis imperialis. Magni vero nomen cur accipiam? quid enim iam magnum feci? cum id Alexander post magna gesta, Pompeius vero post magnos triumphos acceperit. quiescite igitur, venerandi patres, et vos ipsi magnifici unum me de vobis esse censete, quam Magni nomen ingerite'.

[63] SHA, *Alex. Sev.* 12.3–5, 'multo clarior visus est alienis nominibus non receptis quam si recepisset; atque ex eo constantiae ac plenae gravitatis famam obtinuit, si quidem uni iuveni vel adulescenti potius senatus totus persuadere non potuit. sed quamvis senatu rogante non potuerit persuaderi, ut vel Antonini vel Magni nomina susciperet, tamen ob ingentem vigorem animi et mirandam singularemque constantiam contra militum insolentiam Severi nomen a militibus eidem inditum est. quod illi ingentem in praesentia reverentiam, magnam apud posteros gloriam peperit', and 25.2, 'nam et Severus est appellatus a militibus ob austeritatem et in animadversibus asperior in quibusdam fuit'. Cf. below, pp. 210, 262 and nn. The appellation was in fact used to make a point of Alexander's kinship with his predecessor Emperor Septimius Severus.

[64] SHA, *Alex. Sev.* 12.2, 'Dimisso senatu, cum et alia multa eo die essent acta, quasi triumphans domum se recepit'.

he, by the counsel of his wise and virtuous mother Mammea, first purged his own palace, excluding out of his court and all offices dishonest and infamed personages, and by no means would suffer to be in his household any other than by all men should be thought necessary. Moreover, he openly protested, making an oath, that he would never have a superfluous number of servants, to the intent that he would not grieve the public weal with his provision; saying, 'That emperor is a shrewd pupil that feedeth with the bowels of his commons men which be not necessary nor yet profitable to the weal public'.[65]

How much he hated uncleanness of living he well declared when he commanded that no woman infamed should salute or visit his wife or his mother.[66] All his life was a perfect example of temperance. <B4v> His apparel was wonderful clean but not too sumptuous and, after some men's opinion, more meaner than to his estate appertained. Semblable moderation the empress his wife observed. Finally, during his time he used diligent correction of his own manners, wherefore all noble men assayed to follow him; and all honourable women ensued the empress's example.[67]

Moreover, this Emperor was of such an incomparable mansuetude that he commanded that no man should write unto him in any other form than should be written to a private person, reserving the name of emperor; and also prohibited that no man should call him 'Lord'[68] but salute him as one of the

65 SHA, *Alex. Sev.* 14.7, 'fecit cuncta cum matre', and 15.1–3, 'Ubi ergo Augustum agere coepit, primum removit omnes iudices a re publica et a ministeriis atque muneribus, quos inpurus ille ex genere hominum turpissimo provexerat; deinde senatum et equestrem ordinem purgavit. ipsas deinde tribus et eos, qui militaribus nituntur praerogativis, purgavit et Palatium suum comitatumque omnem abiectis ex aulico ministerio cunctis obscenis et infamibus nec quemquam passus est esse in Palatinis nisi necessarium hominem. iure iurando deinde se constrinxit, ne quem adscriptum, id est vacantivum, haberet, ne annonis rem publicam gravaret, dicens malum publicum esse imperatorem, qui ex visceribus provincialium homines non necessarios nec rei publicae utiles pasceret'. SHA, *Alex. Sev.* 15.2–3 is quoted in Eras., *Apoph.* 6.144 (CWE 38, 636). And another translation of some of the same passage (SHA, *Alex. Sev.* 15.1–2) is in Elyot, *Gov.* 3.10 (Watson, p. 232), 'Alexander also, Emperor, for his incomparable gravity called Severus, being but of the age of eighteen years when he first was made emperor, was inclined to so incredible labours, that where he found the noble city of Rome, then mistress of the world, thoroughly corrupted with most abominable vices by the most shameful example and living of that detestable monster, Varius Heliogabalus, next emperor before him, a great parte of the Senate and nobility being resolved in to semblable vices, the chivalry dispersed, martial prowess abandoned, and well-nigh the majestic imperial dissolved and brought in contempt, this noble young prince Alexander, inflamed with the zeal of the pristinate honour of the Romans, laying apart utterly all pleasures and quietness, wholly gave his wit and body to study and travails intolerable'. Cf. also below, n. 108.

66 SHA, *Alex. Sev.* 25.10, 'a mulieribus famosis matrem et uxorem suam salutari vetuit'.

67 SHA, *Alex. Sev.* 41.2, 'prorsus censuram suis temporibus de propriis moribus gessit. imitati sunt eum magni viri et uxorem eius matronae pernobiles'.

68 SHA, *Alex. Sev.* 4.1, 'Dominum se appellari vetuit. epistolas ad se quasi ad privatum scribi iussit servato tantum nomine imperatoris'.

senators, and in this form, *Ave Alexander*/ 'Be glad Alexander'.[69] And if a man had used in gesture or speech any manner of flattery, he was either put back, if the place so required, or else with a great laughter was mocked by them which were present. And forasmuch as he would not be saluted or visited but of them which were honest and of good fame, he decreed that no man should enter into his palace but only such as knew themselves uncorrupted with notable vices; and caused to be proclaimed that no person knowing himself to be a thief or extortioner should be so hardy to salute the Emperor, upon pain of losing his life.[70] He had this sentence oftentimes in his mouth: 'Thieves only complain of poverty, thereby coveting to hide their mischievous living'.[71] Finally, no day passed wherein he did not something charitably, gently, or honourably, but that <C1r> things he did in such wise as therein he neither consumed ne wasted the common treasure.[72]

He procured seldom any condemnations; but those that were done, he never pardoned.[73] The tributes or fee-farms of cities, he often times gave to the repairing and building of the same cities. Moreover, to diverse poor men of whose virtue or wisdom he had perfect knowledge, he lent of his treasure to purchase lands, receiving again his own money only of the rents of the same lands, and let the said persons have the possession and all other profits.[74]

[69] SHA, *Alex. Sev.* 17.4, 'Salutabatur autem nomine, hoc est "Ave, Alexander"'.

[70] SHA, *Alex. Sev.* 18.1–2, 'Si quis caput flexisset aut blandius aliquid dixisset, ut adulator vel abiciebatur, si loci eius qualitas pateretur, vel ridebatur ingenti cachinno, si eius dignitas graviori subiacere non posset iniuriae. salutatus consessum obtulit omnibus senatoribus atque adeo nisi honestos et bonae famae homines ad salutationem non admisit iussitque [...] per praeconem edici, ut nemo salutaret principem, qui se furem esse nosset, ne aliquando detectus capitali supplicio subderetur'. Eras., *Panegyricus* (CWE 27, 41) also quotes SHA, *Alex. Sev.* 18.1 (in a passage where he uses the term *Gnathones* for flatterers), and again in *Institutio principis Christiani* 2 (CWE 27, 249); cf. also Eras., *Adagia* 1.3.41, *Fumos vendere*, 'To sell smoke' (CWE 31, 272): 'If only our princes would take care to imitate Alexander Severus. He [...] was so violently opposed to flatterers, informers, dishonest judges, sellers of smoke and all such pests of Courts, that he was implacable towards them, though otherwise a man of the mildest character'.

[71] SHA, *Alex. Sev.* 18.4, 'erat praeterea haec illius sententia solos fures de paupertate conqueri, dum volunt scelera vitae suae tegere', quoted in Eras., *Apoph.* 6.157 (CWE 38, 640).

[72] SHA, *Alex. Sev.* 20.4, 'dies denique numquam transiit, quando non aliquid mansuetum, civile, pium fecit, sed ita ut aerarium non everteret'; possibly recalling Suet., *Tit.* 8.1, 'Moreover, in the case of other requests made of him, it was his fixed rule not to let anyone go away without hope. Even when his household officials warned him that he was promising more than he could perform, he said that it was not right for anyone to go away sorrowful from an interview with his emperor. On another occasion, remembering at dinner that he had nothing for anybody all day, he gave utterance to that memorable and praiseworthy remark: "Friends, I have lost a day"'.

[73] SHA, *Alex. Sev.* 21.1, 'Condemnationes et raras esse iussit et, quae factae fuerant, non indulsit'.

[74] Cf. SHA, *Alex. Sev.* 21.2, 'faenus publicum trientarium exercuit, ita ut pauperibus

He would not suffer any of his court to wear any garment mixed with gold[75] or otherwise precious or costly, nor he himself delighted in rich apparel, saying that governance was in virtue and not in beauty or costly apparel.

At his table, he used no gold but pure beryl, and crystal, and other like matter to drink in. He exceeded not two hundred pound-weight of silver vessel in all his household.[76]

Precious stones that were given to him he caused to be sold, esteeming it to be a womanly appetite to have such jewels,[77] which he mought neither give to his soldiers ne, in having them, find any profit. Wherefore, on a time when an ambassador had given to the empress two orient pearls of wonderful greatness, he commanded them to be sold; and, when no man could be found that would give as much as the price was esteemed — lest any evil example should proceed of the empress, if she should be seen to wear that thing which no man could buy — he caused them to be hanged at the ears of the image of Ve-<Civ>nus;[78] thereby declaring that such things either for the inestimable price was meeter for gods than for men, or for the unprofitable beauty thereof served only for persons of wanton appetites, whereof Venus was goddess and patroness.

No less temperance used he in meats and drinks, never exceeding four sundry kinds of flesh and fish at one meal, and those with a great moderation and reason. He drank wine not scarcely nor too much, but competently.[79]

In feasts or banqueting, he never would have any wanton pastime. His pleasure was to behold birds fighting together, and therefore he had in his garden places where birds of sundry kinds were enclosed and kept, wherein he took singular pleasure.[80] Notwithstanding, to the intent that he would in

plerisque sine usuris pecunias dederit ad agros emendos, reddendas de fructibus'.

75 SHA, *Alex. Sev.* 34.5, 'auratam vestem ministrorum vel in publico convivio nullus habuit'.

76 Cf. SHA, *Alex. Sev.* 34.1, 'In convivio aurum nescivit, pocula mediocria sed nitida semper habuit. ducentarum librarum argenti pondus ministerium eius numquam transit' and 41.4, 'et cum argentum in ministerio plus ducentis libris non haberet nec plures ministros'.

77 SHA, *Alex. Sev.* 41.1, 'Gemmarum quod fuit, vendidit et aurum in aerarium contulit dicens gemmas viris usui non esse', quoted in Eras., *Apoph.* 6.160 (CWE 38, 641).

78 SHA, *Alex. Sev.* 51.1–3, 'Dona regia in templis posuit; gemmas sibi oblatas vendidit muliebre esse aestimans gemmas possidere, quae neque militi dari possint neque a viro haberi. cum quidam legatus uniones duos uxori eius per ipsum obtulisset magni ponderis et inusitatae mensurae, vendi eos iussit. cum pretium non invenirent, ne exemplum malum a regina nasceretur, si eo uteretur, quod emi non posset, inauribus Veneris eos dicavit'. Something of the same passage is used in Elyot, *Gov.* 3.21 (Watson, pp. 259–60), 'The same prince also would not suffer his empress to use in her apparel any richer stones than other ladies; and if any were given her, he either caused them to be sold or else gave them unto temples, affirming that the example of pomp and inordinate expenses should not proceed of the Emperor's wife'.

79 SHA, *Alex. Sev.* 37.11, 'ipse cibo plurimo referciebatur, vino neque parce neque copiose, adfatim tamen'.

80 Cf. SHA, *Alex. Sev.* 41.5–7.

nothing aggrieve the market in feeding them with corn, he had servants that provided for them eggs of wildfowl and culvers.[81]

In honest recreation, he was marvellous merry and pleasant, amiable in communication, at the table so gentle that every man mought demand of him what he would.[82] And to the intent that he would be the more circumspect, he ordained the wise man Ulpian, one of the greatest interpreters of the law civil, to be in the stead of his tutor, his mother repugning thereat at the first; but after, she gave him therefore great praises.[83] When he dined or supped abroad, he had ever with him Ulpian or other well learned men, to the intent he would then hear histories containing learning, wherewith he said that he was both recreate and also fed. If he sat privily, he <C2r> had a book by him and read therein oftentimes, but that was in Greek, for the more part. In open feasts, he used the same simplicity that he did in his palace.[84]

He so much had flattery in hatred that he would not hear orators or poets speak anything to his praise, calling it foolishness. But he heard gladly orations persuading to virtue, and also the acts of other good princes, as well Romans as Greeks, specially the praise of Alexander the Great, which conquered the more part of the world. He went oftentimes openly to the common schools to hear rhetoricians and poets, Greeks and Latins. He heard also orators reciting causes which they had prosecuted, either before him or before the great officers.[85]

Finally, he so much esteemed and favoured learning that he ordained great salaries to be given to rhetoricians, teachers of grammar, physicians, astronomers, geometricians, musicians, devisers of building °and engines; and provided for them places to read in and scholars also, giving to poor and honest men's children that heard them their commons free. With like charity, he retained advocates in poor men's causes; and such lawyers as freely did help

[81] SHA, *Alex. Sev.* 41.7, 'et ne eorum pastus gravaret annonam, servos habuit vectigales, qui eos ex ovis ac pullicenis ac pipionibus alerent'.

[82] SHA, *Alex. Sev.* 44.1, 'In iocis dulcissimus fuit, in fabulis amabilis, in conviviis comis, ita ut quisque posceret quod vellet'.

[83] SHA, *Alex. Sev.* 51.4, 'Ulpianum pro tutore habuit, primum repugnante matre, deinde gratias agente'. For Ulpian, see above, p. 184 and n. 48.

[84] SHA, *Alex. Sev.* 34.6–8, 'cum inter suos convivaretur, aut Ulpianum aut doctos homines adhibebat, ut haberet fabulas litteratas, quibus se recreari dicebat et pasci. habebat, cum privatim convivaretur, et librum in mensa et legebat, sed Graece magis. Latinos autem poetas lectitabat. publica convivia ea simplicitate egit, qua privata'.

[85] Cf. SHA, *Alex. Sev.* 35.1–3, 'Oratores et poetas non sibi panegyricos dicentes, quod exemplo Nigri Pescennii stultum ducebat, sed aut orationes recitantes aut facta veterum canentes libenter audivit, libentius tamen, si quis ei recitavit Alexandri Magni laudes aut item bonorum retro principum aut magnorum urbis Romae virorum. ad Athenaeum audiendorum et Graecorum et Latinorum rhetorum vel poetarum causa frequenter processit. audivit autem etiam forenses oratores causas recitantes, quas vel apud ipsum vel apud praefectos urbis egerant'.

° \Architecti./] *A* : *B om*

poor men with their counsel and labour, he rewarded them with corn and wine to maintain their household.[86]

He also yearly perused his laws and reformed them, according as occasion changed or happened. And he himself diligently and rigorously executed them in his own person and servants, and therewith was of such gentleness that he would offer to give <C2v> place to the ancient senators that came unto him and would suffer no man of honesty that pressed to speak with him to be repelled. He never did wrong to any person; semblably, of wrongs he was a vehement and sharp persecutor, saving that in his own wrong he was much more tractable than in a stranger's.

If he lay not with his wife, he was in the morning betime in his privy closet, where were set the image of Christ; also, the pictures of Abraham, Socrates, Apollonius, and other °<a>ncient and virtuous men; where, by the space of half an hour, he remained in prayers.[87] And for this devotion and marvellous example of living, he was had of all men in wonderful reverence. Albeit, his temperate and sober living being thought of some men not agreeable nor congruent to his majesty, he was exhorted to advance his estate, both in princely port and more sumptuous manner of living, leaving his affability and straight observation of his laws, as it shall appear by letters following, mutually written between him and his counsellors.

6. The letter of Gordian the senator to the Emperor Alexander.

There was in the city of Rome an honourable senator named Gordian,[88] who

[86] Cf. SHA, *Alex. Sev.* 44.4–5, 'Rhethoribus, grammaticis, medicis, haruspicibus, mathematicis, mechanicis, architectis salaria instituit et auditoria decrevit et discipulos cum annonis pauperum filios modo ingenuos dari iussit. etiam in provinciis oratoribus forensibus multum detulit, plerisque etiam annonas dedit, quos constitisset gratis agere'.

[87] SHA, *Alex. Sev.* 29.2, 'si facultas esset, id est si non cum uxore cubuisset, matutinis horis in larario suo, in quo et divos principes sed optimos electos et animas sanctiores, in quis Apollonium et, quantum scriptor suorum temporum dicit, Christum, Abraham et Orfeum et huiusmodi ceteros habebat ac maiorum effigies, rem divinam faciebat'; cf. below, p. 249 and n. 168, adapting the same passage; also, Eras., *Adagia* 2.1.15, *Leporem non edit*, 'He has not eaten hare' (CWE 33, 26). The Neopythagorean holy man Apollonius of Tyana (*c.* 15–*c.* 100) was the subject of a biography written *c.* 217 by Philostratus at the behest of Iulia Domna, wife of the Emperor Septimius Severus; also, sister of Iulia Maesa, Alexander's grandmother, both mentioned above p. 177 the biography was first printed in 1501 and frequently thereafter.

[88] The figure is the invented 'Aelius Gordianus Gordiani imperatoris pater', distinctive of the Erasmian edition of SHA, *Alex. Sev.* 68.1. Nevertheless, for the characterisation, Elyot appears to use properties of the Emperor Gordian I (imp. 238) as he is represented in SHA, *Gordiani tres*: the family (2.2), the consulship (2.4, 4.1), and reputation for learning (3.1–4, 7.1). For Gordian, see also below, pp. 202, 206, 267–69 with another lengthy oration, and 284.

° ancient] *B* : uncient *A*

had sometime been consul (which was the highest dignity next to the Emperor) and was the richest man of all the city, having the greatest possessions in the countries adjoining that any man had, the Emperor only except, and also was a man of excellent learning <C3r> and wisdom.

Wherefore, during the life of Heliogabalus, this Gordian, having his monstrous life in abomination and perceiving the majesty of the empire to decay by his negligent and dissolute living and that there was no hope of remedy, observing the time, he by little and little withdrew him into such places as he had of his own, far from the city, feigning himself to be grieved with such diseases as did debilitate his wits, and therefore required to be far from resort of company and much noise, which, being in the city, he mought not eschew. This excuse the Emperor Heliogabalus heard gladly, as he that feared and also hated the gravity and authority of Gordian, and therefore licensed him to depart and remain in the country as long as it liked him, thinking by his absence to be more at liberty and to live more wantonly.

So, with the Emperor's favour or, rather, folly, Gordian quietly and also pleasantly passed the time that Heliogabalus lived; and when he heard of the death of that monster, he would not return to the city but sent his consent of election to the Senate after that he knew that, by assent of the people, Alexander was named emperor. And when he was required of the Senate to come personally, he aggravated his impediment, alleging sickness, although, indeed, neither in body nor wit he was in any part diseased; but, knowing Alexander to be very young and also cousin germane to Heliogabalus, he drad in him both the one and the other, fearing lest nature should prevail again education when he should come to an absolute liberty and be out of the state of all correction.

But soon after that <C3v> Alexander was stablished in the empire and that his virtues were commended and published, Gordian, rejoicing thereat, took thereof marvellous comfort, albeit for his native gravity and stately courage he liked not the affability and familiarity that Alexander used,[89] now being the chief prince and sovereign governor of all the world. Wherefore, ere he would make any access to his presence, he would prove his wisdom and virtue in admitting his counsels; wherefore, he wrote in this wise unto him.

[89] The present chapters 6 and 7 make an epistolary closet-drama: the position that 'Gordian' takes in the debate, familiar from Shakespeare, *1 Henry IV* 3.2.39–91, was espoused by Elyot's contemporary Robert Copland, *The Secrete of Secretes of Arystotle* (London: Copland, 1528), sig. C2r, for example: 'And also the king ought not to shew himself too often to his people, nor haunt too much the company of his subjects, and special of villains. And therefore the Indians have a good custom in the ordinance of their realm. For their manner is that their king sheweth himself but once in the year'; the position that 'Alexander' advocates is espoused in Elyot, *Gov.* 2.5, 'Of affability and the utility thereof in every estate' (Watson, pp. 130–36).

NOBLE AND EXCELLENT prince! The fame of your advancement unto the governance of the empire was to me, as it is unto all the world, most joyful tidings, considering the lamentable estate of our public weal, with the certain hope that all men have in you, being moved with your virtues incomparable, which daily more and more ye do manifest by your most honourable example in living, declared to all that do behold not only your royal person but also your servants and familiar companions.

Among which virtues, your affability and gentleness have acquired no small praise among the people, as commonly they delight in sweet countenance and mildness of governors, wherein they trust to find more liberty. But, most noble prince, although for these qualities ye deserve praise and love of your subjects, yet in the imperial majesty requireth to be a more strange countenance and a seld and difficult access unto your person, considering that by the familiarity of him that is a master or governor as well evil men as good do receive boldness to speak; and they which be evil do busily assault him either <C4r> with flattery or with detracting of other, whereby princes, although they be of good natures and well brought up by their parents, yet be they oftentimes transformed into monsters, that is to say, into beastly livers or ravenous tyrants. I omit contempt, which, induced by familiarity, bringeth the subject to disobedience; let it not displease you that I seem to have in your highness any suspicion.

Verily, as a man that hath a fair and honest wife, whereby he is moved to love her entirely, would not have her gladly stand in the marketplace and admit without discrepance every man equally and, with like pleasant countenance, suffer every man to speak to her what he list, although he knoweth her to be virtuous and constant, as well forasmuch as the natural shamefastness that ought to be in a woman may not admit such open resort and communication, as also the ears that be often assaulted cannot ever escape but, be they never so well fortified with wisdom, at the last, like a castle wall, they being sore shaken with many sweet words and long interview, they yield at the last, ill custom expelling shamefastness and finally all wisdom being rejected and nothing set by; semblably, most excellent prince, your person is to the Senate as dear as the wife to her husband, and for your fair virtues we of good reason ought to be so jealous over you that willingly we should not behold you fall into any custom which mought allure you into any ill disposition, remembering the late calamity that the city and empire were brought unto by your most monstrous predecessor, Varius Heliogabalus.

Wherefore, like as now ye be to him most contrarious in living, <C4v> so we desire to have you resist all occasion that mought give never so little a path for flatterers, detractors, and promoters of vice to enter into your counsel or favour. Who can avaunt himself to be well assured from this net of hypocrisy,[90] which hath (as I mought say) sundry and diverse meshes of flatterings, which uneath any man can escape that will tarry until the net be cast over him? The remedy then is either with majesty to repel it; or to cut it asunder with sharp rebukes, and that in the presence of other; or so grievously to persecute alway those hypocrites — I do mean flatterers — with open punishment that all men may know and abhor them and that other thereto by nature inclined may be ever afeared of like experiment.

But the first way is most sure, undoubtedly. For rebuke and punishment cometh after the danger, but majesty precedeth and therefore more profiteth. For such persons rebuked or punished, perchance excusing themself that they do it by too ardent affection and desire to please, or by their youth and lack of experience, or recognising their folly and promising amendment, may happen eftsoons to creep into favour; and then they work their net so finely that it cannot so soon be perceived and pitcheth it more covertly, applying it aptly to their masters' conditions, so that it shall be almost impossible for him to escape but that in one mesh or other he shall be tangled.

Contrariwise, by majesty — that is to say, stately countenance and difficult access — joined with wisdom impresseth such reverence that men not only do fear to approach unto their sovereign lord unless they be called, but also to speak anything whereby they, <D1r> being discovered, should lose their credence, hoping never again to recover it, considering that by majesty and wisdom the access to the prince is made impenetrable, since to them that never offended he is so hard and diffuse to be spoken unto.

Thus to your majesty have I shewed mine opinion; wherefore, if by my counsel ye do leave your affability and familiar access and embrace gravity and princely estate, ye shall be safe from the perils that I have remembered and have equal honour with your predecessors, which would not be seen of the people but seldom and oftentimes with a curtain before their visage, sitting in their place of estate, which they took of the Persians. For things seldom seen be most esteemed, and they that be frequent and often in eye be little regarded; which, as ye increase in age and experience, ye shall find true and to be written of a faithful counsellor that desireth the increase of your virtue, with the public weal of our most noble city and empire.

[90] Cf. Elyot, *Gov.* 2.14 (Watson, p. 193), 'And in this wise pitching their net of adulation they entrap the noble and virtuous heart, which only beholdeth their feigned severity and counterfeit wisdom, and the rather by cause this manner of flattery is most unlike to that which is commonly used'.

7. The answer of Alexander to the letters of Gordian.

When the Emperor Alexander had received and read the said letters of the senator Gordian, he seemed to rejoice more thereat than at all the honours and titles that were given him by the Senate and people, saying with a loud voice: 'Yet there remaineth some hope in the public weal, that it shall not utterly perish, since we have Gordian the senator left to assist us'. And therewith he called for <D1v> his tables and immediately made to him answer, as hereafter ensueth.

GORDIAN, honourable father! How much better had the Senate and people of Rome provided for their public weal if they had taken you to be their emperor, having regard to your ancienty and excellent wisdom, where in me they find nothing but frail youth and lack of experience! For only detestation of the negligence of my predecessor, with the desire that I have to increase virtue, hath sown of me such opinion among the Senate and people that, not remembering you perchance for lack of your presence, they have enabled me to this estate above my merits. Verily, no man doubteth but that ye, being born in the city of a right ancient and noble house of the Romans, as of your father's side issuing from the honourable senators called Gracchus and by your mother descended from Trajan the Emperor,[91] mought, with that gravity and sternness which is in you as it were by nature ingenerate and among the people of Rome above forty year in the principal dignities experienced, most honourably have maintained the imperial majesty; where I, being born a stranger and my blood, although it proceeded of the noble house of Metellus,[92] being to the more part of the Senate and people unknown, am constrained to avale that majesty that in you should be commendable and, in the stead of your gravity and sadness, to use toward all men affability and such form of gentleness which ye seem in me rather to prohibit than to dispraise, lest that my novelty should cease to be pleasant unto the people, if by my sharp-<D2r>ness or strange countenance I should seem to deceive them in their opinion.

Remember you not that the haught countenance and the difficult access which was in Tarquin, the last king °<of> Romans, acquired to him that odious surname to be called Tarquin the proud? And although that he were both valiant in wars and in garnishing the city very industrious, yet when occasion and opportunity happened of rebellion,

[91] SHA, *Gord.* 2.2, 'Horum Gordianus senior, id est primus, natus est patre Maecio Marullo, matre Ulpia Gordiana, originem paternam ex Gracchorum genere habuit, maternam ex Traiani imperatoris, patre, avo, proavo consulibus, socero, prosocero et item alio prosocero et duobus absoceris consulibus'.

[92] SHA, *Alex. Sev.* 44.3, 'Syrum se dici nolebat, sed a maioribus Romanum et stemma generis depinxerat, quo ostendebatur genus eius a Metellis descendere'.

° of] *B* : *A om*

the people, being brought into fury, declared then how much more they hated him than they did fear him, ne had him for his noble acts in any estimation or reverence? Moreover, when they had expelled him out of the city, to the intent they mought have more familiar access unto their governors and find in them more affability,[93] from thenceforth unto the time of Gaius Caesar, °they yearly elected new governors, calling them Consuls, as it were counsellors, supposing that in their time of authority the remembrance that they should be private persons the next year following should cause them to use the people the more familiarly and also gently; and when those officers, being of long time chosen of the nobility only, became in process of time haught-minded and stern toward the commonalty, the people with long sedition compelled the Senate to join at the last with a noble man in that office one of their company.

Julius Caesar[94] with affability, mercy, and gentleness became so puissant that neither the Senate's authority, nor the prowess incomparable of the great Pompey, nor yet the inexpugnable armies prepared against him had power to resist him. Yet shortly <D2v> after that he had decreed that no man should approach him and became in his countenance and words more stately, he was slain in the middle of the city by fifty senators only.

The great Alexander[95] — being so familiar and gentle among his people that he did not only visit homely their pavilions and halls, ministering to them all thing that they lacked, but also suffered them to come to him boldly and oftentimes to speak to him rudely — he drew them with him into the furthest parts of the world, into most barren

[93] Cf. Elyot, *Gov.* 2.5 (Watson, p. 131), 'The pride of Tarquin, the last king of Romans, was more occasion of his exile than the ravishing of Lucretia by his son Aruntius, for the malice that the people by his pride had long gathered, finding valiant captains, Brutus, Colatinus, Lucretius, and other nobles of the city, at the last brast out and taking occasion of the ravishment, although the King were thereto not party, they utterly expulsed him forever out of the city. These be the fruits of pride, and that men do call stately countenance'; also, Plut., *Publicola* 1.3, and Liv. 1.57–60.

[94] Cf. Elyot, *Gov.* 2.5 (Watson, p. 133), 'Wherefore little and little he withdrew from men his accustomed gentleness, becoming more sturdy in language, and strange in countenance, than ever before had been his usage [...]. Thus Caesar, by omitting his old affability, did incend his next friends and companions to slay him'.

[95] Cf. Elyot, *Gov.* 2.5 (Watson, pp. 132–33), 'What availed fortune incomparable to the great King Alexander, his wonderful puissance and hardiness, or his singular doctrine in philosophy, taught him by Aristotle, in delivering him from the death in his young and flourishing age? Where, if he had retained the same affability that was in him in the beginning of his conquest, and had not put to silence his counsellors which before used to speak to him frankly, he mought have escaped all violent death, and by similitude, have enjoyed the whole monarchy of all the world. For after that he waxed to be terrible in manners, and prohibited his friends and discrete servants to use their accustomed liberty in speech, he fell in to a hateful grudge among his own people'.

° they] the *B*

and dangerous countries, and by most gentle persuasions vanquished nature, which abhorred the tedious journeys, the travails intolerable, the venomous stinging of serpents, the hunger and thirst that sundry times happened, and other incommodities and incredible labours, which mought not withdraw them from following their prince, so much his most amiable gentleness subdued their appetites. But after that he, following the kings of Persia, whom ye seem to praise in your letters, used a more pompous estate than he was accustomed and neither would behold or speak to his people familiarly, nor suffer them to speak to him freely, how soon after changed they then their copy? And as his affability decayed and pride increased, so their loving affection toward him in likewise relented, which constrained him to omit part of his enterprise and return unto Babylon, where, among his friends at a banquet, he was destroyed with poison.

The incomparable humanity and gentleness of noble Germanicus — who should have succeeded Tibe-<D3r>rius in the empire if the treason of °Piso had not frustrate the trust of the people — caused his son Caius, being yet in his cradle, to be so favoured throughout the army that they, having him with his mother Agrippina among them,[96] took no less care for him than if he had been proper son to everich of them; which love in such wise remained that, immediately next after Tiberius, they made him emperor; who, in the beginning of his reign using the humanity of his noble father, governed the empire quietly, as he that was marvellously beloved of the people. But when, to advance his majesty, he became strange, counterfeiting his visage in a glass into a terrible gravity, coveting to seem fearful unto the people; and when he was openly seen, which was but seldom, he, sitting in apparel all of gold laded with jewels, compelled the Senate and people to worship him as god;[97] how soon after was his stateliness turned into mockery, and he, being of all men

[96] Cf. Elyot, *Gov.* 1.12 (Watson, pp. 51–52), 'the noble Germanicus (who by the assignment of Augustus should have succeeded Tiberius in the empire, if traitorous envy had not in his flourishing youth bereft him his life)'. The references are to Iulius Caesar Germanicus (16 BCE–19 CE), son of Tiberius by adoption and father of Caligula; Tiberius Iulius Caesar Augustus (imp. 14–37); Cn. Calpurnius Piso (43 BCE–20 CE), whose possible murder of Germanicus so preoccupied Tacitus (*Ann.* 2.43, 2.55–58, 2.69–83, 3.1–19); and Gaius Iulius Caesar Germanicus (imp. 37–41), 'Caligula'. Cf. Suet., *Tib.* 52.3, and 53.1–2, on the treatment of Caligula's mother Agrippina (14 BCE–33 CE).

[97] Cf. Suet., *Calig.* 50.1, 'While his face was naturally forbidding and ugly, he purposely made it even more savage, practising all kinds of terrible and fearsome expressions before a mirror' (used again below, p. 259); and 22.3, 'He also set up a special temple to his own godhead, with priests and with victims of the choicest kind. In this temple was a life-sized statue of the Emperor in gold, which was dressed each day in clothing such as he wore himself. The richest citizens used all their influence to secure the priesthoods of his cult and bid high for the honour. The victims were flamingos, peacocks, black grouse, guinea-hens, and pheasants, offered day by day each after its own kind'.

° Piso] Fiso *B*

abandoned, was like an horrible monster slain and drawn through the city?

Consider the affability and gentleness of the noble Augustus, Titus the son of Vespasian, Nerva, Trajan, Antonine called Pius, and Marcus Aurelius, whom no man can derogate of any part of honour and wisdom,[98] and see where ye may therewith compare any sturdy gravity, or haught and strange countenance of any other emperor or prince.

Certes, Gordian, honourable father, he much erreth in mine opinion that preferreth fear before love, without the which — witnesseth Socrates — nothing either with God or with man may dure or abide.[99] Fear de-<D3v>pendeth on love, and without love it is soon had in contempt. Suppose not ye that he was a wise man that said, °'Men whom they fear they hate, and whom they hate, they would were destroyed'?[100] Wisdom causeth men to be honoured, liberality to be marvelled at, but gentleness and affability only to be heartily loved. Gravity proceedeth of wisdom, and consisteth not in countenance; but is compact of two virtues, constance and prudence. Wherefore, it can never be counterfeit if the acts be well expended and tried. For where it lacketh the said two virtues, it is either niceness and to be laughed at, or else pride outrageous and to be abhorred and hated.

But affability can never be vicious. For though it be in one that lacketh discretion, yet by liberty of speech, which increaseth thereby, he shall be so oftentimes warned that he shall defalcate that thing that seemeth superfluous. Ne the access of flatterers or detractors to him that mortally hateth them can bring any damage. For he is too much a fool that will shew his breast naked unto his enemy. And to him that is surely armed, it is no peril though his enemy assault him; yea, perchance, if his enemy find him invincible, he shall afterward be afeared to approach him.

Thus have ye, father Gordian, not only mine opinion herein but also my determinate sentence; not thereby dispraising your honourable gravity, which, for the causes that I have rehearsed, is in your person

[98] The 'good' emperors listed here but not given biographies in Elyot, *Bibl.* are Titus Flavius Vespasianus (imp. 79–81), called 'Titus', with his father, also Titus Flavius Vespasianus (imp. 69–79), though called 'Vespasian'; M. Cocceius Nerva (imp. 96–98); and M. Ulpius Traianus (imp. 98–117).

[99] Cf. Elyot, *Banquet*, sig. E5v, 'It beseemeth men to fear their prince, but much more to love him' (without attribution).

[100] Quintus Ennius (*c.* 239–*c.* 169 BCE), probably quoted from Cic., *Off.* 2.23, 'Of all motives, however, none is better adapted to secure influence and hold it fast than love; nothing is more foreign to that end than fear. Ennius puts it clearly: "Whom they fear, they hate; and whoever hates someone hopes to see him dead"'; also Elyot, *Banquet*, sig. D2v (with attribution to Ennius), 'Whom men fear they do hate, and every man whom he hated, he desireth to perish'.

° \Quem metuunt oderunt, et quem odiunt perisse expetunt: Ennius/

right laudable; but in me, being not so well knowen in this city among the Romans, which of their nature be free and were never in servitude, it seemeth not to be so expedient. Albeit, if I reigned in Persia, <Dvr> where the people from the beginning have been best governed by tyranny, I would perchance otherwise do, changing affability into strangeness and stately countenance, which improperly — in mine opinion — ye in your letters have named majesty.

Thus fare ye well, and haste you to return unto the Senate, which (with me) desireth the presence of your excellent wisdom.

Soon after the Emperor Alexander being elected consul, he solicited the Senate and people to elect also Gordian into that office, affirming that his youth required for the utility of the public weal to be joined with such a companion as Gordian was, whose wisdom, experience, and gravity was of all men sufficiently knowen.

8. The first practice of Alexander in reducing of the empire into his pristinate honour.

The noble and prudent lady Mammea, mother of the Emperor Alexander,[101] considering her son to be now entered into the most dangerous passage of youth, being but sixteen years old, feared lest the excellency of his estate, as it oftentimes happened to other, should incite him to assay things which frail nature thinketh delectable and, tasting once of them, his tender youth mought not withstand the assaults of pleasant affections, whereby he mought eftsoons bring the empire into ruin and infamy and himself and all his blood to utter destruction.

Therefore, she perceiving him to be obedient to her exhortations — indeed, she was a woman of much wisdom and holiness, but that she <D4v> was somewhat noted of covetise — she with good reason persuaded to him that he could never well stablish his estate imperial but only by reducing of the Senate and people into their pristinate order, which could never be brought to pass except that, first, his own palace were clean purged of personages corrupted with vices and into their places men of approved virtue and wisdom elected; and semblably that, to the example of the Emperor's own household, the sundry dignities and offices in the weal public were aptly distributed; considering that the prince's palace is like a common fountain or spring to his city or country, whereby the people by the cleanness thereof be long preserved in honesty, or by the impureness thereof are with sundry vices corrupted; and until the fountain be purged, there can never be any sure hope of remedy.

Wherefore, Alexander, immediately after that he had received of the Senate and people the name of Augustus, whereunto was annexed the entire power and

[101] See above, p. 177 and n. 14.

jurisdiction imperial, whereby he mought command or prohibit what he thought most convenient; first, he discharged all ministers which the monstrous beast Heliogabalus had undiscretely promoted of most vile and dishonest personages, banishing also out of his palace all such as he mought by any means know to be persons infamed; semblably, flatterers, as well those which therefore were favoured of his predecessor, as them whom he apprehended abusing him with semblable falsehood.

According to that example, he reformed the whole Senate and judges and also all other dignities and offices in the public <E1r> weal. In like manner, he purged his garrisons and men of war, and corrected their liberties and privileges, given undiscretely to them by other emperors or by them misused.

Moreover, with all speed convenient, by the advice of Ulpian his tutor, Frontinus,[102] and other the wisest men of the Senate, he with all diligence elected out of all parts of the empire a convenient and honourable company of wise and honourable counsellors. This number were the most excellent lawyers, of whose sentences is made the text of the law civil, gathered in the books named the *Digests*.[103] There was also Fabius °<S>abinus, surnamed Cato for his singular wisdom; also Gordian, of whom I late did write, a man of much gravity and nobleness, whose son was afterward emperor. Moreover, there was Claudius Venatus, a noble and eloquent orator; also, Catilius Severus, kinsman to the Emperor, most excellently learned above all other; Serenianus, a man of great perfection and gravity; and Caius Marcellus, who was of such virtue and goodness that never history remembered a better.[104]

These good and honourable personages, with many other not of much less estimation, at all times and places attended upon that noble Emperor,

[102] For Ulpian, see above, p. 184 n. 48; and for 'Frontinus' see above, p. 179 n. 32.
[103] *Digesta seu Pandectae* (533), the second part of the *Corpus iuris civilis* codifed in the reign of Justinian (imp. 527–565), is an abbreviated collocation of opinions of already authoritative ancient jurists, having the force of law. Cf. Elyot, *Bibl.*, '*Pandecta,* comprehending all things: it is also the volume of the Law Civil, called the *Digests*'; he also praises it, *Gov.* 1.14 (Watson, p. 67), 'Who readeth the text of Civil [Law], called the *Pandects* or *Digests*, and hath any commendable judgment in the Latin tongue, but he will affirm that Ulpianus, Sceuola, Claudius, and all the other there named, of whose sayings all the said texts be assembled, were not only studious of eloquence, but also wonderful exercised: for as much as their style doth approach nearer to the antique and pure eloquence than any other kind of writers that wrote about that time?' About two-fifths of the *Digest* consists of Ulpian's contributions; another one sixth, of those of Iulius Paulus (fl. *c.* 210), officially 'Prudentissimus', who was mentioned by the SHA and by Elyot below, prominently as Alexander's interlocutor in the inset dialogue on severity in chap. 37: pp. 254, 290, and 301.
[104] The list of counsellors is based on SHA, *Alex. Sev.* 68.1, which Elyot uses for names repeatedly, sometimes in forms distinctive of the Erasmian edition of the SHA. For 'Claudius Venatus', see also below, p. 284. For 'Sabinus', see above, p. 184 and n. 48; and for 'Gordian', p. 193 and n. 88. 'Catelius' or 'Catilius Severus' reappears below, most prominently in the senatorial debate on usury in chap. 30, pp. 266–67, but also pp. 206, 284, 299, and 301. For 'Caius Marcellus', also 'Quintilius Marcellus' (distinctively 'Quintilius Caius Marcellus' in the Erasmian edition), see below, pp. 206 and 274.

° Sabinus] SHA, *Alex. Sev.* 68.1 : Gabinus *A B*

of the which Ulpian was in manner his chancellor or keeper of the imperial monuments; and the Emperor had him for his chief counsellor. <E1v>

9. In what form the Emperor Alexander had his council, which alway attended upon his person.

°The form of Alexander's counsel was as hereafter ensueth.

First, all matters and causes civil of great importance he caused to be examined and brought in order by the great lawyers before rehearsed, of whom Ulpian was chief,[105] and they made true report thereof unto him.

Moreover, he would never make decree or ordinance without twenty lawyers, substantially learned, and fifty other expert men and eloquent,[106] and that was done after this manner: every man's opinion and sentence was thoroughly and quietly heard, without interruption or altercation; thereto were assigned eight secretaries or clerks, men of quick and substantial memory, who, in brief notes or ciphers made for that purpose, wrote every word that by those counsellors was spoken. Moreover, a competent time was given to every counsellor to study and seek for such reason as he would purpose, to the intent they should not speak unadvisedly in things of importance.[107]

It was also this Emperor's custom that, when he treated of laws and matters politic, he called thereto learned men and such as were eloquent and well reasoned. If he commoned of matters touching war and hostility, he called to him old and expert captains which had valiantly acquitted themselves in sundry battles; also, them that were expert in the situation of places, pitching of fields, and preparation of camps. He would also hear di-<E2r>verse which were perfectly and ripely instructed in histories, ensearching by them what the emperors and princes, as well Romans as of other nations before that time, had done in semblable causes as were at that time in reasoning.[108]

[105] For Ulpian, see above, p. 184 and n. 48.
[106] SHA, *Alex. Sev.* 16.1, 'neque ullam constitutionem sacravit sine viginti iuris peritis et doctissimis ac sapientibus viris isdemque disertissimis non minus quinquaginta'.
[107] Cf. SHA, *Alex. Sev.* 16.2, 'et id quidem ita ut iretur per sententias singulorum ac scriberetur, quid quisque dixisset, dato tamen spatio ad disquirendum cogitandumque, priusquam dicerent, ne incogitati dicere cogerentur de rebus ingentibus'.
[108] SHA, *Alex. Sev.* 16.3, 'fuit praeterea illi consuetudo, ut, si de iure aut de negotiis tractaret, solos doctos et disertos adhiberet, si vero de re militari, militares veteres et senes bene meritos et locorum peritos ac bellorum et castrorum et omnes litteratos et maxime eos, qui historiam norant, requirens, quid in talibus causis, quales in disceptatione versabantur, veteres imperatores vel Romani vel exterarum gentium fecissent'. Cf. Elyot, *Gov.* 3.10 (Watson, p. 232), 'this noble young prince Alexander, inflamed with the zeal of the pristinate honour of the Romans, laying apart utterly all pleasures and quietness, wholly gave his wit and body to study and travails intolerable, and choosing out of all parts of the world men of greatest wisdom and experience, consulting with them, never ceased until he had reduced as well the Romans as all other cities and provinces unto them subject, to their pristinate moderation and temperance'; and above, n. 65.

° \Bebius Macrinus/

And after that all their opinions and sentences were written by the secretaries (as is before mentioned) and that they, conferring together, had made thereof one perfect minute of every man's saying and delivered it to the Emperor with as much haste as was possible; then he, in a place secret, perusing the minute and assembling and pondering the sentences thoroughly, after a competent time therein bestowed, either gathering of them one perfect conclusion or else adding to some thing of his invention, he finally opened his conceit among all his counsellors, whom he had before heard; notwithstanding, he gave to them liberty either to allow his sentence or, if any man had anything newly devised, eftsoons to declare it.

And that sentence which was of most wise men approved, that alway prevailed; and he thereto consented and caused it with all diligence to be put in experience. For he was of such moderation of mind that nothing more pleased him than to hear any man with a substantial and true reason to confute his opinion, which caused him to bring to pass things to be marvelled at.

But now will I declare the oration that he made in the Senate, after that he had set in good order his own proper household. <E2v>

10. The oration of Alexander to the Senate.

'The inestimable majesty of this empire — as ye well know, honourable fathers — like as it took beginning and increase of prowess and politic wisdom, so by the same and like means it must be conserved.

'Our most noble progenitor and founder of this empire, the valiant Romulus,[109] being in his tender infancy cast out of the palace and nourished among the poor herdmen, with sustaining much hunger, cold, and continual travail, achieved this little portion of ground wherein now standeth the principal ruler and mistress of all the world. To the aid of his prowess, he added too the quiet and vigilant study of rude shepherds, old and decrepit, whose bodies, being macerate with labours and made feeble with age, although they mought nothing profit in battle, yet their wits being confirmed by long experience and free from the vexation of wanton affections, they no less advanced and set forth the enterprise of the courageous Romulus than did the diligence and prowess of his lusty soldiers.

'Neither his strength or courage, ne the wits of his rude senators, became so excellent, as it seemed at that time to be, by feeding superfluously, by beastly idleness or wanton pastimes, but only by temperance in living, vigilant providence, and continual exercise, whereby strength is nourished and wits be increased, like as by the other the strength of body is resolved and the wits be consumed or unprofitably dispersed. And certes, like as the first is proved to be <E3r> true by the example before declared and many other succeeding that

[109] Cf. Elyot, *Bibl.*, '*Romulus*, the first king of Romans'.

time, so the last is semblably verified by late experience, and whereof the steps yet do remain, to our no little grief and displeasure; considering that thereby this noble empire is like to fall into extreme ruin and perpetual infamy, unless your most excellent wisdoms will diligently and constantly prepare yourselves to the certain remedy against this peril intolerable; which remedy only shall be the purging and reformation, as well of this most honourable company of senators, as of all other dignities and estates in the weal public.

'In the which inquisition, we desire none other prerogative but that it may take his first beginning at our proper palace and household and in our own person to be first executed, to the intent that, the principal fountain being found clean, the remnant of our subjects, whose order of living proceedeth of our example as rivers and sundry lakes from a head-spring which is set on a mountain, may with little difficulty be more easily purged.

'Nor other estate or pre-eminence will I require; but where youth refuseth in me the most reverend name of father of the country, which ye offered unto me, yet condescending to part of your gentle requests, I will gladly receive the names and titles of protector of the Senate and tribune or else, if better do like you, defender of the Roman people.

'And on that behalf, I require you, for the approbation of my sincere love to the public weal, that according to the ancient and laudable custom of this noble city, ye will cause to be chosen censors, or correctors of manners: such personages <E3v> as never were infamed with any vice notable; and whose lives be inculpable; and therewith be sufficiently furnished with wisdom and gravity; void also of all private affection, fear, avarice, and flattery; who, like good surgeons, shall not forbear, with corrosive and sharp medicines, to draw out the festered and stinking cores of old mormals and inveterate sores of the weal public, engendered by the long custom in vice. To the which remedy, as a necessary minister, I shall put to my proper hands and assistance, unto the death, leaving remembrance after me that, in making me your emperor, ye nothing have appaired of the imperial majesty but have advanced it, with the public weal of your city.

'To the ratification of the which judgment of you, noble fathers, I shall apply wholly my study, travail, and diligence, calling God to witness that the Senate and people of Rome shall sooner fail the public weal than I shall leave any part of my duty.'

11. How the correctors of manners called censors were elected and with what rigour they executed their office, by the commandment of Alexander.

The said oration of the Emperor Alexander being finished, a wonderful rejoicing entered into the hearts of the senators which were virtuous and honourable, and, being replenished with joy, they all spake on high with one voice, saying, °[110]'Emperor Alexander, God ever preserve thee! God sent thee unto us! God ever defend thee! God hath delivered thee from the unclean Heliogabalus! God <E4r> keep thee perpetually! Thou didest long tolerate that mischievous tyrant; thou doest lament his abominable living; and, at the last, God hath delivered thee and us also of him, and to this hath brought thee!'

After these and many mo congratulations made to the Emperor, he — giving to the Senate condign thanks — departed to his palace. And shortly after, there were chosen, by the common consent of the Senate and people, four censors: two to remain in the city, and other two for Italy and the provinces under the name of Latins, from whence were elect for the more part senators, judges, and other chief officers which had jurisdiction and authority to give any sentence. °[111]The censors for the city were Fabius Sabinus and Catilius Severus, men of excellent wisdom and gravity; and for the provinces were made Quintilius Marcellus and Caius Manlius, men of ancient nobility and great severity.

°The office of censors was to note the manners of every person which was in any degree of honour — that is to say, above the estate of the common people — wherein was shewed such rigour that no man was spared; so that if a knight, a judge, or a senator had used any unseemly thing, appairing or staining the estimation of the degree which he represented, it was in the authority of the censors to degrade him or discharge him of his office or dignity.

Soon after the said election, they made Alexander consul, who with all diligence procured that Aelius Gordianus, of whom I late spake,[112] was made his companion in the consulate, whereat some of the people grudged, fearing lest the sturdiness and <E4v> haught courage of Gordian should change the incomparable gentleness of Alexander into cruelty and pride. But it succeeded all otherwise; for the wise Emperor, by the exquisite gravity of his companion, reformed so his nature, which was in wise men's opinion more easy and simple than appertained to the imperial estate, that by all men's judgment he became, in moderation of virtues, of all other incomparable.

The censors, immediately after that they were elected, vigilantly and sharply

[110] Aelius Lampridius (mentioned repeatedly below) is the nominal author of SHA, *Alex. Sev.* The *acclamationes* following are abbreviated from *Alex. Sev.* 6.3–4.

[111] The historical public figure Marius Maximus (*c.* 169–*c.* 230), named in the marginal note, was also an imperial biographer, whose work is lost, though it was cited by the SHA. None of the references to him in SHA, *Alex. Sev.* (5.4, 21.4, 30.5, 48.6, 65.4) corresponds to this sole citation in Elyot. Excepting 'Caius Manlius' (here possibly a recollection of the Catilinarian conspirator, though not in the SHA or elsewhere in Elyot), the censors' names are from SHA, *Alex. Sev.* 68.1; see above, p. 202 and nn.

[112] See above, p. 193 and n. 88.

° \Lampridius./
° \Marius Maximus/
° \Office of Censors./

executed their offices. For first, they discharged out of the Senate all such which by Heliogabalus for their abominable living or flattery were thereto promoted. Semblably, they purged the order of knighthood, disgrading all knights which were shameless lechers, maintainers of thieves, or they themselves robbers; in like wise, all those which of bauds, ruffians, carters, cooks, and other like reproachable persons were by Heliogabalus put in authority. The same industry they used in reforming judges and other head officers, as well in the city as about in the provinces. Finally, none estate or degree escaped their rebuke or correction.

Ne the Emperor's palace was exempt from their jurisdiction, in so much as Aurelius Philippus, who was sometime a bondman — notwithstanding that he was manumised and had been the Emperor's schoolmaster and after wrate his life[113] — forasmuch as he did ride in a chariot and would be saluted as a senator, the censors caused him to be led to prison, and prohibited him for coming to the Emperor's palace but only on foot and his <F1r> copped cap on his head, which fashion only was used of them that were enfranchised. And although for his good learning and honesty, some noble men advised the Emperor that he should require the censors that they should withdraw their rigour in correcting Phillip, considering that he had been sometime his schoolmaster, he nothing would do to let or restrain the sharp correction of the censors; but, much extolling their constance, he answered, 'If the commonweal may have ever such officers, in short space there shall be found in Rome mo men worthy to be emperors than I at my coming found good senators'.

And immediately he ordained that there should never libertine — that is to say, any man of a bond ancestor — be of the Senate, saying that the order of °k<ni>ghthood was the place from whence were fetched the plants of the Senate;[114] that is to say, from whence the senators were elected. Notwithstanding, he purchased a goodly mansion, with sufficient revenues, not far from Rome, which he gave to the said Phillip, saying to him, 'Before I was emperor, I disdained not to follow thy doctrine; now be thou as well contented, for the increase of mine honour and of the weal public, to obey to mine ordinance. And although the majesty of the city may not permit thee to be openly received in the number of our familiars, yet privy resort shall approve our favour towards thee, not lost, but increased'.

Of such marvellous severity was this Emperor, that no kind of affection or private appetite mought reflect him from the sharp execution of his <F1v> laws or laudable customs of the city, as more yet shall appear in the chapter following.

[113] On this figure, see above, p. 179 and n. 31.

[114] SHA, *Alex. Sev.* 19.4, 'idem libertinos numquam in equestrem locum redegit adserens seminarium senatorum equestrem locum esse'.

° knighthood] kynghthode *A B*

12. Of the great prudence of Alexander used in the election of his counsellors and officers.

It oftentimes happeneth that, where God doth ornate a prince with natural gifts and also great understanding and sharpness of wit, he, for lack of election, which is a great part of prudence, having about him counsellors, companions, and officers unmeet or unworthy, maketh the said ornaments unprofitable or, peradventure, incommodious to the weal public whereof he hath governance; whereby the renome, which were condign and as it were incident to rare and excellent qualities, is lost and dieth with the body, or else — which is much worse — is turned to perpetual reproach and dishonour. Which the Emperor Alexander circumspectly considering, he, with an incomparable study, prepared for himself certain rules of election, as hereafter followeth.

°First, he determined to love all that was virtue and to hate all that was vice, in what person so ever the one or the other should happen.

Also, whatsoever pleasure or commodity mought come to him by embracing or tolerating of any notable vice, he would rather lack it, though it were to his detriment, than to be seen to change his opinion, lest any man should thereby take occasion to commend vice. <F2r>

And forasmuch as under his empire were diverse and sundry nations, whereof also the people by natural disposition be diversely inclined to virtue or vice, he therefore applied himself to know the sundry wits, manners, affects, and studies of men born in every region, country, and notable city throughout the world; which knowledge he apprehended so exquisitely, as well by studious reading of many histories and other notable works of moral philosophy, as by diligent examining of captains and merchants which had travelled and been in sundry countries; whereby he was wonderfully holpen in his elections and judgments, as it shall hereafter appear.

He would never accept commendation of any person before that he himself had spoken with him and that by secret scrutiny he had been truly informed of him. And yet the commendation that he would afterward hear should be apart, none other man hearing but himself, lest, if many were present and he that commended were in authority, other hearers, although they knew the contrary, should either affirm a false commendation or else fear to say truth if they should be thereof demanded.

In them that were counsellors, he utterly abhorred ambition and flattery. In judges, he hated with extreme detestation covetise and wrath. In both the one and the °other, he loved sincerity, vulgarly called uprightness.

The perfect knowledge of men's conditions, he had not by the report of their superiors or equals, ne by them which dwelled far from the habitation of those whom they praised, but by the examination <F2v> of their nighest neighbours, being men of honesty and not their enemies. And that was practiced by such

° \Rules whereby a prince should elect counsellors./
° \Sincerity./

of his own yeomen as were most ancient and sage; which, finding occasion to ride through the countries where they were neither born nor had possessions, should make this diligent scrutiny or search. And to such manner of persons, the common people would more familiarly and plainly declare their opinions than to gentlemen or men in authority.

But if the Emperor perceived afterward that he had been untruly informed by any of his said espials — which sometime he did, by further experience, as being in his progress or himself hearing and discussing complaints of the common people openly and with a great deliberation and gravity — he then extremely and without hope of remission punished the false reporters, were it in praise or detraction, causing their tongues to be pierced through with a hot brenning iron and to be banished his court and presence forever.

Which punishment, although it will seem to some men sore and cruel, yet considering that, using this mean, he was never deceived by counsellors and also that justice was duly executed by them that were in authority, that manner of rigour may be thought necessary and very expedient. Also, the punishment being in a few executed at the beginning, the severity of the prince became so terrible that men so grievously feared him that neither desire, reward, nor dread of any other man could let the said espials to report truly, according as they had founden by their diligent scrutiny.

One marvellous cautel he used, that is to say: <F3r> one man was not oftentimes in that trust of espial. And those personages were chosen and appointed only by himself, without making any other man privy, until he had deprehended them with some manner of falsehood.

Finally, he was of such a wonderful discretion and soberness that no report could bring him out of patience or into suspicion until he had well tried the report with some praty experience, as it shall be declared hereafter.

And thus I make an end of the first part of his governance, which was in ordering of his own person and court, whereby, principally, he brought not only the city of Rome but also all the whole empire — notwithstanding the beastly license brought in by Heliogabalus — in as good estate as ever it was in the time of any of his most noble progenitors.

13. How extremely Alexander hated extortioners and bribers, and how much he favoured them that were virtuous.

The Emperor Alexander had such indignation towards them that were extortioners or bribers that, if by chance he espied any of them, he was therewith so grieved that he immediately would vomit up choler and, his face being as it were on a fire, of a long time mought not speak one word.[115]

[115] Cf. SHA, *Alex. Sev.* 17.2, 'addit Septiminus, qui vitam eius non mediocriter exsequutus est, tanti sthomachi fuisse Alexandrum in eos iudices, qui furtorum fama laborassent,

On a time, one Septimius Arabinus, who in the time of Heliogabalus was a famous briber, came in the company of senators to salute the Emperor Alexander; who, beholding him, said with a loud voice, 'O lord God, <F3v> behold: Arabinus not only liveth, but also presumeth to be in the Senate! Peradventure, he trusteth in me, judging me to be an ignorant and foolish emperor'.[116]

Moreover, he ordained, that where there were founden any extortioners or bribers, that they should be openly examined and judged and by the governors of countries sent into exile. When he was in his progress, such as were governors or justices in provinces whom he heard worthily commended, without sinister affection, he would in his journey take them into his horse litter, commoning with them of the state of their country and honouring them with rewards, saying that, like as extortioners and bribers are to be impoverished, so good men and just are to be enriched.[117]

In hearing the complaints of his soldiers against their captains, if he found any captain faulty in that thing whereof he was accused, forthwith he caused him to be punished after the quality of his offence, without any hope of remission;[118] semblably did he to his soldiers and servants. For where they injustly grieved any person, he corrected them sharply and with a marvellous austerity. To one of his secretaries, which forged an untrue bill in his counsel, he commanded the sinews of his fingers wherewith he did write to be cut, and so to be utterly banished.[119]

Wherefore, he was called 'Severus', which is as much to say as sharp or rigorous.[120] For severity is rigour in punishment, according to the quality of the offence, having respect to a good purpose, without any desire of vengeance; and it is that part of justice that consisteth in execution, <F4r> the commendation whereof shall appear in the next chapter.

etiamsi damnati non essent, ut, si eos casu aliquo videret, commotione animi stomachi choleram evomeret toto vultu ininardescente, ita ut nihil loqui posset'.

[116] Cf. SHA, *Alex. Sev.* 17.3, 'nam cum quidam Septimius Arabianus, famosus crimine furtorum et sub Heliogabalo iam liberatus, inter senatores principem salutatum venisset, exclamavit: "o Marna, o Iuppiter, o di inmortales, Arabianus non solum vivit, verum etiam in senatum venit, fortassis etiam de me sperat: tam fatuum, tam stultum esse me iudicat"', quoted in Eras., *Apoph.* 6.156 (CWE 38, 640).

[117] SHA, *Alex. Sev.* 22.6, 'praesides provinciarum, quos vere, non factionibus laudari comperit, et itineribus secum semper in vehiculo habuit et muneribus adiuvit, dicens et fures a re publica pellendos ac pauperandos et integros esse retinendos atque ditandos'.

[118] SHA, *Alex. Sev.* 23.1, 'Causas militum contra tribunos sic audivit, ut, si aliquem repperisset tribunorum in crimine, pro facti qualitate sine indulgentiae proposito puniret'.

[119] SHA, *Alex. Sev.* 28.3, 'eum notarium, qui falsum causae brevem in consilio imperatorio rettulisset, incisis digitorum nervis, ita ut numquam posset scribere, deportavit'.

[120] Cf. above, p. 188 and below, p. 262 and nn.

14. A notable example given by Alexander in reproving an ambitious and vainglorious counsellor.

I suppose it shall not be tedious to good men to hear one incomparable example of the severity of this marvellous Emperor, which, although it shall seem to many that shall hear it to be over vehement and grievous, yet, in reading the chapter next following, it shall be sufficiently declared by the words of the same Emperor that his said rigour in judgment was necessarily used, and with equality in justice, deserving in no part to be reproved. But now will I rehearse the said story.

There was about the said Emperor a man of great honour called Vetronius Turinus,[121] whom, for his great wit and sageness in appearance, the Emperor had in singular favour, in so much as he called him to his privy council and used to be with him more familiar than he was commonly with any other; which so much blinded the inward eye of Turinus that he could not see in himself which he not long before had condemned in other. Such incomparable sweetness is founden in the familiar company of princes.

Wherefore, like as when the companions and servants of Ulysses had eaten abundantly of the herb called *lotos* — the taste thereof was so pleasant and marvellous that all that ate thereof, forgetting their own proper country, coveted to remain still in that region where that herb grew, and but only by vio-<F4v>lence they could not be brought to their ships, to return to their proper houses[122] — semblably, Turinus, after that he had been with the Emperor in an inward and secret familiarity, he found it so pleasant that, forgetting from whence he was called and taking little heed of any other part of his office, he put his whole study and delectation to augment the opinion of men that thought that the Emperor would nothing do without his advice, whereby he should be magnified and honoured above all other of the Emperor's counsellors.

And therefore he had continual suit made unto him, as well by them that had suits to the Emperor in their particular causes, as others that looked for offices or great promotions. To every man apart he would promise his favour, and therefore received great rewards and presents. But finally, whom he knew that the Emperor had preferred in office or anything determined in his just

[121] What follows is based loosely (with significant elaboration) on the episode of 'Verconius Turinus' in SHA, *Alex. Sev.* 35.5–36.3, except as indicated at the chap. conclusion below, where the translations are close. Eras., *Adagia* 1.3.41, *Fumos vendere*, 'To sell smoke' (CWE 31, 270–72), quoted the same SHA, *Alex. Sev.* passage in full, with considerable comment; moreover, as noted below, Erasmus referred to the same episode repeatedly in other writings as well. The chap. 15 of debate next is wholly invented, though it seems likely that Elyot's developed interest in the episode was prompted by Erasmus's.

[122] Cf. Hom., *Od.* 9.82–104; also, Elyot, *Bibl.*, '*Lotos*, and *Lotis*, *-tidis*, is a notable tree in Afrike, or herb, of whose fruit if a stranger do eat, he doth incontinently forget his own country'.

cause — for that mought he know, being with the Emperor so secret, although the good Emperor did nothing by his persuasion only but by prudent advice and good deliberation, as it shall hereafter appear — on him would he beck, if he were in the chamber; and often times in a day, he would come from the Emperor into the chamber of presence, or place where suitors awaited, and, of whom he had received money, to them would he say that he had remembered them and in their request or matter received good comfort, when indeed he spake not thereof one word.

Finally, by the colour of this familiar and secret recourse that he had to the Emperor, he gathered much treasure; but at the last, diverse, and in great number, to whom he had <G1r> promised that thing that they sued for, notwithstanding they received nothing in conclusion but nods with the head, found themselves deceived and their great sums of money vainly employed, whereat they murmured; and partly moved with disdain, partly with poverty, they brast forth at the last into manifest grudging, which came to the Emperor's ear, by what means I know not. But such abuses cannot be long hid from princes that have their ears perforate, as is the proverb.

Which the Emperor hearing, he was moved with marvellous displeasure, considering that Turinus, whom he had in so great estimation, abusing his person in feigning him to be his pupil or servant, had sold his determinations and sentences; whereby he had defamed his majesty, in that that Turinus had brought men in belief that the Emperor did nothing but, as it were, at his only beck and commandment. Which opinion to redress, he used this policy.

He caused one to desire a thing of him openly, and afterward to sue to Turinus privily to help him in his demand and secretly to move the Emperor for him; which being done, and that Turinus had promised his good will to him that sued and soon after saying that he had somewhat moved the Emperor therein — where indeed he spake not thereof any one word — and that he abode an answer thereof, whereupon he received of the said suitor a great sum of money.

Which the Emperor knowing, he caused him to call eftsoons on Turinus; but he, as if he had in hand other business, only beckoned on him without speaking anything to him. For indeed the Emperor had given to another that <G1v> thing which this man sued for, which, grudging thereat, discovered openly what Turinus had of him received.

That knowing the Emperor, he caused Turinus immediately to be arrested and openly in his presence to be accused, which was done by a great number whom he had also deceived, taking of them great sums of money for offices, and other things which they never obtained.

Wherefore, after that Turinus was condemned by sufficient and credible witness, in whose presence he had received this bribery and in whose hearing he had effectually promised, he was judged by the Emperor to be led into the open marketplace, where most resort was of the people, and, there being bounden to a stake, with smoke made of green sticks and wet stubble to be smouldered to death. And during the time of his execution, the Emperor commanded a beadle to cry, 'With fume shall he die that fumes hath sold!'[123]

But to the intent that men should not think that for one offence the judgment was too cruel and rigorous, ere ever Turinus was condemned to die the Emperor made diligent search; and, by evident proofs, it was founden that Turinus had often and in many causes received money of both parts, promising to advance their cause to the Emperor.[124]

Moreover, to prove the severity of this Emperor laudable, it shall be declared in the chapter next following.

15. The consultation concerning the punishment of Turinus, and the excellent reason of the Emperor Alexander.

In the mean time that Turinus was accused and before his condemnation, the Emperor Alexander, according to his customable usage, gave <G2r> convenient time to his counsellors to deliberate by themselves, ere ever that they gave any sentence, what punishment should be equal to the offence of Turinus and necessary for an example to other, that they presumed not to do the semblable. After when the council was called, every man was commanded to declare his opinion. Some reasoned that the open rebuke with sufficient satisfaction unto the party should be a convenient punishment; other added to imprisonment for a certain time; diverse would that he should be banished far from the court; many affirmed with vehement arguments that he deserved to be beheaded, considering that, in abusing the Emperor's majesty, in selling great offices to persons unworthy, he had put the public weal in no little hazard.

The Emperor, advisedly hearing all their opinions, last of all, as it was his

[123] SHA, *Alex. Sev.* 36.2, 'in foro Transitorio ad stipitem illum adligari praecepit et fumo adposito, quem ex stipulis atque umidis lignis fieri iusserat, necavit praecone dicente: "fumo punitur, qui vendidit fumum"', quoted in Eras., *Apoph.* 6.159 (CWE 38, 640–41). Eras., *Panegyricus* (CWE 27, 41), praises Alexander's judgement on the occasion: 'What an emperor, worthy of immortal power!'; likewise, Eras., *Adagia* 1.3.41, *Fumos vendere*, 'To sell smoke' (CWE 31, 272), 'If only our princes would take care to imitate Alexander Severus. He was a pagan moreover, and a Syrian by race, and a mere youth'; furthermore, Eras., *Institutio* 2 (CWE 27, 246), proposes adoption of the punishment, with adaptation of it to contemporary circumstances ('it might be possible to construct an example artificially by finding a man who has already been convicted of some other capital offence').

[124] SHA, *Alex. Sev.* 36.3, 'ac ne in una tantum causa videretur crudelior fuisse, quaesivit diligentissime, antequam eum damnaret, et invenit Turinum saepe et in causis ab utraque parte accepisse, cum eventus venderet, et ab omnibus, qui aut praeposituras aut provincias acceperant'.

manner, reasoned in this wise, as hereafter followeth.

'My trusty and well beloved counsellors: we have hitherto attentively heard and thoroughly considered your wise and honourable sentences, declared with free and uncorrupted minds, although by the diversity of your natural inclinations your sundry reasons seem to have no little diversity, as it happeneth in all consultations wherein diverse men do show their conceits freely without fear of blame, as I doubt not but ye do; notwithstanding, forasmuch as, hearing all your opinions and reasons, I have my wit the better instructed to find out and declare — except I be deceived — what should be the most expedient and necessary punishment of Turinus for the offences which he hath committed, wherein ought to <G2v> be no less severity (as I will prove with good reason) than if he had attempted to have slain me or to bren this most noble city of Rome, the honourable mansion of gods, and common refuge of all the world.

'First, ye remember that ye chase me to be your governor not only for the nobility of my progenitors, ne for their images or monuments of thankful remembrance; yea, rather for the beastly and most abominable life of Heliogabalus, my cousin germane, ye had more cause to refuse me.

'Neither ye made me your emperor and prince for the goodliness of my person, or prowess shewed by me in your wars, I being yet for tenderness of age uneath able to do feats of arms, much less to lead an army, specially such one as pertaineth to this noble empire.

'But truly it was for the good estimation and hope that ye had in the towardness of mine education and nature, thinking it to be aptly disposed to virtue; wherein being brought up in °chil<d>hood, I ought to have alway about me such as be of like disposition and, by their assistance and counsel, to moderate and rule the public weal of this city.

'It ought therefore to be kept in remembrance that, as I have said, by the good opinion and hope that all men have conceived of me, this public weal, which being subverted, I found as none, I have reedified and — be it spoken without boast — almost made new from the foundation.

'Then if he that enforceth himself to bren the houses or to beat down the walls of the city by good justice and reason should suffer death, by a much greater reason ought Turinus to die, that hath endeavoured himself to subvert and destroy that <G3r> whereby the public weal as well was begun as is also preserved, considering that the public weal in estimation is to be preferred before the material city, as much as the life of man and renome of virtue be of more value than stone or timber, wherewith the walls and houses be builded. °And therefore Aristotle, in defining what is a city, doth not call it a place builded with houses and environed with walls, but saith that it is a company which hath sufficiency of living and is constitute or assembled to the intent to

° childhood] chyldhode *B* : chylhode *A*
° \City./

live well.[125] Wherefore, it is the people and the weal of them that maketh the city; and the destruction and subversion thereof ought with more rigour and vehement punishment to be revenged, if more sharp punishment may be than death, than brenning and beating down of material houses or walls.

'This well and deeply considered, it shall not be thought that they that have reasoned for the mitigation of Turinus' punishment had before in remembrance and sufficiently examined the grievousness of his offence, according as I have declared it, but only considered his bare act without any circumstance. But yet the treason done also to me aggrieveth the trespass. Is it not treason to conspire the destruction of thy sovereign lord? Most of all, of whom thou art entirely favoured and put in great trust? Is there any diversity between the sticking of him with a dagger or killing him with poison and, by some circumstance, to cause his people to rebel against him and in their fury to slay him? Who, comparing together the form and manner of these offences, will not suppose it reason that the punishments therefore should be <G3v> much more vehement and sharp than for any other transgression, since justice limiteth equal punishment in proportion according to the importance, that is to say, the greatness or smallness of the offences.

'Now let us consider the quality or substance of Turinus' misdemeanour. In the time of the Emperor Severus[126] and Caracalla, he was in small estimation; but after that I was elect emperor, he, craftily smelling out my disposition, by little and little acquainted himself with some of those of whom for their virtues I had best opinion; and counterfeiting their manners, he at the last so aptly set forth such gravity, which he adorned also with a wonderful sharpness and promptitude of wit, that he obtained to be °<h>ighly recommended unto me by the wisest men of my council, by whose advice first I made him one of my treasurers. Finally, I called him near me and made him of my privy council, wherein we found him so necessary that in our opinion his sentences were equivalent and sometime surmounted them that had been in most estimation. And to the intent that he would augment that opinion and credence that we had in him, he ever used a great severity or straightness in his sentences again flatterers, dissemblers, and persons corrupted, namely, such as sold their endeavour or diligence in obtaining our favour in any matter or for any office. And by his industry, diverse were detected unto me and punished according to their merits.

'For these causes, I more and more took him in favour, and, to encourage other to ensue his example, I did advance him, as ye know, to the highest dignities within the city, except the con-<G4r>sul, and have participate with

125 Arist., *Pol.* 1.1 (1252a).
126 i.e. Septimius Severus.

° highly] *B* : kyghly *A*

him our most privy secrets, using him so familiarly that diverse other of our counsellors have partly disdained.

'Now behold what he hath done. First, he hath deceived and mocked us with his hypocrisy, abusing our simplicity and winning our favour, and not our favour only but also our credence and trust, whereby he mought finally work to his private commodity and to our confusion. For, he being with us in such familiarity as none other was, he practiced those things that we most abhorred, that is to say extortion, selling of right and wrong, and merchandising of offices and dignities. To whom is extortion or bribes not grievous, although the giver receiveth great lucre? Is there anything to be more abhorred than selling of justice, which knoweth no reward? How much more intolerable is the selling of injustice or wrong, whereby the one part suffereth damage by sustaining of wrong, the other is more endamaged by leesing of his good name and also his money, if it happen, as it hath done oftentimes, by a good and righteous governor, that he which hath done wrong be compelled to make restitution? But principally and above all other am I most endamaged. For I, unawares and innocent, being brought into the hatred of men, should be destroyed before that I mought know that I were in peril.

'Now consider ye the importance of Turinus' offence, conferring it with all that which I have rehearsed — and by the way, remember that not only he that sleeth his prince or depopulateth his country and maketh it desolate, but also he that conspireth to do it and thereto endeavoureth himself with all his puissance, though <G4v> he be let by some occasion or study, deserveth to die by the determination of justice distributive. By what mean he would do it, it is not material, except peradventure some man mought suppose that the act were more odious of him that procured the people to destroy their own prince or country, whom they are bound by allegiance and duty with all their power to defend, than of him that °do solicit strangers or ancient enemies to invade his country.

'Finally, if any common person, never receiving of me any benefit, would report in the ears of people that I went about to change the estate of the weal public of this noble city, to slay all the senators, to withdraw the people from their ancient liberties, and finally to bring the majesty of the empire into a tyranny, and by such false information exciteth and stirreth the Senate and people to hate me and covet my destruction; such one, proved at the last to have said falsely, I believe ye would not think only worthy to die, but ye would with your own hands dismember him and pluck him in pieces.

'Why should you not then think that Turinus, whom I most favoured and was about me most secret, not by reporting evil of me, which perchance would not be believed, but by actual deeds and openly committing injustice

° do] doth *B*

and tyranny in maintaining, supporting, and comforting wrongs, extortions, oppressions, and other enormities against the weal public; also, advancing evil and ungracious personages to dignities and offices, whereby justice ought to be ministered and the public weal governed, and by these means quenching the good opinion and love that <G4r> all men had toward me and changing it to a fervent grutch and hatred, they thinking that Turinus did all thing by our appointment, stir the hearts of the people against me: why should ye not, I say, think that such one hath deserved to die?

'And, as he was with us in singular favour and trust, and therein like to none other, so ought his death to be singular and strange that, by the novelty thereof, it may be more terrible, whereby other may fear from henceforth to abuse in such manner our affability which, being in us natural, without such a munition, cannot be sure and safely preserved.

'And for this our sentence, no man ought to deem us cruel or to lack mercy, if he consider diligently all that we have spoken. And do also remember that, to keep an infinite number of men from the rigour of justice, I spare not to execute the same rigour on him, whom I specially favoured.'

After that the Emperor had concluded in this wise his reason, there was no man offered to reply thereto, perceiving him rather moved with zeal than with any particular displeasure. And, to say the truth, when they had pondered his considerations, not finding sufficient argument to confound his opinion, finally they all, being in number fifty wise and honourable counsellors, rejoiced that they had so wise and virtuous an emperor, which preferred justice and the weal of his people before any private affection or singular appetite.

Then immediately followed the execution of Turinus, which was appointed by the Emperor, in form as ye heard it declared in the last chapter. <H1v>

16. How Alexander instructed and entertained them that were officers, and of his liberality toward them that did well their duties.

Notwithstanding the severity of this noble Emperor in the sharp punishment of oppressions, extortions, and other offences of semblable importance, yet was he toward such as justly executed their offices for the public weal very favourable, gentle, and bounteous. For if any of them had, peradventure, at the beginning or first entry into his room or authority, used less diligence or omitted something that he ought to have done, either for lack of experience or having not therein sufficient instruction — foreseen alway that he did nothing by corruption or vicious affection — the Emperor, calling such one to him privily and apart from all other, first he would remember him for what cause he had called him to that room or authority, the importance or charge whereof he would also declare; and then would he somewhat commend him for his honesty and temperance, wherewith he would confess himself to be satisfied, according to his expectation; then, sadly and with a wonderful gravity, he would admonish or warn him of his lack in diligence or in omission, shewing what damage the public weal mought sustain by lack of his circumspection and, without that, their virtues should be unprofitable to their office or dignity. After would he exhort and require them with gentle countenance and words to use more study and travail about the affairs of the weal public com-<H2r>mitted unto them, promising to them for their good endeavour his assistance and favour with honest recompense in the end of their travails.

Moreover, although he were thus industrious in espying out the demeanour of every man in his office, yet would he not suffer any other person to rebuke or to scorn them, saying that, where any obedience is due, thence ought to be excluded all rebuking or mocking, considering that thereof ensueth contempt, which, like a pestilence, consumeth all laws and authority, and that he and the Senate were judges of the duties of them that be in authority. Also, he used to say oftentimes that it happeneth sometime that they which be slack in their duties at the beginning, after that they have been monished thereof, either by their friends or by the goodness of their proper wits, they have been industrious and diligent. Contrariwise, other, which at the first have been quick, with a marvellous dexterity and promptness, they have by little and little relented and, having gathered good estimation and abundance of substance, have withdrawn themselves from painful affairs and at the last to be to no man but only to themselves profitable.

When any man had exercised his office duly, uprightly, and circumspectly in the public weal, at the end of his term, when there was a successor unto him (being present) appointed, then would he say unto him that departed out of his office, 'The public weal giveth to you right hearty thanks'. Then would he reward him in such wise as, being private, he mought (according to his degree) live the more honestly. His reward was in land, cattle, horses, grain, iron, stone, <H2v> and other things necessary to build a commodious place,[127] wherein, after great travail about the weal public, he mought refresh both his body and spirits; and ever after the Emperor had him in most tender familiarity.

Verily, in one thing he used an incomparable diligence, wherein he surmounted (in mine opinion) all other emperors. There was no man in dignity or office, either by the assignment of the Senate or by his commission, but that he knew his person and form of living. And, that much more is, he had in his chamber bills containing the number of them which were his soldiers in wages,

[127] SHA, *Alex. Sev.* 32.3, 'si umquam alicui praesentium successorem dedit, semper illud addidit: "gratias tibi agit res publica"; eumque muneratus est, ita ut privatus pro loco suo posset honeste vivere, his quidem muneribus: agris, bubus, equis, frumento, ferro, inpendiis ad faciendam domum, marmoribus ad ornandam et operis, quas ratio fabricae requirebat'.

and also every one of their names, and what time they had served; and when he was by himself, quiet from great affairs, he perused the number of them, their dignities, wages, and fees,[128] to the intent that he would be for all occasions surely provided. And therefore when he had anything to do with his soldiers, he named every man in his communication; and when they were present, he called them unto him. And when he was solicited to promote any person, he marked his name; and then would he search his books of remembrance, wherein were the names of them that had served him, with the time of their service, also their reward or promotion, and at whose request or by whose solicitation they were promoted.[129]

In offices he seldom suffered to be any deputies, saying, 'They only should be advanced, which by themselves and not by deputies could order the public weal'; adding thereto that men of war had their ministrations and learned men theirs,[130] and accor-<H3r>ding thereunto should rooms be disposed, that every man should do that thing whereof he had most knowledge. He had therefore written what he had given; and, that remembering, if he found any man to whom he had either given nothing or that which in value was not equal unto his merits, he called him and said, 'What is the cause that thou askest nothing of me? Desirest thou to have me thy debtor? Ask somewhat, that, lacking promotion, thou complain not of me'.[131] He gave alway such thing as impaired not his honour, as goods of men attainted, not being in gold or silver, for that was alway put in the common treasury. Also, he gave bailiwicks and rules of places civil, but never of war,[132] except it were to them which were expert and approved true captains. Receivers he changed every year and called them an evil that needs must be suffered. As for chief judges, proconsuls, or lieutenants, he gave none of those rooms in reward, but by a deliberate judgment either of himself or of the Senate.[133]

[128] SHA, *Alex. Sev.* 21.6, 'milites suos sic ubique scivit, ut in cubiculo haberet breves et numerum et tempora militantum semperque, cum solus esset, et rationes eorum et numerum et dignitates et stipendia recenseret, ut esset ad omnia instructissimus'.

[129] Cf. SHA, *Alex. Sev.* 21.7–8, 'denique cum inter militares aliquid ageretur, multorum dicebat et nomina. de provehendis etiam sibi adnotabat et perlegebat cuncta pittacia et sic faciebat diebus etiam pariter adnotatis et quis quo esset insinuante promotus'.

[130] SHA, *Alex. Sev.* 46.1, 'eos esse promovendos, qui per se rem publicam gerere possent, non per assessores, addens militares habere suas administrationes, habere litteratos', quoted in Eras., *Apoph.* 6.147 (CWE 38, 637).

[131] SHA, *Alex. Sev.* 46.3, 'cogitabat secum et descriptum habebat, cui quid praestitisset, et si quos sciret vel nihil petisse vel non multum, unde sumptus suos augerent, vocabat eos et dicebat: "quid est, cur nihil petis? an me tibi vis fieri debitorem? pete, ne privatus de me queraris"', quoted in Eras., *Apoph.* 6.148 (CWE 38, 637).

[132] SHA, *Alex. Sev.* 46.4, 'dabat autem haec in beneficiis, quae famam eius non laederent, bona punitorum, sed numquam cum auro, argento vel gemmis, — nam id omne in aerarium reponebat — dabat praeposituras locorum civilium, non militum'.

[133] SHA, *Alex. Sev.* 46.5, 'rationales cito mutabat, ita ut nemo nisi annum conplerent, eosque,

Such was the wonderful and (as I mought say) most curious circumspection of this excellent prince Alexander, which, in mine opinion, cannot be by man's tongue sufficiently extolled.

17. How curious the Emperor Alexander was in assigning of justices in his laws, and how he used liberality or sharpness towards them according to their merits.

Such persons as he assigned to be judges in causes civil, he with good deliberation and proof did choose them which were best learned in the laws, and <H3v> were of much ancienty and therewith having good gravity, and were known to be sincere and of good conscience. And unto them was appointed an honourable stipend, in so much as to them that were judges in provinces was given °to every of them twenty Roman pounds of silver, six silver pots, two mules, two mulets, two horses, a horsekeeper and a muleteer, two robes or habits to sit in judgment, one honourable garment to wear in his house, one for his bain or study; also, a hundred pieces of gold; moreover, one cook, and, if they were unmarried, one concubine. And after that they had left their administration, they should yield again the mules, mulets, horses, muleteers, and cooks, which all the said time were found of the common treasure; the residue they should retain still, if they had done well in their office; and, if they had done evil, they should pay the quadruple or four times so much as they received.[134]

He never would suffer that any office which had jurisdiction or execution of justice should be sold or obtained by giving of money or any other reward. And therefore, where one of his most privy servants had promised to one to obtain of the Emperor for him an office which had civil jurisdiction or administration of justice and therefore had taken a hundred pieces of gold, the Emperor commanded that he should be hanged on a gallows openly in the highway, wherein the Emperor's servants should most often pass to his manors without the city.[135]

etsi boni essent, oderat, malum necessarium vocans. praesides vero proconsules et legatos numquam fecit ad beneficium, sed ad iudicium vel suum vel senatus', quoted also in Eras., *Adagia* 1.5.26, *Necessarium malum*, 'A necessary evil' (CWE 31, 406).

[134] Cf. SHA, *Alex. Sev.* 42.4–5, 'iudices cum promoveret, exemplo veterum, ut et Cicero docet, et argento et necessariis instruebat, ita ut praesides provinciarum acciperent argenti pondo vicena, mulas senas, mulos binos, equos binos, vestes forenses binas, domesticas binas, balneares singulas, aureos centenos, cocos singulos, muliones singulos et, si uxores non haberent, singulas concubinas, quod sine his esse non possent, reddituri deposita administratione mulas, mulos, equos, muliones et cocos, cetera sibi habituri, si bene egissent, in quadruplum reddituri, si male, praeter condemnationem aut peculatus aut repetundarum'.

[135] Cf. SHA, *Alex. Sev.* 23.8, 'qui [sc. a eunuch] de eo fumos vendiderat et a quodam militari

° *Pondo* containeth of our usual groats 125, so the stipend amounted to £41 13s. 4d. of our money/

And when Ulpian,[136] one of the sage men of his council, blamed <H4r> his sentence, as cruel and representing a tyranny, he patiently heard him and answered immediately, saying, 'The residue of my manners declareth me not to be furious or to take pleasure in cruelty, specially to them whom I favour and have next about me.

'See you not what worms and flies would increase to consume the grain and fruits of the earth, if the pleasantness of the springtime and beginning of summer should ever continue and the sharp and terrible winter did not, with his sharp frosts and bitter winds, purge the earth of such evil increase? Who knoweth not that, in all thing that is sweet, worms be founden, which will soon consume all that they breed in, if it be not preserved by laying about it something bitter or very unsavoury?

'If the ancient laws of this city judgeth him to die that spitefully pulleth down or defileth the Emperor's image, or counterfeiteth his coin, seal, or sign manual, of how much congruence and more with justice is it that he should suffer death which, with selling of the administration of justice, plucketh down and defileth among the people the good renome of the Emperor? Or counterfeiteth and changeth the mind of the Emperor, which is his very image immortal, whereby both the prince and the people suffereth incomparably more damage than by forging of money?

'Do not ye, being so wise a man, consider that he which buyeth a thing may sell it?[137] And for my part, while I live, I will never suffer any authority to be used as merchandise. For that which I suffer, I may not with mine honour condemn or prohibit; and I cannot for shame punish a man for selling that thing <H4v> that he buyeth.

'Wherefore, if ye consider everything well, ye shall find no cause to blame me of cruelty or resemble me to a tyrant.'

With these words, Ulpian found himself satisfied and, wondering at the Emperor's wisdom, ceased to speak any more against him in any semblable judgment.

When he made any ordinary judges, advocates, or proctors, he caused them

centum aureos acceperat, in crucem tolli iussit per eam viam, qua esset servis suis ad suburbana imperatoria iter frequentissimum'; quoted also in Eras., *Adagia* 1.3.41, *Fumos vendere*, 'To sell smoke' (CWE 31, 272). The ensuing 'dialogue' of Ulpian and Alexander is wholly Elyot's invention.

[136] For Ulpian, see above, p. 184 and n. 48.

[137] SHA, *Alex. Sev.* 49.1, 'necesse est, ut qui emit et vendat'. Cf. Elyot, *Banquet*, sig. E3r (translating the whole of SHA, *Alex. Sev.* 49.1, with attribution of the remarks to 'Alexander Augustus'), 'The Emperor Alexander would never suffer to be sold the office of a judge or great authority in the execution of laws, saying, "Needs must he sell that doeth buy. And I will not let that there shall be merchants of governance, which, if I do suffer, I may not condemn; for I am ashamed to punish a man that buyeth and selleth"'. SHA, *Alex. Sev.* 49.1 complete is also quoted in Eras., *Apoph.* 6.151 (CWE 38, 638).

to be openly named, requiring the people and giving them courage, if there were cause to accuse them, to prove the crime by open witness — and he was wont to say, 'Since Christian men and Jews, in the election of priests, caused them to be in such form tried, it should be inconvenient, if the same were not used in the governors of countries, unto whom were committed both the lives and substance of men that be under them' — foreseen, if they did not sufficiently prove it and that it seemed to be malicious detraction, the accuser should forthwith be beheaded.

18. Of the great care and diligence that Alexander used about the public weal, and of certain new officers ordained by him.

The household servants and counsellors of the Emperor being well tried and by his own example brought in good order; also, the head officers, judges, and all other that had authority in the public weal being well chosen and instructed by the example of the Emperor's court; it was a wonder to behold with how little difficulty and how soon <I1r> the residue of the weal public was brought into a good fashion, all men delighting in virtue and praising the beauty and commodity thereof in their superiors. Also, rejoicing at the affability and gentleness of the noble Emperor and semblably dreading his severity, they brought at the last virtue in custom, whereby happened that such vices as before seemed little and were nothing regarded became to all men (or, at the least, to the more part) detestable, in so much as the Emperor needed not to send forth any espial to espy men's conditions.

For such as were evil were everywhere noted and of all men disdained, so that by them it happened as it doth by one that is sick in a hot fever: which first abhorreth every medicine that the physician doth offer to give him; but, when he beholdeth the physician drink anything thereof, then is he the better content to assay of the same; but, by reason that his taste is corrupted, to him all thing that is wholesome seemeth unpleasant, be it never so delectable; finally, fearing either to die or to be compelled to receive a more grievous medicine, he taketh the potion by little and little; until at the last, by custom of drinking thereof, he hath brought that potion to be as familiar and agreeable unto his taste as was his common and most usual drink; and then doth he scorn both them that wilfully would die rather than they would take medicine, and also them that be their keepers or rulers, which do suffer them to take only that which contenteth their appetite. Semblably did they who by the Emperor's example accustomed themselves to virtue and honesty, eschewing such vices which before they had haunted. <I1v>

19. How the Emperor Alexander did ordain new officers in the weal public, and what belonged to their authorities.

Now let us return unto the Emperor Alexander. When he perceived that, by the example of him and other great officers, the people began to apply and waxed apt to receive due reformation of the state of their living, he, marvellously thereat rejoicing, gave himself wholly to the restoring of the public weal to her pristinate honour.

Wherefore, to the intent that nothing should escape unreformed, he ordained to be in the city and also in the provinces many officers, somewhat mo than before were accustomed to be, appointing causes civil and criminal to sundry jurisdictions, saying, 'Where one man hath many matters to order of sundry effects, it fareth with him as it doth with a man's stomach; for the stomach receiveth meats, diverse in qualities and effects, which all together cannot be by one man's nature duly concoct and digested. For some meats be in operation hot and be not apt but for a cold stomach; some, contrariwise, be very cold and in a cold stomach will never be boiled; other meats be of gross and hard substance and require a strong and mighty stomach to endue it; other be soft and delicate, and, being too hastily digested, it nothing profiteth. Notwithstanding, any one of the said meats, being in one stomach, are better prepared to digestion than many, considering the travail that nature must have in the separation of sundry qualities that be in diverse meats, to prepare them to their effects whereto they were <I2r> ordained. And if the natural heat in man's body be not thereto sufficient, that which is ordained for nourishing of life is converted to corruption of blood and other humours, which is cause of sickness. But if any meat happen to come into the stomach, which meat is apt for his temperature, there shall he be perfectly concoct or boiled, and by a natural digestion made apt for the nourishing and preservation of other members.

'According to this similitude, if one man, being in authority, which I resemble unto the stomach, be he never so well learned or wise, if he take upon him the ordering and discussing of all manner causes, his wit, which is in the stead of nature, shall be therewith so much encumbered that, being studious or occupied about one matter, in the mean time another is appaired; and if he leave the first, to reform the second or third, the first is then in worse case than he found it, the parties contending being chafed and in a more fervent contention. Or in a criminal cause, the offenders being left uncorrected, putting all fear apart, not only do persevere but also increase in their evil doings. Finally, where one man hath the depeaching of many matters, none one of them may be brought to a perfect conclusion, forasmuch as to every act belongeth opportunity, which can never be found where many matters be interlaced, opportunity being only espied by a vigilant and constant study. Moreover, where many men be in authority, good wits shall not be hid nor unrewarded, and many shall apply them to virtue and study, upon hope of preferment; and whereas be many particular authorities, there shall sundry matters be the sooner <I2v> depeached.'

This was the saying of Alexander; and therefore, by the consent of the Senate and people, he ordained first, according to the counsel of Plato, certain persons, which were named 'Conservators of the Weal Public',[138] to whose office it appertained to see that the children of the Romans were well brought up and instructed, according to the capacity of their wits, from the age of seven years unto sixteen, and that in their plays and recreation were nothing dishonest; also, that at certain times appointed they were exercised in riding, if they were sons of gentlemen; also, they and the residue were exercised in swimming, running, wrestling, and to occupy all weapons of war; semblably, that the maidens, during the said age, were brought up in shamefastness, humbleness, and occupation necessary for a housewife; and that they were not seen out of their fathers' houses, but only in the temples unto the which women only resorted, and that in the company of their mothers or such other as were in their places.

Moreover, it pertained to the said Conservators to control every householder, of what estate or degree so ever he were, if there were found any excess in his fare, or that he had resort of riotous persons, or that he kept any mo servants than had rooms in their houses or in some necessary business were continually occupied. Also, that no man, neither in himself, his wife, nor his servants, should exceed or in any part change the apparel that by the laws or the Emperor's ordinances had been provided. Moreover, to see that no vittling house nor bordel <I3r> house should have their doors open or receive any person either before the sun risen or after the sun set, which was done to the intent that every man should be known that repaired to such places. And much good happened by that provision.

These Conservators were three score in number, that is to say, for every tribe two, Rome being divided into thirty tribes.[139] And twice in the week, they assembled and did communicate such defaults as they had founden; and forthwith, all they certified to the Provost of the city all the defaults, reserving the education of children, which they themself reformed by sharp admonition given to their parents; whom if they found disobedient or negligent, they certified thereof the Senate, who caused the said parents to be punished as enemies of the public weal of the city. Them which offended in the other articles, the Provost of the city punished according to the statutes and ordinances in such cases provided.

[138] Φύλακες, from Pl., *Resp.* 2.374d–376d.

[139] Cf. SHA, *Alex. Sev.* 33.1, 'Fecit Romae curatores urbis quattuordecim, sed ex consulibus viros, quos audire negotia urbana cum praefecto urbis iussit'. By tradition, the *tribus* were regal-period divisions of the populace of Rome for purposes of administering suffrage, described in Liv. 1.13.7–8, 1.42.4–1.44.2.

The praetors, quaestors, and other like offices and authorities, he augmented in number, albeit he divided their jurisdictions. To some, he appointed only contracts, in the which word were comprehended all things wherein bargain or promise was contained; and that he caused to be extremely examined and discussed by the said officers. And in whom was founden to be any deceit or faith broke he, without hope of any remission or pardon, was immediately beaten with whips; which was also the punishment of them that had stolen privily, without any violence, the Emperor saying that it was but a fantasy and a thing to laugh at, to make a dif-<I3v>ference between stealing and deceit or breaking his bargain, where it appeareth to be no diversity but only that this hath trust and credence joined with it and the other hath none, but is a single injury; wherefore in reason it is the lighter offence, where, by the other means, not only the thing is gotten with as much injustice as if it were stolen, but also faith, otherwise called trust, which is the foundation of justice and consequently of the public weal, is dissolved; and therefore it ought to be revenged with no less punishment than simple theft.

Purveyors for grain to the city, he made of honest and diligent persons, and to them he assigned particular auditors. Notwithstanding, at the end of the year, both the purveyors and auditors left their offices and other were chosen. To them that were his bailiffs, receivers, surveyors, and other that procured or gathered the revenues of his crown, he gave competent salaries; but he favoured them not, calling them a necessary evil. Wherefore, if he perceived that any of them had gathered much richesse, he would take all from them, saying, 'Let it suffice you that ye have taken so long pleasure with my goods, and beware that ye take not from other men injustly, lest ye make me more angry with you'. Albeit, if he perceived any of them afterward to live uprightly and to have good wit and learning, he advanced them to some other rooms, wherewith they confessed their service to be recompensed.

Finally, he never punished any man grievously for his own particular causes. And the sharpness that he used in punishing offences against the <I4r> weal public, when his considerations were well examined and pondered, it was thought by all wise men to be right expedient. To the Provost, he joined fourteen which had been consuls, calling them governors of the city, commanding them to hear, with the Provost, the affairs of the city, and that no sentence were given nor act made but that they all, or the more part, were thereat present.

20. The detestation that Alexander had unto idleness and the vices thereof proceeding, and of diverse provisions that he made against it.

This most noble Emperor was so rooted in virtue and fervent zeal toward the weal public that all vice was to him almost intolerable. And forasmuch as he perceived that idleness — that is to say, ceasing from necessary occupation or study — was the sink which received all the stinking canals of vice, which, once being brimful, suddenly runneth over through the city and with his pestiferous air infecteth a great multitude of people ere it may be stopped and cleansed; and that notwithstanding, the people, being once corrupted with this pestilence, shall with great difficulty and with long tract of time be delivered; and yet ere that shall be brought well to pass, a great part of the people shall perish.

Which this wise and virtuous Emperor considering and having thereof marvellous care, to the intent to withdraw men from all excuses of idleness, he, with an °incompar<a>ble prudence, ordained <I4v> for every estate some form of exercise to be necessarily or virtuously occupied, beginning at the base people or commoners, which were most in number, and preceding forth to every other degree or condition.

First, all vile occupation or labour whereby nature mought be corrupted or bodily strength decayed, he caused only to be exercised by bondmen or strangers, that is to say, not being citizens. Semblably, he would not suffer any citizen to be a merchant adventurer, nor to sell anything by retail that he himself wrought not or were not made by his own provision or study; saying that the Romans, by travelling into sundry countries, gathered and brought into the city with their merchandise the vices of other people, which, apprehended by other — as the more part of men do delight in newfangleness — is the cause of more damage to the public weal than a hundred times the value of the merchandise may be commodious. Moreover, finding once a delight to accumulate treasure and desiring to exceed one another in richesse, they attend so much to their own particular lucre that they abandon all liberality, benevolence, and charity, except it be very few; finally, they be never to the public weal profitable.

Also, they that retail that which is bought of the craftsman that worketh it, they not only defraud other of the just price, contrary to the direct order of equity, but also do consume the time idly, being not occupied neither in bodily exercise nor in virtuous or commodious study. Therefore, to such practice or mystery, he admitted only strangers; and also to bring out of other countries and to sell to the citizens all such <K1r> things as thereof was none growing in Italy, or not in sufficient quantity, as wools, metal, and silk, foreseen that none of it were wrought in any place out of Italy. And of such strangers, it was leeful to the Romans to buy in gross and retail, albeit there should no mo retail than were appointed by the Senate; and those also should be examined and assigned by the Provost of the city and such as were to him associate.

And the said merchant strangers were by the Emperor's commandment very courteously entertained — and so were all other strangers which repaired to the city to buy there anything or else to practice any excellent cunning or craft — and were exonerate of all charges for the wars, except it were only for the defence of the city. But of them he suffered to be but a certain number, which

° incomparable] incomparble *A B*

was not lawful for them to exceed; and unto them were assigned of the Romans certain judges and officers, which yearly also were changed.

But now, to treat how he kept the people from idleness: first, he provided that °there was not any artifice or craft necessary but that it mought be found within the city, which he ordered in this wise. He knew every year once by the officers called *censores* how much people were dwelling in the city of every age; also, by them which were called *aediles*, how many households there were of every craft. Then would he diligently ensearch of what perfection their works were, wherein they were occupied; and if he found therein much lack, so that the buyers should suffer detriment, then enjoined he the seller thereof that he should no more work to sale until he were instructed <K1v> more perfectly; notwithstanding, that person was compelled to work under another man, which was more perfect, until his work were commended.

Moreover, he ordained that, after that the children of the commoners could write and read perfectly, they were set to some artifice or craft; but, if within one year it appeared that they were unapt thereunto or that it were much contrarious unto their nature, then the Conservators, examining as much as they could to what craft or science necessary their wits were most apt, unto that should they forthwith be set, to learn of them which were good workmen. And therefore, he gat out of all parts of the empire the most cunning and perfect craftsmen in every science to dwell in the city, not only compelling them by his authority but alluring them, with yearly stipends of grain, to the finding of their households; and also, to be free from all manner exactions in peace or war, to instruct in their crafts perfectly the youth of the city.

The crafts which he would that the more part of Romans should occupy were those wherein both the body and wit mought be exercised, which he said pertained to men that were free of condition; other occupations, wherein was bodily labour only, he said was for bondmen and beasts. And therefore, within the territory of the city of Rome and in the manors and farms of the gentlemen Romans, he ordained that bailiffs and surveyors of husbandry should be free men and citizens and that the plowmen and laborers should be bondmen and strangers. In other cities besides Rome, some of these things <K2r> were changed after the necessity and nature of the people, wherein this Emperor alway had a marvellous consideration.

After this diligent provision, if any one of the people had been found idle by the space of one whole day, except in feastful days and other times of solace appointed, he was forthwith examined; and having no leeful and approved excuse, he was first whipped and after by the Conservators committed to one of the crafts that he was of; and for every day that he was openly seen to be idle, the person unto whom he was committed should for a month set him to any labour

° there] where there A B

that he list as his slave or bondman, giving to him meat and drink only. And it was not to any other man leeful during that time to give him meat or drink, or to speak with him otherwise than to rebuke him. And after the said correction, the said Conservators should see that he were bestowed where he mought work with a competent living.

The semblable order was diligently and (as I mought say) exactly kept by the Emperor's straight commandment, both in Greece and Italy. And where execution any time failed or was neglected, the officers were deposed with open reproach and forfeiture of the third part of their substance, which was employed immediately on grain and distributed equally and freely among the people well occupied within the city or town where such thing happened. And with great difficulty, the said officers in such wise deposed could ever after obtain of the Emperor to come in authority. By the fear whereof and the said distribution unto the people, this ordinance <K2v> was never omitted during the life of Alexander. Wherefore, it was a wonder to behold how suddenly idleness was everywhere excluded and cunning in every occupation augmented.

21. Of bains and places of exercises made for the people of Rome by the Emperor Alexander.

Moreover, to the intent that the people should not be too much fatigate with continual labour, whereby their bodies should become decrepit and unapt to the wars, he not only amended and enlarged the hot baths made by diverse emperors and princes before him, wherein the people of Rome accustomed to refresh and make clean their bodies, but also made new baths, more pleasant and sumptuous, joining them to those that were made by Nero the Emperor, conveying into them water naturally hot, running by conduits of marble from mountains in Naples by the space of two hundred miles from the city of Rome;[140] and also, he brought into some parts of the bains cold water from the most pure and delectable springs, the people to use the one or the other at their own pleasures.

Moreover, he bought certain houses which stood nigh to the said bain and caused them to be pulled down; and that place he made to be levelled and to be set with young trees in the most pleasant fashion, having there large places wherein the people, after that they were bained, mought run, leap, or wrestle, or use any other semblable exercise, to the which places the said trees gave a commodious and pleasant umbrage; and in the wrestling pla-<K3r>ces, the

[140] Cf. SHA, *Alex. Sev.* 25.3–4. The *thermae Alexandrinae* on the *campus Martius* in Rome, mentioned also in Elyot, *Gov.* 1.17 (Watson, p. 75), were the *c.* 227–229 rebuilding and extension of the *thermae Neronis* constructed in 62. The baths were fed by the 22.4 km long *aqua Alexandrina* built at the same time.

ground was thick covered with camomile, origanum, and other like grasses, both sweet in savour and soft to fall upon. Also, the said Emperor much delighted in the beholding of the said exercises, wherefore it was the most part of his pastime or solace to see the people exercised in form aforesaid or else the gentlemen to assay themself in form of battle, as hereafter shall be declared.

To the said bains and places of exercise were assigned a number of keepers and ministers, to whom were given sufficient salaries. And those places were alway kept so neat and delectable that, to the eyen or nose, was never anything unpleasant or noyful; by the which cleanness the city was marvellously preserved from sundry sicknesses, which undoubtedly do grow of corrupt exhalations venting out of men's bodies.

And for that cause, to avoid occasion of pestilence and other horrible diseases, this Emperor prohibited, by special laws, ingurgitations, banquets, late suppers and long; moreover causing the controllers of markets — of whom there were diverse, which were every year chosen of special honest men, and not avaricious or needy — to have a vigilant eye on the market, that not only vittles were sold by a due weight and measure and at prices set by the Senate, but also that they were not in any part corrupted in savour or substance and that no such thing were sold for vittle wherein any poison naturally mought be engendered and hid, as musherons, frogs, and other like things, founden out rather by wanton appetites than by nature engendered to serve for man's sustenance.

And in these things, if any lack <K3v> were perceived to be, the Emperor and Senate, with a diligent scrutiny, found out the person by whose default it happened, with also the controller which seemed to be negligent, and the seller was according to the laws sharply punished. The controller or other officer, if there were founden in him negligence, was with great rebukes expelled from his office and had the tenth part of his movable goods confiscate, which, being brought into money and bestowed on wheat, was distributed among the people which dwelled in that part of the city where the offence was committed.

It is here to be considered that such sums as were forfeited by corrupt or negligent officers came never to the use of the Emperor, nor he gave them to any person; but, employing it on corn, he caused it to be distributed among the people, which, in mine opinion, was a marvellous policy. For thereby he declared that he used severity not for his own particular advantage; and also, the people which suffered detriment by the lack of the officers received the benefit of that which was forfeited, which caused a multitude to lie alway in await to find some misdemeanour in the officers, to the intent they mought thereby be the better relieved. And the officers at the last became marvellous circumspect; and finally the prince, for his wisdom and charity not only praised but also as a universal father of all his people, was most °ent<ire>ly beloved.

Touching such persons as were in extreme poverty and, either by grievous

° entirely] enterly A : entierly B

sickness or feeble age, were decrepit or otherwise not able to labour, I will, after the next chapter, declare the incomparable prudence of this excellent Emperor. <K4r>

22. Of the magnificence of the Emperor Alexander in sumptuous and necessary works, and in what exercises he caused the nobility and gentlemen of Rome to be occupied.

Besides the bains which I late remembered made in the city of Rome, Alexander made also in every realm, being subject to the empire of Rome, common bains.[141]

He also made great and strong barns in many cities for the people to keep in their private stuff and goods, such as had not of their own private houses of sufficient strength for that purpose.[142]

He made also many fair houses and mansion-places, which immediately he gave to his friends whom he perceived to be most trusty and honest.[143]

In a place called *Baianum*, he made works magnific or sumptuous, garnished with images of them which were joined to him by any affinity. He made meres and pools to be wondered at, bringing the sea unto them[144] and causing them to be replenished with strange and principal fishes.

Also, he edified great and wonderful bridges and repaired all them which were made by Trajan, leaving notwithstanding to Trajan the name and honour thereof.[145]

In the market place of Nerva, he set up great images of the most noble emperors, some on foot and some on horseback, with their titles over their heads, and between every image a great pillar of brass, containing all their gests and acts worthy remembrance.[146]

141 SHA, *Alex. Sev.* 39.4, 'balnea omnibus regionibus addidit, quae forte non habebant'.

142 SHA, *Alex. Sev.* 39.3, 'Horrea in omnibus regionibus publica fecit, ad quae conferrent bona hi, qui privatas custodias non haberent'.

143 SHA, *Alex. Sev.* 39.5, 'fecit et domos pulcherrimas easdemque amicis suis maxime integris viris donavit'.

144 SHA, *Alex. Sev.* 26.10, 'fecit et alia in Baiano opera magnifica in honorem adfinium suorum et stagna stupenda admisso mari'. *Baianum*, 'the Baian territory', in the region of Baiae on the Gulf of Naples, was traditionally the Roman elite's favourite resort: cf. Elyot, *Bibl.*, '*Baiae, arum*, a town in Campania, on the sea side, between *Puteolos*, and *Misenum*, for the temperateness of air and fairness of building, much haunted of the ancient Romans, where also been hot waters natural, which are both pleasant and wholesome, and therefore it hath been supposed, that all other hot baths natural, were called *Baiae*'.

145 SHA, *Alex. Sev.* 26.11, 'pontes, quos Traianus fecerat, instauravit paene in omnibus locis, aliquos etiam novos fecit, sed instauratis nomen Traiani reservavit'.

146 SHA, *Alex. Sev.* 28.6, 'Statuas colossas vel pedestres nudas vel equestres divis imperatoribus in foro divi Nervae, quod Transitorium dicitur, locavit omnibus cum titulis et columnis aereis, quae gestorum ordinem continerent'.

He made also a basilic, or place where civil controversies were heard and judged, which contained in breadth one hundred feet, and in length a thou-<K4v>sand, and stood all upon pillars[147] of porphyry, which is a stone of purple colour, and the pillars were garnished with images of noble princes, Greeks and Romans, wrought in pure white marble, with their names over their heads, and, under their feet, their acts wrought also in very small images of copper, in a most lively and quick demonstration.

But in one kind of magnificence, he passed all other. For where diverse cities by earthquaves had been frushed and therewith deformed, he, of the revenues of the same countries, gave great sums of money to the re-edifying of them.[148] And many he °eftsoons restored to their pristinate beauty and strength; diverse he made more substantial and sure. There was no town of reputation in his time decayed, but that he caused the occasion thereof to be searched for and to be forthwith reformed.

The havens of Italy and Sicily, he caused not only to be cleansed and repaired, but also to be made more stronger, to defend outward hostility.

Moreover, for the exercise of them which were above the estate of the common people, he repaired and new made many places and things necessary, which is expedient to be put in remembrance.

First, he visited all the libraries that were in the city. And where he found any books deformed, either with ancienty, or by negligent keeping, or by any other means, he caused them to be new written and laid in their places, and the houses to be not only cleansed, but also made more ornate and necessary, as making for every book an hutch locked, to the intent that, when any man came to study there, he should have no mo books to look on than one of the keepers of the libra-<L1r>ry — whereof there were a good number retained to give their attendance, having therefore competent salaries — should deliver unto them; and before they departed, the said keeper should peruse the leaves of the books that they looked in, to the intent that, if they did cut or rend any out of the volume, they should be apprehended and by the officers called *aediles* committed unto prison, and there should remain until they had repaired sufficiently the books that they had defaced and also caused another like book

[147] SHA, *Alex. Sev.* 26.7, 'basilicam Alexandrinam instituerat inter campum Martium et saepta Agrippiana in lato pedum centum in longo pedum mille, ita ut tota columnis penderet'.

[148] SHA, *Alex. Sev.* 44.8, 'multis civitatibus, quae post terrae motus deformes erant, sumptus ad instaurationem operum et publicorum et privatorum pecuniam ex vectigalibus dedit'. Cf. Elyot, *Gov.* 2.10 (Watson, pp. 159–60), 'The noble emperors Antonine and Alexander Severus gave of the revenues of the empire innumerable substance to the re-edifying of cities and commune houses decayed for age or by earthquaves subverted, wherein they practiced liberality and also beneficence'.

° eftsoons] efetsones *A* : eftesones *B*

to be written and bestowed in the said library; and if any such person had escaped by negligence or favour of the keeper and the default founden by some other, the keeper was expelled from his office without hope of remission and was also compelled to redub the harm in likewise as he should have done which committed the offence if he immediately had been apprehended.

He made also a new library, garnishing it as well with most principal works in every science as also with the images of the authors, wrought most excellently both in embossed work and portraiture; which library was divided into sundry galleries, according to diverse sciences, all builded round, in the form of a circle, and being separate with walls one from another. And in that portion that belonged to Geometry and Astronomy were about the walls great cartes and tables, containing sundry lines, figures, descriptions, dimensions, or measurings, conversions of stars' motions and revolutions of planets, spheres, and imaginary circles, with also material spheres, quadrants, astrolabes, and all other instruments belonging to those sciences. Semblable tables were <L1v> in that portion that pertained to Arithmetic and Music, containing the sundry proportions of numbers and tunes, and thereto was added harps, lutes, organs soft in sowning. For all instruments that were loud and made great noise were excluded thence; the cause appeareth to wise readers.

The place which was compassed about with the said libraries was also round, and decked with pleasant imagery, and having seats commodiously about it, where they that came to study in the libraries mought walk or sit at their pleasure and communicate, each with other, that which they had read or perceived. And to these places, there failed not to come daily a great number of gentlemen.

For other necessary exercise, the Emperor enclosed with a high wall a ground joining to his own palace, containing in circuit one Italian mile and a half, which, within the wall, was environed with a gallery of three heights for men to stand in and behold, which galleries were also of stone. And in the space that two men mought stand and talk, there was a small pillar of marble, decked with images of men that deserved noble remembrance. The place was divided or set out with many large alleys, plain and straight, containing in brede one hundred feet, and in length one thousand feet. Those alleys were floored with plaster, and the residue was thick spread with fine grass and camomile, having here and there banks for men to rest them when they were weary.

The young gentlemen of the city, when they repaired to the palace to give their attendance, they, in the meantime that the Emperor was in preparing him for-<L2r>ward, exercised themselves, some in the said alleys in running or casting the ball, some in the green places wrestling, leaping, and casting of the dart. And in the galleries stood other of the nobility and gentlemen, such as listed to behold them. And without the walls were great and high trees of cypress and fir, with broad tops, conveyed thither with great industry; which trees did cast over the walls a pleasant umbrage or shadow, and defended them that did exercise from the vehement heat of the sunbeams, and also, in winter, kept the place more mild and temperate, in resolving or breaking the violent and cold blasts of the northern and western winds.

Oftentimes, the Emperor himself delighted to come and behold the said exercises. But in his own person, he never exercised himself but privily and a few being present, to the intent that, if he were vanquished in any feat — as sometime it happened, although few men surmounted him in strength and deliverness — he would not give occasion to be dispraised and had in contempt of his subjects.

When by extreme heat in the summer or by rain and other vehement tempests of winter, the said exercises mought not be used, then the young gentlemen some repaired to the said libraries and passed the time virtuously in reading, writing, or playing on instruments; diverse haunted the schools of philosophers, rhetoricians, and poets — of the which sort there were at that time in Rome a great number — and heard them either recite their own works or expound other old authors. Many would resort to the common houses called theatres and, purposing some matter of philosophy, would there dis-<L2v>pute openly; other would pick out of some ancient story some question concerning martial or civil policy and, in commending or discommending it, declare their opinions and sentences in the form of a consultation; which exercise was of no little importance to the increase of wit and provision of counsellors. And at such exercise, the Emperor principally delighted to be present in his own person, as well to have knowledge of other men's wits and towardness as also to gather of their reasons some sentence or matter, which, being kept in remembrance, mought perchance profit him in matter more serious or earnest occasion.

Besides these persons, there failed not to be some more given to play than to study, which also had a fair and large place in the palace, where they played at the chess and other like games, wherein they mought be pleasantly occupied, wherein the winning was, neither gold nor silver, but only victory and commendation of wit or diligence. Notwithstanding, it was leeful for them at such games to play for money, so it exceeded not a sum certain which was assessed by the Emperor and Senate.

At dice it was not to any man leeful to play, the Emperor having this sentence alway in his mouth: 'Our forefathers trusted in wisdom and prowess and not in fortune, and desired victory for renome and honour and not for money; and that game is to be abhorred wherein wit sleepeth and idleness with covetise is only learned'. And for the mortal hate and indignation that he bare to this loss of time — for so ought it rather to be called than a play — he made a law, which was ratified by the authority of all the Senate and people, <L3r> that, if any man were found playing at dice, he °should be taken for frantic or as a fool natural, which could not well govern himself; and his goods and lands should be committed to sage and discrete personages appointed by the whole Senate, which, employing on him that which was thought necessary for his estate or degree, should bring truly that which remained to the common treasury, to the intent that, when he returned to thrift or was seen by a good space of years to use good husbandry in employing well and honestly that portion that he had, he should be eftsoons restored as well to his lands and goods as to the revenues and profits that were growen in the mean time while they were confiscate or in the rule of his tutors. Finally, next to thieves and extortioners, the Emperor most hated them which, after the said law being made, were found to be dice-players and would not have any of them called either to office or council.

23. Of hospitals and other provision made by Alexander for men that were decrepit, or so diseased that they could not labour.

On a time, the Emperor Alexander, visiting all parts of the city of Rome to behold how the temples and other solemn edifices were kept and repaired, in passing through the streets, he beheld a great number of persons, some defaced with horrible diseases and some mutilate of their members, as lacking arms or legs or the necessary use of the one or the other; which he, considering with a <L3v> severe and grave countenance, at the last said to a noble man called Julius Frontinus,[149] who at that time was praetor or governor of the city under the Emperor, 'What sort of people be these, which, being horrible and noyous to behold, do seem unprofitable to the weal public, since they cannot labour but consume those things which are ordained for them that can defend the weal public and us when occasion requireth?'

Then answered Frontinus, 'Sir! They be your natural subjects, whereof part be deprived of their members by chance of war, wherein they have served you and your noble progenitors, emperors of Rome; some do lack the office of their members by natural infirmities; the residue, which to your majesty and all other seemeth to be an horrible spectacle, are men attached with grievous sicknesses, which do happen to them — as physicians do say — by the putrefaction of natural humours.'

[149] For Frontinus, see above, p. 179 n. 32. The ensuing dialogue uses principles from Elyot's *Castle of Health*; it also exemplifies the principle articulated in *Gov.* 3.26 (Watson, p. 285): 'And therein governors shall not disdain to be resembled unto physicians, considering their offices in curing and preserving be most like of any other. That part of physic called rational, whereby is declared the faculties or powers of the body, the causes, accidents, and tokens of sicknesses, cannot always be sure without some experience in the temperature or distemperature of the regions, in the disposition of the patient in diet, concoction, quietness, exercise, and sleep'.

° \Dice playing/

'And whereof', said the Emperor, 'proceedeth such putrefaction of humours, suppose you?'

'Truly', said Frontinus, 'as I have read and heard say, it cometh of one of these causes: either forasmuch as great abundance of superfluous humours, thick and clammy, be dispersed in the body, whereby the pores — which are little holes in the skin, throughout all the body, that be invisible — be stopped, so that the exhalation or breath enclosed in the body may not issue out by the same pores, whereunto a strange or unnatural heat being joined maketh the said putrefaction. Sometime it happeneth of meats or drinks, being corrupted ere they be received; sometime where as well the air as the bodies of men be distem-<L4r>pered. Also, it happeneth sometime by the wrath of God, where he is offended or neglected in such duty as belongeth unto him, as it hath been perceived oftentimes in this city and declared by prophets.'

'Ye have answered right well', said the Emperor, 'unto my demand. But yet, forasmuch as I suppose that ye call them superfluous humours which are more than convenient to the natural proportion and temperature of the body wherein they be, I pray you tell me, if ye can, whereof cometh that superfluous abundance? And by what occasion do they become thick and clammy, whereby the pores, as ye say, be stopped?'

'Truly', said Frontine, 'as I have heard of physicians — and also, daily experience and reason declareth it — it proceedeth of repletion and idleness: that is to say, by eating immoderately above that which natural heat may concoct in the stomach; also, engorging meat upon meat, ere that meat which was first eaten be fully digested; also, by not using competent exercise, whereby nature is comforted and prepareth herself to labour about the concocting and digesting of that which the body receiveth.'

'Ye have now satisfied me', said the Emperor, 'and well to the purpose. Now behold', said he, 'Frontine, honourable father, what a pernicious negligence was in our predecessors' emperors (besides the ill example of diverse of them)! Which have, like ill tutors, suffered the people of Rome, their pupils, so many years daily to consume themselves by licence in living! Which hath brought into the city such horrible sickness! Which I will provide to expel thence, if it be possible.'

The next day following, he assembled his coun-<L4v>cil, which as I said before was of fifty reverend personages, to whom he declared the communication between him and Frontine, who at that time was present, being one of the counsellors, affirming that he was fully determined as well to provide for them which either were attached with the said horrible sicknesses, and for those which were by wars for the weal public mutilate in their members or maimed, as also to put clean away or at the least way to minish the original occasions of the said sicknesses; which noble enterprise being of all them that heard him commended.

Finally, it was thought expedient by the noble Emperor and by all his said council approved that, within the city of Rome, there should be two fair and large hospitals builded to receive and keep them which were so mutilate or maimed in the wars that they could not exercise themselves in manual occupation; for all other labours were done by captives, bondmen, and slaves, and the Romans were thereof discharged. Also, without the city, in some village nigh to it whereby passed some river, should also be edified two other hospitals, ample and necessary for five hundred sick persons, unto whom should be appointed five physicians, substantially learned in physic and well experienced; also, five expert surgeons, with two apothecaries, men of good credence and trust, which should be bounden to have alway all necessary drugs, vigorous in their force and virtue, without sophistication or other deceit in simples or compounds; also, that they should burn or utterly reject all things which were either corrupted, or so dried that it should seem to the physi-<M1r>cians — who should as oft as they list examine the wares — to be noyous or to medicine unprofitable.

The meat which was ordained for these sick persons should be so little in quantity that it was less than sufficient for any whole person; and when it was asked of the Emperor why he would that they should have so little a pittance, he answered merrily that he did it for three special considerations. \1/ The first was that he had read in the books of Galen, the most excellent physician, that the more one nourished bodies unclean and not sufficiently purged, the more he did hurt them.[150] \2/ Also, if the meat were more than the sick men could eat, the ministers about them would sell that which was left; and when they had gathered thereby much money, either they would live therewith riotously and neglect their duties in attending the sick folk, or else with that gain provide for themselves some more wealthy and easy living, so that in conclusion the sick people should be destitute of convenient ministers to await on them. \3/ The third consideration was that if the sick men had abundance of good meat, many of them remembering that, when they were whole, they should be constrained to some occupation and that they should not then eat so much meat and so good as they eat in the hospital where they lay well and at rest; wherefore, perchance when they were whole, they would find the means to fall eftsoons in their said sickness or other like, that they mought be brought again to the hospital. Such miserable nature remaineth in some men that, to live idly and voluptuously, they will choose rather to be sick than to be healed. <M1v> These allegations of the wise Emperor was then confirmed by diverse which had known it by long experience.

[150] Galen of Pergamum (129–216), physician to the Roman emperors from Marcus Aurelius to Septimius Severus, from whose commentaries on the Hippocratic corpus is probably taken the quotation of Hippoc., *Aph.* 2.10 used here, as also in Elyot, *Banquet*, sigs C8r–C8v (unattributed), 'Unclean bodies, and they which of superfluous humours be not well purged, the more ye nourish them, the more do ye hinder them'.

Concerning them which were mutilate or maimed in wars for the weal public, they should have a more plenteous entertainment if he were in poverty or lacked friends. But they which were not in that necessity should have appointed by the Senate and the Emperor's consent an honest proportion in corn and wine to spend in their own houses, as a thankful remembrance of the Senate and people for their good endeavour whiles they were able.

Moreover, to provide for time to come, that is to say, that the causes before remembered whereof the said horrible sicknesses proceeded, he affirmed that the best and most sure mean was to pacify the ire of God and to make him benevolent unto the people, which should be most assuredly done by excluding horrible vices and abominations out of the city, and to honour God purely. As for the disposition of men's bodies, made apt by surfeits and idleness to receive corruption and consequently horrible sicknesses, he determined to make an edict or imperial ordinance, confirmed by an act of the Senate, that no man should use mo than two meals in one day and that there should be at the least six hours between every meal. Also, that the censors, or correctors of manners, should take diligent heed that, if they found or were informed that any man of the commonalty went to his meal before he had wrought sufficiently in some occupation, that the same censors should cause him to be apprehended and kept in some prison, by the space of three days, having but once in <M2r> the day only one ounce of bread and a little water, without any other nourishment; the Emperor here rehearsing a proverb whereof he had heard part of the Christian men: 'Let him eat that laboureth, for he that laboureth not is not worth that thing that he eateth'.[151] And such as mought not be withdrawn from idleness, he would have them sent into Spain, to dig for gold, or into the isles called *Cassiterides*,[152] to labour in tin works. And if within a while they laboured well without coercion or grutching, those should be revoked into the city, there to apply diligently their occupation.

He would also that the common people should not have at one meal but one kind of flesh or fish, and that should not be either delicate or in great quantity; and if any man were found doing otherwise, he should forfeit to the common treasury double the value of the meat which he had for that meal provided; and that no gentlemen should have mo than three sundry dishes at one meal, besides fruit, nor any senator above four diverse dishes and one kind of fruit, if he list. Which number he himself did not exceed, although no law did thereto compel him.

[151] Proverbially, 'Qui non laborat non manducet', usually attributed to Paul, on the basis of 2 Thes. 3. 10, 'nam et cum essemus apud vos hoc denuntiabamus vobis quoniam si quis non vult operari nec manducet': 'For even when we were with you, this we commanded you, that if any would not work, neither should he eat'; cf. Elyot, *Banquet*, sig. E4r (with attribution to 'Paulus'), 'He that will not work shall not eat'.

[152] The legendary 'Tin Islands' of ancient Greco-Roman geography, e.g. in Plin., *NH* 34.156; cf. Elyot, *Bibl.*, '*Cassiterides* be ten Isles in the Spanish sea, wherein was digged much tin, and they be not far from the west part of Spain'.

He would not that any citizen should resort to open tavern, but that every man should have his provision in his own house, and that taverns and common cooks should serve only for them which dwelled out of the city and came thither for some necessary business. And if any citizen were found in tavern, eating or drinking, he should be sent for to the censors and be sharply rebuked; at the second time excluded out of all assemblies and noted ever after as a man out of <M2v> credence or possibility to any preferment; at the third time, he should be sent to the mines and there remain until he seemed to have amended his manners. A gentleman should be at the first time rebuked; at the second time lose the name of a gentleman and be reckoned among the base people; the third time, his goods should be committed to a tutor, whereof he should have no portion until it were well perceived that he had utterly left resorting to taverns. A senator, being found in such places, should incontinent be discharged out of the Senate, being during his life without hope to be thereto restored.

When the Emperor Alexander had concluded these things with his own counsellors, he soon after came into the Senate and there recited in an eloquent and sober oration the said articles, declaring what fervent desire he had to save the people of Rome, not only against outward hostility, but also against inward perils and consumption of their bodies by horrible sicknesses; which oration finished, all the Senate, with tears in their eyes for gladness, in the name of themselves and the people, rendered most hearty thanks to the Emperor's majesty, and forthwith, without any exception or misliking of any one thing, they confirmed it by an act of the Senate.

And the next day, the tribunes assembled the people and declared to them all that preceded; which they so joyously heard and received that they ratified it with their common consents, with these acclamations: 'Noble Alexander, we pray the gods that they have no less care of your majesty than ye have for us! Most happy be we that we have you among us! Noble Alexander, the <M3r> gods preserve you! The gods defend you! Proceed forth in your purpose! We ought to love you as our father, to honour you as our lord, to marvel at you as a god here living among us.'

Thereto they added, 'Noble Emperor, take what ye will of our treasure and substance, to accomplish your purpose'.

The Emperor, hearing of this liberal offer, caused to be answered in his behalf by Frontine his praetor: 'The Emperor thanketh you, but nothing will he charge you with, touching the building and furnishing of the said four hospitals; for he will do it of his own treasure. Only two things he requireth of you, which shall not be burdenous to you: first, that ye cease not to pursue and obey continually all the said statutes and ordinances; the second, that ye will be content that such common revenues which seem to him vainly employed and against the weal public may, without any grutching of your part, be laid to the maintenance of the said hospitals.'

Thereat, all the people eftsoons with one voice cried, 'Do, noble Emperor, what shall seem to you good! For your most blessed nature cannot err or do amiss any thing that ye purpose!'

Hereat, the Emperor rejoicing and remembering that, long time before, he thought that the plays called *Florales* and *Lupercales* and the abominable ceremonies of Isis — in the which were shewed by men and women, naked, most abominable motions and tokens of lechery — were provokers and nourishers of beastly vice,[153] he therefore, by the consent of the Senate, abolished the said plays and ceremonies; and, the revenues which belonged to the maintenance of them being very great, <M3v> he appointed to lay them unto the said hospitals, with some part of his own possessions, which he had purchased.

Finally, the said four hospitals, within the space of one year, were builded on the river of Tiber in the most ample and magnific fashion, so that all the chambers of the sick people were so made that the floors of them were ten feet above the ground and distant one from another twenty feet, every chamber having his bain and fresh water conveyed into every one of them by a conduit, their places of easement over the river, the windows lying north and northeast, the floors of great thick planks close joined. In the nether story were the cellars, larders, wardrobes, and such other offices. At the south side were like many chambers, the windows opened toward the north. The kitchens and lodgings of officers and ministers which should serve the sick men were at the west end. At the east end, having a prospect into the north, was the warehouses, which served for medicines. To them were joined the lodgings of the apothecaries, physicians, and surgeons, and they were right fair and honestly furnished. Of no less magnificence were the two hospitals in the city, but rather more costly, whereby the beauty of Rome was much augmented.

These things being stablished, the Senate took on them the governance of them, appointing every year by lot ten senators to be thereof surveyors and controllers of all the officers and other ministers, and the same senators at the end of their year to make accompt openly to the tribunes and people of the employment of every parcel of the said revenues; and if any were found in arrearage, he should be compel-<M4r>led immediately to pay to the treasury of the said hospitals four times as much as the arrearage amounted to.

Finally, so much commodity happened unto the city of Rome by the said hospitals and other ordinances before rehearsed that, within very few years after, no foul sickness was perceived to be in the city nor idle person, by occasion whereof a great part of the chambers in the said hospitals were vacant and much of the revenues were saved; which, being brought to the common

[153] The *Floralia*, the *Lupercalia*, and the *Isidis navigium* rite were historical spring celebrations of fertility at Rome; cf. Elyot, *Bibl.*, '*Floralis, florales ludi*, plays made in the honour of Flora an harlot, which gave a great treasure unto the people of Rome', and '*Lupercalia*, sacrifices and plays made to Pan'.

treasury, afterward eased the people of taxes in time of war, to their no little comfort and quietness.

24. In how sundry wise Alexander exercised his own person, so that he was never unprofitably occupied.

The mind of this noble Emperor was so fervently set and determined to the good governance and advancement of the weal public and the conservation of the same that, in eight the first years of his empire, which was the most part of his reign, inasmuch as he reigned but thirteen years and nine days,[154] he did almost none other thing but continually sit with his counsellors, which were never fewer than fifty men, excellent in learning and virtue, treating and devising things expedient for the weal public. And by the example of Augustus the Emperor, he reported to the whole Senate once in a month such things whereupon they were concluded, with the principal reasons which thereto induced them, which, if the more part of the Senate sem-<M4v>blably liked, then were the provisions or ordinances devised by their sentence approved and incontinently enacted and published.

And to the intent he would not have his labours and the authority of the Senate frustrate by the lack of execution (notwithstanding that he had many espials, as I said before, to await the defaults of officers), he used many times to disguise himself in diverse strange fashions, as sometime in the habit of a scholar of philosophy comen out of Greece and speaking nothing but Greek, which he did most exquisitely; oftentimes, like a merchant come out of Syria or Persia, which had then but one language, and that spake the Emperor naturally, forasmuch as he was born in Syria. And having with him one or two men of that country which he did counterfeit, he, like a scholar or servant, would one day haunt one part of the city, another day another part, and most politicly find occasion to see the state of the people, with the industry or negligence of them that were officers. Which progress he would never discover to any man, but only to Ulpian[155] or one or two mo of his most secret counsellors or servants, neither before that he began it nor after; and to them that accompanied him he commanded that they should keep it ever secret, as they would avoid his most grievous displeasure. And, indeed, during his life, it was by them never discovered; but sometime, he could not so escape unknowen but that he was sometime perceived; but, dreading his severity, they that met with him and knew him °darst not salute him or make any sign of knowledge unto him. But when that they had disclosed it, all they that heard it examined <N1r> their own acts; and all they which at that time had done anything worthy to be reproved lived in dread, looking to be therefore corrected, or at the least ways blamed;

[154] SHA, *Alex. Sev.* 60.1, 'Imperavit annis XIII diebus VIIII'.

[155] For Ulpian, see above, p. 184 and n. 48.

° darst] darste A : durste B

contrariwise, they which had done anything worthy commendation took marvellous comfort, doubting not but that their good acts should either with benefit or with the Emperor's praises be shortly rewarded, whereunto soon after was added to profit either in some office or in other yearly revenues.

After that he had reduced the city to this honourable state, he then, by the advice of his most discrete counsellors, once or twice in the week, used to solace out of the city with a great company with him of honourable personages. For he never shewed himself openly as emperor but with a great and honourable presence, above any other king of the world, albeit then he expressed a marvellous familiarity to all men indifferently that list to approach him, without repulse to any man being in honest vesture and not diseased with infective sickness.

In this solacing, he hunted the hart, the wild boar, or such as be called *alces*,[156] brought for the nonce out of the great woods of Germany, which be in quantity higher and longer than any ox. He hunted also oftentimes the bear, but that never saving only when he was in the parts where they were bred, saying that, forasmuch as the bear was of his nature a devourer of cattle, he desired not to have of that kind in those places where cattle is nourished. In hunting these beasts, he sometime on horseback proved his strength, sometimes shooting, otherwhiles casting at them javelins which served for that purpose. Oftentimes, he only beheld other <N1v> young gentlemen hunting, which he divided into sundry companies and appointed to them a number certain of arrows or javelins, to the intent that one should not be more exercised or take more solace in hunting than another.

The lions, leopards, tigers, panthers, and other like strange and furious beasts he had in great numbers, which were kept only to the intent that, at certain times, in the amphitheatre and other like places in the city ordained to the purpose, the people mought take pleasure in beholding them, and also seeing some such desperate persons as would adventure their lives fight with some of the said beasts or one beast to fight with an other. But never would he let any gentleman Roman to do such battle, saying that he esteemed none so little that he would put him in danger for such a beast, whose body, being dead, was nothing profitable.

He took also pleasure to hunt the fallow deer, the roe, and the hare with greyhounds, enforcing his horse (wherein he much delighted) to give as many turns to the game that he hunted as the greyhounds should do. And in that pastime, having to every beast of venery but two dogs at the most, he contended

[156] Elks: Elyot, *Bibl.*, '*Alce*, a wild beast in the woods of Germany, in fashion and skin like to a goat, but greater, which have no joints in their legs, and therefore they do never lie, but only do lean to trees, when they do rest them, which the hunters knowing, do saw the trees that they lean to, half asunder, whereby they fall down, and be taken'.

with many other young gentlemen on horseback, which were by himself only appointed to shew himself most deliver and ready to encounter and check the game at the most advantage, wherein was a right pleasant and also profitable exercise, shewing a visage or representation of a skirmish in wars, specially when he hunted the hart and the beasts named *alces*, for then there required to be shewed much strength and hardiness, and in the pursuit labour and <N2r> painfulness.

And in this solace he used much prudence, for they which one day hunted with him should not hunt the next day, but behold other hunting and mark diligently the lack of them that hunted in too much haste or slowness, to the intent that they mought refrain such default, and they that did best were praised. And by him that was the provost of hunting, it was registered in the Emperor's presence how many times every man was commended, to the intent that, as rooms of captains and petite captains were void in any of the Emperor's garrisons, they which in the said huntings were judged most active, if other good manners were in them founden according, should be preferred to such rooms, after their merits. But alway this good Emperor had a vigilant respect to the form of their livings and advanced no man suddenly, but with long deliberation and good advisement.

Moreover, notwithstanding his hunting or other recreation, he never would let any day pass without either consulting some thing for the weal public, or giving some true sentence in judgment, or reading some place in good authors to augment his wisdom, or writing some story or other thing worthy remembrance. He was such a niggard of time that he was marvellously grieved if he spent any day in solace without doing of any of those things that I have rehearsed, notwithstanding that, in the mean time, all the affairs of the empire were treated and ordered by men, assured good and faithful, whom he knew well would not be corrupted. And when need required, he heard matters before it was day, and prolonged the <N2v> time until it were late and within night. And notwithstanding, he never shewed countenance of weariness, ne to be in any part froward or angry, but had alway one manner of visage, and in all things seemed merry and pleasant.[157] Undoubtedly, he was of an excellent prudence, as in whom no man could find any lack, and of so ready a wit, that if any man merrily would taste him with a pretty taunt, he should shortly perceive that he understood him.[158]

After the common affairs, as well civil as martial, he gave the more part of his study to the reading of Greek authors, reading the books of Plato, *Of*

[157] SHA, *Alex. Sev.* 29.5, 'sane si necessitas cogeret, ante lucem actibus operam dabat et in longam horam producebat neque unquam taediavit aut morosus aut iratus resedit, fronte semper pari et laetus ad omnia'.

[158] Cf. SHA, *Alex. Sev.* 29.6, 'erat enim ingentis prudentiae et cui nemo posset inponere et quem si aliquis urbane temptare voluit, intellectus tulit poenas'.

a Public Weal; and, when he would read any Latin books, he read specially the books of Tully, *Of a Public Weal*, and also his *Offices*. Sometimes he read orators and poets, among whom was Serenus °<S>ammonicus, whom he knew and favoured, and also Horace. He read much the life of the great Alexander, whom specially he followed, notwithstanding he abhorred his drunkenness and cruelty, albeit the one and the other is defended and excused by some good authors, whom oftentimes the Emperor much believed.[159]

After his study, he applied himself to wrestling, running, or throwing of the ball, moderately. After his exercise, he, having his body anointed with precious and wholesome ointments, as it was at that time the use, entered into a bain or stew, not hot, where he tarried sometime by the space of one hour, not only to wash him but also to exercise himself in swimming.[160] And when he was come out of the bain, he would eat a good quantity of milk, sopped with fine manchet, and a few eggs, and thereto would he drink meath, and taking this for his breakfast, <N3r> sometime he would dine also, and oftentimes he abstained until supper.[161]

Always at after noon, he applied the time to signing and reading of letters and bills, they which were called remembrancers standing about him; and if, by the reason of sickness or age, it were painful for them to stand, he caused them to sit down, having the secretaries or clerks reading the said letters or bills unto them. Alway, the Emperor, having a pen, with his own hand added to that which was necessary, but that did he by the advice or sentence that seemed best or most convenient.

When he had perused all these things, all his friends were let in together, and who that list mought freely and boldly speak then unto him, and he merrily and comfortably gave ear unto them, albeit he would not hear alone any man, but only his great master, or Ulpian the lawyer, and such as were associate with him

[159] SHA, *Alex. Sev.* 30.1–3, 'Post actus publicos seu bellicos seu civiles lectioni Graecae operam maiorem dabat, de Re Publica libros Platonis legens. Latina cum legeret, non alia magis legebat quam de Officiis Ciceronis et de Re Publica, nonnumquam et orationes et poetas, in quis Serenum Sammonicum, quem ipse noverat et dilexerat, et Horatium. legit et vitam Alexandri, quem praecipue imitatus est, etsi in eo condemnabat ebrietatem et crudelitatem in amicos, quamvis utrumque defendatur a bonis scriptoribus, quibus saepius ille credebat'. Caracalla's murder of the near contemporary, exceptionally learned poet Serenus Sammonicus, 'many of whose books dealing with learned subjects are still in circulation', is described in SHA, *M. Ant.* (Caracalla) 4.4.

[160] SHA, *Alex. Sev.* 30.4, 'post lectionem operam palaestrae aut sfaeristerio aut cursui aut luctaminibus mollioribus dabat atque inde unctus lavabatur, ita ut caldaria vel numquam vel raro, piscina semper uteretur in eaque una hora prope maneret'.

[161] Cf. SHA, *Alex. Sev.* 30.5, 'egressus balneas multum lactis et panis sumebat, ova, deinde mulsum atque his refectus aliquando prandium inibat, aliquando cibum usque ad cenam differebat, prandit tamen saepius'.

° Sammonicus] Ammonicus A B

in some special cause of justice; but yet he never talked with any of them but that he caused Ulpian also to be present.

In this form, this noble Emperor passed his time, interlacing therewith other manner of solace.

25. How the Emperor Alexander, at the request of his mother Mammea, sent for the most excellent clerk Origen, and of the diverse notable sentences spoken by the same Emperor concerning the receiving of the Christian faith.[162]

°At this time, there was in the city of Alexandria, in Egypt, a man excellent in all manner of learning, and therewith wonderful eloquent in the Greek tongue, whose name was Adamantius Origenes, in so much as, when <N3v> he was but of the age of eighteen years, he was in all the liberal sciences and in philosophy learned exactly, above all men's estimation. He was son of one Leonidas, who for the Christian faith was beheaded. Also, this Origen was christened and from his tender age most perfectly brought up in the rules of that religion, which he alway most exactly observed, as well in all kinds of abstinence as in example of humility and contempt of things worldly. He was for his great learning and severity of life appointed by the bishop of Christian men in Alexandria to preach and expound the books which they called the Bible, by occasion whereof he drew a great number of people daily to the said Christian faith, which, although the Emperor Alexander knew, after that he did perceive that they were exquisite followers of virtue and peace, he would not suffer that any of them should be apprehended or punished but had them in great admiration and reverence.

[162] The episode is largely Elyot's invention, elaborated from the suggestion of the *c.* 325 *Ecclesiastical History* of Eusebius, 6.21.3–4: 'The mother of the Emperor, Mammaea by name, was a most pious woman, if there ever was one, and of religious life. When the fame of Origen had extended everywhere and had come even to her ears, she desired greatly to see the man, and above all things to make trial of his celebrated understanding of divine things. Staying for a time in Antioch, she sent for him with a military escort. Having remained with her a while and shown her many things which were for the glory of the Lord and of the excellence of the divine teaching, he hastened back to his accustomed work'. Having also the biographical information on Origen (Origenes Adamantius, *c.* 184–*c.* 255) that Elyot uses — e.g. Euseb., *Hist. eccl.* 6.1.1, 6.2.7–8 and 14, 6.2.12, 6.3.1–3 — the work was widely known in the West in the Latin version of Rufinus (*c.* 345–411), and it was cited by Jerome in *De viris illustribus* (*c.* 393) 54, which reports the same incident: 'How great the glory of Origen was appears [...] from the fact that he went to Antioch, on the request of Mammaea, mother of the Emperor Alexander, and a woman religiously disposed, and was there held in great honour'. Most likely, Elyot's imputation of this matter to 'Eucolpius' — including the repeated first-person intrusions of 'Eucolpius' below — is Elyot's oblique way of signalling his invention. On 'Eucolpius', see above, p. 171 and n. 1.

° \Eucolpius./

The fame of this great clerk Origen came to the ears of Mammea, the Emperor's mother, who (as some men supposed) was already persuaded to embrace that profession. Wherefore, to be the more perfectly instructed therein, she most affectionately coveted the presence of the said Origen. And therefore, she, awaiting opportunity, came to the Emperor her son and desired him that he would send for the said Origen, whose famous learning was only by report knowen unto him. To the which request he easily granted, and he himself endited letters to be directed to Alexander, then being the bishop of Christian men in Alexandria,[163] the tenor whereof hereafter ensueth. <N4r>

> °Alexander, Emperor Augustus, etc., to Alexander, the chief bishop of Christians in the great city of Alexandria, well to do.[164]
>
> The fame of the virtue and °wonderful learning of Adamantius Origenes, your great philosopher, soundeth continually in our ears; which maketh us desirous to behold and hear him, whose name contendeth in honourable renome with our imperial majesty. We, notwithstanding, not envying his glory but coveting to be partakers of his inspired learning and followers of his virtue, do require you to license him to come unto us to Rome at his leisure, without festination or travail.
>
> We have written to our Provost of Egypt, that he provide for him all thing expedient for his journey toward us.
>
> Fare ye well.

After that the bishop had received these letters, he, much rejoicing thereat, sent for Origen. But with great difficulty mought he persuade him to take that journey, he alleging by diverse arguments that it should be more necessary that he continued his preachings and lessons, where a great part of the people were already informed in the Christian faith, and daily increased, and waxed desirous of the interpretation of divine mysteries, than going to the city of Rome, where abounded all vice, pride, and tyranny, there to sow precious seeds, as it were, in the sand, or to give orient pearls to swine.

Yet finally, when the bishop and other sage personages had °credibly informed him of the most excellent virtues of the Emperor Alexander and in what sort he had reformed the state of the city of Rome, he condescended to go thither. Which being intimate unto the Provost of <N4v> Egypt, he, according to the Emperor's commandment, provided for him a ship with all things necessary unto his journey. And because he beheld him simply apparelled, he ordained

[163] Presumably the sainted Alexander of Jerusalem, martyred in 251 (Euseb., *Hist. eccl.* 6.11), is meant, though he was not a bishop of Alexandria.

[164] Translating the standard Greek epistolary salutation, Εὖ πράττειν, 'enjoy well-being, do well', as in the nearby sidenote; equivalent to Latin *salutem dicere*.

° \The letters of Alexander the Emperor/

° \Ευ πραττειν/

° credibly] credyble *B*

for him sundry garments in the most honest sort that philosophers then used; but Origen would not receive any part thereof, not so much as hosen or shoes; but, like as he alway accustomed to go from his childhood — that is to say, in a single garment of cloth and barefooted — so went he to Rome.[165] And when at his arrival there were brought unto him a mule and a chariot, to ride in the which he best liked, he answered that he was much less than his master Christ, which rode but one day in his life, and that was on a seely ass-mare; wherefore, he would not ride except he were sick or decrepit, so that his legs mought not serve him to go.

The Emperor and his mother, hearing of the coming of Origen, caused him to be brought in their presence, where he, according to his duty, right °humbly saluted the Emperor, kneeling, but the Emperor, with most gentle countenance, embraced him and enforced him to stand on his feet. Semblably, the Emperor's mother devoutly saluted him, rejoicing much of his presence. And when the Emperor had beholden his native gravity and most assured countenance, he in his heart judged him to be a reverend personage.

Then demanded he of him what thing he professed.

He answered, 'Verity'.

The Emperor asked of him what he meant thereby.

He said it was the word of the living god, which was infallible.

The Emperor asked which was the living god and why he so called him. <O1r>

Origen answered that he did put that distinction for a difference from them whom men, being long drowned in error, did call their gods, whom they confess to be once mortal and to have died; but the god whom he preached was ever living and never died, and is the life of all things that be, like as he was the creator of them.

And when the Emperor had required him to declare the unity of God the creator, he devoutly lifting up his eyes, after a short meditation, with an incomparable and most compendious eloquence, he forthwith opened that mystery in such wise that, as well to the Emperor and his mother as to all other standing about them — of whom I, Eucolpius, most happily was one — it seemed that we were brought out of a long sleep; and then did we see things as they were indeed; and that which before we esteemed and honoured were but vain dreams and imaginations.

Yet the Emperor, after a little pause, said unto Origen that he much marvelled why men of such wonderful knowledge should honour for god a man that was crucified, being but of a poor estate and condition.

'O noble Emperor!', said Origen. 'Consider what honour at this present time

[165] Cf. Euseb., *Hist. eccl.* 6.3.10–12.

° humbly] humble B

the wise *Athenienses* yet do to the name and image of Codrus, their last king of Athens,[166] forasmuch as at the time that war was made by the two people called *Peloponenses* and *Dorienses* against the *Athenienses*, answer was made to them which counselled with Apollo at Delphos that the Peloponenses and Dorienses, if they slew not the king of Athens, they should have the victory. Whereof Codrus hearing, preferring the <O1v> safeguard of his people before his own life, took on him the garments of a slave, and, bearing on his shoulder a burden of sticks, he went to the host of the enemies, and, there of a purpose quarrelling with some of them and in the press hurting one with his knife, he was by him which was hurt stricken through the body and slain; by occasion whereof, after that it was perceived and knowen of the enemies, they being confused, raised their camp and departed. And for this cause, the Athenienses have ever since had the name of Codrus in reverence and, as all men do think, worthily and not without reason.

'Now, then, consider, most excellent prince, how much more worthy, with what greater reason and bounden duty ought we and all men to honour Christ, being the son of God, and God; who, not only to preserve mankind from danger of the devil, his ancient enemy, but also to deliver man out of his dark and stinking dungeon of error, being sent by God the father from the highest heavens, willingly took on him the servile garment of a mortal body, and, hiding his majesty, lived under the visage of poverty; and finally, not of his enemies immediately, but, much more against reason, of his own chosen people the Jews, unto whom he had extended benefits innumerable and after his temporal nativity were his natural people and subjects, he, quarrelling with them, by declaring unto them their abuses and pricking them with condign rebukes, at the last he was not slain with so easy a death as Codrus was, but in most cruel fashion was scourged until no place in his body was without wounds and then had a crown of long and sharp <O2r> thorns set and pressed on his head; and, after long torments and despites, he was constrained to bear

166 The tale of this legendary figure was widely recirculated in antiquity (e.g. Val. Max., 5.6.ext.1), and Elyot himself has another retelling of the same version of it in *Gov.* 2.9 (Watson, pp. 152–53); also, Elyot, *Bibl.*, '*Codrus*, the proper name of a king of Athens, which to save his country, willingly lost his life'; cf. Eras., *Adagia*, esp. 2.8.33, *Generosior Codro*, 'As nobly born as Codrus' (CWE 34, 60–61), though also 2.8.15, *Cur non suspendis te?*, 'Why not hang yourself?' (CWE 34, 54). The analogy with Christ developed immediately below is in Origen, *Contra Celsum* 1.31, 'Therefore, let those who would disbelieve the statement that Jesus died on the cross on humankind's behalf say whether they also refuse to accept the many accounts current both among Greeks and foreigners of persons who have laid down their lives for the public advantage, in order to extirpate evils which had fallen upon cities and countries', and in the letter traditionally ascribed to Origen's teacher Clement (Titus Flavius Clemens, *c.* 150–*c.* 215), 1 Clem 55.1, 'To adduce examples of Gentiles too, however: many kings and rulers, when some season of plague pressed upon them, being taught by oracles, have delivered themselves over to death, that through their own blood they might rescue their fellow citizens'.

an heavy cross, whereon afterward his both hands and feet were nailed with long and great nails of iron; and the cross, with his naked and bloody body being lift up on height, it was let fall with violence into a mortise, that all his joints were dissolved. And notwithstanding all this torment and ingratitude, he never grudged, but, lifting up his eyes unto heaven, he prayed with a loud voice, saying: "Father, forgive them, for they know not what they do."[167]

'This was the charity most incomparable of the son of God, employed for the redemption of mankind, who, by the transgression of Adam, the first man that ever was created, was taken prisoner by the devil, that is to say, kept in the bondage of error and sin, from the actual vision of God's majesty, until he were in this wise redeemed, according as it was ordained at the beginning.'

At these words of Origen, all they that were present were wonderfully astonied, and therewith the Emperor, with a sturdy countenance, said unto Origen: 'Ye have wonderfully set forth a lamentable history! But yet notwithstanding, therein be things dark and ambiguous which do require a more plain declaration. For what maketh you bold to affirm that Jesus, which in this wise was crucified, was the son of God and God, as ye have called him?'

'Sir', said Origen, 'sufficient testimony, which of all creatures reasonable ought to be believed and for the most certain proof to be allowed.'

'What testimony is that?', said the Emperor.

'Truly', said Origen, 'it is in diverse <O2v> things.

'First, the promise of God, by whom all this world was made.

'Also, by his holy spirit speaking by the mouths of prophets, as well Hebrews as Greeks and other whom ye call *vates* and *sybillas*.

'Thirdly, by the nativity of Jesus of a pure virgin, without carnal company of man; the most pure and clean form of his living, without sin; his doctrine divine and celestial; his miracles most wonderful and innumerable, all grounded on charity only, without ostentation; his undoubtful and perfect resurrection the third day after that he was put to death; °his glorious ascension up unto heaven, in the presence and sight of five hundred persons which were virtuous and of good credence. Also, the gift of the holy ghost in speaking all manner of languages and interpreting scripture, not only by himself but also afterward by his apostles and disciples and given to other by imposition of their hands.

'And all these things ordinarily followed, according unto the said promises and prophecies. I omit to speak of the confession of devils, which by Jesus and his apostles in his name were cast out of people which were obsessed. The oracles and answers of them, whom ye untruly call gods, do remain in confirming this testimony.'

And when Origen had said all this, he forthwith began there and disclosed the answers of Apollo made at Delphos, affirming Jesus to be God. Afterward, he

[167] Lc 23.34, 'Iesus autem dicebat: Pater, dimitte illis: non enim sciunt quid faciunt'.

° \How many were at the ascension of Christ/

recited and declared the prophecies, as well of the Hebrews as of the sibyls and other; last, the promise of God unto the patriarchs, by the which it manifestly appeared that Jesus was Christ and God, and that, by his temporal °nativity, he was King of Israel, <O3r> and that the Jews were his natural subjects.

Which declaration of Origen was so evident and plain, and set forth with such wonderful eloquence, devotion, and learning, that it persuaded the Emperor and diverse other which then were present — whereof I, Eucolpius, was one — to embrace the profession of Christ's faith and doctrine, for the which I give most humble thanks unto God, by whose only grace I was called.

And for that time, the Emperor gave licence to Origen to return unto Alexandria, forasmuch as he darst not attempt to publish the Christian faith by his authority, the persecution of Christian men being but late ceased and they being yet odious to the Senate and people.

°Notwithstanding, in his privy closet he had the images of Christ, of Abraham, and of Moses; and, being by himself, he honoured one god,[168] as I myself, being often times secret with him, did well perceive. And at the last, he made request to the Senate that there mought be made a temple to Christ; wherewith they all were sore grieved and did obstinately deny it, saying that they had counselled with the gods, of whom they had answer that, if that were suffered, all men should be Christians and all other temples should be made desolate.[169]

Wherefore he ceased his enterprise, but alway he was studious in the books of Christian men and oftentimes used their sentences. As when any man went out of the highway and would pass through another man's ground, breaking his enclosure and riding over his corn or grass, if he perceived it, he would cause him to be beaten with staves or rods in his presence, after the quality of his trespass, or, if he were a man of honour <O3v> or worship, he would give to him great rebukes and say unto him, 'Wouldest thou have that done unto thee that thou doest to another?' And when a man was punished for any such trespass, he would cause it to be openly proclaimed, 'That which to thyself thou wouldest not have done, do not in any wise unto another'.[170] Also, when cooks

[168] Cf. SHA, *Alex. Sev.* 29.2, 'in larario suo, in quo et divos principes sed optimos electos et animas sanctiores, in quis Apollonium et, quantum scriptor suorum temporum dicit, Christum, Abraham et Orfeum et huiusmodi ceteros habebat ac maiorum effigies, rem divinam faciebat'; and above, p. 193 and n. 87, adapting the same passage.

[169] SHA, *Alex. Sev.* 43.6–7, 'Christo templum facere voluit eumque inter deos recipere. quod et Hadrianus cogitasse fertur, qui templa in omnibus civitatibus sine simulacris iusserat fieri, quae hodieque idcirco, quia non habent numina, dicuntur Hadriani, quae ille ad hoc parasse dicebatur; sed prohibitus est ab his, qui consulentes sacra reppererant omnes Christianos futuros, si id fecisset, et templa reliqua deserenda'.

[170] SHA, *Alex. Sev.* 51.6–7, 'si quis de via in alicuius possessionem deflexisset, pro qualitate loci aut fustibus subiciebatur in conspectu eius aut virgis aut condemnationi aut, si haec omnia transiret dignitas hominis, gravissimis contumeliis, cum diceret, "Visne hoc in

° nativity] nativitte A : nativitie B
° \Lampridius./

of the city claimed a certain place which Christian men had and his pleasure was therein required, he wrate in his rescript that it were better that God were there honoured in any manner of fashion than that cooks should have thereof possession.[171]

Eucolpius writeth that on a time he said to him and to Philip his bondman:[172] 'I perceive ye do wonder at the learning of Origen, whereby ye be induced to embrace the Christian profession. Truly, the humility and charity of the Christian people, which I have heard of and do daily behold, do much more steer me to believe that their Christ is God than the residue of all his persuasion.'.

And on a time when two Christian men contended proudly together, and they accused each other of speaking reproachful words of the Emperor, he called them before him and prohibited them to name themselves Christian men, saying, 'Your pride and malice do declare that ye be not the followers of him whom ye profess. Wherefore, though ye find lack in me, the which I will gladly amend, yet will I not let you against justice reprove by your acts him whose life and doctrine ye all do affirm to be uncorrupted and without any lack'. Which words being once spread among the Christ-<O4r>ian men in the city of Rome, it made them all afterward more circumspect and in humility and charity to be the more constant.

26. How Mammea the Emperor's mother exhorted him to be married, and what wise answers he made; and finally took to wife the daughter of a noble and ancient senator.

When the Emperor was come to the age of twenty years, his mother Mammea exhorted him to take to his wife some maiden of a noble and ancient house, to the intent that he mought have generation, which should be for the sure tranquility of the city and empire and to the principal comfort of him, the Senate, and people of Rome. After that he had diligently heard his mother say all that she would, he made to her an answer, in form following.

'I dare well say, madam, that ye have given to me this counsel of a sincere and natural love that ye bear toward me, your only son. But forasmuch as it is the matter which, within myself, I have much more debated than I suppose ye have

agro tuo fieri quod alteri facis?" clamabatque saepius, [...] idque per praeconem, cum aliquem emendaret, dici iubebat, "Quod tibi fieri non vis, alteri ne feceris"', quoted in Eras., *Apoph.* 6.153 (CWE 38, 639). The scripture lying behind the remark is Mt 7. 12: 'Omnia ergo quaecumque vultis ut faciant vobis homines, et vos facite illis. Haec est enim lex, et prophetae': 'Therefore all things whatsoever ye would that men should do to you, do ye even so to them: for this is the law and the prophets'.

[171] SHA, *Alex. Sev.* 49.6, 'cum Christiani quendam locum, qui publicus fuerat, occupassent, contra popinarii dicerent sibi eum deberi, rescripsit melius esse, ut quemadmodumcumque illic deus colatur, quam popinariis dedatur', quoted in Eras., *Apoph.* 6.152 (CWE 38, 638).

[172] On this figure, to whom a biography of Alexander is elsewhere imputed, see above, p. 179 and n. 31.

done, although perchance ye have thought more on it, I will declare unto you how I find in my fantasy that the taking of a wife should be to the public weal and to myself more dangerous than fruitful, specially at this time. For where ye will me to take a maiden, if she shall be much younger than I am, perchance she shall not be so apt for generation of children, strong and lusty, as if she were of mo years. And I covet not to deface the imperial majesty with children weak and unlusty. Also, the sturdiness of the Romans may <O4v> not sustain to be governed but of them which, as well in personage as wisdom, be convenient and seemly.

'If she shall be as old or elder than I am, then shall I bring myself to much unquietness and trouble of mind. For ye know well, it is not yet passing four years agone, that the abominable monster my kinsman Heliogabalus left not only the city of Rome but also all the country of Italy so polluted with detestable lechery that with much difficulty mought one find an house wherein had not been committed some kind of that vice, either voluntary or else by enforcement. Wherefore, if I should marry one of the said city or territory, although I found her by fame and experience a maiden, yet should not that discharge my mind of suspicion, thinking alway that she was rather so kept by restraint of liberty than by her own chastity, considering that she did hear or see daily such wanton allectives and provocations to lechery that the custom thereof did assault the mind so continually that it were well-nigh impossible to escape uncorrupted, although the body by vigilant custody abode undefiled. And this suspicion should wrap my heart in such melancholy that I should seldom be merry or pleasant with her, whom for mistrust I could not love perfectly.

'And to take a wife of any other country, ye know well it hath not been the use of emperors or other noble men of this city. I suppose it hath been for the wars, which hath and mought eftsoons happen to be between us and these outward countries. Wherefore, if the women thereof should be married to the Emperor and other of the nobility, and that soon after should happen hostility between them <P1r> and those countries, much inconvenience mought come to the city and public weal by means of the women, in favouring their parents. The means I will not rehearse, for offending of you and other ladies; and also since you and all that are wise may shortly conject what I mean. Finally, I am determined not to alter that custom, which is both ancient and honourable.

'Moreover, I cannot be sure to have generation when I am married, and then the only cause thereof is utterly frustrate; and, to me, which shall be alway in study and business about the weal public, the wife remaineth a tedious impediment and charge superfluous. Semblably shall I be unto her an unpleasant cumber-house, finding little idle time to be in her company; and, being fatigate with business about the weal public, I shall be less diligent and pleasant with her than she would have me, whereof mought proceed not only contention between us, but also matter of worse occasion.

'And, where ye seem to affirm that my generation should be for the tranquility of this city and empire and for the comfort of me, the Senate, and people, truly, when I remember what daughters the most noble Augustus had — whom for their corrupted living and for the griefs which he thereby sustained, he was wont to call them his botches and boils[173] — when I think what sons the reverend Vespasian, the wise and most virtuous prince Marcus Antoninus, the honourable Severus left for their successors in the empire of Rome — which were all slain for their detestable livings[174] — O how little care I for children! Yea, how glad would I be alway to lack them, that my benefits, which I intend to em-<P1v>ploy on the weal public, by the folly or vice of my children be not consumed, men more hating my name for that I have begotten and left unto them, in the stead of a governor, a ribald or tyrant for to succeed me, than they will praise me for mine own charity! O what sorrow and pain shall my soul suffer — if there be any care among them which be passed out of this world — when I shall behold with immortal eyes my child, which is of mine own substance, to abandon that thing which I loved, to embrace that which I hated, to be of the Senate abhorred, of the people detested, and of all foreign princes disdained, and, finally, of all honest men persecuted like a serpent or monster, like a wolf or a tiger, infamed for lechery, pursued for tyranny! O happy sterility, whereby lacketh annoyance! O hateful fertility, whereof cometh sickness or pestilence! I am sure that sterility can no more hurt me but only take from me the name of a father, or the doting pleasure to see my little son ride on a cockhorse or to hear him chatter and speak like a wanton.

'And I am not sure that fertility shall bring to me any more quietness than I have already. For my child, being of such inclination as best shall content me, if death take him from me, then shall I languish in torments incurable, considering that I cannot well sustain the death of my servants. If he live with me and be either a fool, a ribald, or tyrant, then should I, like Oedipus, scratch out mine eyes rather than I would behold such a monster proceed of my body; yea, rather slay him with mine own hands than to let such one to succeed me.

[173] Augustus's daughter Julia the Elder (Iulia Augusti filia, 39 BCE–14 CE) and his granddaughter Julia the Younger (Iulia Caesaris minor, 19 BCE–*c.* 29 CE) were both arrested for adultery and treason and exiled, with Agrippa Postumus (12 BCE–14 CE). Elyot is quoting Suet., *Div. Aug.* 65.4, 'nec aliter eos appellare quam tris vomicas ac tria carcinomata sua'; also quoted in Eras., *Adagia* 4.10.75, *Tota hulcus est*, 'The whole thing is a festering sore' (CWE 36, 528).

[174] The three 'good' emperors listed here were each succeeded (though not always immediately) by a notoriously 'bad' emperor, who was his biological child, casting hereditary successions into disrepute: Vespasian by Domitian, Marcus Aurelius by Commodus, and Septimius Severus by Caracalla. Elyot's remarks derive from SHA, *Septimius Severus* 20.4–21.12, but are not a translation; cf. Eras., *Adagia* 1.6.32, *Heroum filii noxae*, 'Great men have trouble from their children' (CWE 32, 26), 'Aelius Spartianus holds forth on this theme in his life of the Emperor Severus, showing with many examples how it often happens that men who are distinguished for courage or literary gifts or the favours of fortune either have no children at all, or leave offspring of such a kind that it would be better for humanity if they died childless'.

Or if he escaped me, I would ask that only reward of the Senate and <P2r> people that they would sacrifice him on my tomb when I were buried.

'Therefore, mother, I pray you, cease from exhorting me unto marriage until I be thereto better disposed; which shall be when, in beholding one which perchance I have not yet seen, some affection, ere I be ware, may in me, as it hath in other, surmount both learning and wisdom.'

With these words the wise lady, shewing herself as she were content, departed unto her lodging, but it was not long after that she bode the Emperor unto a supper and banquet; and, against his coming, she had assembled a great number of the fairest maidens in Rome, attending upon their mothers or on some other ancient and sad gentlewomen, whom, when the Emperor beheld, he forthwith conjected the intent of his mother. Notwithstanding, he most gently countenanced them all and shewed him content well with their company, although it were not correspondent unto his fantasy. But after that he had eaten and drunk more wine than he was accustomed to do, being chafed in body and spirit, in casting his eyes hither and thither, he at the last beheld an excellent fair maiden, named Memmia, which was daughter of a noble man called Sulpicius. And, after that he had devised with her and found her to be wise, sober, and of singular humility, he much loved her. And, at the last, by the continual provocation of his mother and consent of his council, he afterward married her. But she died shortly after, wherewith he took no little discomfort, saying oftentimes, 'So great a treasure as I have lost, a man seldom findeth. Death were gentle, if he took nothing but that that offendeth.' <P2v>

Eucolpius will not be known that he had any mo wives; but Lampridius useth the authority of one Desippus, who saith that Alexander had another wife, who was daughter of one Martianus, but, when it was found that he would have slain the Emperor by treason, he was put to death and his daughter separate from the Emperor.[175] Herodianus affirmeth that all that was done by the malice of Mammea, the Emperor's mother, without other cause; only because she could not sustain her son's wife to be called Augusta, and therefore she caused her to be exiled into Africa, and all the lands and goods of her father Mammea took and converted unto her own profit;[176] which report I suppose not to be true,

[175] SHA, *Alex. Sev.* 49.3–4, 'Dexippus dixit uxorem eum cuiusdam Macriani filiam duxisse eundemque ab eo Caesarem nuncupatum. verum cum vellet insidiis occidere Alexandrum Macrianus, detecta factione et ipsum interemptum et uxorem abiectam'. The historical figure P. Herenius Dexippus (*c*. 210–273) was the author of a twelve-book *Chronike Historia* (continued by Eunapius) surviving only in fragments; uses of his work by the SHA are dubious, however, and, in any case, Elyot is only following 'Lampridius'.

[176] Cf. Hdn. 6.1.9–10, 'His mother provided a wife for him from a patrician family; nevertheless, though he lived with her and loved her, Mamaea banished her from the palace with insults. Since she wished to be the only empress, Mamaea was jealous of the title of Augusta going to the girl. The abuse went so far that the father of the girl, despite his position of great honour as father-in-law to Alexander, could not stand the insults

considering that Mammea was so wise and virtuous a lady, and, being well instructed in Christ's religion, knew well how detestable unto God is envy and cruelty.

27. Of the severity that Alexander used, as well toward them that were proud, as to them that were malapert and did not their duty.

On a time, he being *censor* — or, corrector of manners — with Julius Paulus[177] and Callidius Rufus, and walking in the streets of Rome with a few other, disguised like commoners, he happened to meet with a senator's son, having with him a great train of young men, whom he and they that were with him saluted, doing to him reverence. The young man beheld them disdainfully and with a proud countenance, without saying anything, and they which were with him did also the semblable.

Where-<P3r>fore the Emperor, at his return home to his palace, incontinent discharged the father of the said young man out of the Senate, saying that he was not worthy nor meet to be of that reverend company, whereby the weal public ought to be governed and the Emperor himself to be chiefly counselled, since he had so ill brought up his son that not only he himself lacked humanity and extended a more stately fashion than pertained to his degree but also by his example caused them that were with him to embrace pride, which is captain of vices and chief confounder of all public weals.

Soon after, he sent for the said young gentleman and his companions and sharply rebuked them, saying that pride is the most horrible monster, and of all men so hated that it is not had in detestation of good men only but also to them which be proud. They that be less proud be indeed of all other most odious. And as pride sleeth love, provoketh disdain, kindleth malice, confoundeth justice, and subverteth weals public, so gentleness and affability do stir up affection, augment benevolence, incend charity, support good equity, and preserve most surely countries and cities. And after that he had charged them to abandon and leave the said vice and other, and to embrace virtue and gentle manners, whereby they should acquire more estimation than by high countenance; and menacing them that, if the said fault were eftsoons spied in them, he would not only exclude them from hope of all dignity, but also from the name of nobility and put them in the number of the base commoners; and so he let them depart. <P3v>

This sharp correction availed many a proud heart, so that, by custom of

Mamea offered him and his daughter. He took refuge in the military camp and, while acknowledging his gratitude to Alexander for the honours, he laid charges against Mamaea for her insults. Furious at this, the empress ordered him to be executed and the girl, already turned out of the palace, was exiled to Libya'.

[177] For Paulus, see above, p. 202, n. 103.

gentleness, pride was so much abhorred throughout the city that if any man, perchance by a natural habit or fashion, or unadvisedly and not of a purpose, seemed to them that beheld him to have a proud countenance, he was either laughed at or disdainfully wondered at, so that he was constrained, had he never so sturdy a courage, to be ashamed. Whereof preceded a proverb: slaves and bondmen have only this liberty, to use a proud countenance, because they be shameless; and noble men be knowen alway by their gentleness.

It was not long after that the Emperor, looking out at a window of his palace, perceived certain gentlemen exercising themselves in wrastling, running, and leaping, to whom came certain commoners of the base people, and, without any sign of reverence or asking leave, they mingled themselves with the gentlemen and malapertly enterprised to contend with them in those recreations, with arrogant boastings and words of presumption. And when the gentlemen, being therewith offended, bade them be content with their degree and elsewhere to pass the time with their companions and equals, the said commoners, taking that in despite, with countenance bragging and sturdy proudly made answer that every of them was better able to live and had more abundance to use liberality and to haunt pleasures than the best of the other. And if the Emperor's guard had not come the sooner, the commoners had fought with the gentlemen and put them in danger; for they were mo in number.

This, as it happened, <P4r> the Emperor beholding, he took therewith a vehement displeasure, being therefore so angry as erst he was never. Wherefore, he caused the said commoners to be kept in safeguard and straightly commanded that nothing that was done should be rehearsed until he had further declared his pleasure. And forthwith he sent for the Provost and tribunes and required them to send their ministers to summon all the commoners of Rome, being men, to be the second day following in the Theatre of Pompey,[178] where the Emperor in his own person would also be present and declare to them things concerning the most dangerous state of the weal public.

The Emperor's commandment accordingly was executed, and a haltpace made at the end of the Theatre, where the Emperor should sit in his majesty and all the people should plainly behold him and perfectly hear him. For the Theatre was a place made in the form of a bow that hath a great bent, and in all the round part were many benches, one behind another and over another, for it was narrowest beneath and upward grew larger and larger; and there sat all the people. At the straight end, which was to the other part as the string to the bow, were the seats of the senators and, behind them, of the gentlemen.

At the time appointed, the people being in the Theatre as they were

[178] The *theatrum Pompeii* on the *campus Martius*, dedicated in 55 BCE, was a gift of C. Pompeius Magnus to the republic; it appears to have been much as Elyot describes it just below.

commanded, the Emperor came, accompanied only with the Provost and tribunes, leaving all his guard at the gate of the Theatre. At his coming, all the people did rise and, with most joyous acclamations, did salute him; but he, contrary to his old custom, with a displeasant <P4v> countenance passed by them. Whereat they were not a little abashed and, with hearts full of a loving dread and constant silence, they prepared their ears to hear attentively what the Emperor would say. Who, after that he had long beholden the people, at the last, with a grave countenance, full of majesty, he spake unto them as hereafter followeth.

28. The oration of the Emperor Alexander to the people of Rome.

'We wot not how to begin to speak unto you, for we know not by what name we shall call you. For if ye were senators, we would call you "fathers"; if ye were gentlemen, we would call you "friends"; if ye were as ye should be, good commoners, we would call you "good people of Rome", as we were wont to do. But since election hath not made you senators, nor nature gentlemen, nor your merits good commoners, we be in no little doubt what we shall call you. For if we should call you "Romans", we fear lest Romulus, of whom proceeded that name, if he be deified as ye do suppose, being therewith offended, will be avenged as well on us as on you for abusing his glorious name on such people which goeth about to dissolve this noble empire, destroy this city, which he first began with his most excellent prowess and wisdom, and, that worse is, if any thing may be worse, extinct utterly the most honourable and glorious fame of this city and people thereof, which hath pierced the clouds, flowen over the high mountains, and passed the perilous seas and large rivers, run through the great <Q1r> deserts and wildernesses, and touched the furthermost bounds of the world. We will therefore omit to call you by any name until we can find one meet and according unto your merits.[179]

'Perchance, at our coming, ye, beholding our countenance toward you more strange than it hath been, thought that we were moved with some private displeasure, for something touching our person, or that we were altered from our late temperance unto a tyranny, conceiving suspicion of our nature by the remembrance of that monster, our late predecessor, forasmuch as we both came of one lineage, which I deny not. Truly, if this were your fantasy, we will soon acquit ourself thereof, and set all your minds at a more liberty. We will say this much unto you, as touching our person and family: no man with words

[179] The remarks imitate those of C. Iulius Caesar to the mutinous Tenth Legion in 47 BCE (Suet., *Div. Iul.* 70), which reportedly were imitated by Germanicus Iulius Caesar (15 BCE–19 CE) to mutinous troops in Lower Germany (Tac., *Ann.* 1.42), and had themselves imitated the remarks of P. Cornelius Scipio Africanus maior (236–183 BCE) to mutinous troops in Spain (Liv. 28.27.1–4).

hath offended us, no man hath taken aught from us, no man (that we know) hath gone about to betray us, nor there is any other thing privately done to our incommodity that hath displeased us. And as for our accustomed manners, which did content you, we have not nor intend not to alter them. Tyranny, as we have ever had it in extreme detestation, so do we now most abhor it. The corrupt nature of our predecessor had never place in us. One garden at one time bringeth forth both poison and wholesome medicine. We see one woman which by one man hath many children: of them, some be fair and personable, some ill-favoured and crooked, some be wise and apt unto doctrine; other be fools and dull witted; one is courageous and hardy, another is a dastard and coward; this child is gentle and inclined to virtue, the other is fierce and wrap-<Q1v>ped in vices. This is not a rare thing, but in daily experience. If this diversity happeneth to be in one garden and in the generation of one father and also one mother, then may we well escape the cause of your suspicion, we and Heliogabalus having diverse fathers and diverse mothers, and they as diverse in their conditions as ye yourselves can bear witness, which have knowen and seen proved the chaste living, sanctimony, and prudence of our reverend mother, and in what honesty and virtuous discipline she hath nourished us and brought us up unto the time that by God we were called unto this dignity. This ought to be enough, as well to persuade you that neither anything concerning ourself hath moved us to displeasure toward you, as also to exclude out of your minds all suspicion of tyranny.

'Now shall ye know the very cause why we be discontented with you, for although we said at the beginning that ye went about to dissolve this empire, destroy this city, and extinct the glorious fame thereof, which indeed is the cause of our displeasure and heaviness, yet in those general words ye do not perceive, I suppose, what we mean thereby. Wherefore, take good heed, and ye shall hear it declared more specially.

'Romulus after that he had builded this city, he by his divine reason considered and, as I doubt not, in the time of the building experience declared that, in a confuse multitude of people, they being of diverse wits and conditions, if order lacked, there mought not be a perpetual concord, but, by continual variance and discord, the people of necessity should be compelled either to abandon the city and, dividing <Q2r> themselves, to seek for sundry places to dwell in, or, abiding there in continual sedition, should shortly and easily be subdued or destroyed by their neighbours dwelling about them.

'Wherefore he, issuing of a gentle and noble house, excelling the residue of the people in noble courage and fineness of wit, first devised and stablished this order, that the company which he had assembled, as well of them which he had brought with him, as of those which he out of diverse parts had allured unto him, should generally be called Romans for ever; and that of them should be three states or degrees, every one of them necessary for the weal public of his noble city, in their sundry administrations, duties, and exercises.

'To the first state, he chase out of the whole congregation one hundred of men, ancient in years, which, in moderation of living, soberness of manners, and sharpness of wit, were of the principal personages of all that number. Of them, he ordained and stablished a council, whereby the affairs of the city and appendances thereof should be ruled and ministered; and these counsellors for their age should be called "senators" — for *senes* in Latin are old men — notwithstanding, being saluted or spoken to, they should be named "Fathers". Also, the college or company of them was incorporate by the name of "The Senate". Moreover, of this college should be elected the great judges and officers in the weal public, to whom should be committed the determination of justice, the execution of ceremonies and solemn sacrifices, and other authorities which do belong unto governance. Wherefore he would that in this state there should be a majesty which of all <Q2v> other men should be had in a singular honour and reverence.

'Semblably, like as this state was ordained for counsel and governance, so elected he out of the residue, which were lusty in years, valiant, and hardy, a greater number; whom, because in wars they should be on horseback, he called them *Equites*, and the order he called *Equestris*. To them should chiefly pertain the defence of the city against the invasion of enemies, with other small administrations about the necessary provisions and ornaments of this noble city. And this state also would he have honoured of the rest of the people; and to the intent that they should be knowen from other men, he assigned them to wear a ring and to bear in their hands javelins, whereof afterward they were called *Quirites*, which, in the old tongue of this country signified spearmen. Of this state should be elected the senators, when the just number of the Senate decayed.

'The third state was of the base people or commoners, to whom severally should not be committed any authority but should apply their occupations and be ready to execute the statutes and ordinances made by the Senate; also, be obedient to the great officers in that which pertained unto the weal public; moreover, when wars required that they should go forth, then to be obedient and diligent at the commandment of their captains and leaders.

'This order being stablished by Romulus, as long as in every degree it was duly observed, how marvellously did this city prosper! Yea, how wonderfully did a few Romans in regard not only defend this little territory against the great number and puissance of diverse and sundry people confe-<Q3r>dered against them, but also beat them back unto their own houses, entered into their cities, despoiled them of their substance, and also compelled them not only to desire perpetual peace but, moreover, at the last, to become their subjects and tributaries?

'And when this good order began to be broken, your state aspiring to governance and rule where ye were ordained to obey only, what year can ye find clear from sedition and discord among you? Who can number the Romans which have been slain in the civil wars and commotions? Who could without tears recite the dolorous estate of this city in the time of Cinna and Marius,[180] whom, for disdain that ye had unto the nobility, ye did elevate unto the highest dignities? By this, your disorder, came unto the city sundry calamities.

'Ye chase Caligula to be your emperor, and where mought there be found a more horrible tyrant? In the which name he so much delighted that, looking in a glass, he would most diligently form his visage into the most terrible fashion. Also, in recompense of your kindness, he wished that all the people of Rome had but one neck, that he mought strike it off at one stroke.[181]

'I am ashamed to rehearse my predecessor and kinsman Heliogabalus, the detestable vessel of abomination. But ye ought to be more ashamed that ye, setting apart so great a number of honourable personages as were then in the Senate, for their experience, wisdom, and prowess worthy every of them to be emperors, chase the said Heliogabalus, a stranger born, a boy in years, a fool in regard of their wisdom, to be your sovereign lord, who brought you to the most vile subjection that any people were in the world. For <Q3v> is there any thing in mankind so vile, as to be under the condition of brute beasts? What beast can ye name that will suffer in his presence another beast to occupy in the act of generation her whom he hath chosen for his make and companion, but to his power will resist and fight with him? Heliogabalus held you in such captivity that, partly to avoid his displeasure, partly to flatter him and get somewhat of him, ye not only suffered him to abuse your wives and your children such as best liked him, but also increased your bordel houses and with open eyes let your wives and your children daily and nightly to haunt them, and openly in the streets — which I abhor to rehearse — to apprehend men and provoke them to lechery.

'I omit for the shortness of time many such other elections which have preceded of your gross and presumptuous wits, after that ye had transgressed the order wherein Romulus left you and exceeded the terms of your office or duty. Which, at the last, was perceived by you, as I did suppose, when ye, being tedious of that beastly license which that beast Heliogabalus gave freely unto you, had slain him and took me to be your emperor, although with all my power I refused that burden, until I was by the Senate and you constrained to take it.

180 L. Cornelius Cinna (d.84 BCE) and C. Marius (*c.* 157–86 BCE).

181 Suet., *Calig.* 50.1, quoted above, p. 199 and n. 97; and 30.2, 'Angered at the crowd for cheering a faction which he opposed, he cried: "I wish the Roman people had but a single neck"'.

'And then desired you me to reduce the state of this city unto the first order; whereabout I have travailed these eight years with not a little pain, study, and labours; beginning at mine own household, to the intent that as well by the example of my servants and officers ye and other, being under my rule, mought the sooner reform yourselves, as also <Q4r> that ye mought the better perceive and be less offended with my severity.

'And because I did see much ill example proceed of the Senate — also, that ye were oppressed with the pride and corruption of judges and officers — I using much diligence weeded them out and discharged them of their authorities; ne they went not unpunished, according unto their merits.

'I purged also the state of gentlemen of ribalds and rioters; and advancing thereunto other, I caused them to be daily exercised in acts of prowess, or else to hear lessons in such manner of doctrine as thereby they mought acquire more wisdom to be officers or counsellors in the weal public.

'Only the state of the people I did not visit, saving in punishment of thieves, forasmuch as I judged that ye had least liberty to do any great evil, being (as I said) oppressed with tyranny, and that those vices which were among you, like as they were taken by the example of your superiors, so trusted I that, by their punishment, the said ill manners should be forsaken and by the virtuous example of such honest men as I have put in their places good manners should be as gladly embraced.

'But now I perceive all hath happened contrary to mine expectation. For the sparing of you and the correction of my servants, with the sharp reformation of the Senate and gentlemen, hath brought you unto such a presumption and arrogance that ye contend to be equal with gentlemen, using no form of reverence unto them, either that ye think that I fear more your puissance than I favour their honesties, or else that your richesse do make you so proud which, ye abusing in excessive usuries, ye there-<Q4v>with devour the patrimonies of many young gentlemen and have made them beggars or, by the severity of the ancient laws of this city, taken them in bondage and slain them in irons. And by such colourable ravin, ye have bought great possessions, in Grecia, Sicily, and Spain, whereby ye accumulate treasures and pleasures like to great princes.

'If ye think me to be afeared of your puissance, your opinion is false. For above all things, I most desire to die for the defence of the weal public of this noble city; and indeed, rather will I die than see the calamities which needs must ensue thereunto if order be not kept, as I before have declared.'

At that word, all the people cried with one voice, pouring out tears from their eyes, 'Live, most noble and gracious Emperor! He that would your death, let him die! Let him be rent into pieces! Our puissance shall not annoy you, but unto death shall defend you! Ye have restored us unto life that were dead, unto liberty that were in thraldom, unto honour that were dishonoured! Live, virtuous Emperor! And, what lack ye find in us, reform it, and we shall obey you; and he that will resist or rebel, let him be slain and drawen with a hook through the city and throwen into Tiber! Ye be in governance our father, whom we chiefly will honour. In age, ye be our most dearest son, whom more than our own lives we do favour.' And then eftsoons they cried, 'Live, most gentle and rightwise Emperor!'

Hereat the Emperor relented and, with much pain, retained the tears of his eyes. And after that he had settled his spirits and countenance, he spake then <R1r> unto them in this wise.

'I am well content that ye have declared that there is yet in you some portion of virtue, which giveth me hope that neither the noble renome of this city, begun by Romulus and augmented by other honourable governors, nor my labours in restoring thereof when it was decayed and likely to perish, shall fall into ruin. But if ye be constant in this affection, I trust that right shortly the public weal shall flourish and that this city and people shall be in as much estimation as ever it was in the time of any of our progenitors.

'And now have I found again your old name, whereby I will call you: Ye children and successors of the virtuous Romans! I say you most victorious people, branches of Romulus, subduers of realms, samplers of virtue and prowess to all the world!

'Mitigate your covetous appetites; expel from you avarice; avail your high courages, I mean in exceeding the bounds of your popular state and comparing yourselves with your superiors; be charitable and merciful to your own countrymen where their necessity may be relieved with your abundance.

'Be you ashamed that people of other countries, people barbarous and rude, should condemn you of cruelty for destroying your gentlemen, the chief ornament and defence of this noble city, that they should reproach you of rudeness and pride, in omitting to do reverence to them which do in order excel you.

'Remember that, like as if the state of senators do decay, of the gentlemen are elected into the Senate such as be virtuous; so ye that shall be found equal to them in virtue — for your substance only cannot make you gentle — shall <R1v> be advanced to the state of gentlemen according to reason.

'Then consider if ye would not then also require to be preferred in reverence. Nothing shall more cause a man willingly to do his duty than to think what he would require of him that is inferior unto him. And it hath been said of wise men that he which would be a ruler should first learn to be a good subject.[182]

[182] Cf. Elyot, *Banquet*, sig. F3v, 'Theopompus the King of Lacedemonia, to one which said that the country was well kept because that kings there knew how to govern, he answered, "No, not so; but rather because the people knoweth how to obey them"'; and sig. G5v (with attribution to Aristotle), 'It is the virtue of an honourable personage, commendably to rule and also be ruled'.

For truly, a proud and covetous subject shall never be a gentle and temperate governor.

'Now have I no more to say to you, but apply yourselves with good wills to restore this city to the ancient and most laudable order, as I shall endeavour myself by example and diligence to bring it eftsoons unto his perfection.'

Thus ended the Emperor's oration, and therewith he arose and departed, all the people pursuing him with this acclamation: 'The gods immortal keep and defend you, most noble Emperor! Ye are the crown of our glory, of our wealth and prosperity! Hated be he, of gods and of men, that would you displeasure. Do what best liketh you! The gods immortal defend you!'

29. The severity that the Emperor Alexander used in chastising as well the pride of the people, as also his men of war or soldiers.

After that the Emperor was returned home to his palace, he decreed that the said commoners should be deprived of their liberty and name of Romans, and to be delivered as bondmen unto the said gentlemen with whom they presumptuously <R2r> had contended, and so to remain in that state except they redeemed themselves by making the said gentlemen in possessions and movables better than they themselves were when they contended — for, indeed, the said commoners were very rich men, as well in substance movable as yearly °re<v>enues; that done, they should be eftsoons restored unto their liberty, adding thereto that it should not be leeful unto the said gentlemen to enfranchise them in any other condition. Finally, the said commoners, abhorring servitude, incontinent redeemed their heads according to the Emperor's decree; which example was found afterward so profitable to the weal public in retaining the ancient order and restraining sedition, which before that time now and then happened, that it was thought of all men that there was never decree or law made that was more beneficial unto the city; and the Emperor was therefore not only feared, but also more honoured and loved of all the people which were good citizens and chiefly favoured the weal of their country.

°Like severity he used to all other states, as partly it is before rehearsed[183] and partly I will now briefly declare. He so heard the complaints of soldiers against their captains that, if he found any captain in fault, he punished him according to the quality of the act, without purpose to pardon him.[184] °Like austerity he used to them that served him in wars. For on a time, when he heard that one of them had done wrong to a poor old woman, he discharged him of his retainer

[183] See above, pp. 188, 210 and nn.

[184] SHA, *Alex. Sev.* 23.1, 'Causas militum contra tribunos sic audivit ut, si aliquem repperisset tribunorum in crimine, pro facti qualitate sine indulgentiae proposito puniret'.

° revenues] renenues *A* : reuenues *B*

° \Lampridius/

° \Lampridius/

and gave him to the woman to be her bondman, that he, being a carpenter, should <R2v> with his craft and labours relieve her. And when the residue of the soldiers were therewith grieved, he persuaded them to be therewith contented and did put them in fear to grudge at it.[185] Oftentimes, he discharged whole legions, never fearing his army, forasmuch as never man could reprove him that, in his life, any captain or petty captain took or detained anything of their soldiers' wages.[186]

When he came to the city of Antioch, his men of war fell to wantonness, haunting women's bains and other riotous pastimes. Which being brought to his ear, he caused them all to be apprehended and put in prison; which being knowen to them which were of the fellowship of those that were taken, they began to make a commotion. Then the Emperor went to the place of judgment and caused the prisoners to be brought before him, the residue of men of war standing all armed about him; and then began he in this wise:[187]

'Companions in arms! — so that the acts of your fellows do discontent you: the discipline left to us by our ancestors maintaineth and keepeth the weal public, the which, if it be let to decay, we shall lose as well the name of Romans as also the empire. We may not suffer things to be done which late were supported by that unclean beast Heliogabalus. The Roman soldiers, your fellows and my companions in war, they haunt brothels, taverns, and bains in the Greek fashion, and thereto one provoketh another: shall I suffer this any longer, and not strike off their heads?'[188]

[185] SHA, *Alex. Sev.* 52.1, 'idem cum quandam aniculam adfectam iniuriis a milite audisset, exauctoratum eum militia servum ei dedit, quod artifex carpentarius esset, ut eam pasceret; et cum dolerent hoc milites factum, persuasit omnibus, ut modeste ferrent, et eos terruit'; cf. Elyot, *Banquet*, sig. E1v (translating the same first clause), 'The Emperor Alexander, hearing that a poor old woman was ill intreated with one of his soldiers, he discharged him and gave him in bondage unto the woman to get her her living with his craft, for as much as he was a carpenter'.

[186] Cf. SHA, *Alex. Sev.* 52.3, 'severitatis autem tantae fuit in milites, ut saepe legiones integras exauctoraverit, ex militibus Quirites appellans, nec exercitum umquam timuerit, idcirco quod in vitam suam dici nihil posset quod umquam tribuni vel duces de stipendiis militum quicquam accepissent', quoted in Eras., *Apoph.* 6.154 (CWE 38, 639). The episode following, to the end of the chap., is translated from SHA, *Alex. Sev.* 53.2–54.7, as indicated; the same passage is quoted in full in Eras., *Apoph.* 6.155 (CWE 38, 639–40), at uncharacteristic length.

[187] SHA, *Alex. Sev.* 53.2–4, 'nam cum Antiochiam venisset, ac milites lavacris muliebribus et deliciis vacarent eique nuntiatum esset, omnes eos comprehendi iussit et in vincula conici. quod ubi compertum est, mota seditio est a legione, cuius socii erant in vincula coniecti. tum ille tribunal ascendit vinctisque omnibus ad tribunal adductis, circumstantibus etiam militibus et quidem armatis ita coepit'.

[188] SHA, *Alex. Sev.* 53.5–8, '"Commilitones, si tamen ista vobis quae a vestris facta sunt displicent, disciplina maiorum rem publicam tenet. quae si dilabitur, et nomen Romanum et imperium amittemus. neque enim sub nobis ista facienda sunt quae sub impura illa bestia nuper facta sunt. milites Romani, vestri socii, mei contubernales et commilitones, amant, potant, lavant, et Graecorum more quidem se instituunt. hoc ego diutius feram? et non eos capitali dedam supplicio?"'

Therewith arose a great rumour and noise in the people. Then said he again: 'Ye that be here, cry out when it is necessary in battle <R3r> against your enemies, not against your emperor and sovereign lord. I dare say, your captains taught you to use those cries against the Polans, Germans, and Persians, not against him that hath given to you meat, livery, and wages. Cease, therefore, of your terrible cries, which only be necessary in war and battle, lest that I with one mouth and one voice discharge you Romans, and yet I doubt where I may so call you. For ye be not worthy to be of the people of Rome, if ye know not the law of the Romans.'[189]

And when they cried louder, and also menaced him with their weapons, he eftsoons said to them: 'Put down your hands, which, if ye be valiant, ye should advance against your enemies, for these things do make me nothing afeared. And if ye slee any man, the public weal, the Senate, and people will not fail for to revenge us.' But when they brawled and murmured never the later, he cried to them with an high voice, saying, 'Get you hence, Romans, and put off your harness'.[190]

A wonderful example: they, all putting off their harness and soldiers' coats, departed every man to his lodging. There was it perceived how much his severity profited.[191]

Then the Emperor's guard brought all the standards into the camp, and the people themselves brought all their armour to the Emperor's palace. And the legion which he had discharged, after that he was sued unto, thirty days before he went toward Persia, he eftsoons restored into his place, and, by their prowess most specially, he afterward vanquished his enemies. Notwithstanding, ere he departed, he commanded all the captains of <R3v> the said legion to be beheaded, because that, through their negligence, the soldiers passed their time riotously in a place of excellent pleasure called Daphnis and had made the sedition, they winking at it.[192]

[189] SHA, *Alex. Sev.* 53.9–11, 'tumultus post hoc ortus est. atque iterum: "Quin continetis vocem in bello contra hostem, non contra imperatorem vestrum necessariam? certe campidoctores vestri hanc vos docuerunt contra Sarmatas et Germanos ac Persas emittere, non contra eum, qui acceptam a provincialibus annonam, qui vestem, qui stipendia vobis adtribuit. continete igitur vocem truculentam et campo ac bellis necessariam, ne vos hodie omnes uno ore atque una voce Quirites dimittam et incertum an Quirites. non enim digni estis qui vel Romanae plebis sitis, si ius Romanum non agnos citis"'.

[190] SHA, *Alex. Sev.* 54.1–3, 'et cum vehementius fremerent ac ferro quoque minarentur, "Deponite", inquit, "dextras contra hostem erigendas, si fortes sitis, me enim ista non terrent. si enim unum hominem occideritis, non nobis deerit res publica, non senatus, non populus Romanus, qui me de vobis vindicet". cum nihilo minus post ista fremerent, exclamavit, "Quirites, discedite atque arma deponite"'.

[191] SHA, *Alex. Sev.* 54.4–5, 'mirando exemplo depositis armis, depositis etiam sagulis militaribus omnes non ad castra, sed ad deversoria varia recesserunt. tuncque privatim intellectum est quantum eius severitas posset'.

[192] SHA, *Alex. Sev.* 6–7, 'denique etiam signa stipatores et ii qui imperatorem circumdederant

30. How the Emperor Alexander reformed the usury, whereof he spake afore in his oration made to the people.

Soon after that Alexander had chastised the pride of the common people of Rome as before is rehearsed, he himself came into the Senate and there declared the sundry inconveniences which had happened as well to the city as unto the countries thereunto subject by the detestable practice of usury, which utterly repugneth against all humanity, charity, and natural benevolence that ought to be among people that do live in a mutual concord, but most specially among them which live under one obedience, under one law or policy.

The inconveniences which happened he shewed to be these. First, where the gentlemen and the more part of men of war were from their cradles brought up in idleness, being not instructed in any occupation or science, save only in feats pertaining to war, in the time of peace and tranquility, or when the wars be not so great that they require the whole puissance of Rome, then they which be not sent forth to battle, some do pass their time in dalliance and banqueting with wanton women, or at dice and other chargeous solacing, or in both, with the one and the other shortly consuming their <R4r> substance; some do delight in other excessive pleasures, as to have great and beautiful houses, large and ample orchards, and walks enclosed with high and strong walls, great ponds and meres, conveying thereunto by a long distance the salt water through rocks and mountains, and to have in them diverse strange kinds of fishes. In the which enterprises, they also have not only consumed their goods and patrimony, but also, the work above their expectation, far exceeding their power, they have been constrained to borrow great sums of money. Other there have been which, of an ambitious courage, have used prodigal expenses as well in continual feasts and banquets, as in distributions of great sums of money among the people, and giving great rewards to corrupt senators and other great officers, to attain, before their time or not being worthy, to some high place or dignity; whereby they, being brought into poverty, have been also constrained to seek help of other, to maintain their folly.

'All these persons, how unprofitable they be unto the weal public, report me unto you; specially if ye consider also that, when they have borrowed so much, and the sums borrowed being so increased by usury that they be not only in desperation to borrow any more of their creditors, but also in the state to be grievously punished according to the laws; then desire they some alteration in the weal public; then fish they out the ambitious courages of them which are

in castra rettulerunt, arma collecta populus ad Palatium tulit. eam tamen legionem quam exauctoravit rogatus post dies xxx, priusquam ad expeditionem Persicam proficisceretur, loco suo restituit eaque pugnante maxime vicit, cum tamen tribunos eius capitali adfecit supplicio, quod per neglegentiam illorum milites apud Daphnem luxuriati essent, vel per coniventiam seditionem fecisset exercitus'.

in authority; and, between whom of the noble men is envy, disdain, or private displeasure, then seek they matter of sedition within the city which, not being wisely repressed, <R4v> hath at his back division of parts, civil commotions, oftentimes battle and destruction of people. Read the histories of Rome, and see how often they called for new tables, that is to say, that the instruments and obligations made for debt should be cancelled and those debts acquitted, and, until it was done, the commotion ceased not.

'Now see ye that the chief cause of this inconvenience was the said pestilent practice of usury, which, as the occupiers did see the wantonness and prodigality of the nobility, gentlemen, and other increase, so did they augment it, more esteeming their proper lucre than the weal public, charity, benevolence, or natural humanity. Wherefore, in my judgment such usurers among the Romans ought not to be numbered, but, if they be not willingly reformed, they should be taken and used as pernicious enemies unto us all.'

Here all the Senate, except a few, with one voice commended the zealous intent of the Emperor and offered their consents in making such a law as should seem to the Emperor and them expedient, unto the redress of so great an enormity.

°Then, one Catelius, a noble senator and a man of great virtue,[193] said in this wise: 'Mine opinion is, noble Emperor and reverend fathers, that no kind of usury shall be here practiced within this city! But, first, I would that search be made diligently how many Romans and who they be which are entered into bonds for the payment of usury, and likewise who be the creditors; and, the principal debt being knowen, the creditors to be compelled by an edict of your majesty to hold them content <S1r> with repayment of the sum or value of the thing that they lend; and then, by an ordinance of this council, the said principal debts to be paid out of the treasure of the city, the debtors bringing in pawn or surety to repay it within five years unto the treasuries.

'Also, that no man shall lend money or any thing else which the debtor shall be constrained to change into money to serve his commodity, upon any condition, bargain, or promise, to have lucre by the said loan; and, if that he do, all his movables to be immediately forfeited to the common treasury.

'Moreover, that if any Roman shall happen to be in necessity, by any misfortune or casualty, or by necessary charges which he could not escape, that he should come to the Provost of the city and treasurers, bringing with him one senator and two of the people, men not suspected of infamy, which shall swear by the gods, preservators of the city of Rome, that they know that the necessity doth not proceed of the said ill occasions. That done, he shall lay in his sufficient pawn, or bring in two able persons to undertake for the repayment of the money which he will borrow, °<and> the treasurers shall deliver so much to

[193] For 'Catelius' or 'Catilius Severus', see above p. 202 and n. 104.

° \The sentence of Catelius./

° and] *A om B om*

him as to the Provost and them shall seem to be sufficient for his necessity.

'And if any other man will benevolently lend them that which they will desire without practice of usury, if the borrower hath consumed his goods in such folly as before is declared, that then he shall not be charged with the repayment of that that he borrowed, but that the creditor be clearly excluded from thenceforth to have for his said loan any manner of remedy.

'But if constraint or misfortune do cause <S1v> the necessity, and any man lend to another for a benevolent charity, without any colour of usury, then if the debtor neglect the repayment thereof and willingly let the day pass when it ought to be paid, then he without mercy to sustain the rigour of the common laws of the city.

'And so, this law being well executed and never omitted, we shall neither have usurer dwell in this city, nor gentlemen landless, nor persons seditious which shall be able to annoy the universal weal public.

'Now ye have heard mine opinion, whereto ye may add or make something less, as it shall seem best to your excellent wisdoms.'

°Then the Emperor desired Gordian, an ancient senator, who is named before,[194] to shew his opinion; and he, risen out of his place, pausing a little, said in this wise: 'I learned, when I was young, noble Emperor and fathers, that he which shall give counsel, specially to the making of laws, ought to consider four things: that his counsel be honest, that it be necessary, profitable, and possible.

'Three of them have be remembered by Catelius Severus; the fourth, it seemeth that he had forgotten. I do well agree that the thing that he would have done is charitable and therefore is honest; also, that it is necessary to repress the riotous and prodigal living of gentlemen. It is profitable unto the weal public to have all occasions of sedition and seeds of war civil to be extirpate. And truly, no better device may be found than Catelius, according to his great learning and wisdom, hath right well declared.

'But let us see if the relief appointed by Catelius for them whom he nameth worthy to have <S2r> it shall be alway certain and possible; and if not, then must we instead thereof find some other provision, more certain though it be not so easy, that good men in their unwilling necessity be not disappointed.

'Is it possible, trow ye, that the common treasure shall be alway abundant, that is to say, able to furnish all things necessary for the weal public, and in the overplus to be also sufficient to relieve the said private necessities? Consider the greatness of this noble empire: the great number of realms, countries, and cities, whom the prowess of our noble ancestors have by force constrained to be subject unto us; and by force we keep and retain them. Think you that they all will ever remain in peace and tranquility? Do you not know that all living things desire liberty, and mankind most specially? Remember you not that will

[194] See above, p. 193 and n. 88.

° \The sentence of Gordian./

constrained seeketh ever opportunity to slip off his collar?

'Forget you that almost yesterday the Moors began to rebel and had shaken off their yoke, had they not been quickly repressed by Furius Celsus? Also, the great country of Illyria, from whence we have our chief men of war, made late a commotion which had been no small danger and loss to this empire, had they not been valiantly and wisely pacified and brought in good order by the noble captain Varius Macrinus, kinsman unto your majesty, most noble Emperor. Armenia was in peril to be lost, if it had not been well defended by the prowess of Junius Palmatus;[195] and it is doubted of some whether the Germans will continue the league that they made with us. It is privily muttered among the people that Artaxerxes, King of Persia,[196] doth gather much people and trea-<S2v>sure, intending not only to subdue all Armenia but also the whole country of Asia unto the sea of Propontis, which divideth Asia from Europa, claiming it in the ancient right of the kings of Persia. What other people will do, we be uncertain; as uncertain be we what treasure will be sufficient to furnish all things necessary against those perils.

'Yea, we be not so sure of our provinces and ancient dominions, from whence we have our yearly revenues, pensions, and tributes; but if other rebel and prevail against us — which the gods forbid! — puissance failing us and good fortune forsaking us, it is to be supposed that they will rather pay nothing than aught, °<and> be also governed rather by their own countrymen than by us that be strangers. Then what have we left us to keep this noble city, to defend us, our children, our wives, the temples and altars of gods immortal, if our common treasure be not rich and abundant, wherewith we may get succours in some place, provide vittles sufficient, and strongly fortify our munitions and fortresses?

'Also, we be not sure where war shall assail us, either by land or by sea. If it happen to be by the land, yet know we not whether it shall be in diverse countries or one. If in sundry countries, then must we have diverse armies and diverse provisions, according as the state of the countries requireth, some being fervently hot, some exceeding in cold; the one full of mountains unapt for carriage, the other thick of woods; this lacking fresh water, that drowned in fens. If it be on the water, then be the charges greater and much more uncertain, ships with their tackling and ordinance above all <S3r> other things being most costly and oftentimes, ere their enemies meet them, they be either devoured

[195] Cf. SHA, *Alex. Sev.* 58.1, simply reporting 'Actae sunt res feliciter et in Mauretania Tingitana per Furium Celsum et in Illyrico per Varium Macrinum adfinem eius et in Armenia per Iunium Palmatum, atque ex omnibus locis ei tabellae laureatae sunt delatae'.

[196] The founding dynast of the Sassanian empire, Ardashir (*c.* 180–241), against whom Alexander campaigned, as discussed below, pp. 310–11.

° and] *A om B om*

with storms or by contrary winds constrained to run on quicksands or rocks. Wherefore, we must alway have a great number of ships in making, and a great number of persons retained to furnish them.

'I will not omit the most necessary provision of grain for this city, which oftentimes, by scarcity in the countries adjoining unto us, we have been compelled to make in countries far distant from us at very high prices; which, if the like necessity happen unto us, undoubtedly it will exhaust wonderful treasures.

'These things considered, it shall seem, I doubt not, expedient that the common treasure remain alway untouched but only for common necessity, the incertainty whereof proveth it impossible that the common treasure shall be ever sufficient to relieve the private necessity of them that are spoken of, since misfortune and other constrained means unto poverty shall every day happen to some man.

'Wherefore now let us devise a more certain provision. And truly few men have so much compassion and charity (the more pity is it) that they will lend their goods to another man, have they never so much, except thereby may return to them some advantage or profit. And to constrain them to lend, except it were for defence of the weal public, it were against justice.

'Wherefore, finally, this is my sentence: let a certain gain be limited by the Emperor's majesty, which, being thought by us tolerable to the borrower and competently sufficient unto the creditor, let it be declared by the tribunes unto the people, with the re-<S3v>sidue which was indifferently and wisely devised by Catelius Severus. And I doubt not but that it will lightly pass and be enacted by all their voices.'

This oration and sentence of Gordian was well commended, as well of the Emperor as of all the Senate.

In conclusion, after a little debating, it was appointed by the Emperor that the creditors should have, for the forbearing of every *sestertium* (which, in English money of old groats, whereof eight made an ounce, amounteth to four pounds, sixteen shillings, eight pence) for every day loan, the third part of *as*, called *triens* (which was the third part of an old Roman penny, called in Latin *denarius*, which was the poise of an old English groat); and so the usury for the whole year amounted in Roman money to twelve pence, one *as*, and two *trientes*; in accompt of English money, twelve groats, the tenth part of a groat, and two parts of a tenth part divided in three parts, which sum mought be more easily compted by the Romans, which had the said small money *trientes* coined, than by us that have no such money. Notwithstanding, forasmuch as it well appeareth that the gain by the loan of one hundred pounds sterling by the whole year amounted not by this reckoning but to four pounds, twelve pence, and the third part of a groat or thereabout, compting by the old groats, whereof went but eight to the ounce; of the money current, whereof do go eleven groats to the ounce, the usury amounteth to five pounds, ten shillings, seven pence and a half, or thereabout; which will seem to all men, not being usurers, to be a gain sufficient and reasonable.

But now to return to our matter: this sentence of the Emperor and Senate, being declared by the tri-<S4r>bunes as it was appointed, all the people, with most joyous spirits and as loud as they could cry, consented that it should be made a law perpetual in every point, according as the Emperor and Senate before had devised it, whereupon incontinent the act was drawn and published as hereafter followeth.

31. The law concerning usuries made by the Emperor, Senate, and people of Rome.

'No necessity be considered from henceforth in them that consume their substance in dice playing, outrageous expenses, or lechery. Whosoever lendeth to them, let it be at his jeopardy and without hope of remedy.

'Whom fortune perverse, long sickness, service, friendship, disloyalty of them that he trusted, thieves, or oppressors have brought unto poverty, to him let men extend their compassion and charity.

'Or if his necessity do constrain him to borrow, let him come to the Provost of the city and declare his necessity and whereof it preceded, having with him one senator and two of the commoners, persons well known and credible; which, being deposed that his words be true and unfeigned and what they suppose shall be sufficient to relieve his necessity, the Provost shall assign one rich man of the city, if the party himself name not another; to whom or to him that is named, the Provost shall direct his letter in the name of the Senate and people, willing him to deliver to the said person the sum that he needeth, taking of him sufficient surety for the repayment of the sum <S4v> that he lent; with the increase for every day, sparing of one *sestertium*, twelve Roman pence, one *as*, and two *trientes*, and so after that rate in all other sums above the sum of *sestertium*, and not to exceed that gain in any manner condition.

'He that refuseth to lend for this gain, let him, as unworthy the name of a Roman or to take any benefit by the weal public, be of the censors deprived of the name of a citizen and noted forever with the crime of ingratitude.

'This law, decreed by the Senate, enacted by the people, confirmed by the imperial majesty, be forever established, and never by any other law, custom, or ordinance to be abolished.

'And who that with violence resisteth against it, let him be taken for rebel and enemy unto the weal public'.

32. What love and benevolence the Emperor shewed to the people of Rome, and of other of his wonderful virtues.

Ye have heard much declared of the virtuous severity or sharpness of this noble Emperor Alexander; now shall you hear as much of his gentleness, patience, and affability. After that the said act was proclaimed throughout Rome and Italy, the Emperor, calling to his remembrance that the said law was made only for them which hereafter should be constrained to borrow and that there were many at that time in danger whom by that act should take no benefit, he, being moved with pity, caused suddenly search to be made by the censors how many were in the danger of usury. And then sent he for all the usurers; and after that he had a little blamed them <T1r> for their avarice and ingratitude toward their country, at the last altering his countenance and speech unto a more mildness, he desired them all, at his contemplation, to take for that time their principal sum that was borrowed and clearly to remit all the residue, promising that the money should be paid to them out of his treasure. Which request of the Emperor was pronounced in so gentle a fashion that the creditors with one voice not only granted unto it, but also promised to remit part by his arbitrement, where he thought convenient; which the Emperor most thankfully taking, gave the creditors leave to depart, commanding them to keep the thing secret until they knew more of his pleasure.

Then commanded he that all such as were run in the danger of usury should be warned to come before him, not at one day or time, but first they which were reputed and knowen to be men of honesty and by some misadventure were brought unto poverty. And being truly certified what goods or lands they had in possession, he remembered to them what peril they were in and lamented the state of the city, that the gentlemen, by negligence or lack of good husbandry, should be in bondage and captivity unto the commoners, which ought to be inferiors to them and do to them reverence.

'O!', said he, 'where is the noble courage of Romulus's progeny? Who followeth °Quinciu<s>, Publicola, Curiu<s>, Fabritiu<s>, noble senators? Which, after that they had vanquished princes and achieved sundry great victories, been diverse times consuls and dictators, the highest dignities within this city, they lived so moderately, <T1v> that rather than they would be subjects to the avarice of other, they chase to live in poor houses of husbandry out of the city, with a pot full of worts and such a small pittance for them and their wives as now our servants would disdain to be fed with. And lest abundance at any time should provoke them to live more delicately, they refused not only great sums of money sent to them by strangers, but also possessions offered them by the Senate and people for their endeavour and labours about the weal public. Thus I say unto

° Quincius, Publicola, Curius, Fabritius] Quincium, Publicolam, Curium, Fabritium *A B*

you whom, although misadventure or charges enforced have exhaust some or the more part of your substance or patrimony, yet have ye not therefore abated your diet, nor abstained from pleasures, nor minished your family; but, without using good husbandry, and without circumspection, have, contrary to the said honourable senators, chosen rather to spend your old age in misery and to be in bondage unto your inferiors, than ye would retain in captivity your wanton appetites.'

But here, when the Emperor perceived that they were ashamed and made heavy countenance, then said he unto them: 'Would ye not gladly be eftsoons at liberty? At the least way, out of the danger of usury?'

They, with a voice most lamentable, answered: 'Yea, noble Emperor'.

'Will ye', said he, 'with good will pay to your creditors the principal duty, having time convenient that it may be levied of your possessions, having left unto you some portion to live on?'

They answered, 'Yea, noble prince, else were we unhappy', notwithstanding among them were some, and <T2r> not many, which had not left either goods or possessions to pay the whole duty.

Then the Emperor withdrew him into his chamber and caused them severally to be brought unto him, one after another; and, according to their substance in possessions or movables, he rated them to pay off the principal debt, some all, some more, and some less. And because they had not the money then ready, he, promising to discharge them of the said payments by their consents, assigned to them which had possessions two parts thereof, and the third part he reserved to himself, until the sum were thereof received whereto they were rated. Of them that had goods and no possessions, he appointed that the sum whereunto they were rated should be valued in their said movables by their own friends and be brought unto some place where, by the Emperor's officers, it should be received. And ere they departed, he caused in their presence every sum to be severally told out of his coffers. And then sent he for all the creditors; and putting them in remembrance of their gentle promise made unto him and declaring also what he had done, he caused every man's portion according to the said rate to be delivered unto them. And for them which had neither good nor possessions, he paid half of the principal debt out of his own coffers, with a clear acquittance unto the party, and, commanding the creditors to bring to him, cancelled the obligations and instruments belonging to the said duties; and giving to them hearty thanks, he let them depart.

Semblably, persuading the debtors to frugality or moderate living, he also prayed them to foresee <T2v> as much as they could that wilfully they commit not themselves to the hazards of fortune. He, then, embracing them all, bade them farewell; who, giving to him most humble thanks and for joy pouring out abundance of tears, departed with glad tidings home to their houses.

As for them which at dice playing, in riot and lechery, had consumed their substance, he, if any were left, caused it to be valued, as well possessions as movables, and to be divided among their creditors according to the quantity of the true debt; and in satisfaction of the remnant, he adjudged them bond, so that, for a certain time as the Emperor would apportion him, having regard to the debt, he should serve one creditor and afterward another, in most vile services, receiving therefore nothing, but only meat, drink, and clothing, belonging to slaves, and that the creditors should have over them equally as much authority as they had over them which they had bought or taken in battle. Notwithstanding, it was at the liberty of the creditors to acquit them of their service but not to enfranchise them, until the time were expired which was by the Emperor appointed; but, during that time, they ware continually the habit or apparel assigned to bondmen, ne were esteemed for Romans nor enjoyed any privilege. If they obediently served and contented their creditors, at the end of the term which the Emperor appointed, they were set at liberty and restored to their first estate and condition; but if they fled from their master or contemptuously withstood his commandments, fighting with him or doing to him any nota-<T3r>ble injury, they were condemned to perpetual servitude during their lives.

They which had left nothing to pay their creditors, to them he appointed a longer captivity, esteeming the value of his service as well to the faculty of the person as to his estate and condition, as if he were very witty, well learned, or a perfect artificer, by reason whereof his service mought seem very commodious or profitable. Also, being a gentleman, the more estimation that he were of, the more grievous and odious to him should be his service and punishment. Wherefore, to the one and the other, less time was thought to be sufficient than to them which were of gross wit, or ignorant of good occupation, or else base or vile of condition.

This ordinance being put in due execution, it was thought at the first of some men to be very cruel. But after that it was once perceived what a marvellous frugality or temperance of living was suddenly found, as well in the city of Rome, as also throughout all Italy; also, what delight men took to beseen themselves moderate in apparel, honest in living, also exercising themselves in pastimes convenient, not dishonest or chargeous; also, to have them in derision whom they found in any manner of wise attempting the contrary; then extolled they the excellent wit and virtue of the most noble Emperor. And, where afore they called him cruel and tyrannous, they ceased not to name him equal to the gods, most benign and most gracious, confessing that, had not been his severity, they all, with the city and empire, had utterly perished. <T3v>

33. Of the circumspect curiosity of the Emperor Alexander in admitting counsellors, and of his answers touching that matter.

The incomparable diligence of this noble Emperor about the weal public is to be marvelled at and of all princes to be observed and followed. For what by his own travail and excellent prudence, what by his continual scrutiny by wise and honest espials, he assuredly knew the qualities, manners, and appetites of all men, except very few, dwelling in Rome or Italy, which, either by reason of their possessions or substance or for any other estimation among their neighbours, were likely to be called to some authority; also, of all those which in other regions and provinces were for some cause notable or famous. This knowledge caused him to be circumspect in admitting counsellors and other great officers. As among many examples, I will declare one, whereof I myself can bear witness.

After the death of Quintilius Marcellus, a man in great authority about the Emperor — as he was well worthy for his singular wisdom and virtue, in so much as it was thought that there was never a better man born in Rome, and therefore the Emperor did extremely lament his death — the noble man Frontine,[197] whom also the Emperor entirely loved, awaiting his time, advanced to him with a commendable report an honourable personage, who was named Fabius Macrinus,[198] to be in the place of Marcellus. After that the Emperor had heard and well considered the words of Frontinus, whereby was set forth the ancient stock <T4r> from whence Fabius descended, his great possessions and substance, the gravity of his personage, his great experience in sundry authorities, the Emperor did cast on Frontine a displeasant countenance; and, after that he ceased to speak, the Emperor made answer in this wise.

'How much hath your judgment deceived us, Frontine? How could ye this long dissemble with us? I had thought that ye had ever esteemed the stock by the fruit, and not the fruit by the stock! No man commendeth the boughs or branches, because the stem of the tree is great, long, or straight; but if they be well spreading, thick of green leaves, and well set with good fruit, then men say, "that tree hath a fair top!", "that tree beareth good fruit!"; and although the tree be never so misshapen or crooked, the owner will dig about it and use all diligence for to preserve it. But if the stock be never so fair, if the boughs be rotten or sere, the owner will shred them and throw them into the fire. If the fruit be unsavoury or withered, who taketh any great heed of the tree? Who will

[197] For 'Marcellus', see above, p. 202 and n. 104; for 'Frontine', p. 179 n. 32.

[198] The figure appears to have been invented for purposes of this inset dialogue on patronage. The ancestral distinction and wealth attributed to him below precludes his being a relation of the Mauretanian *eques* Macrinus, who became emperor nevertheless, 217–218 (see above, p. 178); or of the Illyrian conqueror 'Varius' Macrinus, a relation of the Syrian Emperor Alexander (see above, p. 268); or of the 'Bebius' or 'Baebius' Macrinus, who was one of Alexander's tutors in rhetoric (see above, p. 179). It is the case, however, that the *gens Fabia* (below, 'the house of Fabius') was particularly old and distinguished in Rome.

gather the fruit, but rather let them rot on the tree or fall down, for he careth not for them? Who loveth rotten groundsel or post, because that it was part of an ancient house? Who °setteth by a ragged, a resty, or ill-favoured colt, because that the haras whereof that kind is comen, two hundred years past, won the prize of running at the game of Olympus? I confess that long continuance in any thing that is good addeth an admiration but no praise to the thing, albeit the thing founden good praiseth the continuance or long enduring thereof. A good child rene-<T4v>weth and also augmenteth the praise of his parents; the ill child raseth out of men's hearts the father's honour and benefits.

'Also, great possessions or substance maketh virtue suspected, because they be ministers of pleasant affections and also nourices of wanton appetites. Moreover, the gravity of the personage is not proved by stately countenance or disdainful silence, but by constance in virtue and words alway apt for the time and purpose. And experience which is not commended by laudable acts doth deserve no more praises than the gate of a blind horse about a wide horse-mill which grindeth no corn; and that old captain which in many battles and journeys hath been found alway negligent deserveth no garland. Many authorities do require an exquisite trial, forasmuch as authority doth abate fear and minister boldness, boldness draweth in licence, licence is mother of mischief, which needs must be suffered until favour relenteth.

'These things considered, Frontinus, either your judgment is not so perfect as I would have taken it to be, or else ye, secretly winking at the said faults, have dissembled long with me and kept things from my knowledge, contrary to your allegiance and duty.'

With these words Frontinus, °being afeared, kneeled down and besought the Emperor to pardon him of his folly, confessing that he had not perfect knowledge of the disposition and manners of the said Fabius; but forasmuch as he had been favourable toward him and his friends in his ministrations, he mutually desired his advancement.

Thereat smiled the Emperor and said, 'Shall <U1r> this plague never cease, which in realms and cities hath so long reigned, that mutual beneficence blindeth men's judgments? And whiles power with pleasures getteth great acquaintance, virtue is unknown and in the court friendless.

'I know, Frontinus, that pride in Fabius Macrinus is a domestical vice. For in all the house of Fabius, it hath been exceedingly noted and in some histories remembered. And in this man as well, the remembrance of his ancient nobility, as his long continuance in authority, hath more increased it, as I myself have marked and also heard other murmuring at it, when I have secretly walked in the city in a private apparel. Wherefore, I will not that he be in our counsel nor palace, that either his pride should be of young men followed or of old men

° setteth] setteh *B*
° being] beinge *A* : binge *B*

disdained, or of us suspected.

'His great possessions and riches declareth that he cannot be with a little contented, since the more part thereof he hath gathered under the colour of his authorities, being not left unto him by his own parents, nor received of our liberality, nor by the gift of our predecessors. And very seldom, where honour encreaseth, avarice abateth.

'I hate not Fabius in the state that he now is, although I favour not in him the said notable vices; but if he were nearer unto us, we could neither sustain them nor suffer him unpunished, if he then used them. Also, in his long experience, I never heard him for justice commended; but I have heard his arrogance, his long delaying of suitors, and his partiality, of many dispraised. Truly, such a man is neither meet to be a nigh counsellor nor, to say the truth, in any great office.

'These things considered, Fron-<U1v>tinus, speak no more of him, but search for some other, in whom sincerity and temperance be joined with wisdom. Such one, if he be of an ancient house, shall bring to our palace an honourable remembrance of his noble progenitors and, as well to noble as unnoble, shall be an excellent pattern or precedent. If he be but late come to worship, his advancement shall engender in noble men an honest envy, either to exceed him in virtue or at the least to be judged equal unto him; to poor men it shall be an allective and root of good hope, that they be in the rank where the reward of virtue is dealed.'

And thus ceased the Emperor to speak, and Frontinus departed, being both ashamed of his enterprise and abashed at the wisdom of his noble master.

34. The most noble answer of Alexander, made to Alphenus, concerning the disabling of Sextilius Rufus in his absence.

°The Emperor had a custom, which was very commendable, that he never made any senator without the counsel of the whole Senate, and every senator should give his sentence; also, testimony of his living and credence should be brought in by honourable personages. But if either the senators that spake or the witnesses were founden to have spoken untruly, they were rejected into the lowest place of estimation among the people, being also condemned as deceivers or forgers, without hope of remission.[199]

There was dwelling in a village by Rome a gentleman called Sextilius

[199] SHA, *Alex. Sev.* 19.2, 'senatorem numquam sine omnium senatorum, qui aderant, consilio fecit, ita ut per sententias omnium crearetur, testimonia dicerent summi viri ac, si fefellissent vel testes vel hi, qui sententias dicebant, postea in ultimum reicerentur locum civium in condemnatione adhibita, quasi falsi rei adprobati sine ullius indulgentiae proposito'.

° \Lampridius/

Rufus,[200] which was right <U2r> well learned in all parts of philosophy and also in the sciences liberal. But forasmuch as he considered the frequent alteration of the weal public, with the manifold perils and troubles in the administration thereof, he of purpose withdrew him therefro as much as he mought, although his father had been a senator in his life, and he among his neighbours and diverse of the nobility was had in good reputation. Notwithstanding, for the causes before rehearsed, and that he desired nothing so much as quietness of mind and to solace himself in the most pleasant °arbour of science; and, visiting the most delectable warks of ancient writers, he seldom came to the Emperor's court, or resorted to plays or banquets, ne did come to salute the great officers nor men in authority, as the use was at that time; and among the young gallants, he was not beloved because he favoured not their riotous pastimes; and the men of law had him in disdain because he repugned against their subtle glosses and blamed their avarice. Finally, he, being fully content with the golden mean, lived right honestly, in a manor which he had competently furnished with possessions sufficient for the provision of his mean household, which was to his neighbours more bounteous than sumptuous.

After that the Emperor had purged his palace and the Senate of unworthy persons, corrupted with detestable vices, and with much difficulty found other to set in their places, it happened that some good man named to him Sextilius Rufus, declaring the common report which he had heard of him. The Emperor, who knew all to be true that was spoken, held <U2v> his peace notwithstanding, harkening what should be other men's sentences. The more part of them which were present affirmed that Rufus, for his honesty, wisdom, and learning, was meet to be of the Senate; but three or four said nothing.

[200] The following highly developed tale of 'Sextilius Rufus', with its long inset dialogues (chaps 34–36), is not in the sources, though Elyot's invention of it may have been suggested by SHA, *Alex. Sev.* 19.1, adjacent to the passage cited immediately above: 'He appointed as another praetorian prefect a person who had fled to avoid taking up the office, saying that it were rather the unwilling than the seekers after office who ought to be allotted positions of responsibility in the republic'. The conduct of an unscrupulously mercenary P. Sextilius Rufus is discussed in Cic., *Fin.* 2.55, who would have been a relation of or the same person as the famously scrupulous P. Sextilius of Plut., *Mar.* 40.3–4. Elyot's characterisation may have more to do with the orator and jurist Ser. Sulpicius Rufus (d.43 BCE), whom Cicero publicly mocked in the *Pro Murena* (esp. 15–30), but praised in *Brutus* (150–57) and in the ninth of the *Philippicae*: cf. Cic., *Mur.* 16.1, 'But your nobility, O Servius Sulpicius, although it is most eminent yet it is known rather to men versed in literature and history, but not much so to the people and to the voters'; also, Elyot, *Gov.* 1.14 (Watson, p. 67), 'Also, Servus Sulpitius, in his time one of the most noble orators next unto Tully, was not so let by eloquence but that on the civil laws he made notable comments, and many noble works by all lawyers approved'.

° arbour] herbar *A B* (*fortasse* MnE 'harbour')

At the last, Alphenus, a great lawyer[201] and in good estimation with the Emperor, objected, saying that Rufus, notwithstanding that he was learned in diverse sciences, yet was he neither profoundly learned in the laws civil nor much experienced in affairs of the empire; and that his little husbandry and small provision about the increase of his living declared him to be a man of no great policy nor of any dexterity about things of importance; and that the aptitude of his nature was only in studious meditation of sundry sciences and in writing more than in doing; adding to that, philosophers were never good practisers in a weal public nor yet good men of war. Wherefore, in as much as he that is a senator not only ought to be a man meet for politic governance, as well in giving counsel in matters thereto pertaining, as also, being chosen to be praetor or to any other ministration of justice, not to be ignorant in giving judgment in causes brought before him; but also, he ought to have some experience in martial affairs, that, being chosen consul or leader of the host of the Romans, he mought see the men of war to be well instructed and exercised, and that, in all things belonging to war, the state of the city be sufficiently furnished; moreover, that in battle joined, either by his ignorance or baseness of courage, the Roman army be not destroyed. These things considered, it <U3r> seemed to him that it was not expedient to receive Rufus into the number of senators.

The Emperor, hearing Alphenus and beholding that no man proffered to speak after him, except three or four mo, which were lawyers, and one Ovinius Camillus, a noble man,[202] who had some displeasure toward Rufus for one of his servants: these seemed by their countenances to approve the saying of Alphenus; that perceiving the Emperor, he, looking on Alphenus, spake in manner as hereafter followeth.

'I see well, Alphenus, that not only the vulgar and unlettered people be angrily steered and do retain displeasure against them which, without malice, do rebuke in a generality the vices and faults which be founden among them; but also, which I do lament, men specially chosen for their wisdom and learning do disdain them that rebuke the abuse of that study or exercise which these wise men most chiefly have haunted. I know that Sextilius in one of his books hath sharply noted the detriment done unto justice by covetous lawyers, which, by

[201] The name occurs in a list of persons, who 'omnes iuris professores discipuli fuere splendidissimi Papiniani et Alexandri imperatoris familiares et socii', in the engrossed list of Alexander's counsellors in the Erasmian SHA, *Alex. Sev.* 68.1, to which Elyot had recourse for names (see above, p. 202 and nn.), but in this chap. 34 only. It may be that, for the characterisation, Elyot was using the historical jurist P. Alfenus Varus (cos. suff. 39 BCE), 'a great lawyer'; also, a student of the Ser. Sulpicius Rufus mentioned above: see Aul. Gell., *NA* 7.5.1, 'Alfenus iureconsultus, Servii Sulpicii discipulus rerum antiquarum non incuriosus'. This Alfenus was also responsible for the land confiscations in northern Italy that so concerned the Mantuan Vergil (cf. *Ecl.* 6.6–12, 9.26–29).

[202] For 'Ovinius', see below, p. 291 and n. 221.

their subtle wits, have involved the laws civil into such obscure and ambiguous sentences that no man, without their declarations, may know how to do or minister justice in cases for the which the said laws have provided, nor they that make laws can expound them afterward without a lawyer which perchance was not first privy to the law-making.[203] These and like annotations of Rufus do not a little offend you that be lawyers, although ye have abandoned practice. And that displeasure only hath caused you to make this conclusion, that Rufus is not meet to be of <U3v> the Senate, the residue of your argument doth sufficiently prove it.

'First, the diversity of sciences, wherein yourself do confess that he is well learned, doth not disable him to be a senator, but maketh him more convenient and necessary for so noble a council. °For to whom doth it more appertain to use words in their proper signification and to set them in order, so that they make not the sentence perverse or doubtful, than to a senator or one having rule in a weal public? And that is the thing which grammar teacheth. °Logic is none other but the science of reasoning, helping natural wit to find truth more quickly out of diverse opinions, by affirming or denying, which in a senator may not be spared. °A man shall not well govern a city or country and set in good order the manners of people (as Plutarch saith), except he be well furnished with eloquence,[204] wherewith only he may persuade, affectuously steer, incline, and lead where he listeth the minds of the multitude; and that is best learned by rhetoric.

°'How many things happen in the state of a city or realm which requireth a diligent and exact computation with numbers? And that by arithmetic is best perceived. °In assigning of bounds and limits; also, to the making of munitions and fortresses; also, in devising of engines for wars: who dare say that geometry is not expedient, which describeth equality and inequality, aptness and unaptness, good proportion and deformity? °Also, without harmony, nothing is seemly or pleasant; and by concord and discord, all public weals do stand or decay. Yea, and as some philosophers have written, by them all things had

[203] Cf. Cic., *Mur.* 25–29, e.g. 27.1, 28.1, 'Although many things have been excellently settled by the laws, most of them have also been corrupted and degraded by the genius of the lawyers. [...] the dignity of a consul has never been consistent with that science, since it consists wholly of fictitious and imaginary formulas'.

[204] Plut., *Prae. ger. reip.* 5 (*Mor.* 801E), 'how is it possible that a private man [...] should ever be able to prevail over and govern the many, if he is not endowed with alluring and all-persuading eloquence?'

° \Grammar./

° \Logic./

° \Rhetoric./

° \Arithmetic./

° \Geometry/] *B* : *A om*

° \Music./

<U4r> their beginning. And this is best understand by the science called music. °Moreover, he that leadeth an army, if he be instructed in the diverse temperatures of sundry countries; by the natural discourse of the sun; by the five circles; the alteration of hours in day and night; by the distance of climes and pararels, which be sensible lines and spaces whereby the sun passeth about the firmament; also, the moon, with her mutable figures and special authority over waters and humours; the natural influence of other celestial bodies and signs — I mean in plenty or scarcity of things concerning man's sustenance and in storms or calmness of weather; all which things be knowen by the divine science called astronomy.

'I say, if a captain be therein instructed and not too much curious or arrogant, he shall the more safely keep alway his army. Julius Caesar, being therein exactly learned, vanquished by celerity and sundry preventions not only the fortune and most expert chivalry of valiant Pompey, but also the incomparable wits of five hundred senators.[205] And our noble progenitor Hadrian the Emperor was thought to have exploited things in battle by the help of this science, above men's expectation. I omit Hercules, which became disciple to Atlas for the commodity which he thought to find in astronomy. Finally, as ye all know, I have had no little delight in these four mathematical sciences and yet have, for the utility that I find in them when I do contemplate the perfect state of a weal public; and the same is approved both by Plato and Aristotle, which shapeth their examples by proportions of arithmetic, geometry, and <U4v> music, where they write of concord in virtues or politic governance.

'This well considered, a senator, either for giving of counsel or for being a captain in wars, shall find none impediment by having these sciences; but, using them moderately and as occasion requireth, they shall be to him not only an excellent ornament but also a necessary treasure, and to all sorts of governance a thing right expedient.

'What although Sextilius be not profoundly learned in the laws civil? Is that a good argument that therefore he may not be a good counsellor or in other authority about the weal public? Consisteth all the Senate of lawyers? Or standeth the weal public and all her affairs only by laws already stablished? May no public weal be without lawyers? How many noble senators have there been and yet are, which never read over all the Twelve Tables?[206] And yet have

[205] Plut., *Caes.* 43.4, 'On the night before the battle, moreover, as Caesar was making the round of his sentries about midnight, a fiery torch was seen in the heavens, which seemed to be carried over his camp, blazing out brightly, and then it fell into Pompey's. Then, during the morning watch, it was noticed that there was in fact a panicked confusion amongst the enemy'.

[206] The *duodecim tabulae* was the basic law of Rome. Liv., 3.33–37, has the story of the law's establishment *c.* 450 BCE; cf. Elyot, *Bibl.*, '*Decem tabulae*, were the old laws of the Romans

° \Astronomy/

they be found to reason wittily and minister prudently. Be laws anything else than rules of justice, whereby she commandeth what should be done and what ought not to be done, where a weal public should prosper? Then is it evident that justice maketh laws, and not law justice. Also, he that readeth the law seeth the commandment of justice; but seeing the law only in that that he seeth it, he doth not know justice. But contrariwise, he that knoweth justice by her may discern what is right or wrong, what is equal or unequal, and by the pattern of justice may invent a remedy, propice and necessary, which, expressed in word or writing, may be called a law.

'The knowledge of justice either happeneth by special influence from the high God, or else it is gotten with <X1r> the study of wisdom, comprehended in the books of wise men, who of Pythagoras were called *Philosophi*, which doth signify the lovers of wisdom.[207] Wherefore, they which either by divine inspiration or by study of the warks of excellent wise men have the truest knowledge of justice, and have best understanding what is just and what is unjust, and consequently can provide remedies according to justice; which remedies, if they once be made universal, they be laws, how so ever they be pronounced, be it by a multitude or by one person, as the edict not only of the Emperor but also of him that is praetor, is a law, as well as that which is made by all the whole Senate, or enacted by the tribunes and people of Rome.

'And where ye say that philosophers were never good practisers in a weal public, nor yet good men of war, if ye do mean by practice that detestable exercise which is subtle deceiving, crafty entermining, maintenance of injustice, perverse counselling, and unmeasurable getting, I confirm then your saying. For a philosopher abhorreth such practice and, as much as he may, doth and persuadeth the contrary.

'But if ye do intend by that word practice, only the laudable exercise in the

fetched out of Greece, whereunto afterward were two tables added by them which were called *Decem uiri*', and '*Decemuiri*, after that the laws of the Greeks were brought unto Rome by Spurius Posthumius, Publius Sulpitius, and Aulus Manlius, ambassadors sent for that purpose to Athens, then were there ten men chosen and appointed which of the same laws and ancient customs of the city should make laws, write them, and publish them. And their authority was above all other, that they mought make laws, and, if need were, interpret them. And where before were but ten tables of laws, they added unto them two mo, and so all those laws together were called *Leges duodecim tabularum*, and the dignity of those men was called *Decemuiratus*, and every of them called *Decemuir*, and their authority *Decemuiraleius*'. Elyot praises the *tabelae* in the words of 'Tully' (*De oratore* 1.195), *Gov.* 1.14 (Watson, p. 68), 'Although men will abraid at it, I will say as I think: the one little book of the *Twelve Tables* seemeth to me to surmount the libraries of all the philosophers in weighty authority and abundance of profit, behold who so will the fountains and heads of the laws'.

[207] Cf. Elyot, *Bibl.*, '*Pythagoras*, a man of excellent wit [...]. He was the first that named himself a philosopher, where before men of great learning were called wise men: and, because he would eschew the note of arrogance, when one demanded of him what he was, he said *Philosophus*, which signifieth a lover of wisdom'; also, Diog. Laert. 1.12.

administration of a weal public, truly ye be in a great error and folly and do speak as if ye were one of the vulgar people, ignorant of letters; yea, and that more is, private displeasure hath caused you to forget what ye yourself hath seen, contrary to that which now ye have spoken. I will not rehearse all them which, being studious in philosophy, have governed public weals or have executed their ministration therein substantially; but some <XIV> will I speak of.[208]

'Who governed Egypt and Libya more nobly than did Hermes, called Mercurius Trismegistus? And what philosopher was in all sciences equal unto him? Who ever kept his country in such a quietness and made it so rich as did Solomon, King of the Hebrews? Which — as it is founden in their histories translated into Greek by the commandment of Ptolemy, called Philadelphus, King of Egypt — was so great a philosopher that he disputed of all things natural and supernatural; and for his wonderful knowledge, there came to hear him out of all parts of the world men and women, being at that time in most reputation of learning?[209]

'Was ever this city of Rome in so good order as it was during the time of Numa Pompilius, which was forty years? Who, being an excellent philosopher and a private person, was chosen to be king; and so much more is his governance to be commended that he brought the people, which were rude, fierce, and ever continually in wars with their neighbours, into so good an order and temperance of manners that they which before were their enemies had them in admiration and reverence.[210]

'Who made better laws, or better ordered the commonweal of the city of Athens than Solon, the great philosopher, as long as they could sustain their own wealth? The same city had never a more noble captain nor a more valiant than was Pericles, who with Anaxagoras continually studied philosophy.[211] And, to descend to a more late time, where was there a better captain, or a more

[208] See above, p. 174, where, 'for the confutation of that pestiferous opinion that great learned men be unapt to the ministration of things of weighty importance', a similar list occurs, though with less development; also *Gov.* 1.12 (Watson, pp. 51–52), listing some of the same ancients, to illustrate 'how much excellent learning commendeth, and not dispraiseth, nobility' (p. 52); and likewise *Gov.* 3.24 (Watson, pp. 278–80), having still more coincidence with the lists herein.

[209] 'Hermes' is the legendary-divine figure regarded as author of the writings collected in the *Corpus Hermeticum* (cf. Elyot, Bibl., '*Hermes, -is*, and *Hermetis*, Mercury. *Trismegistus*, the name of Mercurius, in Latin *Ter maximus*'); Solomon, the biblical King of Israel; and the historical pharaoh, Ptolemy II Philadelphus (308–246 BCE) (cf. Elyot, *Bibl.*, '*Philadelphus*, called Ptolomeus, king of Egypt, who made a library in the which were fifty thousand books. He also caused the five books of Moses to be translated into Greek by seventy-two interpreters, doctors of the Jews').

[210] In addition to the *Bibl.* art. 'Numa' in the appendix below, see also Elyot, *Gov.* 2.4 and 3.2 (Watson, pp. 128 and 197–98). The tale of the election is in Plut., *Num.* 3.3–6, 5.1–7.3.

[211] On Solon, see Diog. Laert. 1.2.45; and on Pericles and his studies with Anaxagoras, Diog. Laert. 2.3.13.

noble warrior, than Scipio African? Who had alway with him <X2r> Polybius the philosopher; and in vacant times from battle, he either heard him read or disputed with him.[212] Semblably, Lucullus was so studious in all kinds of learning, as Plutarch writeth, that, where he heard that any great learned men disputed together, thither would he go and studiously hear them; and, as the same author saith, he haunted and embraced all kind of philosophy with most familiar acquaintance and custom, specially that which was called *Academica*, or the doctrine of Plato. And was there ever a more noble, a more politic or more valiant captain, and more esteemed and drad of most puissant princes than he was?[213]

'Lord God, what a senator was Cato, called Uticensis? Whose virtue was wondered at through the world, whose magnanimity and incomparable severity more profited unto the public weal of the city than the victories of Pompey and Caesar. And was not he so studious in °philo<so>phy that he could not temper himself, but that he must needs read Greek books when he sat in the Senate?

'What consul can ye compare to Marcus Tullius? Who, only by his divine and most excellent wisdom, preserved the public weal and city of Rome from utter subversion, which needs must have happened by the conspiracy of Catiline and his confederates if it had not been by the incomparable wit of Tullius found out, and by his divine eloquence plainly convinced, and by his wonderful wisdom suppressed and clean extinguished.[214] And how studious he was and exactly learned in all kinds of philosophy and eloquence, his most noble warks do declare with fame immortal.

[212] Cf. Vell. Pat., 1.13.3, 'Scipio was a cultivated patron and admirer of liberal studies and of every form of learning, and kept constantly with him, at home and in the field, two men of eminent genius, Polybius and Panaetius. No one ever relieved the duties of active life by a more refined use of his intervals of leisure than Scipio, or was more constant in his devotion to the arts either of war or peace. Ever engaged in the pursuit of arms or his studies, he was either training his body by exposing it to dangers or his mind by learning'. The self-justifying *Historiae Romanae* of the dubious military man Velleius Paterculus (*c.* 20 BCE–30 CE) was only discovered in 1515, by Erasmus's intimate Beatus Rhenanus (1485–1547), who published the first edition (Basel: Froben, 1520).

[213] L. Licinius Lucullus (118–56 BCE), in Elyot, *Bibl.*, '*Lucullus*, the name of a noble Roman'. Probably, the reference here is to Plut., *Luc.* 42.1–2, 'His libraries were thrown open to all, and the cloisters surrounding them, and the study-rooms, were accessible without restriction to the Greeks, who constantly repaired thither as to an hostelry of the Muses, and spent the day with one another, in glad escape from their other occupations. Lucullus himself also often spent his leisure hours there with them, walking about in the cloisters with their scholars, and he would assist their statesmen in whatever they desired. And in general his house was a home and *prytaneum* for the Greeks who came to Rome. He was fond of all philosophy, and well-disposed and friendly towards every school, but from the first he cherished a particular and zealous love for the Academy'.

[214] L. Sergius Catilina (d.62 BCE), whose conspiracy was the subject of Sall., *Cat.*, and the four surviving Ciceronian *Orationes in Catilinam*.

° philosophy] *B* : philophy *A*

'I pass over Nigidius, Varro, Thrasea, and many o-<X2v>ther sage and honourable senators, which were not only excellent philosophers but also prudent counsellors and valiant captains;[215] yet will I rehearse some, which were in the time of your remembrance.

'The Emperor Hadrian was so profoundly learned in all philosophy that he disputed openly at Athens with the chief philosophers of all Grecia and vanquished Phavorinus, who at that time was of all other most famous.[216] And to what prince or captain giveth he place, either in martial prowess or civil governance?

'What more honour ever happened to Rome than that Marcus Aurelius Antoninus succeeded immediately Hadrian, whose life was confessed to be the most certain law unto all people, to rule or be ruled? And he, for his exquisite knowledge in all philosophy, was most commonly called Antonine the philosopher, not by reproach, as some would suppose it, but for a most excellent and rare commendation. And what man did ever more increase the weal public or better defend it than did this most noble and virtuous Emperor?

'And be it of you received without suspicion of boast, as it shall be spoken of me without any vainglory: I, which may not be compared with the most inferior of them before named, either in learning or prowess, yet how much I have amended the state of the weal public, ye all can bear witness. And that I have nothing appaired the imperial majesty, it hath been of the Senate and people in your presence confessed. And this could I not so well have done, if I had not instructed my wit with the doctrine of philosophers.

'What say you by Gordian, Venatus, Aelius Serenianus, Catilius Severus, Frontinus, <X3r> Tacitus, and Aurelianus, honourable senators and our trusty

[215] The philosopher-counsellors listed are P. Nigidius Figulus (d.45 BCE) (Elyot, *Bibl.*, '*Nigidius Figulus*, an ancient Roman which was a great philosopher of the sect of Pythagoras and wrote wonderful subtly. About the year of our Lord forty-eight, he died in exile'); M. Terentius Varro (116–27 BCE) (Elyot, *Bibl.*, '*Varro, -ronis*, was a noble Roman, of all other most excellently learned'); and the eminent Stoic, who features in Tac., *Ann.*, P. Clodius Thrasea Paetus (d.66).

[216] Favorinus (*c.* 85–115); cf. *Bibl.* '*Phauorinus*, a famous and eloquent philosopher', etc. The episode to which Elyot here refers and recounts in *Bibl.* (in the appendix below) is from SHA, *Hadrian* 15.12–13, though evidently Elyot also knew the *Epitome de Caesaribus* 14.2–4 (attributed to S. Aurelius Victor in the Erasmian edition of the SHA, which includes it) and possibly Philostr., *VS* 489. Cf. Elyot, *Gov.* 1.12 (Watson, p. 51), 'Who ever reproved the Emperor Hadrian for that he was so exquisitely learned? Not only in Greek and Latin but also in all sciences liberal, that openly at Athens, in the universal assembly of the greatest clerks of the world, he by a long time disputed with philosophers and rhetoricians, which were esteemed most excellent, and by the judgment of them that were present had the palm or reward of victory. And yet, by the governance of that noble Emperor, not only the public weal flourished but also divers rebellions were suppressed, and the majesty of the empire hugely increased'.

counsellors? And Sabinus,[217] which sitteth here with us? Have they not right well shewed themselves to be apt unto governance, when they have been consuls, tribunes, and praetors? Yet be they no lawyers, but the more part of them be studious in philosophy and other liberal sciences.

'And now, to make an end of this matter, wherein I have tarried the longer to the intent that I would extirpate this vain opinion which men have had against philosophers and them that be studious: truly, that which ye do note in Sextilius to be little husbandry and small provision proceedeth not by lack of good policy, as ye have supposed. But he advisedly doth neglect to be rich or to aspire to any authority by ambition or flattery, preferring temperate and sure quietness before dangerous and unthankful labours, and more esteemeth to be an honest liver than a malapert craver.

'Also, by his study in philosophy, it seemeth that he hath acquired a great magnanimity or noble courage, not extending the force of his wit and knowledge in things which are but of little importance; wherein he fareth like to the puissant greyhound which was sent to the great Alexander by the King of Albany,[218] unto whom, when there was brought a great bull, he therefore would not once move. Afterward, a mighty and fierce lion was likewise shewed to him, which he only beheld and moved his tail, but he would not therefore arise out of his place. Finally, there was brought forth a marvellous great elephant. Then stood he on his feet, and did set up his bristles, and shewed his teeth; and, being <X3v> comforted by Alexander, he leapt to the elephant, and bit him, and after a few assaults killed him. Likewise Sextilius, being content with his estate, extendeth not his wit to augment it; but if he be favourably called to things of greater importance and therein well comforted, I doubt not but that he will shew that his study hath not been vainly employed.

'I marvel that ye do not consider that authority and favour not only sheweth a good wit, but also doth polish that which is rude. Fullers, tailors, horsekeepers, and mariners were by the Emperor Commodus and my predecessor Heliogabalus advanced to be consuls, praetors, and tribunes, which, as I heard say, were so changed in their wits that it seemed unto them which knew them before that, saving their visage and personage, they were altered and made other men, so much in their words and proceedings they excelled, above their accustomed wits, all men's expectation. How much more hope is there of those men which by education and study have their wits holpen? Suppose ye not that there be within our empire thousands of men which, being but of mean reputation, if they were set in authority or about our person, would set forth noble wits, equal to yours and perchance better? Which I speak, not displeasantly, but only to warn you to eschew arrogance.

[217] Excepting 'Tacitus' and 'Aurelianus' (both soon-to-be imperial names), the list is from SHA, *Alex. Sev.* 68.1, again: see above, p. 202 and nn.

[218] Plin., *NH* 8.149–150. The tale is used in Elyot's preface, above p. 174.

'Truly, God giveth wisdom; but favour and authority most chiefly sheweth it in a weal public. Earth nourisheth the root of the tree, but the comfortable sun bringeth forth the blossoms; and if storms do not let, he with his wholesome heat ripeth the fruit and maketh it pleasant. In <X4r> like wise, study and labour bringeth in knowledge, which, by the comfort of princes, appeareth abroad in some ministration; and, if envy or displeasure bring none impediment, the increase of favour maketh learning fruitful and profitable unto the weal public.

'Ye all, hear my sentence. And forasmuch as the more part of you, as I well do perceive, esteem no less Sextilius Rufus than I do, I will that he be sent for, and received into the Senate, and his name registered in the table of senators.'

Whereunto all the council according, it was for that time dissolved.

35. How Sextilius, hearing that he was made praetor, fled; and what the Emperor said concerning that matter.

After that it was declared unto the Senate that the Emperor had chosen Sextilius Rufus to be a senator and what he had said on his behalf, they all rejoiced in the Emperor's wisdom and judgment; and at his next coming into the Senate, they all did arise and gave thanks unto him for bringing into that college such a man as Sextilius was.

Soon after, Sextilius, being sent for by the Emperor's most gentle letters, came into the Senate and, as his learning and honest manners required, was beloved and commended of all men, except very few, whom envy and private displeasure continually fretted. Which, the wise Emperor perceiving, to the intent as well that the virtues of Sextilius should be more knowen and also be increased by his comfortable assistance, as also <X4v> to manifest to the comfort of other how much he was inflamed in the favour of virtue and doctrine, he caused Sextilius to be chosen praetor, which then was the highest office next to the Emperor in the ministration of justice.

Thereof hearing Sextilius, he, being thereat abashed and marvellous sorrowful, privily withdrew himself out of the city; and, not making long abode at his own house, in a strange habit, having but one man with him, went unto Athens, determining to pass his time there in study until the fame of him were somewhat decreased and another chosen unto that office.

Of this, the adversaries of Sextilius gathered no little occasion not only to pursue him with mocks and derision, but also to accuse him unto the Emperor of disobedience and obstinacy contrary to his allegiance, and also to blame him for his departure without asking licence.

All these accusations the Emperor heard without being anything moved against Sextilius; and, at the last, beholding the accusers with a displeasant countenance, he said unto them as hereafter followeth.

'How dare ye thus presumptuously assault our patience with your false accusations? Or how may ye for shame pour out your malice thus in our presence? What giveth you boldness to be thus malapert in attempting our reason with your envious persuasions? Think ye us to be so dull and gross witted that we cannot perceive your conspiracies? Or so deaf that we cannot hear your false rumours, which ye have spread of Sextilius? Or so blind that we see not your cankered affections and passions sparkling in your eyes, <Y1r> inflaming your visage, blasting out with your words, which for anger and haste be so set out of order that in them do appear your detestable folly?

'I tell you, Sextilius, by this his departing, hath nothing offended us or minished the opinion that we have had of him but hath augmented it and right well contented us. For if envy and malice hath not made you forgetful, ye may remember that, when we chase him to be a senator, one thing wherein we commended him was that he neglected to be rich or to aspire to authority. See ye not how he hath confirmed my saying, and that I spake it not for special affection? He hath not only neglected authority but (that more is) he is fled from it when it came toward him. When we sent for him, he came unto us and, being appointed to be a senator, he did obey us and gladly applied his study and counsel thereto pertaining; only hearing that he was chosen praetor before that he had monition thereof, he fled, as if he had been pursued with such force as he had not been able to strive with, fearing (as I said when I praised him) the dangerous and unthankful labours which he supposed to be in such offices. And whither or to whom is he fled? Not to the Persians, not to the people of Barbary or other our enemies; but he is peaceably gone unto Athens, which city, next unto Rome, we most favour. And there, in a private habit, he liveth in study, in that exercise which he supposeth that he can better sustain than the governance of a weal public.

'But notwithstanding, shall we herefore reject him and judge him unworthy to be called to authority? Nay, then were we ill advised and mought be noted variable in our opi-<Y1v>nion, since we judged him once able for neglecting thereof, we now deem him more able for the refusing. Ne we will be therefore more slack in the offering; yea, we also will thereto gently require him.

'For truly, authority ought to be given to such as careth least for it, and kept from them which press fastest toward it. For he that desireth would have it for his only commodity; he that looketh not for it considereth that he is chosen for others' necessity. Therefore, how diverse is their ministration it ever appeareth, whereas both happeneth.

'Leave your vain enterprise to bring us in displeasure with him, who is worthy more honour than we can give him, and by his laudable flight hath vanquished your envy, and to your great reproach hath published your folly.

'We therefore command you to avoid out of our presence, and that we see you not until we call for you.'

36. The letters of the Emperor Alexander sent to Sextilius, and how unwillingly he returned to Rome and received the office of praetor.

Forthwith, the Emperor himself indited letters unto Sextilius, in manner following:

> Alexander Augustus, etc.
>
> The tidings of your sudden departing, honourable Sextilius, was to the Senate and people grievous, to your enemies (although they be few) pleasant and joyous, dolorous to your friends, of whom there be many; but to us not strange, displeasant, nor marvellous, forasmuch as we longer have knowen your notable temperance than we have used your presence. Wherefore now, we more con-<Y2r>sider your humility and virtuous shamefastness than that which your enemies do call obstinacy and disobedience.
>
> Persuade now to yourself that, where before we did favour you, now do we most heartily love you and have no less ardent desire to have the fruition of your virtue and learning than hath the true lover of his wife or companion. What such love is, ye that have been at Socrates's banquet do know most certainly. Return, therefore, with honour, gentle Sextilius; satisfy the desire of me that am both your emperor and lover; rejoice the Senate and people; shame your enemies and recomfort your friends. Let it suffice unto shamefastness that she hath caused you to jeopard not only your estimation and credence but also your life and substance, if there had been a Senate uncircumspect, a people disordered, or an emperor a tyrant. Let her now give place to prudence and magnanimity. Her time of rule is expired in you; theirs is now come; for divine providence hath so provided and willeth it be so, since she hath called you to the dignity which ye well have deserved.
>
> In vain were your long travail in study and learning, if actual experience did not shew forth their fruits. I confess that the books which ye have made have well instructed other to governance; but yet, when the public weal calleth you to be ready in your own person to serve her, it is your chief office and duty. For so God hath ordained you, nature commandeth you, your country compelleth you, and philosophy biddeth you.
>
> Return, therefore, hardily, and accept with good courage and thankfully the reward of your virtue. Ne the ministration shall be strange unto you

that in study have had with <Y2v> justice such familiarity and have read so many books of good policy. Also, which ought much to comfort you, ye have a favourable emperor, expert assistants, diligent ministers, and people obedient. Ye being praetor, how many men expert in that office shall desire your company and be glad to participate with you that which experience or custom hath usurped from learning? Where law civil is necessary, among your assistants shall ever be some which therein shall counsel you. But finally, if ye have alway respect unto justice, and consider the causes with a prudent and diligent scrutiny, the great knowledge of the law civil shall not much trouble you.

Lay, therefore, all dread apart, and be not seen for faintness of courage to forsake that which the Emperor, Senate, and people — lords of the world — have with so great affection and judgment prepared for you. Take heed of your health, and let us shortly embrace you.

These letters were sent by post and in short time delivered to Sextilius, then being at Athens in the house of Sextus Cheronensis,[219] with other philosophers; which he receiving with reverence opened and read, and in the reading of them, partly stirred with the loving persuasions of the most noble Emperor, partly oppressed with dolour seeing that he mought make no longer defence against his election and that he must needs enter the dangerous race of authority, pight full of perils, he let the salt tears trill down by his cheeks. But when they that were present understood why that he shewed such countenance, contrariwise they rejoiced exceedingly, as well at the wonderful wisdom of the young Emperor, as that the <Y3r> virtue and learning of Sextilius was in conclusion so well considered, calling Rome a city most blessed that should have such a praetor. And with one consent, they so pressed on Sextilius with invincible arguments that he accorded to return toward Rome and to receive the said office.

Notwithstanding, after that he had sit a good space without speaking, he abraided out at the last and complained him in this wise.

'O what miserable estate shall I now come to? wherein diligence shall be cause of displeasure, negligence of reproach; sharpness shall be dreadful, pity unthankful; familiarity suspicious, friendship dangerous; every man's countenance pleasant, many men's minds offended; flattering openly, disdaining secretly; against my coming attendance, in presence much courtesy; being out of office or favour, lack of acquaintance. But, of force, I must obey that the Emperor commandeth; and yet he commandeth not, but most gently allureth,

[219] Cf. SHA, *Marc.* 3.2, where this 'nephew of Plutarch' is mentioned as one of the teachers of Marcus Aurelius; also, Eutropius, *Breviarium* 8.12 (in the Erasmian edition of the SHA), and M. Aur., *Med.* 1.9.1–3. He is also Guevara's falsely imputed source for the *Libro Aureo.*

whereto my friends also consenten and reason determineth. I therefore commit all unto God, who with his providence all thing disposeth.'

And so he departed and in short space arrived at Rome, where, with many noble senators and the chief of the people, he was gladly received.

Many other wise and well learned men did this noble prince elect and most gently invite into the ministration of the weal public, by occasion whereof oppression, extortion, bribery, and other corruption of justice were out of the city of Rome during this Emperor's life utterly exterminate. <Y3v>

37. A notable question moved by Julius Paulus unto the Emperor Alexander, and the wise answer which he thereunto made.

Ye have heard before what austerity and sharpness in punishment the Emperor Alexander used toward all them which by any manner corruption gave untrue sentences. Semblably, against thieves and oppressors of people, he was no less rigorous, punishing them sharply and openly, without remission or hope of pardon. Touching treason, he did never alter or add anything to the punishments which were afore ordained; and in conspiracies against his own person, he oftentimes suspended his sentence or deferred execution, as well to try out the counsels and practices of the offenders, as the first occasion of their displeasures; also, whether their natures were obstinate or proud, aspiring unto supremity, or if they were mild and easy and seemed to be incended thereto by the provocation of other; and diverse such.

Some he pardoned and, with most gentle persuasions, not only reduced them to due obedience but also bound their hearts to him in a perfect allegiance. Some he caused for a time to sustain imprisonment or exile; and, as he found them repentant, so did he relieve them. In their exile, it was punishment of death to give to them anything but meat and drink, and that but coarse and of small quantity; also, to be in their company longer than they °<who> brought them meat, or to speak with them, or to receive letters of them; so that they lived alone among people, in a prison unclosed, <Y4r> and, in a common resort, in most painful solitude. He had, notwithstanding, in those places of exile some trusty persons abiding, who marked in what form they sustained that punishment, whether they were very repentant or sturdy; and, according to such men's intimation, he caused the exile to be shorter or longer; and here about, he was very curious and diligent.

On a time, Julius Paulus, a noble counsellor,[220] marvelling that the Emperor was so pitiful toward them which offended his person, being so rigorous against all other transgressors, he, finding the Emperor at leisure, said unto him in this

[220] For Paulus, see above, p. 202, n. 103.

° who] *A om B om*

wise. 'Sir, if it shall stand with your pleasure, I would be fain satisfied in a thing which causeth me °to much wonder at you.'

'Speak on', said the Emperor.

'Sir', said Paulus. 'In all the time that I have served your majesty, I have considered that your proper nature is mild, facile, gentle, and witty, and therewith adorned with incomparable patience and constance. Wherefore, when I behold you in public or civil matters alway so bent to the rigour of justice that ye will pardon none execution, the offender being justly condemned; yet in transgressions against your majesty, be they never so grievous and leefully proved, ye oftentimes do give your most gracious pardon, and sometime unasked. And some have I knowen which have been condemned for committing acts against their allegiance to whom ye not only remitted your grace's displeasure but also received them familiarly and entertained them with great liberality, as Ovinius Camillus, who by secret means aspired to the <Y4v> imperial majesty.[221] When he was therefore brought afore the Senate all trembling, his conscience disclosing his trespass, ye, giving to him thanks that he willingly would take on him the charge of the weal public, which other good men refused when it was proffered, and calling him copartner of the empire, led him from the Senate unto your palace and caused him to sit with you at supper, in more richer apparel than ye ware at the time, with much other benevolence shewed unto him at your going in wars toward Persia.

'This thing maketh me and many other to marvel; wherefore, the causes which hereunto moveth you I am most desirous to know, which by mine own wit I cannot determine, and many other as well as I be therewith perplexed. I therefore most humbly beseech your majesty that by your own mouth it may be resolved.'

The Emperor, after a little pause, thereunto answered, 'Truly, Paulus, we be nothing offended with your demand but are right well contented to declare unto you and other men, of like wisdom, the reason and cause that doth move us to do anything in our office imperial, that thereby we may exclude all ill suspicion and approve our benevolence toward the weal public; albeit if ye had seen as

[221] SHA, *Alex. Sev.* 48.1–3, 'Cum quidam Ovinius Camillus senator antiquae familiae delicatissimus rebellare voluisset tyrannidem adfectans eique nuntiatum esset ac statim probatum, ad Palatium eum rogavit eique gratias egit, quod curam rei publicae, quae recusantibus bonis inponeretur, sponte reciperet; deinde ad senatum processit et timentem ac tantae conscientiae tabe confectum participem imperii appellavit, in Palatium recepit, convivio adhibuit, ornamentis imperialibus et melioribus, quam ipse utebatur, adfecit. et cum expeditio barbarica esset nuntiata'. SHA, *Alex. Sev.* 48.1–5 is quoted in Eras., *Apoph.* 6.150 (CWE 38, 638). This is the only mention of an 'Ovinius Camillus' in the SHA, and such a person is not known otherwise; Elyot uses the name above, p. 278 and, with reference to the imputed rebellion, repeatedly below, chaps 38–39, pp. 294 and ff.

° to much] much to B

much of philosophy as ye have done of the laws civil, ye should not have had need to have made this demand. But now, to your question.

'Ye must confess, Paulus, that in our person be two states or conditions: one, by nature, common with other men; the other, by election, private and from the people excepted. In the first, we be resembled to beasts for the affections and passions wherein we <Z1r> communicate with them. In the other, we be like unto gods immortal, in supreme dignity excelling all other men, which is to us happened, and not ingenerate, by the prerogative of virtue, which is supposed to be more excellent in us. °Which virtue is none other thing but disposition and exterior act of the mind agreeable to reason, and the moderation of nature. The supreme dignity that we have received is only in governance of men, which do participate with us in nature, wherein they alway remain equal with us; but by reason they be made inferior unto us. For they, supposing it to be more abundantly given us, have therefore willingly submitted themself unto our governance. And what that governance ought to be, our names of dignity, which the people hath given us, do express it sufficiently.

'For they gave to us first the surnames of "Caesar" and "Augustus", for remembrance of the prowess of the one and the wisdom of the other; which, like as they desired, so they trusted to be °abundantly in us.

'They call us also "emperor"; which dignity, among the ancient Romans, consisted in the principal governance of hosts and armies, not only in leading them unto wars — which was also the office °of a duke — but also to see them ever well exercised, keeping alway and in every place good order and justice.

'Moreover, the Senate and people have given us a name excelling all other in honour and dignity, calling us °"Father of their country". May there be imagined any name greater or higher? For where ye have withsave liberally to consecrate many of our progenitors and, calling them gods, have made them equal one to another, only Jupiter, whom <Z1v> Orpheus doth call "life", you and your progenitors have called "Father", as it were by a special prerogative above all other; which name is agreeable unto his property. For of life, all things have being and moving; which act of creation, or (more naturally to speak it) generation, is incident to the name of father; like as also his office is to preserve and keep safe that which he himself hath engendered.[222]

[222] Cf. Elyot, *Gov.* 3.23 (Watson, p. 272), explicating an Orphic hymn, 'Moreover, Jupiter was alway taken of the poets and philosophers for the supreme god which was the giver of life and creator of all things, as it appeareth in all their warks. Wherefore, sometime they call him omnipotent, sometime the father of gods and of men, so that under that name they knowledged <him> to be a very god, though they honoured not him as one only god, as they ought to have done'.

° \Habitus contemplativus et practicus./

° \Imperator./

° \Dux./

° \Pater patriae./

'Considering how inestimable an office and dignity are included in that divine and most reverend name of father, making me thereby the mortal image of the living God, how circumspect ought I to be, that I do nothing unworthy that name so liberally given me?

'Ye know well, Paulus, that in men's children be diverse and sundry dispositions. Some be apt of their nature to virtue and towardness; some have not nature so prompt and benevolent, wherefore they must be by education thereunto formed; some be quick of wit, some dull in capacity. Of sharp wits, some most do resplendish in acts that be honest; other seem quickest in malice and shrewdness. The good and diligent father of everich of them is equally careful and assayeth first by education to make them all conformable unto his appetite. And therefore, at the first, with sweetmeats and pretty gifts, he allureth them all for to love him; and where they offend (as none or else very few are perfect in virtue), correcting them with a little sharp rod, he maketh them also to fear him. And if he beat a shrewd boy, it is done as well to put other in fear to offend as to make him amend. And sometime, the father, to restrain the prompt disposition that he seeth in his children to vicious qualities, doth <Z2r> abdicate now and then one; that is to say, putteth them out of his family and clearly excludeth them from any hope of inheritance. Sometime, perceiving their shrewdness to cease, if any transgresseth against himself only, either he correcteth him moderately or, by a wise and gentle persuasion, assayeth to induce him to know well his duty and to pluck from him opinion of a false liberty.

'Next unto God, who is so great a father as he which is father of a whole country? that is to say, father of them that be fathers, their children and family? How much, then, ought the care of him exceed far the cares of all other? The charity of him, the love of all other? The wisdom of him, the prudence of other?

'The studious father more careth how to bring up his children in honesty than how to live pleasantly.

'The loving father hath more solicitude about his children's health than about his own wealth.

'The wise father more considereth what his son shall be in the estimation of other men than how he may content his singular affection.

'I have shewed to you the office of a private father. What will ye now say to me, that in office am the universal father of all the whole country? Will ye say that I should have less care, less love, or less wisdom and policy? I suppose, no. I know therein your opinion sufficiently.

'Then take good heed what I say! The rigour of justice, which ye seem to note in me, in punishing offenders against the weal public is but a form of discipline, convenient and necessary, having regard to such children as I found in this city, corrupted with all kinds of vice and having their minds and wits all disposed to folly; which, being a <Z2v> general detriment, I have used therein a more sharper remedy; and therefore, consequently it hath been found the more convenient and speedy.

'In offences touching our only person, we have descended in our mind from the imperial majesty and considered our first estate left us by nature; wherein looking as in a mirror, we behold the same matter that other men be of and therein the seeds of sundry affections. This causeth us, where we find hope of amendment, in lamenting the misery of mankind, to be moved with a fatherly pity; and, much less esteeming the danger of our person only than of the whole country, we endeavour us, by mercy and gentleness, to restore that unkind child, which hath offended us, eftsoons to his brethren and company. Notwithstanding, if he be so malicious and arrogant that he will not cease to abuse our patience, we then refuse him to be our child; and, as an enemy unto the weal public (for so be all that intendeth hostility against him which is head and father thereof), we commit him to the Senate and people, for his malice and treason, to be justly condemned. And thus doing, we accomplish all the parts of a father; and, keeping the people in a moderate fear and good order, we execute the office of a good emperor.

'Thus have ye, Paulus, a just accompt of our ministration. I wot not how it contenteth you; sure I am that mine own conscience therein was never offended, nor the public weal grieved, nor any good man thereby oppressed; whereof I have the Senate and people my witness, and him only my judge, who, being in heaven, faileth not to punish all them that abuse <Z3r> his image.'

Herewith, Julius Paulus seemed to be satisfied and, most humbly thanking the Emperor and marvelling at his great wisdom and temperance, for that time departed.

38. Of a great exclamation made against a gentleman called Marcus Geminus by his libertines, and the oration of Junius Moderatus made in the Senate.

Likewise as this Emperor Alexander was rigorous and terrible to corrupt judges and oppressors of justice, so was he most favourable and bounteous unto all such as were sincere in their ministrations and supporters of equity.

On a time as he went toward the Senate, there came against him a great number of persons, homely apparelled and of a rude presence; which, as the Emperor approached them, they fell down on their knees and, in a most lamentable form, with one confuse cry, accused a gentleman called Marcus Geminus of oppression; and, to bring him more into displeasure and envy, they added to their complaint that he was one of them that conspired with Ovinius Camillus.[223]

[223] 'Marcus Geminus' is not implausible, though there appears to be no such historical person; possibly, this is one of the series of figures, in this episode only (chaps 38–39), whose

The Emperor heard them and diligently marked their gesture and countenance, wherein he perceived to be more rancour than dolour, more sturdiness than humble shamefastness, more obstinate cruelty than reason or honesty.

He then asked of them what people they were.

They answered, saying that they were husbandmen of Campania.

He commanded them to withdraw them until they were sent for, and, shewing to them a right gentle visage, he passed <Z3v> from them.

The people, receiving a more arrogant courage of the comfortable countenance which it seemed that the Emperor made to them at their departing, leaving for the while their counterfeit sorrows, they spent the days in taverns and vittling houses, the nights in places of bawdry, promising unto themselves victory against Geminus; adding thereto, with most despiteful arrogance, that his torments and death should be a dreadful example to gentlemen and that from thenceforth their plowmen and tenants should be fellow like with them; which menaces and boastings were soon after reported unto the Emperor.

But first, as soon as he was come to the Senate, he shewed there all that was happened, and then he demanded the senators if any of them knew Marcus Geminus. Diverse of them answered, in order, that they knew him well and that he had been alway reputed a man of much honesty; and, having a competent living for his degree, had ever lived therewith temperately, without note of reproach unto this time.

Herewith, as the Emperor sat marvelling at the fury of the said clamorous people and the commendation given to Marcus Geminus, an ancient senator, named Junius Moderatus, who was reputed to be a man of great worship and was of the age of one hundred years or thereabout,[224] did stand up on his feet and said in this wise.

°'Most noble Emperor, albeit that I am not required nor do now intend to take on me the defence of Marcus Geminus, with whom I have no manner acquaintance, yet to the intent that your most gentle and <Z4R> pitiful heart, tempered with justice, should be no longer perplexed as it appeareth to be by your countenance, I will, by remembering your majesty of the general state and condition of them which have complained on Marcus Geminus, in some part, I

names may be allegory or paronomasia; for it emerges that there are two distinct views of the character of the doubtful 'Geminus': cf. Elyot, *Bibl.*, '*Didymus*, is in Latin *Geminus*, in Hebrew Thomas, in English, a twin in birth or double a man'. For 'Ovinius' and the plot against Alexander mentioned repeatedly below, see above, p. 291 and n. 221.

[224] Again, not an implausible name (the proper name of the Roman *agrimensor* whose work was known to Elyot was L. Iunius Moderatus Columella, fl. 50); but again, its irreal properties may be indicated by the punning of the first *nomen* of 'old Moderatus': cf. Elyot, *Bibl.*, '*Iunius*, a proper name of the Romans, as *Iunius Brutus*, *Iunius Columella*. It is also a month called June: for when Romulus had first divided the people into old men and young men, called in Latin *Maiores et Minores*, he honoured them with two months, calling the one *Maius*, or May, the other *Iunius*, of young men called in Latin *Iuuenes*'.

° \The oration of Junius Moderatus/

trust, resolve the importance of your admiration and study.

'Ye do well perceive that the complainers be all of Campania,[225] a country most plenteous of all thing that the earth may bring forth, and therewith so fertile that it doth not require great toil or labour, but only good diligence in observing the opportunity of time in sowing and planting, with the preservation of the things whiles they be growing. With this fertility, the bodies do become fat and lusty and thereby are made ill-disposed to labour, the which disposition the goodness of the soil alway supporteth.

'Thereof proceedeth obstinate sturdiness against their superiors and oftentimes commotions and sudden rebellions; and with great difficulty hath that people be brought unto a perfect obedience, which was after that they had rebelled against the Romans, being confederate with Hannibal and the *Carthaginensis*. At the which time, they being vanquished by Fulvius, many were slain, the multitude were sold in bondage unto the Romans, among whom the fields and possessions were at that time divided.[226]

'It dured a long time that the Romans, being good husbands themselves, overseeing their tillage and husbandry, keeping the Campans in servitude, burdening them with continual labours, feeding and clothing them moderately and more nearer to scarcity than superfluity, leaving them no more vacation from labour than the festival <Z4v> days which the laws have appointed; the country abode in continual quietness, and justice was there sufficiently ministered by one only magistrate, sent unto them yearly out of this city. There dwelled Sacerna, Tremillius, Julius Atticus, and diverse other gentlemen, as well in husbandry as in other wisdom and policy noble and famous, without exclamations unto the Senate. Moreover, the gentlemen brought up in that country, for their temperance in living and prudent governing of their own family, were oftentimes elect into the Senate and esteemed alway for the best senators.

'But after the subversion of Carthage and that all Greece and Asia were in our jurisdiction, Spain made tributary, and Gallia brought under subjection, idleness, with delicate appetite, entered together into this city and so much abounded that it was from thence distributed into all the whole region of Italy. And then the gentleman of Campania left their ancient frugality and diligent governance and did set all their study only about things pleasant and delectable, not being contented with the commodities of the same country, ne with the same measure and quantity which they before used; but, with outrageous expenses,

[225] Elyot's description of the history of Campania and the character of its inhabitants hereafter appears to depend on Eras., *Adagia* 4.8.14, *Campana superbia*, 'Campanian arrogance' (CWE 36, 361–63); cf. 4.10.18, *Peristromata Campanica*, 'Campanian curtains' (CWE 36, 496), 'Campania in its heyday indulged excessively in soft living and luxuries'.

[226] Reference is to the notorious 211 BCE reduction of Capua by siege and the city's treatment afterwards by the consul Q. Fulvius Flaccus, during the Second Punic War, in Liv., 26.15 esp.

sending into other countries far off for other kinds of things which they had not growing, they unsatiably fed therewith themselves and their servants; and, contemning the exercise of husbandry, they negligently have suffered their servants to be oppressed with gourmandize, and to reject their accustomed fare, and to have it more delicate; also, to increase sleep and pastime, and to minish their labours and diligence. °Moreover, by private contentions a-<2A1r>mong the same gentlemen — which alway happeneth where temperance lacketh — by ambition and envy, they that were bondmen were enfranchised and made libertines, to the intent that their lords would be seen puissant of men, to maintain their quarrels.

'Whereby it is happened that the progeny of the said bondmen are now of such sturdiness that they disdain and take scorn to be corrected, ne will otherwise labour than it shall like them. And if their lord will sharply call on them, they will not let boldly to make resistance. And where they be not thereto sufficient, they will suborn some false quarrel to make a commotion, trusting thereby to rob and destroy their lords. Or if they cannot bring that to pass, at the least they will make injust exclamations, where they find a prince whom they suppose to have his ears open to tales and reports and will condemn in his opinion men complained on before perchance that he knoweth them.

'Hereof have we too many examples, as well in the time of Tiberius, Nero, and Domitian, as in the time of my remembrance. Were not Dulius Sillanus and Antius Lupus, men of great honesty, condemned to death by the Emperor Commodus upon the false complaints of their libertines? Which grudged against them because that Sillanus was a stern man and of the ancient severity, wherefore they mought not sustain him punishing them continually for their idle and riotous living. Lupus, because he would not suffer his libertines to encroach upon his possessions and to retain certain portions of land which, after the death of Petilius Rufus, his mother's uncle (whose heir Lupus was), they had taken by stealth, whiles he was <2A3v> in Asia; wherefore they appeached him unto the Emperor, saying that he was of familiar counsel with Caius Regilius, whom a little before Commodus had put unto death. Petronius,[227] in the time of Caracalla the Emperor, was also put unto death by a like occasion.

'And to speak of mine own experience, by the space of forty years, so long I

[227] The names of these imperial victims, though not the causes of their condemnations, appear to be drawn from SHA, *Comm.* 7.4–5, including the 'Petronius' whose death Elyot imputes to Caracalla: 'As successors to Cleander [sc. in the office of *praefectus praetorio*] Commodus appointed Julianus and Regillus, both of whom he afterwards condemned. After these men had been put to death he slew the two Silani, Servilius and Dulius, together with their kin, then Antius Lupus and the two Petronii, Mamertinus and Sura, and also Mamertinus' son Antoninus, whose mother was his own sister'.

° \Libertines were of like conditions, as our copy-holders were of old time./

continued in keeping of husbandry in the country of Umbria, having therein much delectation, I found the rustical people, my neighbours, prompt to injuries, murmuring at justice, grudging at labours, desirous of pleasures, ingrate against benefits.

'At the first, I was with them familiar and homely; then found I them alway carlish and sturdy. Then, against mine own nature, I changed my copy and became toward them more strange in countenance, more rare in speaking, more seld in pardoning, more quick in revenging such injuries as they willingly did me; moreover, I was more frequent in commanding my libertines and would myself see them to do truly their services, nothing omitting. Then had I little and seldom any occasion to be offended with: there was none injuries offered me of my neighbours, which, beholding me so sharp to my libertines and so rigorous in justice, feared to displease me; my libertines, forgetting all pleasures, studied with labour and diligence to get some praise of me.

'Then considered I well that good debtors, oftentimes spared, become ill payers; small injuries, oftentimes pardoned, maketh of neighbours pernicious enemies. A servant made malapert will kick at his duty, and labour by custom becometh easy. Behold that gentle masters have alway proud <2A<4>r> servants; and of a master sturdy and fierce, a little wink to his servant is a fearful commandment. The nature of libertines is much contrarious to that which is gentle. The gentleman, gently entreated, is content to do all thing; the vile nature, familiarly used, grudgeth at everything. This is every day proved, but no wit can make straight which nature made crooked.

'Geminus is a gentleman of an old house of the Latins, whose great grandfather Rubellius Geminus was consul in the late days of the Emperor Tiberius. He hath his possessions in Campania, as I have heard say, by an ancestor of his mother called Pomponius Sura.[228] Perchance, his novelty there may be disdained, and the moveable people, lacking somewhat of their wills, may be comforted by some of equal degree unto Geminus, by their exclamations to bring him out of credence and consequently unto some jeopardy.

'Wherefore serveth the praetor Triphonius, who is knowen to be a man very discrete, well learned, and of a great judgment?[229] If they came to him, why did he not hear them? If he would not hear them, why complain they not of him? If

[228] It is the case that L. Rubellius Geminus and C. Rufus (*recte* Fufius) Geminus were consuls in 29 (Tac., *Ann.* 5.1.1), traditionally the consulate of the crucifixion of Christ; also, the *gens Fufia* to which these persons belonged was of Campanian origin. The name 'Pomponius Sura' may only have been confected from elements in the above cited passage of the SHA, *Comm.* 7.5.

[229] The name occurs in a list of persons, who 'omnes iuris professores discipuli fuere splendidissimi Papiniani et Alexandri imperatoris familiares et socii', in the engrossed list of Alexander's counsellors in the Erasmian SHA, *Alex. Sev.* 68.1, to which Elyot had recourse for names (see above, p. 202 and nn.), but in these chaps 38–39 only.

he did hear them, why is Geminus left still unpunished? If he be punished, why is he eftsoons accused?

'Mine advice is, most noble Emperor, that Marcus Geminus be hastily sent for, that he have no leisure to solicit the praetor Triphonius; and that, immediately afterward, a letter be directed to the same praetor, willing him to advertise your majesty, with all expedition, what may be proved in the ratification of such articles as been objected in the accusation of Geminus; which proves, being sent up unto us, if Geminus <2A4v> cannot refel them, then let the laws of the city proceed against him. If the suggestion be found false and malicious, then shall your majesty do like a virtuous governor and father of the country, if, by your excellent wisdom and rule of justice, ye provide that the false accusers and their abettors may be so punished that they and other persons of like inclination may be afeared to abuse your clemency and most gentle nature.

'And now hath your majesty heard all mine opinion.'

This sentence contented the Emperor, who therefore commended the substantial wisdom and compendious eloquence of the old Moderatus. And according thereunto was Geminus sent for by an officer; and soon after, a letter was sent to Triphonius, according to the minute before rehearsed, which was delivered to the praetor incontinent upon the departing of Geminus.

39. The wonderful prudence and equity shewed by Alexander the Emperor, in the determination and sentence in the matter preceding.

At the coming of Geminus to Rome, he was forthwith committed unto Catelius the senator,[230] to be secretly kept, with comfort given unto him that, if such things as he was accused of could not be proved by witness or matter sufficient, his accusation should be to him an happy displeasure.

In the mean time, Triphonius the praetor, when he had read the Emperor's letters, fearing his rigorous justice to rulers and judges corrupted or negligent, he forthwith sent unto the most honest inha-<2A<3>r>bitants, not being gentlemen, which dwelled in towns and villages next adjoining to the habitation of Geminus. Whom, not being yet ware of the departing of Geminus nor for what cause they were sent for, the praetor calling unto him one of them after another, he severally examined them: what they knew or supposed of Marcus Geminus; in what condition he used himself, first concerning his faith to the Emperor, Senate, and people of Rome; also, in justice and equity touching his neighbours; moreover, frugality and temperance in his own family; finally, in oppression and cruelty to his tenants and libertines; adding thereunto that the Emperor's majesty was informed that Geminus in all the said points was

[230] For 'Catelius' or 'Catilius Severus', see above p. 202 and n. 104.

grievously noted, which, being sufficiently proved against him, his punishment should be to all other men a dreadful example, whereby poor men should afterward live in the more surety and out of the danger of cruel affections.

Every one that was examined apart, freely, without alteration of words, affirmed that Geminus was a man of great honesty and that they did never suspect his faith °<or> allegiance, although he repaired sometime to Ovinius, when he sojourned nigh to him, which he seemed rather to do for the honouring of Ovinius's dignity than for any special affection that he had toward him, considering that they were most unlike of conditions. For Ovinius was proud, ambitious, and prodigal; Geminus was gentle, moderate in living, and temperate in spending. The other was almost ignorant of letters, delighting in riot and lechery; this man, well learned and having his principal pleasure in reading or writing. So diverse <2A<3>v> conditions could never join hearts in a fervent affection. Moreover, they could never perceive that Geminus at any time praised Ovinius otherwise than is the general praise given to men in authority, calling him honourable.

Concerning justice and equity, they said that therein he was ever found notably earnest, in so much as by keeping his promise and touch, he sustained oftentimes no little detriment. Also, he remitted oftentimes a good part of his duty, which the laws gave him, sometime of gentleness, sometime moved with the person's necessity. The measurable fare and good order of his family was to all his neighbours an excellent pattern.

To his tenants and libertines, at his first coming he was of much affability. But after that he had perceived by the ancient tables and muniments belonging unto his patrimony that his libertines had withdrawn some part of their services and craftily interlaced his dominical lands with their servile possessions, he first assayed to persuade them to restore unto him his inheritance, offering to remit unto them their wrongful intrusions with all the profits which they had thereof received, if they would willingly depart from that which by justice they mought not keep from him. But they, little regarding his honest request, obstinately denied to leave the possession of those lands which they had so long occupied and became, in all their acts toward him, sturdy and malapert. Wherewith being displeasantly moved, he, with his household servants and friends, expelled them from the possession of such lands as they wrongfully occupied.

Wherewith, they being exasperate and desirous to be revenged, supposing <2A4r> that, if they complained to the praetor, the truth shortly appearing unto him, they should nothing prevail but be for ever excluded from their unjust occupation; they, conspiring together, went unto two gentlemen dwelling hereby, the one called Duillius, the other Cotta,[231] who alway had envy at

[231] Both 'Duillius' and 'Cotta' are widely attested as elements of historical Roman *nomina*;

° or] of *A B*

Marcus Geminus and mought not sustain his commendation but used to speak reproachfully of him.

When they had heard what the libertines purposed, they exceedingly rejoiced thereat and gave to them not only comfort in their proceedings but also sums of money toward their charges, with secret letters unto their friends and acquaintance in the city of Rome, desiring them to assist and solicit the cause of the libertines. They said, moreover, that there remained yet in the town of Geminus as well libertines as men free of condition, his tenants, which, being of a more honest nature and persuaded at the first with the reasonable request of their lord, would by no means consent unto the conspiracy, notwithstanding that they were thereunto pressed as well by the said gentlemen as by the libertines, which persons they thought expedient to be also examined.

That hearing the praetor, commending their truth and modesty, he depeached those deponents for that time, commanding them to keep all thing secret; and immediately, he sent for the said residue of the tenants and libertines of Marcus Geminus, who, being likewise examined, in all and every thing agreed with the first witnesses.

Then Triphonius incontinent caused horses to be provided and those persons, without any longer abode, to be conveyed to Rome with his letters unto the Emperor, contai-<2A4v>ning the true report of the said examinations; which letters the Emperor reading himself, commanded that those men which were come to the city should be forthwith brought to his presence, in most secret wise, which was performed.

Then the Emperor, calling to him Ulpianus, Catelius, Paulus, and Sabinus,[232] who at that time were in the palace, he commanded the said persons to be brought forth; and, himself demanding like questions of them, as Triphonius had done but in another order and fashion, he found their words in every condition like as they had deposed, saving that they thereunto added that the complainers, before their departing and after that they were come from Duillius and Cotta, had importunately desired these men to go with them, saying that they nothing doubted but that Geminus at the least should lose his head, and that they for their travails should have his goods or a good part thereof divided among them, and that Duillius and Cotta trusted to have his lands by gift or by purchase.

That hearing, the Emperor, with visage inflamed and eyes sparkling as fire, brast out in these words following:

'O villain nature, bestial and monstrous! O cruel envy, foul and malicious!

the information supplied is inadequate to enable identifying either of Elyot's characters with a historical figure.

[232] For Ulpian, see above, p. 184 and n. 48; for 'Catelius' or 'Catilius Severus', p. 202 and n. 104; for Paulus, p. 202, n. 103; and for Sabinus, p. 184 and n. 48.

The one never vanquished with gentleness, the other never contented with virtue and soberness! How often have wise men been by such falsehood deluded; emperors, kings, and other potentates by such serpents abused, justice oppressed, mercy sklandered, good people destroyed, false harlots advanced! God forbid that I should live emperor of Rome if I would not see this enor-<2B1r>mity punished, whereby all public weals may be shortly subverted. For where order faileth, obedience decayeth, boldness increaseth, deceit escapeth, injury prevaileth, avarice corrupteth, the state of a weal public soon after perisheth.'

When he had said thus, he, commending the truth and sincerity of them which had spoken, commanded that they should remain still in his palace, in a place secret, until it were his pleasure for to call for them.

Then caused he to be published throughout the city that Marcus Geminus was likely shortly to be condemned. Which being comen to the ears of his accusers, they, replenished with joy, roamed about the city, embracing their friends and confederates with mutual congratulations, making banquets one to another, for exceeding joy forgetting to sleep, but passed forth the nights in drinking and singing and devising torments for Marcus Geminus.

Of all this heard the Emperor, who dissembled his anger, albeit he had no less solicitude in providing the means how their mischief and falsehood mought be in such wise corrected as good men mought be free from such perils and the example mought utterly drown the malice of wretches.

As soon as Duillius and Cotta had heard of the bruit of the condemnation of Geminus, with all speed they both came unto Rome, bringing with them great presents to give unto such as were nigh about the Emperor, to the intent that they by their means mought attain to the possessions of Geminus. But these noble men, unto whom they offered to give the said presents, refused to take them, fearing the Emperor's severity.

As soon as the Emperor had heard <2B1v> of the coming of Duillius and Cotta, he sent for them; and, in the presence of diverse senators, after that he had taken them by the hands with a familiar countenance, he dissembled to them that he was much grieved with the unkindness of Geminus toward his person, and also his oppressions and injuries toward his libertines and tenants. With that, Duillius and Cotta, being much comforted toward their purpose, to aggravate the complaints against Geminus and seeming to do well, dispraised the rigorous tyranny of Geminus and commended the simplicity of his libertines, saying that they would not so soon have complained on Geminus if they had not been by them vehemently stirred and provoked thereto.

After that the Emperor had been a while in a study, as it were to say some thing against Geminus, at the last, with a familiar visage, he said unto them: 'Ye have knowen in how much detestation I have alway had the oppression of innocents, the injuries done with extreme malice and violence; and yet, notwithstanding the sharp corrections which have been executed against such malefactors, as well by ancient laws of this city as by our own decrees and ordinances, yet, as it seemeth, that pestilence in the weal public ceaseth not.

'Wherefore, we now would that some new and strange correction were devised for Geminus, which should be such as, to all men of every degree, it mought be the most fearful example to offend in like condition. And as touching the offence toward me, I shall hold me content with the judgment which the laws have provided.

'And moreover, to the intent that men shall perceive how much <2B2r> we favour them that do support true men against tyrants, I would that some reward were also devised for such supporters, equal and convenient unto their merits; and herein will we first hear your sentences. Forasmuch as ye do seem to be men of zeal and are reported to be wise men and politic about your affairs, wherefore we intend to have of you better acquaintance, that the public weal by you may be amended.'

These words of the Emperor Duillius and Cotta took to be all for their benefit; and thinking that they had good opportunity offered them to achieve their desire, thinking that, the more sharp and vehement punishment they did devise for Marcus Geminus, the better it should content the mind of the Emperor; first Duillius, forgetting himself, with face all inflamed with malice, declared his sentence in this wise:

'Forasmuch as the Emperor had referred the offence committed against his majesty to the judgment of the laws civil — albeit that such punishment were insufficient for such a traitor as Geminus was — concerning his oppression of innocents, his correction mought be no less than that he, being all naked, should by his libertines be first of all whipped throughout the city of Rome with whips full of rowels, called "Scorpions"; and afterward, his nose and ears being cut off, so with reproaches to be conveyed unto the town of his habitation, and there to be eftsoons whipped by all his libertines; and from thence to be carried into the isles called Hebrides and never to return into Italy; his children also to be banished forever out of that territory; restitution also to be made to the <2B2v> libertines of all that which was bereft them. As concerning the residue, they which were accusers of traitors and supporters of the same accusers should have divided among them the one half deal of their goods and possessions, so that the one half thereof should be to the accusers, the other half to the supporters of them; the other half deal of the whole should be confiscate to the Emperor's treasure.'

Cotta agreed in everything with Duillius, saving the deforming of Geminus and banishment of his children, saying that therein was too great a visage of cruelty. In the disposition of the goods and possessions, he added unto the sentence of Duillius that, if the accuser or supporter were a bondman or libertine, he should have no part of the possessions but only the fourth part of the movables. In the residue, he agreed with Duillius.

When they had spoken, the Emperor and other that were with him seemed to commend their zealous affection; and the Emperor, finding occasion by the lack of time and that his supper abode then for him, did depart from them, saying that he would advise him on their wise counsels, and licensed them to depart with a familiar beck. Who, being returned to their lodgings and sending for the libertines and other of their acquaintance, after that they had declared what they had spoken, and how nigh the confusion of Geminus did approach, and what trust they had to enjoy his goods and possessions, there was made among them joy without measure, with revel and banqueting, so that the report thereof came to the ears of the Emperor and of all the Senate, which remained in a great expectation of the Emperor's judg-<2B3r>ment.

Afterward, the Emperor commanded his place of estate to be made ready in the Theatre of Pompey[233] and that the people of Rome should be summoned to be ready there the third day following, which was accomplished. And the Emperor being set with his noble counsellors with him, he commanded that as well the libertines as Duillius and Cotta should prepare them to the accusation of Geminus; who came into the place bringing with them one Rutilius Lupus, a subtle rhetorician,[234] to be their advocate. But Geminus, only trusting on his own conscience, refused to have any other patron than the true examination and justice of the Emperor and other which were his judges. And the Emperor was therewith right well contented, considering that the time of the controversy should be made thereby the shorter.

First, Lupus began his oration with a great praise of the Emperor's virtues, which the Emperor in no wise sustaining, but being therewith offended, interpelled Lupus and commanded him to enter into his narration and to declare immediately the state of the matter contained in the complaint of the libertines.

Then Lupus, being partly abashed, forasmuch as his beginning was to make the Emperor and hearers benevolent toward the libertines and to make the cause against Geminus to seem more grievous, he coldly entered into the matter and generally objected against Marcus Geminus his familiar resort unto Ovinius Camillus before that he was detected of treason; and thereunto he brought in for witnesses Duillius and Cotta, whom he called men of great worship, Geminus

[233] See above, p. 255 and n. 178.

[234] There was a Tiberian-period rhetor named P. Rutilius Lupus, mentioned by Quintilian (*Inst.* 9.2.101), some of whose work survives. The figure here may be intended as a relation of the 'Antius Lupus' mentioned just above as an imperial victim (from SHA, *Comm.* 7.5). Most likely, the name would be Elyot's allegorical invention for immediate purposes: it means something like 'The Ruddy Wolf'.

speaking yet nothing, nor changing his countenance.

Duillius and <2B3v> Cotta, by too much malice and covetise forgetting themselves, pressed forth and said that they had oftentimes seen Geminus not only at super with Ovinius in the time of his conspiracy, but also talking familiarly and secretly with him.

Therewith the Emperor, taking occasion, demanded of them what it was that Geminus spake to Ovinius.

They said they wist not, for they stood far from them and mought not hear them.

The Emperor demanded if they did see when Geminus came and departed.

They answered that for the more part they came before him and abode long after him.

He asked, moreover, in what form Geminus departed from Ovinius.

They said, for the more part, with no pleasant countenance of the one or the other.

The Emperor asked if Geminus were desired by Ovinius to come or if he came to him unsent for.

They said they could not remember but that Ovinius sent alway a servant for Geminus.

The Emperor demanded if he did likewise with them.

They answered no.

The Emperor immediately sent for Ovinius, who, being reconciled to the Emperor, was then in the Senate, and for Carnilius his servant,[235] who had detected his treason; and in the meantime, the Emperor turned him unto Geminus and said that, if he were the man that he shewed to be, he would less esteem death than the loss of his credence and that, for his part, he more esteemed the confession of truth than the avenging of his displeasure; wherefore, he charged him, upon the faith of an honest man, to tell plainly whereof was the communication between him and Ovinius.

Geminus answered that the first access that he had to him <2B4r> was voluntary and unsent for, only to salute him because he was a senator and in great estimation, not knowing anything of his traitorous affection; but perceiving his qualities and natural appetites not to be agreeable to his opinion and study, he ceased to come until he was desired of Ovinius, which, as he after perceived, was for his incommodity. For Ovinius desired of him a mansion place which he had joining to the gardens of Nero, from the which he would in no wise depart, albeit often and sundry times Ovinius sent for him, and, as well by offering great sums of money and friendship as sometime by menaces, he assayed to get of him the house; but last of all, he threatened him that, having

[235] 'Carnilius' is no part of a Roman name; possibly, Elyot derived it from *caro* or *carnis*, 'flesh', as in *carnalia*, 'things of the flesh', as opposed to *spiritualia*.

all thing at commandment as he doubted not but that he should see it come to pass shortly, he would leave him neither house nor life. With the which words, Geminus said that he was astonied and so departed with his displeasure, but yet not thinking that Ovinius intended any conspiracy, considering that he was allied unto the Emperor and was by him advanced unto great riches.

Thus ceased Geminus to speak any more; and by that time, Carnilius was comen, who, being demanded what acquaintance he had knowen to be between Ovinius and Marcus Geminus, he answered that he knew none acquaintance between them but that oftentimes he had heard Ovinius his master say to his secret friends, after that he had a long time talked with Geminus, that he was a sturdy and obstinate person and would not conform him to his requests concerning a house which he had nigh to the city, wherefore, if he mought <2B4v> bring his purposes to pass, he would leave him neither house nor head on his shoulders.

The Emperor demanded if Geminus were any of them that Ovinius counselled with concerning his conspiracy.

Thereat smiled Carnilius and said that Ovinius never had him in so much reputation, for he ever esteemed him to be most unapt to any such practice.

Then came in Ovinius and, the Emperor commanding him, sat down by him. And the Emperor asked him if he knew Marcus Geminus. And he, fearing that he had complained of him, blushed and said that he could never find kindness in him and that his nature was overthwart and alway against his desires; wherefore, he desired the Emperor not to give too much credence unto him in such things as he complained of him, other than touching the request made for his house in the city, which he confessed to have desired importunately, and for that cause only had often times convented him when he repaired into that country.

The Emperor with that answer was well contented and demanded if he had any better opinion of Duillius and Cotta.

He said that they were of another sort, and more conformable unto his appetite.

Thereat the Emperor laughed in his heart, as he after declared unto his familiars, marking the folly as well of Duillius and Cotta as of Ovinius Camilius, which unawares had disclosed their secret affections and declared the innocency of Marcus Geminus.

And licensing Ovinius to return to the Senate, he commanded Lupus to resort to the residue of the accusation of Geminus; who, partly being discouraged, with a weak eloquence alleged the injury and cruel op-<2C1r>pression of Geminus extended unto his tenants, taking from them their ancient possessions and annexing them to his dominical lands.

Therewith Geminus, being somewhat moved, plainly denied that it was their ancient possessions but affirmed that it were his proper dominical lands, which, between the death of his uncle and his entry, they had unjustly usurped and falsely concealed; wherefore, not only he by the law mought justly expulse them from that which they unleefully occupied, but also by their ingratitude they had forfeited their manumissions; and consequently, the lands given to them by his ancestors of good right ought to resort eftsoons to his possession.

This hearing the Emperor, he demanded of the complainants of what state and condition they were.

They all confessed to be the libertines of Marcus Geminus and that such lands as they had were servile, as for the which they were bounden to certain observances; but they plainly denied that they had forfeited anything and with great exclamations and out of order cried out on Geminus.

Then commanded the Emperor that the gentlemen and residue of the libertines and tenants sent by Triphonius should be brought in; who, being in likewise examined, declared openly the stealing of Geminus' dominical lands by the said libertines which were accusers, the conjuration of them to the destruction of Geminus, their privy solicitation of other, the malicious supporting of Duillius and Cotta with their secret confederacies, and all other things as before they had shewed to the Emperor at home in his palace; which as well the accusers as Duillius and Cotta hearing disclosed <2C1v> contrary to their expectations, they all were confounded and, in their amazed countenance sudden and °silence, seemed to the Emperor and all that were present to confess their untruth and malice.

And therewith Cotta, fearing the Emperor's severity, fell on his knees, and besought the Emperor to pardon him, and likewise desired Geminus to forgive him his malice, confessing all to be true which was now spoken on his behalf.

Herewith, the Emperor was fervently stirred with displeasure toward the accusers.

After that he had spoken with the residue of the judges, he gave sentence in this wise: 'Forasmuch as it appeareth unto us that thou, Marcus Geminus, art innocent of that treason which thy cruel libertines, with the supportation of Duillius and Cotta, have falsely accused thee of, we declare thee to be a true gentleman, loyal to the weal public and majesty imperial, and denounce unto all men that none be so hardy to renew this suspicion, whereof thou art purged. And for thy patience, wisdom, and temperance, we deem thee worthy to be admitted into the college of senators.'

Then the Emperor, turning him to the libertines, said: 'Ye villain generation, full of pestiferous malice, rude and most bestial of nature, void of all courtesy, false and deceitful toward your sovereign, cruel and vengeable against justice and reason; forasmuch as ye with all your will and puissance have endeavoured yourselves by your false accusation not only to have brought to a shameful

° silence] silente *B*

death Marcus Geminus, your natural lord, a true and innocent gentleman and a necessary member of the weal public, which, if it had happened, thereof <2C2r> should have succeeded unto the weal public notable damage, and to our person perpetual reproach and burden unto our conscience; we therefore judge you all worthy no less to suffer than Duillius, one of your captains, gave in his sentence at home in our palace against Marcus Geminus; that first ye shall be whipped throughout the city with Scorpions, and then your noses and ears to be cut off, and so to be brought into Campania, and there to be eftsoons whipped in every town, and last of all, to be hanged in chains on high gibbets, as ye be sixteen in number, in sixteen of the greatest towns of that country; and that your children shall lose the privilege of the manumission of you and your ancestors, and that none of your blood be from henceforth manumised by any consul or praetor; moreover, all your possessions wholly to remain to Marcus Geminus, your movables, by the consent of Geminus, whereunto we exhort him, to be equally divided and given to his other tenants and libertines which refused to be consenting or party to your proceedings.'

Then looked he on Duillius and Cotta and first said to Duillius: 'Thou detestable serpent of villain progeny, which nature in thee neither mought be subdued with authority nor altered with riches; forasmuch as by envy only thou hast maligned against Marcus Geminus and with all thy power hast supported his libertines to accuse him most falsely of treason; and moreover, thyself hast in such wise appeached him that in thine own words it appeareth that thou were of a more familiar resort unto Ovinius than Geminus was and by Ovinius's confession more conformable unto his appetite — and what is declared by <2C2v> those words but thou and Cotta were consenting unto the conspiracy? Thou shalt therefore receive thine own judgment which thou wouldest have given on Marcus Geminus, that is to say thou shalt be disgraded of all honour and despoiled of thy garments in the middle of this city, and from thence whipped with Scorpions unto the highway called *Via Appia*; and from thence, thou shalt be carried unto Tarentum and, being there eftsoons whipped, thou shalt be rendered with thy children in servitude to Marcus Geminus, and all thy possessions to remain forever to him and his heirs.

'And as to thee, Cotta, although that thou hast desired pardon, yet forasmuch as thou hast polluted the noble and ancient blood whereof thou camest, embracing villain conditions and choosing rather to be confederate with villains and malicious wretches than to favour virtue and justice, it were not expedient that thou shouldest be so pardoned, that thou shouldest clearly escape without punishment, specially considering that thy nobility was a cause that Geminus was much more suspected than if thou hadest not joined thyself with his libertines. Thou shalt, therefore, sustain part of thine own judgment which thou wouldest have given on Geminus, that is to say thou shalt forthwith lose all thy movables, which also with the goods of Duillius shall be equally parted, the one half to be brought into the common treasury, the other half to be given indifferently among those gentlemen which honestly have declared unto us the innocency of Marcus Geminus; and as for thy lands, during thy life to be confiscate, afterward to return to thine he-<2C3r>irs; moreover, that thou thyself shalt never return into Campania but remain still here in this city, except we upon other considerations hereafter moving us shall clearly pardon thee.'

This was the end of the Emperor's sentence, wherewith all the people rejoiced and cried with one voice: 'Happy is Rome, that hath such a governor! Happy is the world, that it hath such an emperor! But most happy be we, that have such a father! Live, noble Alexander! For the gods do favour thee, all princes doth honour thee, all ill men do dread thee, all good men love thee! Live and prosper, most excellent Emperor!'

With these and other most joyous acclamations, the Emperor issued out of the theatre and departed toward his palace, having with him Marcus Geminus, all the streets being full of men, women, and children, casting before him innumerable roses and other sweet flowers.

The next day was the Emperor's judgment put in execution, and Geminus admitted into the Senate.

This was the last judgment that the Emperor gave openly in his own person; diverse other judgments he gave, which were in tables, according as other emperors used to do.

HITHERTO is the report of Eucolpius:[236] much more he wrate, as it seemed; for diverse quires lacked in the book. Wherefore, to make some perfect conclusion, I took the residue out of other, which wrate also the life of this Emperor. <2C3v>

Herodianus, a Greek author, writeth that the journey made against Artaxerxes, the King of Persia, was lost through the slackness of Alexander, whom he supposeth to be retained from his enterprise by his mother Mammea, who would not let her son jeopard his person against the Persians;[237] but Lampridius, who gathered his work out of the books of Accolius and °E<n>colpius, who

[236] See above, p. 171 and n. 1.

[237] Cf. Hdn. 6.5.8–9, 'But Alexander failed by not invading with his army. Perhaps it was due to fear — no doubt he wanted to avoid risking his own life and limb for the Roman empire. Or his mother may have restrained him because of her womanly timidity and excessive love for her son. She used to blunt Alexander's efforts to behave bravely by convincing him that it was other people's job to take risks for him, not his to get involved in the battle. It was this which brought about the end of the invading Roman army'.

° Encolpius] Eucolpius *A B*

were alway in company with the Emperor Alexander,[238] writeth in this wise.

He being such an emperor, in his house and abroad, he enterprised the journey of Parthia, whereunto he prepared all things with such discipline and reverence about his own person that it mought be said that senators went and not soldiers. Wheresoever the host was, the chief captains were circumspect, the captains honest, the soldiers beloved; and therefore, the inhabitants of countries received him as god. The men of war loved the young Emperor as their brother, their son, and their father; they were honestly clad, conveniently hosed and shod, richly armed, very well horsed, with harness and bridles accordingly trimmed, that he which beheld the Emperor's army should have perceived the state of the weal public. He himself laboured to be judged worthy to have the name of Alexander and to surmount him of Macedon.[239]

In such form, he went into Persia and vanquished King Artaxerxes,[240] who came against him with seven hundred elephants, bearing on their backs towers of wood full of archers and artillery; also, a thousand and five hundred chariots armed with scythes, and people innu-<2C4r>merable. And afterward, Alexander returned unto the city of Antiochia, and, with the prey that he took of the Persians, he made all his men of war rich.[241] Then first began Persians to be slaves to the Romans; but because that the kings of Persia do disdain that any of their people shall live in servitude, he was content that they should be redeemed, the money being given to them which took them prisoners.[242]

Being returned to Rome, °<he> was conveyed unto his palace with all

[238] The five paragraphs following are each based on several diverse sections of the *Alex. Sev.* of 'Lampridius', as noted, who names as his sources the probably invented 'Acholius' (64.5, 'Acholium, qui et itinera huius principis scripsit'; cf. 14.6) and, with him, 'Encolpius' (17.1, 'Encolpius, quo ille familiarissimo usus est'), at 48.7, 'et Septiminus et Acholius et Encolpius vitae scriptores ceterique'.

[239] SHA, *Alex. Sev.* 50.1–4, 'Cum igitur tantus ac talis imperator domi ac foris esset, iniit Parthicam expeditionem, quam tanta disciplina, tanta reverentia sui egit, ut non milites sed senatores transire diceres. quacumque iter legiones faciebant, tribuni taciti, centuriones verecundi, milites amabiles erant, ipsum vero ob haec tot et tanta bona provinciales ut deum suspiciebant. iam vero ipsi milites iuvenem imperatorem sic amabant ut fratrem, ut filium, ut parentem, vestiti honeste, calciati etiam ad decorem, armati nobiliter, equis etiam instructi et ephippiis ac frenis decentibus, prorsus ut Romanam rem publicam intellegeret quicumque Alexandri vidisset exercitum. elaborabat denique ut dignus illo nomine videretur, immo ut Macedonem illum vinceret'.

[240] SHA, *Alex. Sev.* 55.1, 'Magno igitur apparatu inde in Persas profectus Artaxerxen regem potentissimum vicit'.

[241] SHA, *Alex. Sev.* 55.2, 'qui cum septingentis elephantis falcatisque mille et octingentis curribus ad bellum venerat et equitum multis milibus, statim Antiochiam rediit et de praeda, quam Persis diripuit, suum ditavit exercitum'.

[242] SHA, *Alex. Sev.* 55.3, 'tumque primum servi Persae apud Romanos fuerunt, quos quidem, quia indigne ferunt Persarum reges quempiam suorum alicui servire, acceptis pretiis reddidit pretiumque vel iis qui manu ceperant servos dedit'.

° he] *A om B om*

the senators, gentlemen, and people, the wives and children of his soldiers environing him and his triumphal chariot following him, being drawn with four great elephants. And entering into his palace, he was lift up with the hands of the people, so that during the space of four hours he mought not walk on his feet, all the people crying about, 'Now is Rome safe, for Alexander is safely returned!'[243]

Afterward, he lived in most tender love of the people and Senate; but at the last, the Germans wasting and destroying the country, he being ashamed that, the Parthians now being vanquished, that nation should press so nigh to the head of the weal public — which people were subdued by petty emperors — he prepared his voyage toward them, and departed against all men's wills, every man bringing him a hundred and fifty miles on his way, with hope of victory and soon return to the city.[244]

But being in France and finding the legions seditious, he commanded them to be rejected. By which occasion, the French men's stomachs, as they be alway obstinate and froward and oftentimes displeasant unto the em-<2C4v>perors, would not suffer any longer his rigorous gravity.[245]

Wherefore certain soldiers, which were enriched by Heliogabalus,[246] by the comfort and aid of that monstrous muleteer Maximus, whom they made afterward emperor,[247] they, suddenly entering into the pavilion of Alexander, slew both him and his mother, he nothing fearing their malice.

Other opinions there be of his death; finally, the rage of unthrifty persons,

[243] SHA, *Alex. Sev.* 56.1, 'Post hoc Romam venit', and 57.4–6, 'Post hoc cum ingenti gloria comitante senatu equestri ordine atque omni populo circumfusisque undique mulieribus et infantibus, maxime militum coniugibus, pedes Palatium conscendit, cum retro currus triumphalis a quattuor elephantis traheretur. levabatur manibus hominum Alexander, vixque illi per horas quattuor ambulare permissum est, undique omnibus clamantibus: "Salva Roma, salva res publica, quia salvus est Alexander"', omitting the intervening oration and *acclamationes*.

[244] SHA, *Alex. Sev.* 59.1–3, 'Post haec cum ingenti amore apud populum et senatum viveret, et sperantibus victoriam cunctis et invitis eum dimittentibus ad Germanicum bellum profectus est, deducentibus cunctis per centum et centum quinquaginta milia. erat autem gravissimum rei publicae atque ipsi, quod Germanorum vastationibus Gallia diripiebatur. pudoremque augebat, quod victis iam Parthis ea natio inminebat rei publicae cervicibus, quae semper etiam minusculis imperatoribus subiecta videbatur'. SHA, *Alex. Sev.* 59.1 is quoted in full in Eras., *Panegyricus* (CWE 27, 12–13).

[245] SHA, *Alex. Sev.* 59.4–5, 'sed cum ibi quoque seditiosas legiones comperisset, abici eas praecepit. verum Gallicanae mentes, ut sese habent durae ac retorridae et saepe imperatoribus graves, severitatem hominis nimiam et longe maiorem post Heliogabalum non tulerunt'.

[246] SHA, *Alex. Sev.* 59.7, 'quidam milites et hi praecipue, qui Heliogabali praemiis effloruerunt'.

[247] SHA, *Alex. Sev.* 59.8, 'multi dicunt a Maximino inmissos [...] eum occidisse, multi aliter'. This successor was C. Iulius Verus Maximinus (imp. 235–238), sometimes called Maximinus Thrax; for Elyot's characterisation, cf. SHA, *Max.* 2.1–2.

which mought not sustain his excellent virtues, traitorously slew this most noble Emperor, whose death all Rome lamented, all good men bewailed, all the world repented; whom the Senate deified, noble fame renomed, all wise men honoured, noble writers commended; whose life may worthily be a pattern to knights, an example to judges, a mirror to princes, a beautiful image to all them that are like to be governors, whereby they may have in continual remembrance to embrace and follow his most excellent qualities.

FINIS.

LONDINI
IN OFFICINA Thomae Bertheleti
typis impress.
Cum priuilegio ad imprimen-
dum solum.
ANNO. °M.D.X.L.

° M.D.X.L.] M.D.XL *B*

EXEMPLARY ANCIENTS INDEX & BIOGRAPHIES

This is a biographical index of the ancient figures whom Elyot mentions more than once in the writings edited herein, who are exemplary in some quality or other, and for whom Elyot also wrote biographies, usually brief. The headings are from the standard sources, chiefly *OCD*, though supplying also some indication of the variant name-forms and nicknames that, like others, Elyot sometimes uses. The biographies are edited here, without annotation, from *Bibliotheca Eliotae* (*sub uerbo* but without other indication), though in a few cases biographical matter from *Governour* is introduced (as indicated).

Alexander III of Macedon, 'the Great' (356–323 BCE).

'*Alexander* was the name of many noble princes; but among other, one was most excellent, which was the son of Philip king of Macedonia; who, in his childhood was brought up by Aristotle in learning, wherein he profited wonderfully; and was of such courage that, after the death of Philip his father, being but twenty years old, he took on him the enterprise to conquer all the world; and first gat Illyria, now called Slavonia, and after subverted the city of Thebes; and brought in subjection all Greece and entered into Asia; and vanquished in sundry journeys the great and puissant king Darius king of Persia, and had his mother, his wife, and daughter prisoners, and never would company with any of them, notwithstanding that they were most excellently fair; finally, he conquered India and all the east part of the world. And all this did he in little more than twelve years. But when he had pacified the world from all rebellions, he fell into such cruelty and pride, slaying his most trusty counsellors in his fury and commanding himself to be called a god, he became so odious to his own people that they, desiring his destruction, at the last being in his most glory at the city of Babylon, where he abode the ambassadors from all realms at supper with one of his physicians, was poisoned by drinking out of a cup, which was supposed to be made of a horse's house — which was thought to be done by the device of Aristotle, sometime his master, and Antipater, his lieutenant in Macedonia, whom a little before he had grievously threatened. Thus Alexander, abounding both in excellent virtues and notable vices, after most happy fortune, by his outrageous pride and cruelty, shortened his life, being at his death little above thirty-three years old, which was afore the Incarnation of Christ 322 years.'

M. Aurelius Severus Alexander, 'Alexander Severus' (imp. 222–235).

'*Alexander Severus* was emperor of Rome, the year of our Lord 224. This man from his childhood was of wonderful gravity and prudence, in so much as where the city of Rome was before brought by his cousin, the monstrous emperor Heliogabalus, into all abomination of living and dissolution of manners, this man by his virtue, prudence, and continual justice, reduced it unto a perfect public weal, reformed the order of his army, stablished laws, restored honesty, expelled vicious persons and bribers, advanced men of virtue and learning to great offices and dignities, renewed the Senate, prepared also a great and a noble counsel about his person, and so hated corrupted judges that he did not only put them to torments, but when any came in his presence he was ready with his two fingers to put out their eyes. And yet this noble and gentle prince, by the false treason of one Maximus, whom of a muleteer he had made a great captain, he was in a sudden commotion slain of his own people at Moguntia [Mainz] in Germany, with his mother Mammea, a wise lady and virtuous. Some supposed that it was because, by her counsel, he was become avaricious and was not so liberal as he and other emperors had been before.'

Antoninus Pius, 'Verus Antoninus' (imp. 138–161).

'*Antonius*, a name by the which was called diverse emperors of Rome. And among other, one was called *Antonius Pius*, which succeeded Hadrian, the year of our Lord 141, and reigned two and twenty years and three months, with Aurelius and Lucius. His progenitors were Spaniards, as Capitolinus saith. He was a marvellous good man; for after that he was Emperor, he governed with such moderation and gentleness that he was therefore called *Pius* and "father of the country". He was never cruel for any private or common cause. He used often this saying: he had leaver save one subject, than destroy a thousand enemies. For his devout living, sweetness of manners, mercy, justice, and temperance, he was compared to Numa. Wherefore, many kings and princes of diverse nations, laying war apart by his commandment, committed all their contentions unto his judgment and held them therewith contented. For both love and fear of him caused them to eschew wars, honouring him for his virtue as a god. Yet was not he so desirous of glory or richesse that he would attain thereunto by other men's damage. He died at the age of seventy years.'

Aristides (fifth century BCE).

'*Aristides* was a noble man of Athens, in wisdom, justice, and temperance excellent. For where in the governance of the commonweal of Athens, he was joined with Themistocles, a man of great prowess and richesse, who, saying in the council that he knew a thing which was expedient to the commonweal, but it was not necessary that it should be openly knowen, and desired to have one appointed unto whom he should disclose it, the council assigned to him Aristides; to whom he shewed that the navy of the Lacedaemonians mought be shortly set on fire and so should their puissance be abated; which Aristides hearing, he returned unto the council and said that the advice of Themistocles was profitable, but it was not honest. The *Athenienses*, hearing that it was not honest, judged that it mought not be profitable and would not let it then to be disclosed, such credence had they in Aristides. Also, notwithstanding that the *Athenienses* had exiled him without any cause, but only because he excelled in justice, yet at his departing, he prayed to God that, whatsoever they desired, it mought come to good effect and conclusion. And when he was called again out of exile, he never remembered any old displeasure, in so much that he alway honoured Themistocles, with whom he ever contended in the weal public. Of his temperance, this was a great token that, notwithstanding that he had been in the greatest dignity and offices in the commonweal of Athens, yet died he so poor that he left not sufficiently to bury him worshipfully, and his daughters were married at the charge of the city. And to his son Lysimachus was given by the people one hundred *minae*, which amounteth of our money to two hundred thirty-nine pounds, eleven shillings and eight pence. Oh! how may Christian men be ashamed when they read this story, beholding in his temperance, justice, and charity a more resemblance of Christ's doctrine than is in them, which will do nothing unhired, measure justice by their affections. Of this name were four other, which deserved not so good a remembrance. He was afore the Incarnation 474 years.'

Aristippus (late fifth century BCE).

'*Aristippus* was disciple to Socrates, notwithstanding he did put the chief goodness in volupty or pleasure, wherefore Diogenes called him "the royal dog", because he alway followed them that were rich and taught for money. On a time, he being on the sea, when a storm came that the ship was in peril, he was sore afeared; after that the peril was past, men asked of him why he feared so much since he was a philosopher; "the peril", said he, "in loss of an ignorant knave and of a noble philosopher is not of like estimation". The followers of him were called *Cyrenaici*. Saint Augustine saith of him: "It is not requisite to answer *Aristippum*, who in every part lived so as between him and a beast was no diversity". His sect, by other disciples of Socrates and noble philosophers, was utterly exterminate. He had a daughter called *Arête*, excellently learned. He was afore Christ three hundred sixty-six years.'

Aristotle (384–322 BCE).

'*Aristoteles*, son of Nicomachus the physician, born in Stagira in Greece, consumed his youth riotously. Afterward, he was scholar to the noble Plato twenty years continually. He excelled all men in sharpness of wit and knowledge in diverse sciences; wherefore, King Philip of Macedon sent his son Alexander to him to be taught, saying that he thanked God that he had a son born in his time. This man began a sect, the followers whereof were called *Peripatetici*, and taught after the death of Plato twenty-three years. He was banished out of Athens because, it was supposed, that he deemed not well of their gods. It is written that he died by this occasion. As he went by the sea-side, he perceived fishermen, sitting and doing of somewhat. And when he asked what they did, they told him a riddle; which when by long study he could not assoil, for shame and sorrow he died. Of him Quintilian writeth in this wise: "What say you by Aristotle, whom I wot not whether I may judge more excellent in knowledge of things, or in abundance of writing, or in sweetness of eloquence, or in sharpness of wit, or else in diversity of works". Notwithstanding, he was little of personage, crook-backed, ill shapen, and stutting. He was 345 years before Christ's Incarnation.'

C. Iulius Caesar (100–44 BCE).

'*Caesar*, the emperor. It was the surname of a noble house of the Romans, of whom came Julius Caesar, the first Emperor of Rome.'

C. Iulius Caesar Germanicus, 'Caligula' (imp. 37–41).

'*Caligula*, the surname of an emperor, called also Gaius, who succeeded Tiberius the emperor, and was son of the noble Germanicus, and had the name of Caligula given to him by the men of war which were with his father. Forasmuch as to allure the love of the people toward him, his mother sometime would shew him to the army with greaves on his legs, like to the fashion of war, which greaves were named in Latin *caliga*; and because they were little, they were by a diminutive called *caligula*, which the soldiers in disport and rejoicing applied to his surname. This man at the beginning of his reign was of manners right commendable; but soon after, he became of conditions detestable, as well in lechery as in beastly cruelty. Whereof happened this proverb: there was never a better prince than Caligula at the beginning, nor a worse tyrant than he at his later ending. Whereby — notwithstanding that at the beginning he was most dearly beloved of the Senate and people — afterward he was so deadly hated that they slew him when he had reigned but four years, being then thirty-eight years old, after the Incarnation of Christ forty years.'

M. Porcius Cato, 'Uticensis', 'of Utica' (95–46 BCE).

'*Cato Uticensis* was so called because he slew himself in the town called *Utica* in Africa. His great grandfather was the other Cato, called *Censorius* [M. Porcius Cato, 'Censorius', 'Cato the Censor' (234–149 BCE)]. This man in childhood shewed a wonderful constance and gravity, seldom very merry or seen to laugh, and, if he did, it was a very little smiling; nor would lightly be angry, but if he were angry he was not shortly appeased. Also, he was hard to learn; but that which he learned, he perfectly retained; and was very studious in all moral philosophy, practicing in his acts and living that which he read of virtue and honesty; and also studied eloquence, only to the intent that in counselling and reasoning he mought add unto philosophy more force and ornament; and yet would he not shew it or practice it openly. And when one said to him, "Men dispraise thine obstinate silence", he answered, "I force not, so that they dispraise not my living. But I will break out of this silence when I can speak that which is not worthy to be unspoken". Being *Tribunus militum* — that is to say, captain of a thousand men, or, as Budeus resembleth, marshal of an army — and being sent in to Macedonia, he with his marvellous gravity, prudence, and painfulness, made all them which were under him fierce and hardy against their enemies, gentle to their fellows, fearful to do injury, prompt to get praises. And himself labouring with them, and using his apparel, feeding, and going like unto them, he, contrary to men's expectation, notwithstanding his severity, won the hearts of them, going on foot and talking with every man. And was of such constance and so far from ambition and flattery that neither by Pompey nor Caesar in their chief pride, when all men either for dread or for favour inclined to their desires, he mought be by no means persuaded to agree to their minds, in cases where it seemed to be against the weal public; nor any manner of menacing or dreadful tokens mought from that constance remove him; in so much that, when he heard that Julius Caesar had vanquished Pompey and that his friends would have sent to Caesar to desire his favour, Cato answered, "They which are vanquished or have any wise trespassed ought to make suite". But since he in all his life was never vanquished, and in innocency he surmounted Caesar, which in making war against his own country had condemned himself to have done that thing which he had often denied; finally, not for malice of Caesar but because he would not behold the weal public destroyed, he slew himself at *Utica*, having with him at supper, the evening before, the greatest officers of that city and many of his friends. Also, this sentence being spoken, among other: "Only a good man is a free man; all ill men are bounden", when one happened to reason against it, Cato, being therewith chaffed, disputed with the other so vehemently and long that all men suspected that he would not long live. He died afore the Incarnation of Christ 44 years.'

M. Tullius Cicero, 'Marcus Tullius', 'Tully' (106–43 BCE).

'*Cicero, -onis*, the surname of Marcus Tullius, whose divine eloquence, abundant learning, sharpness of wit, dexterity in acts, and most ardent love to the commonweal of his country cannot be sufficiently expressed by no mortal man's tongue or pen. He was lineally descended from the ancient kings of the people called *Volsci*; albeit time and occasion wearing out dignities in blood, his name continued long in the state of worship. His ancestors were named *Cicerones*, because that Tullius Appius, a noble king of *Volscis*, one of them, had on his nose a mark like a chich-pease, called *cicer*. In his childhood, he so excelled in wit all other children that the fathers of them, moved with his fame, went purposely to the school to behold and hear him. He so profited in the eloquence of Greek and also of Latin that not only his companions were in a marvellous admiration of him, but also Apollonius [Apollonius Molon (first century BCE)], the most excellent orator at that time, in hearing him, being sore abashed and not speaking a great space, said at the last, "Truly, Cicero, I praise thee and marvel at thee, but I lament the fortune of Greeks when I consider that by thee learning and eloquence, which only was left unto us, is even now translated unto the Romans". Which saying of Apollonius was founden afterward true. For look what subtlety is in logic, what commodity in moral philosophy, what secret knowledge in philosophy natural, he knew it, as Tacitus writeth, and declared it in Latin in most perfect eloquence. And — which is to be wondered at — notwithstanding that, being a very young man, he came to practice in Rome, and had studied abundantly the civil laws, and was marvellously occupied in great and weighty causes, and, after that he was senator, was continually, as it seemed, most busy about the weal public; yet, he that doth exactly read and study his works shall think that he never did anything but read great authors and write books. For there was no sect of philosophers, none orator, no poet afore his time, that escaped him but that he read his works, as in his books sufficiently it appeareth. And yet how many books made he! Since we have not the third part of them, yet such as we have of them, if any man now did write so much and so well, we should think him to have spent the more part of his time in writing. And yet noble Cicero, lord God!, how many things did he exploit by his wisdom and diligence in most weighty affairs, as well in war as in peace? How did he by his dexterity and prudence save the city and people of Rome from the most pernicious confederacy and rebellion of Catiline and many other of the nobility, which went about to destroy the weal public and rob the city? How preserved he the same city and people after the death of Caesar, that they were not oppressed by Marcus Antonius? For his incomparable acts, the whole Senate and people gave to him, first before any, the name of father of the country. What trouble and misery sustained he, being exiled, by the procurement of Clodius, only for the putting of the said rebels to death? Such is the reward of people unstable. Likewise, for driving Antonius out of Rome and by his sharp orations causing him to be proclaimed enemy to the weal public, he made Antony so much his enemy that, in the treaty of peace between him and Octavius, he demanded Cicero, to do with him at his pleasure. Which being granted of the unkind Octavius, whom Cicero had brought up and by his means caused him to be made the chief governor of the Romans; finally, Antony sent one Herennius, whom Cicero had saved from death by his eloquence, who pursued him as he fled. Which Cicero perceiving, abode his coming, lying in a horse litter for weakness; and with constant eyes, prepared his throat to Herennius, who, all other men thereat abhorring, strake of his head and his hands and brought them to Antony. Who rejoicing thereat, caused the head and the hands to be set over the place of civil judgments at Rome, which, beholden of the Senate and people, was daily lamented. This have I purposely written to the intent that this most noble counsellor should not be hid to such as cannot yet understand his life written in Greek or Latin; and that all men should be inflamed to read and understand his works, which, afore all other gentiles, would be chiefly read and followed of Christian men, finding in them incomparable wisdom and eloquence. And truly I will affirm Quintilian's saying: he may well think that he hath much profited, whom that Cicero specially liketh. He flourished about forty years before the Incarnation of Christ.'

Croesus, king of Lydia (560–546 BCE).

'*Croesus* was king of Lydia, son of Alyattes, who subdued many great countries in Asia and Greece and gathered innumerable riches. He on a time demanded of the wise man Solon, "Who was the happiest man that ever he see?" He said, "Tellus, a man of Athens, who had honest and good sons", and they also had like good children, all which he saw in his life. And when he had lived a good time honestly, he at the last fighting against the enemies of his country, after that he had vanquished them, he died a fair death, and in the same place was honourably buried of the *Athenienses*. And when Croesus asked who was most happy next Tellus, he said, "Cleobis and Biton", which were Argives, and had a competent living, and were of such strength that, in all games in proving of strength, they obtained the prize. On a festival day of Juno their goddess, their mother, being an old woman, would be carried unto the temple in a wain; but the oxen which should draw it were not come from the field. Wherefore, her two sons, taking the beam of the wain, drew their old mother therein seven miles and more and so brought her to the temple of Juno, all men marvelling and commending the young men, all women praising the mother for bringing up of such children. The mother, being surprised with joy, as well for the act of her sons as also for the fame and commendation thereof, standing afore the image of Juno, prayed that her sons mought have that thing given them which were the best thing that ever mought happen to men. When they had sacrificed, eaten, and drunk with much pleasure and joy, they fell on sleep and never awaked — whose images all the people of their country did set up with much honour at *Delphos*. Croesus, being abashed, said unto Solon, "My friend of Athens, settest thou so little by our felicity that thou preferrest before us these private persons?" Solon answered, "Truly, Croesus, in process of time, many things are seen which men would not see, and many things be suffered that men would not suffer". And after that he had much spoken of man's calamity, at the last thus he concluded his saying, "The end of every thing is to be looked on, whereto it shall come; for God plucketh up by the roots many men unto whom he gave all fortune at pleasure". Croesus made hereto no countenance but, esteeming Solon to be but a fool, considering that he, passing so light upon the things which appeared to be good, bad him to take heed of the end of all things, he, setting little by Solon, let him depart. A good space after, Croesus, by the comfort of the answers of Apollo at *Delphos* attempting war against Cyrus king of Persia, at the last was taken of him, who caused a great pile of wood to be made ready and Croesus, being in gyres, to be set on the top thereof. Then forthwith Croesus remembered the words of Solon, that no man living was blessed or on all parts happy, and therewith lamenting, he cried, "O Solon, Solon, Solon". Which Cyrus hearing caused to be demanded of him who it was that he named. Croesus with much difficulty at the last told what he was and finally declared all that before was rehearsed. Which after that Cyrus had heard, he, recognizing himself to be also a man, sore repented that he went about to burn him, which was equal to him in honour and richesse, and commanded him to be taken from the fire, which then began to flame; and so with great difficulty he was delivered. And afterward, Cyrus entertained him honourably and used his counsel, which in many things he found very profitable. Much more Herodotus the noble historian writeth hereof in *Clio*, which I would God were read oftentimes of kings and their counsellors, for whose commodity I have written this epitome or abbreviation, to no man tedious which hath a good nature.'

M'. Curius Dentatus (d.270 bce).

'*Curius*, the surname of noble Romans. Of who chiefly was one called Marcus Curius, a man of marvellous honesty, constance, and gravity, which, after many great victories which he, being captain, had against the Samnites, Sabines, and the noble king Pyrrhus, he divided among the people of Rome the fields, appointing to every man forty acres, and retained by their consents as much to himself. And when they would have given to him more, he refused it, saying, "He was an ill citizen that thought it not enough for him, which was enough for other". When the ambassadors of Samnites brought him a great sum of gold, he, sitting by the fire boiling of rapes, said unto them, "I had liefer eat in my earthen dish and have dominion over them that have so much gold". When he was accused of withholding of money, he brought forth a tree barrel, which he occupied when he did sacrifice, and took a solemn oath that, of all the pray that was gotten of them whom he vanquished, he kept no more but that barrel to his own use.'

Cyrus (Kuruš) 'the Great', king of Persia (reigned c. 557–530 BCE).

'*Cyrus* was a noble king of Persia, the son of Cambyses and Mandanes, which was daughter of Astyages, king of Media; who, because that he dreamed that he saw spring out of the secret places of his only daughter a vine, with whose branch all Asia was covered, he caused the child to be throwen in to a desert to be devoured of beasts. But by God's providence, a bitch gave it suck until it was found by a shepherd, who brought it up. At the last, he was king of Persia and Media and subdued the more part of Asia. This man excelled all men in his time in goodly personage, gentleness, prowess, liberality, wisdom, and memory. Solinus [C. Iulius Solinus (fl. *c.* 200)] writeth that of the exceeding multitude of men which were in his host, he so retained the names that, coming daily among them, he named every man by his proper name when he spake unto them. The residue of his wonderful virtues be written by Xenophon most eloquently in Greek. At the last, he, being unsatiable in coveting countries, was slain by Tomiris, the queen of Scythia, with two hundred thousand Persians.'

Demosthenes (384–322 BCE).

'*Demosthenes* was the most excellent orator of the Greeks and was first a disciple of Plato; but after, he followed Ebulides, an orator, and used such wonderful diligence and labour to attain to the perfection of eloquence that, where he had an impediment in his pronunciation, he by putting small stones into his mouth and enforcing him to speak treatably, he at the last attained to most perfect form of speaking. Of his wisdom remaineth among other this pretty example. When King Philip, the father of great Alexander, besieged Athens and sore distressed it, upon certain treatises offered by them, he required to have delivered unto him ten orators, of the which Demosthenes was one, and then would he raise up his siege. That hearing Demosthenes and coming into the common council, he rehearsed this fable. "On a time, the wolves exhorted the shepherds to be in league with them, whereunto the shepherds accorded. Then, the wolves required to have delivered unto them their mastives, which were the cause of debate between them. The shepherds thereunto granted and delivered to the wolves their dogs, the most vigilant keepers of their flocks. Afterward, the wolves, being without any fear, not only did eat now and then a sheep to allay their hunger, but also for their pleasure did tear and rent other in pieces. In likewise", said Demosthenes, "King Philip, after that he hath taken from you your orators, which by their wise advertisements have hitherto preserved you from his tyranny, he will do the semblable". Which the *Athenienses* hearing, they agreed to his counsel and valiantly defended and preserved the city. This man was afore the Incarnation of Christ 345 years.'

Dion (c. 408–353).

'*Dion* was son of a noble man of Sicily called Hipparinus and brother to Aristomacha, wife to the elder Denyse. Wherefore, he was long time in great favour with him, insomuch as Denyse commanded his officers that they should give to Dion all that he would ask. But after that Dion had been the hearer of Plato and followed his doctrine and gravity, Denyse no more favoured him. Semblably the second Denyse, notwithstanding that Dion with all diligence endeavoured himself to bring him up in virtue and honour, yet because he was grave in manners and of great severity and was not pleasant, the favour little and little relented; and at the last, Denyse, gathering suspicion of Dion, sent him in exile. Who, returning after diverse conflicts for the liberty of his country, being often betrayed of his friends and deceived by them whom he trusted, finally was slain in *Syracusis*, the chief city of Sicily. He was a man of excellent virtue and wisdom, and of a great courage; and therefore was above all other favoured of Plato. But by too much liberty in speech and procuring liberty unto the common people — more than was necessary — he brought himself to perpetual inquietness and, at the last, to confusion. The time of his being shall be declared in the life of Plato.'

Dionysius I (c. 430–c. 367 BCE) and Dionysius II (c. 396–c. 343 BCE).

'*Dionysius*, read in "Bacchus". It was also the name of two kings of Sicily, which for their cruelty and avarice were called tyrants. The first was son of Hermocrates, a rich man of Sicily, whom for his valiantness in arms the Sicilians ordained to be their captain against the *Carthaginenses*, which invaded them, and menaced to destroy their country, and take from them their liberty. But after that the enemies were vanquished, Denyse, which preserved his country from bondage, of a benefactor became a cruel tyrant. This man, desirous to see the wise Plato, who then was famous, with importunate requests caused him to come to Sicily from Athens. But having with him communication in the which Plato commended righteous governance and dispraised tyranny, Denyse, being therewith offended, would have slain him; but being let by the intercession of Dion and Aristomenes, he gave him to Polides, the ambassador of the Lacedaemonians, to sell when he came into Greece. The residue ye may read in my book of *The Knowledge which maketh a Wise Man.* The other Dionysius, or Denyse, was son to this man, like in conditions but that he was better learned. He also made means to have Plato come unto him, and a good space had him in much reverence and heard his lessons in philosophy. Finally suspecting him, that he conspired against him with Dion and other, whom he had expelled, uneath at the desires of Archytas prince of Tarentum and other, he suffered him to return unto Athens. So lightly are the minds of great men toward learning satisfied and for small occasions offended, except such as do set all their delight in virtue and do esteem it above other pleasures. The time of this man shall appear in the life of Plato. The father was noted of ravin and cruelty, for the which he was once driven out of Sicily and by poverty constrained to teach children in Italy. Also, he was reproved for having his ears always open and ready to hear detractors; for his timorous and suspicious living, that he would be environed with a great guard of strangers and bondmen, mistrusting his own people and kinsmen; that he would speak to the people from the top of a tower; that he would have his beard neither shaven or clipped by any man, but only with walnut shells, very hot, he caused it to be burned. And yet at the last was he slain of the people, curiosity not so safely keeping him as benevolence mought have done, if he had followed the doctrine of Plato, as he seemed to do.'

C. Fabricius Luscinus (fl. 284–275 BCE).

'*Fabritius,* a noble Roman; who, being wonderful poor, notwithstanding refused a great sum of money sent to him by King Pyrrhus, touching with his hands all his members and saying unto the king's messengers, as long as he mought rule all that which he touched, he could lack nothing.'

P. Aelius Hadrianus, 'Hadrian' (imp. 117–138).

'*Adria<n>us*, a noble emperor of Rome, about the year of our Lord one hundred nineteen. He was Traianus's sister's son: a man of excellent wit and diverse in manners; marvellous in learning, specially in mathematicals; also in music, in carving and graving; in deeds of arms cunning and valiant; a great favourer of well learned men and liberal toward them. He was so great a traveller that there were few countries but that he went through them. He lived sixty-two years, and reigned twenty, and died in torment of the bowels'; and '*Hadrianus*, a noble emperor, which in all sciences was excellently learned. He was after Christ's Incarnation one hundred nineteen years, and reigned twenty-one years.'

Hannibal (247–182 BCE).

'*Hannibal* was son of Hamilcar, the most noble and valiant captain of the

Carthaginensis, who, making war with the Romans sixteen years, contended with them in prowess and policy, winning from them their dominions in Spain and Italy. Finally, being vanquished by Scipio, he fled to Antiochus, king of Asia; afterward, to Prusias, king of Bithynia, of whom under the colour of amity he was betrayed and should have been delivered to Flaminius, that time ambassador to Prusias. But Hannibal perceiving it, choosing rather to die than to come into the hands of the Romans, took poison, which he kept for that purpose, saying, "Let us deliver the Romans from the care and fear which they have of us", with a few mo words of indignation; and so died before that he mought be delivered. Some do write this name without "h".'

Helen 'of Troy' (Homeric hero, n.d.).

'*Helena* was daughter of Jupiter and Leda, the wife of Tyndarus, king of Lacedaemonia. She for her wonderful beauty was twice ravished; first, at the age of nine years, by Theseus; afterward, by Paris the Trojan, she then being wife unto Menelaus. The which was the only occasion of the ten years siege of Troy and finally the destruction of the most famous city, with the death and loss of most noble princes and of people innumerable. Look more in *Troia*.'

Hesiod (fl. c. 700 BCE).

'*Hesiodus*, an ancient poet of the Greeks, which first wrote of husbandry, whom Vergil followed in his *Georgics*.'

Homer (? fl. c. 700 BCE).

'*Homerus*, the chief of all poets, and was named *Melesigenes*; but because he was blind, he was called *Homerus*, which in the tongue called *Ionica* signifieth "blind". Cicero, *Tusc.* 5, saith in commendation of Homer: "It is written", saith he, "that Homer was blind; yet see we his picture and not his poem. For what country, what marches, what host, what navy, what motions of minds, as well of men as of beasts, are expressed in such wise that he maketh us to see that he saw not?". Plutarchus, in the book which he wrote of him, saith that, in his two works, he comprehended both the parts of a man. For in *Iliad*, he described strength and valiantness of the body; in *Odyssea*, he doth set forth a perfect pattern of the mind. Notwithstanding, for his undiscrete fabling of gods and goddesses, Plato excluded him out of his weal public, which he devised.'

L. Caecilius Metellus (fl. 49 BCE)

The tribune who resisted C. Iulius Caesar's looting of the state, in Luc., *BCiv.* 3.112–68; Plut., *Caes.* 35.6–11, and *Pomp.* 62.1; but cf. Elyot, *Bibl.*, '*Metellus*, the proper name of divers noble Romans'.

Nero Claudius Caesar (imp. 54–68).

'*Nero*, called also Domitius, an emperor; son of Gn. Domitius Nero, adopted into the empire by Claudius, who married his mother Agrippina. This man, although he were brought up by the reverend and wise Seneca, yet by the inevitable corruption of his nature he became horrible vicious, insomuch as he caused himself to be gelded and cut in the form of a woman and so to be abused; and by his cruelty, made his own mother to be slain and the city of Rome to be burned, he in the meantime playing on a harp and singing the destruction of Troy; finally, he being hated of all men was slain in a cave whereinto he fled, when he was but thirty-two years old and had reigned fourteen years, in the sixty-seventh year after the Incarnation of Christ'.

Numa Pompilius, king of Rome (traditionally 715–673 BCE).

'*Numa* was king of Romans next after Romulus, that is to say, the second king; and was chosen by the people and Senate of Rome, of a poor gentleman dwelling in a town of the Sabines called *Cures*, for his excellent virtues and learning, being of the discipline of Pythagoras. He being king by his policy and ceremonies by him invented, he brought the Romans, which during the time of Romulus were continually occupied in wars, in such a wonderful quietness and honest form of living that the countries environing them by the space of forty years had them in such reverence that they did never during that time move war against them.'

Origenes Adamantius, Origen (c. 184–c. 255).

'*Origines*, called also Adamantius, born at Alexandria in Egypt, was son of one Leonides the martyr. A man of most excellent cunning and virtue from his childhood, wherein he so wonderfully prospered that, being an infant he lying on sleep, his father came into the chamber and, taking away softly the clothes, he kissed the child's breast as a temple having within it the holy ghost, giving thanks to God that had sent to him such a son. At the time that his father was martyred, Origen, being also desirous of martyrdom, yet a young child, ran in among other which were led to be slain and by all means proffered himself to die with them. Which his mother perceiving, who most entirely loved him, she first lamentably entreated him to withdraw him; but he therewith was more inflamed toward martyrdom than withdrawen. Wherefore, his mother used this craft: at night when he was in his bed, she stale away his clothes, so that in the morning, when he would have gone forth, he mought not come by them, wherefore he was constrained to tarry at home. Which deceit of his mother he complained to his father, then being in prison, desiring him to persist constantly in his good purpose. After the martyrdom of his father, he continually gave himself to the study of holy scripture, which he had tasted before, in reading gentiles' works by his father's instruction; albeit, in philosophy and all other sciences, he did excel all other men of his time, before that he was twenty years old. At eighteen years old, he expounding openly gentile authors, he so interlaced holy doctrine that he converted to the faith of Christ many great learned men, which were his hearers. His living was also so straight and virtuous that he drew many until him and was among all men had in a wonderful reverence. Yet he never ceased in all persecutions to comfort and confirm men in the embracing of martyrdom, and did continually read openly, and also write innumerable books in the expounding of holy scripture, notwithstanding that he also learned the Hebrew tongue perfectly. He went into diverse countries preaching, and, for the great fame that was of him, Mammea, the mother of the Emperor Alexander Severus, sent for him to Rome, and heard him, and, as some do suppose, was by him converted. Whereof ye may read in the book which I translated out of Eucolpius and called it the *Image of Governance*. He most straightly observed all the precepts of the Gospel in continual fastings and watchings, having but one garment and going alway bare footed, and counselling all his hearers to renounce all that they had and to give it in alms. He also gelded himself, not only to be the more chaste; but also for because that in the time of persecution he taught the word of God, as well privily as openly to men and women, he mought let that the paynims should not speak dishonesty of him and of those which repaired to his sermons and lessons. Which although he did secretly, yet God would not have it hid, so that it came to the ear of Demetrius, the bishop of Alexandria. Who, first wondering at the stomach and virtue of the man, praising the ferventness of his faith, he said unto him, "Now stick to thy doctrine and preaching, since thou hast not left unto thine adversaries any occasion of suspicion". But afterward, the same Demetrius, stirred with envy against Origen, laid it in reproach against him openly, finding nothing else wherewith to dispraise him. He that will know more of Origen, let him read the sixth book of Eusebius *In historia ecclesiastica*, and Saint Jerome, *De scriptoribus ecclesiasticis*. He was after the Incarnation of Christ two hundred four years.'

Penelope (Homeric hero, n.d.).

'*Penelope*, the daughter of Icarius and wife of Ulysses, most chaste wife and constant above all the women of her time; who, in the twenty years in the which her husband was absent, she being assaulted with diverse wooers which, would she or no, abode in her house, she mought never with fair means nor menaces be induced to marry or to consent to commit any folly.'

Pericles (c. 495–429 BCE).

'*Pericles*, a noble and valiant captain of the *Atheniensis*, excellent in wit and natural eloquence, and was instructed in philosophy by Anaxagoras, so that thereby he attained to marvellous great knowledge, and noble courage, and patience; insomuch as when a lewd person followed him to his house, reviling him by all the way, when he was come to his door, then being night, Pericles commanded one of his servants to take a torch and bring him which had rebuked him home to his house. Also, he, being in great estimation and authority among the people of Athens, would never be at any feasts or banquetings, nor receive of any man any presents or gifts, nor did go to every assembly or counsel, <n>or being there, did speak or reason in every matter, but reserved himself to things of very great importance; and yet then seemed he to be very timorous. But yet was his eloquence so excellent, his voice and pronunciation so pleasant, his sentences so ponderous and vehement, that he never spake but that thereto all men consented; and therefore, it is written of him that he did fulminate his words; that is to say, that they proceeded from him as thunder and lightning. He was of such temperance that, although he seemed to have all the *Athenienses* at his commandment, yet he never increased his own revenues the worth of one farthing, but augmented the common treasure exceedingly; and such spoil as came to his part in the wars, he did employ upon grain and vittle, dividing it among the people in the time of necessity. Only he was unfortunate in his own children. His eldest son Xantippus persecuting him with sundry displeasures and openly mocking him, notwithstanding as it was reason, he died miserably before his father. Finally, Pericles being sick unto death, the noble men comen unto him to comfort him; speaking softly, they commoned of his prowess, where he had victory in nine great battles. He, hearing what they spake, said unto them that he much marvelled that they extolled so much that thing whereof the more part pertained to fortune and had happened to diverse other captains, as well as to him; and that which was most to be praised they spake nothing of it. "For never man", said he, "by mine occasion had cause to put mourning garments upon him" (Plutarchus, in *Vitae*). He was afore the Incarnation of Christ 441 years.'

Phocion, 'the Good' (402–318 BCE).

'*Photion*, a noble *Atheniense*, which had been disciple to Plato and Xenocrates, afterward one of the chief governors of the city of Athens, was a man of such wonderful gravity and constance that he was not lightly seen to change his countenance, either to laugh or to mourn, nor to have his hands out of his habit, except in war. And when he was in the country, he went alway bare footed, except it were in the cold winter, whereof there was no better token than to see Phocion go shod. His speech was short, grave, vehement, and full of quick sentences; and therefore, the most eloquent orator Demosthenes called him the hatchet that did cut off his words. He was of such a constance that, where Apollo at Delphos made answer that one man in Athens was of a contrary opinion to all the city, when that was reported, Phocion rose up and said, "Leave", said he, "countrymen, to search whom our god meaneth! For I am that one man, whom nothing liketh which is now done in the commonweal of this city". When he had made an oration unto the people and they, praising him, consented unto him, he turned him to them that were next him and said, "Alas! What have I done? I fear me lest some foolish word hath escaped unwitting me", signifying that the people seldom allowed anything that was good or not foolish. On a time, when he reasoned contrary to the mind of the people, wherefore they murmured and would have let him, "It is at your pleasure, countrymen", said he, "to compel me to do that that I would not. But to speak otherwise than I think, that no man living can cause me!" He was so reverend a personage that the great King Alexander, in the beginning of his letters after that he had vanquished Darius, he saluted no man but him and Antipater. He refused infinite treasure sent unto him by Alexander. And although he had been the general captain of the *Athenienses* in sundry wars and honourably achieved his enterprises, yet was he best content to live poorly. Finally, he was of his unkind countrymen condemned to death, whereto he went with the same countenance that he had in authority, when one which was condemned with him lamented and feared to die. Phocion turning unto him said, "Why art thou not glad, that thou shalt die with Phocion?" And when one of his friends asked him if he would anything to his son, "I would", said he, "that such wrong as the *Athenienses* do to me, he shall not remember". What a wonderful word of a paynim was this, who followed Christ's doctrine ere Christ was borne, 333 years!'

Plato (c. 429–347 BCE).

'*Plato*, the prince of all philosophers, in wisdom, knowledge, virtue, and eloquence far exceeding all other gentiles, was born in Athens; whose father was named Ariston, of an ancient and honourable house; his mother was called Perictione, descended from Solon, the maker of laws to the *Atheniensis* and one of the seven wise men of Greece. Lying in his cradle, bees were founden to bring honey into his mouth without hurting the child, which diviners did interpret was a signification that from him should flow eloquence most sweet and delectable. The night before that he was brought unto Socrates to be instructed, Socrates dreamed that he held between his knees a white cygnet, who, having feathers quickly growen, flew up toward heaven and filled the air with most sweet tunes. The day after, Plato being brought by his father to Socrates, he beholding the child, "this is", said he, "the bird whose image I beheld the last night". His name first was Aristocles; but after, he was called Plato, as some do suppose because that he was broad in the shoulders; other do write for as much as he had a broad visage. In his youth, he exercised his body in wrestling and other feats of activity, and, until he was twenty years old, he gave himself to make amorous verses; which, after that he came to hear Socrates, he threw into the fire and burned, and then most ardently and attentively he heard Socrates's doctrine during the time that he lived. And after that, he did not only hear the most famous philosophers and geometricians in *Grecia*, but also he went into Italy, into Africa, and Egypt, to hear the mystical sciences. And it is thought that he heard some of the prophets which at that time lived, since there be founden in his works sentences not abhorring from our catholic faith. He was not ignorant of martial affairs, for he had fought in three great battles. He chase a place by Athens called *Academia*, wherein he taught, and therefore his disciples were called *Academici*. There was in him a marvellous sharpness of wit, with an incomparable dexterity in disputing and making of answers. His constance, temperance, and gravity, with courtesy in language, were of all other incomparable. He was so desirous of knowledge that he was no less studious to learn than he was to teach other. Wherefore, he being scorned of one which asked of him how long he would be a scholar, "so long", said he, "as I shall not repent to be wiser and better". He is called *Diuinus Plato* for his excellent doctrine, which containeth many things (as Saint Augustine saith) which doth accord with holy scripture, in so much as therein is perceived the first part of Genesis unto *Spiritus domini ferebatur super aquas*; and the mystery of three persons in divinity is therein expressed. He died as he was writing, being of the age of four score and one years, afore the Incarnation of Christ three hundred forty-two years. Read more of him in Dionysius.'

Cn. Pompeius Magnus, Pompey, 'the Great' (106–48 BCE).

'*Pompeius*, called *Magnus* for his sundry and incomparable victories, whose father was called Pompeius Strabo, had so good a grace in his visage that from his childhood he moved the people of Rome most entirely to favour him for his singular benevolence, continence of living, martial experience and knowledge, pleasantness of speech, fidelity of manners, and easiness in speaking to. He never required any thing without shamefastness nor granted any thing but with a glad countenance. In his visage appeared alway both nobility and gentleness, so that when he was in his flourishing youth there shined in him manners both princely and reverend. Scilla [Sulla], the cruel and proud tyrant, had him in such estimation that, where he would not arise to any other man, were he never in so high a dignity, he met with Pompeius coming toward him and, putting off his bonnet, saluted him by the name of great captain, called at that time in Latin *Imperator.* He triumphed for his victories in Africa, being almost a child nor yet admitted into the Senate, contrary to the ancient order of Rome. He vanquished the valiant captain Sertorius, a man at that time most famous in prowess, being an exile in Spain and before was invincible. He also vanquished Mithridates, the great king of Pontus, and where a great number of the concubines of Mithridates, women of excellent beauty, were taken and brought unto him, he would not company with any of them but sent them unto their friends. He subdued these realms: Armenia, Cappadocia, Paphlagonia, Media, Colchis, Iberia, Albania, Syria, Cilicia, Mesopotamia, Judea, and Arabia; for the which, he triumphed, after that he had twice before triumphed for the winning of Spain and Africa. In this triumph, he brought into the common treasure, of gold and silver, in money and plate, twenty thousand talents, which, if they were common talents, it amounted to twenty hundred thousand pounds; if they were the great talents, twenty-seven hundred, twenty-six thousand, six hundred ten pounds, thirteen shillings and four pence, in our money, besides that which was given to the men of war which had served him, and that was, to every one, a thousand and five hundred brazen pence, of our money six pounds and five shillings, which, in so great an host as pertained to the conquest of so many countries, extended to a wonderful sum of money; whereby may appear the riches of the Romans. Afterward, by the mediation of the friends of both parts, Pompey took to wife Julia, the daughter of Julius Caesar, which lived not long. And the amity between Pompey and Caesar decreased; and at the last, the insatiable ambition of them both brast out, the one not sustaining the other's honour. Whereof came the war civil between them, wherein Caesar, with a fewer number, vanquished Pompey; who privily fled by sea into Egypt where, under the safe-conduct of the king Ptholomeus, he was slain in a boat, his head stricken off, and his body cast on the strand, where it was poorly buried; when he had lived sixty years and above, and from his youth in most high honour, wealth, and prosperity, on whom it seemed that fortune had most prodigally dowered all her treasure.'

P. Valerius Poplicola (Publicola) (d. 503 BCE).

'*Publicola*, a favourer of the people, the which name was given to Valerius, which was one of the first consuls of Rome.'

Pythagoras (c. 580–c. 500 BCE).

'*Pythagoras*, a man of excellent wit, born in an isle called *Samos*. Which being subdued by Polycrates the tyrant, Pythagoras forsook his country and went into Egypt and Babylonia, to learn mystical sciences, and afterward came into

Italy, where he continued the residue of his life. He was the first that named himself a philosopher, where before men of great learning were called wise men; and because he would eschew the note of arrogance, when one demanded of him what he was, he said, "*Philosophus*", which signifieth a lover of wisdom. He was in sharpness of wit passing all other and found the subtle conclusions and mysteries of arithmetic, music, and geometry. Plato wondereth at his wisdom. His doctrine was divine and commodious, the which he, teaching to other, enjoined them to keep silence five years and hear him diligently, ere they demanded of him any question. He never would do sacrifice with any blood. He would eat nothing that had life, and lived in a marvellous abstinence and continence, and was in such authority among his disciples that, when in disputions they maintained their opinion, if one demanded of them why it should be as they spake, they would answer only "*Ipse dixit*", "He said so", meaning Pythagoras. Which answer was reputed as sufficient as if it had been proved with an inevitable reason, so much in estimation was he for his approved truth and incomparable learning. He was noted to be expert in magic, and therefore it is written of him that, nigh to the city of Tarentum, he beheld an ox biting the tops of beans there growing and treading it down with his feet; wherefore, he bade the herdman to advise his ox that he should abstain from grain. The herd, laughing at him, said that he never learned to speak as an ox; "but thou", said he, "that seemest to have had experience therein, take mine office upon thee". Forthwith, Pythagoras went to the ox and, laying his mouth to his ear, whistered something of his art. A marvellous thing! The ox, as if he had been taught, left eating of the corn nor ever after touched any; but many years after, mildly walked in the city and took his meat only of them that would give it him. Many like wonderful things is written of him. Finally, his disciples for their wisdom and temperance were always had in great estimation. He was before the Incarnation of Christ 522 years.'

L. Quinctius Cincinnatus (fl. 460–439 BCE).

Elyot, *Gov.* 2.4 (Watson, pp. 128–129), 'Quintius, having but thirty acres of land and being plowman thereof, the Senate and people of Rome sent a messenger to shew him that they had chosen him to be *dictator*, which was at that time the highest dignity among the Romans and for three months had authority royal. Quintius, hearing the message, let his plough stand, and went into the city, and prepared his host again the Samnites, and vanquished them valiantly. And that done, he surrendered his office and, being discharged of the dignity, repaired again to his plow and applied it diligently.'

P. Cornelius Scipio Africanus 'the Elder' 236–183 BCE.

'*Scipio*, the surname of diverse noble Romans, of the which three were the most excellent personages of their time, as well in martial prowess as also in other most notable virtues. The one called Scipio *Nasica*, son of Gnaeus Scipio, who had been both Consul and triumphed, and, being a very young man, was deemed of all the people of Rome to be the best man in that city. The other two were brethren, sons of Publius Scipio. The one of them, for subduing Asia, was called Scipio *Asiaticus*; the other, for vanquishing Hannibal and the people of Africa, was named Scipio *Africanus*. This Publius Cornelius Scipio, from his childhood, was of a wonderful towardness; for being but seventeen years old, in a great battle by Pavia in Lombardy, he rescued his father, being environed with enemies and in danger to be slain. Also, after the discomfiture at Cannae where the more part of the flower of chivalry was slain, wherefore the residue of the young men concluded to have forsaken Italy, this Scipio drew out his sword and compelled them to swear that they should not leave the city but defend it. After that his father and uncle were slain, all men fearing to be captains in so dangerous wars, he stepped forth with a noble courage, proffering himself to take that charge in hand; whereunto the Senate and people consented, he being than but twenty-two years old, they beholding in his personage and visage a beauty incomparable, his countenance merry and gentle, and to be in his gesture and pace a wonderful majesty. Which was had in such admiration throughout all the world that, after he had driven Hannibal out of Africa, subdued the city of Carthage, and constrained the great king Antiochus to desire peace of the Romans, the wars being ceased, men came out of all countries to Rome only to see him and honour him, as one exceeding the state of mortality. Whereby he stirred such envy toward him that he was accused for detaining of certain treasure, which should have been brought into the commune treasury; but he, with a noble and valiant courage, came before the people and, remembering what he had done for the weal public, required them to go with him unto the Capitol to give thanks to God for his victory; and so departed all the people, following him and leaving the judges alone. But notwithstanding, he so grievously took the ingratitude of the Senate and people that he abandoned all common affairs, and went out of the city of Rome to a manor-place which he had at Linternum, and there ended his life, when he had lived fifty-four years, a notable remembrance to them that do trust on fortune or favour of people.'

Socrates (469–399 BCE).

'*Socrates*, an excellent philosopher, son of Sophroniscus the mason and Phaenarete, a midwife. Who, being first studious in natural philosophy, finally gave himself to moral philosophy, teaching openly virtue; and so diligently ensued it in his living, and in disputing was so sharp and assured against them that were called *Sophistae*, that Apollo, the question being demanded who was the wisest man living, he answered, "Socrates". He was master to Plato, Xenophon, Xenocrates, and other the greatest philosophers at that time living. Besides his excellency in virtue and knowledge, he was of a rare and marvellous nature. For he mought sustain heat, cold, labour, hunger, and thirst above any man of that time, as Alcibiades declareth in *Plato*. He affirmed that there was alway with him a spirit or spiritual power, called *Daemonium*, the which as often as he was moved to do any thing not convenient or necessary, that spirit touched him and did prohibit him to do it. Under sharp and merry taunts, in the form of argument called induction, he caused men to perceive their ignorance, where before they thought themselves to be wise. Finally, being envied of them which then did bear chief rule in Athens, he was accused of Anytus, Melissus [Meletus] the poet, and Lycon the orator, that he spake against their gods and corrupted their children with perverse doctrine. But he, contemning death, would suffer no man to speak for him; and so drinking poison with a joyous countenance and saying to Anytus, "I bring thee good luck", died incontinent. But soon after, the people were so sorry for his death that, of his accusers, some they slew and some exiled, and did set up openly the image of Socrates made of copper. He was before the Incarnation of Christ three hundred sixty-seven years.'

Solon (c. 630–560 BCE).

'*Solon*, a noble man of Athens, which by his mother lineally descended from Codrus, the last king of Athens. He was a man of excellent wit and called one of the seven wise men of Greece; and was in such authority in that city that he made and gave to them laws, which were never repealed. Notwithstanding, when Pisistratus his kinsman went about to change the form of that commonweal, which was popular, into a monarchy, he willingly went in exile and so died. Read of him in *Croesus*. When he was writing of his laws, Anacharsis the philosopher said that Solon's laws should be like to cobwebs, that little flies should be fast tied with them, but great flies should make holes and break through them.'

Zeno of Elea (early fifth century BCE).

Elyot, *Gov.* 3.11 (Watson, p. 233), 'Which was well proved by Zeno Eleates, a noble Philosopher, who, being a man of excellent wisdom and eloquence, came to a city called Agrigentum, where reigned Phalaris, the most cruel tyrant of all the world, who kept and used his own people in most miserable servitude. Zeno first thought by his wisdom and eloquence to have so persuaded the tyrant to temperance that he should have abandoned his cruel and avaricious appetite. But custom of vice more prevailed in him than profitable counsel. Wherefore Zeno, having pity at the wretched estate of the people, excited divers noble men to deliver the city of that servile condition. This counsel was not so secretly given but that notice thereof came to the tyrant, who, causing all the people to be assembled in the market place, caused Zeno there to be cruciate with sundry torments, always demanding of him who did participate with him of his said counsel. But for no pains would he confess any person, but induced the tyrant to have in mistrust his next friends and familiar servants; and reproving the people for their cowardice and dread, he at the last so inflamed them unto liberty that suddenly, with a great violence, they fell on the tyrant and pressed him with stones. The old Zeno in all his exquisite torments never made any lamentable cry or desire to be relieved.'

WORD LIST

abode n. The action of waiting or delaying; a delay. Esp. in 'without abode': without delay, immediately
abraid v. To break out abruptly into speech; to burst into a cry; to cry out
accompt v. and n. = 'account'
adust ppl. a. Scorched, seared; burnt up, calcined; dried up with heat, parched
advertise v. To call the attention of (another); to give notice, to notify, admonish, warn, or inform, in a formal or impressive manner
advoutry n. = 'adultery'
afear v. To frighten, terrify, or make afraid
affectuously adv. With earnest feeling or desire; earnestly, ardently, eagerly
afore prep. Before, in front of; in advance of
aforesee v. To see previously, beforehand
again prep. = 'against'
agone adv. In the phrase 'long agone': a long while ago, in time long gone, long since
ahem int.
alce n. Elk
allective n. That which has power to allure
alway adv. = 'always'
ampliate v. To enlarge, extend, increase in size, amount, or dignity; to amplify
ancienty n. The quality of being ancient, ancientness, antiquity
and cond. If; even if; as if
appair v. To make worse, less valuable, weaker, or less; to injure, damage, weaken; to impair
appall v. To wax faint or feeble in any characteristic quality; to fade, fail, decay
appeach v. To charge with crime, accuse, inform against; impeach (a person); asperse (honour, character, etc.)
appendance n. A dependent possession, a dependency
approve v. To make good (a statement or position); to show to be true, prove, demonstrate
askes n. = 'ashes'
assay v. To put to the test
assoil v. To absolve from sin, grant absolution to, pardon, forgive
astony v. To stun, paralyse, astound, amaze
avale v. To degrade, abase, humble; to lower
avaunt n. A boast, vaunt; boasting, vainglory
avaunt v. To speak boastfully or proudly of
avow n. A vow, a solemn promise made to a deity, etc.
avow v. To vouch for, guarantee
await n. Watching, watch, watchfulness; heed, caution

await v. To keep watch, watch for; esp. to watch stealthily with hostile purpose; to lie in wait for, waylay
aye adv. Ever, always, continually; at all times, on all occasions
bain n. A quantity of water or other liquid placed in a suitable receptacle, in which one may bathe
basilic n. Basilica: literally and originally, a royal palace; thence, a large oblong building or hall, with double colonnades and a semi-circular apse at the end, used for a court of justice and place of public assembly
bawdry n. Unchastity, fornication
beck n. A mute signal or significant gesture, esp. one indicating assent or notifying a command; e.g. a nod, a motion of the hand or fore-finger, etc.
beck v. To make a mute signal, or significant gesture, as by nodding, shaking the fore-finger, etc.
beholding ppl. a. Under obligation, obliged, indebted, beholden
beseen v. To see to, provide for, attend to; hence, to deal with, treat, use (well or ill). To provide, arrange, ordain, determine
bethink v. refl. To occupy oneself in thought; to reflect, consider, think; also, to call to mind, recollect
betime adv. In good time, early, seasonably. At an early hour, early in the day
bode = pa. tense of v. 'bid': ask pressingly
bordel house n. A house of prostitution, a brothel
bourd v. To say things in jest or mockery; to jest, joke; to make fun, make game
bourding ppl. a. That jests, jokes, mocks, or trifles
bourn v. To set a limit or bounds to; to bound; to check
brake v. = 'broke'
brast v. = 'burst'
brede n. Breadth, width
bren v. = 'burn'
bruit n. Report noised abroad, rumour, tidings; matter noised abroad
burdenous a. Constituting a burden, burdensome; onerous, cumbersome; oppressive
carlish a. Of or pertaining to a carl or carls; churlish, clownish, vulgar, coarse; rude, mean
carrain n. A dead body; a corpse or carcass (cf. 'carrion')
carte n. A chart, map, plan, diagram
caul n. A kind of close-fitting cap, worn by women; a net for the hair; a netted cap or head-dress, often richly ornamented
cautel n. A crafty device, artifice, stratagem; caution, wariness, heedfulness; a precaution
cavillation n. Cavilling; the making of captious, frivolous, quibbling, or unfair objections, arguments, or charges, in legal proceedings; the use of legal quibbles, or taking advantage of technical flaws, so as to overreach or defraud; hence, chicanery, trickery, overreaching sophistry
certes adv. Of a truth, of a certainty, certainly, assuredly
chafe v. To inflame (the feelings), excite, warm, heat
chargeous a. Burdensome; expensive, costly; troublesome
chase v. = 'chose'

chid v., pa. ppl. of v. 'chide'
cinder v. To burn to a cinder, reduce to cinders
clout n. A small piece or shred produced by tearing or rending; in later use chiefly a shred of cloth, a rag
commodity n. Conveniency, suitability, fitting utility; commodiousness
common v. To talk over in common, confer about, discuss, debate; to converse about, talk of
compt v. = 'count'
concoct v. To prepare by the action of heat, to boil, cook, bake, etc., lit. and fig.; to digest (food)
confeder v. To unite in alliance; to ally, league, confederate
confuse pa. ppl. and a. Confounded, disconcerted, abashed, perplexed
conject v. To conjecture, or to suppose
conjuration n. Banding together by oath, conspiracy
consolidate ppl. a. = 'consolidated'
contion n. (from Lat. *contio*, *-onis*, contraction of *conventio*) = 'convention': an agreement creating legal relations
convent v. To cause (persons) to come or appear; to call to a meeting or interview, to summon
cool n. A cool breeze, a light and refreshing wind
copped a. 'Rising to a top or head' (Johnson); peaked
copy n. In the phrase 'to change one's copy': to change one's style, tone, behaviour, or course of action; to assume another character
costermonger n. A person who sells fruit, vegetables, fish, etc. in the street from a barrow (a term of contempt or abuse)
cothed ppl. a. Coed (from v. 'coe': to give (sheep) the coe or rot), diseased
covetise n. Ardent, excessive, or inordinate desire; lust. Specifically, inordinate or excessive desire for the acquisition and possession of wealth, etc.; esp. of possessing what belongs to another
cumber v. To hamper, embarrass, hinder, get or be in the way of
cumber-house n. One that encumbers or inconveniently occupies a house
declare v. To make clear or plain (anything that is obscure or imperfectly understood); to clear up, explain, expound, interpret, elucidate
defalcate v. To cut or lop off (a portion from a whole); to retrench, deduct, subtract, abate
deliver a. Free from all encumbrance or impediments; active, nimble, agile, quick in action
deliverness n. Lightness, activity, nimbleness, agility, quickness
depeach v. To send away, get rid of, dispose of, finish off expeditiously; to dispatch
deprehend v. To seize, capture; to arrest, apprehend
descrive v. To describe
difficile a. Difficult
discourse n. Onward course; process or succession of time, events, actions, etc.
disgrade v. To depose formally, as a punitive measure, from honourable rank, degree, or dignity
displeasantly adv. In a displeased or offended manner.
dizzard n. A jester or fool; a foolish fellow, idiot, blockhead

dominical a. Belonging to a demesne or domain; domanial
drad pa. ppl. = 'dreaded'
draught n. A privy; a cesspool, sink, or sewer
drouth n. = 'drought'
dure v. To last, continue in existence
earthquave n. = 'earthquake'
eftsoons adv. A second time, again; afterwards
embraid v. To upbraid, taunt, mock, reproach
endamage v. To inflict damage or injury upon
endue v. To digest
enfarce v. To stuff
enforce v. To compel, constrain, oblige
ensearch v. To look carefully through; to examine, pry into, scrutinize, search; to inquire into, investigate
ensue v. To follow in (a person's steps); to follow (a leader, etc.)
entermine v. To drive mines between or in an interval
ere prep. and conj. Before
erst a. First in time or serial order
erst adv. Earliest, soonest, first in order of time
espial n. A body of spies; hence (chiefly in pl.) a spy, scout
espy v. To discover by spying or by looking out
everich a. = 'every'
except v. To receive, accept
experience v. To make trial or experiment of; to ascertain or prove by experiment or observation
expulse v. To drive or thrust out from a place; to eject, evict from a possession or holding; to turn out of an office, community, etc.
extinct v. To extinguish; to put an end to, make void; to abolish, suppress
fare n. Mode of proceeding, bearing, demeanour; appearance, aspect. In particular, food regarded with reference to its quality; supply or provision of food, regarded as abundant or scanty
fatigate a. Fatigued
feastful a., in the phrase 'feastful day' = 'festival'
fervence n. Warmth of the emotions, intensity of feeling or desire, fervency
festination n. Haste, speed
forbare v. = 'forbore'
franked ppl. a. Fattened in a frank or pen (from v. 'frank': to shut up and feed in a frank; to feed high; to cram)
fret v. To chafe, irritate. Chiefly with regard to the mind: to annoy, distress, vex, worry
froward a. Disposed to go counter to what is demanded or what is reasonable; perverse, difficult to deal with, hard to please; refractory, ungovernable; also, in a wider sense, bad, evilly-disposed, 'naughty'
frush v. To strike violently so as to crush, bruise, or smash
fume n. The volatile matter produced by and usually accompanying combustion; smoke. Figuratively, a fit of anger, an irritable or angry mood
gat v. = 'got'

gentilesse n. (frequent in Chaucer). The quality of being gentle; courtesy, politeness, good breeding; an instance of courtesy
gest n. Pl. notable deeds or actions, exploits (later also sing., a deed, exploit); esp. the deeds of a person or people as narrated or recorded, history
glozer n. A flatterer, sycophant
gnap v. To bite in a snapping fashion; fig., to find fault
goodly a. Of good appearance; good-looking, well-favoured or proportioned; comely, fair, handsome
gormandize n. Excessive and voracious eating; gluttony
gramercy int. and quasi-n. Thanks; thank you.
groat n. A coin, taken as the type of a very small sum
groundsel n. The lower framing-timber of a door; a door-sill, threshold
grudge v. To murmur; to utter complaints murmuringly; to grumble, complain; to be discontented or dissatisfied
grutch n. Complaint; ill-will or resentment due to some special cause, as a personal injury, the superiority of an opponent or rival, or the like
guard v. To ornament (a garment, etc.) with 'guards'; to trim, as with braid, lace, velvet, etc.
gyve v. To fasten with, or as with, gyves (shackles or fetters); to fetter, shackle
halidom, n. A holy thing, a holy relic; anything regarded as sacred. Much used, down to the sixteenth century, in oaths and adjurations
haltpace n. A part of the floor of a hall, etc., raised one or more steps above the level of the rest; a dais
haras n. An enclosure or establishment in which horses and mares are kept for breeding; hence, a stud, breed, or race of horses
haught a. High in one's own estimation; bearing oneself loftily; haughty. Of exalted character, esp. in the matter of courage; high-minded, noble; lofty
haviour n. The action of having or bearing oneself; deportment, bearing, behaviour, manner
hay n. A net used for catching wild animals, esp. rabbits, being stretched in front of their holes, or round their haunts
headling adv. With the head foremost; headlong
hem int.
holpen pa. tense and ppl. of v. 'help'
illecebrous a. Alluring, enticing, attractive
imbrue v. To stain, dirty, defile. To soak, steep in, or saturate with any moisture; to infect
incend v. To inflame, excite (the mind, passions, etc.); to incite to action
incontinent adv. Straightway, forthwith, at once, immediately, without delay
indite v. To put into written words, write, pen (a letter, etc.); to inscribe, set down, or enter in writing
infame v. To render infamous; to brand with infamy or dishonour; to hold up to infamy; to reprobate
ingenerate a. Inborn, innate
ingrate a. Not grateful
ingurgitation n. Greedy or immoderate swallowing; excessive eating or drinking; guzzling or swilling

interpel v. To interrupt (a person) in speaking; to break in on or disturb
involve v. To envelop within the folds of some condition or circumstance; to environ, esp. so as to obscure or embarrass; to beset with difficulty or obscurity
jape n. A device to amuse; a merry or idle tale; a jest, joke, gibe
japery n. Trickery, deception. Jesting speech; ribaldry; a jest
jeopard v. To put in jeopardy; to expose to loss, injury, or death; to hazard, risk, imperil
kind a. Natural, native; implanted by nature; innate; inherent
knack v. To break or crack with a sharp sound
leasing n. Lying, falsehood
leeful a. Permissible, right, lawful, just
leese v. To lose
let v. To hinder, prevent, obstruct
libertine n. An emancipated slave; a freedman
list v. To wish, desire, like, choose
lenitive n. A lenitive medicine or appliance. Also fig., anything that softens or soothes; a palliative
long v. To belong
lyam n. A leash for hounds
macerate a. Wasted, weakened
magnific a. Renowned, glorious; sumptuous, splendid
make n. A person's husband or wife, a spouse; (also) a person's lover or mistress. The breeding partner of an animal, esp. a bird; a mate
malapert a. Of a person, quality, action, etc.: presumptuous, impudent, saucy
mallender n. Originally: a sore located behind a horse's knee. Later: a kind of chronic dermatitis of horses, characterized by the presence of such sores. Fig. and ironic
manchet n. Wheaten bread of the finest quality
manumise v. To free (a slave), release (a captive)
marry int. Expressing surprise, astonishment, outrage, etc., or used to give emphasis to one's words
measurable a. Of a person, action, etc.: characterized by moderation, esp. of diet; moderate, temperate; (occas.) modest
meath n. Meed, an alcoholic liquor made by fermenting a mixture of honey and water
meet a. Suitable, fit, proper for some purpose or occasion; of an action: fitting, becoming, proper
milt n. The semen or the testes of a male fish
minish v. To diminish; to reduce in number, amount, or degree; to reduce in power, influence
ministration n. The exercise of a public office or official function; a ministerial office or employment
mischieving n. The action of causing ruin, damage, or injury; an instance of this
mislike v. To be displeased at; to disapprove of; to dislike
mitigate a., freq. as pa. ppl. Mitigated; alleviated, soothed
mo adv., pron., and n., and a. = 'more'
mockage n. The action of mocking; mockery, ridicule, derision; a mocking or derisive utterance or action

monish v. To warn or exhort (a person)
monition n. An official or legal notification, esp. one calling on a person to do something specified
mormal n. A sore or ulcer, usually with a dry crust or scab, found esp. on the legs
mought v. = pa. tense of v. 'may'
mulet n. A mule, esp. a young or small one
munition n. The action or an act of fortifying or defending something. Also: a fortification, a defensive structure; anything that serves as a defence or protection. Also in extended use
musheron n. Mushroom
ne adv. = 'not'; and conj. = 'nor', 'lest'
nere = contraction of 'ne were'
nourice n. A woman who takes care of a child; a wet nurse, nursemaid, or foster-mother
noyful a. Annoying, troublesome, tiresome. Also: harmful, hurtful, noxious
noyous a. Causing annoyance; vexatious, troublesome. Also, causing harm or injury
nuzzle v. To train, educate, nurture (a person) in a particular opinion, habit, custom, etc.
oliphant n. Elephant
orient a. Of a pearl or other precious stone: of superior value and brilliancy, lustrous, precious
overplus n. That which remains over; an amount left over from the main amount, or from what is allotted or required; an additional or extra quantity; a surplus
pantile n. A roofing tile curved to an ogee shape, one curve being much larger than the other so that the greater part forms a concave channel for the descent of water while the other forms a narrow ridge overlapping the edge of the adjoining tile. Also: a simply curved tile laid so that a convex one overlaps the join of two adjacent concave ones
pararel n. = 'parallel'
participate v. To take part; to have a part or share with a person, in (formerly also of) a thing; to share
paynim n. and a. Non-Christian; pagan
pelfry n. Booty, spoils, plunder; junk, rubbish, trash
peradventure adv. Perhaps, maybe, possibly; by chance, by accident, as it happens or happened; by chance or accident; as may happen, as may be the case, as is possible
percase adv. By chance, as it happens or happened; it may chance or be the case that, perhaps, maybe, possibly; by any chance, as may happen, as may be the case, as is possible
perchance adv. Maybe, perhaps, possibly
perdie int. 'By God!' (as an asseveration). Hence: 'certainly!', 'without a doubt!', 'indeed!' Also occas. as adv.
petty captain n. An officer ranking next below a captain; a lieutenant. Also (with reference to other military cultures): an officer of comparable minor rank or status
pight ppl. of v. 'pitch': crammed or filled

pip v. To crack (as of the shell of an egg)
pirrie n. A sudden, strong blast of wind; a squall; a storm
poise n. Definite or specified weight; the amount that a thing weighs
Polan n. A native or inhabitant of Poland, a Pole
possede v. Possess
pothecary n. Apothecary
prater n. A person who talks foolishly, pompously, or at great length, esp. to little purpose; a mere talker; a chatterer, ranter, preacher. Formerly also: a boaster, or a person who speaks about or against someone
pratery n. Foolish or idle talk, prating
prating n. (Originally) idle or foolish talk, esp. of a tediously lengthy nature; (now usually) pompous or overbearing talk, 'preaching'; an instance of this. Formerly also: boasting or malicious talk
praty a. = 'pretty'
pricksong n. Descant or melody devised to accompany a plainsong or simple theme
pristinate a. Pristine
privy a. Private, personal; familiar, acquainted
propice a. Favourable, advantageous
prospective n. The art of drawing in perspective; (also) an image so conceived or drawn, a scene or view in perspective; perspective
proves = pl. of n. 'proof'
purpose v. To put forward, propose, present
purse net n. A bag-shaped net, the mouth of which may be drawn together with cords, used chiefly in fishing and for catching rabbits or other burrowing animals
questing n. The action of baying at the sight of game, or barking
quotha int. Used with contemptuous, ironic, or sarcastic force after repeating words said by someone else: 'he said?', 'she said?'; (hence) 'indeed!'
rail v. To complain persistently or vehemently; to utter abusive language; to rant
railer n. A person who rails; esp. one who rants, or is argumentative or abusive
rase v. To pull, pluck, snatch
ravin n. Rapine, robbery, pillage
redub v. To remedy, redress (something suffered); to requite
refel v. To refute or disprove (an argument, opinion, error, etc.); to prove to be false or untenable
reflect v. To direct into or away from a course, to divert; to turn aside, deflect
refrain v. To restrain, hold back, check (a person or thing)
refricate v. To reopen (a wound) by rubbing. In earliest use and chiefly fig.: to renew or stir up again (an old antagonism, grief, a memory, etc.)
remember v. To cause a person to think about or recall (a thing or person); to inform (a person); to cause (a person) to have a memory or recollection, remind
remembrancer n. A person who reminds another or others of a thing, esp. one engaged or appointed for that purpose (common in the sixteenth and seventeenth centuries). Also: a memoirist, a chronicler
renome n. Renown
renome v. To make famous, spread the fame of; to honour

rent v. To rend, tear, pull apart or to pieces
replication n. The action or an act of replying, esp. in disagreement or defence; the giving of a rejoinder or retort; (also) argument, protest
repugn v. To be contradictory or inconsistent
resplendish v. To shine brightly; to be resplendent
resty a. Refusing to go forward, refractory, resisting control
richesse n. Wealth, riches
rightwise a. = 'righteous'
room n. An office, function, appointment; a post, situation, employment
round v. To whisper, to speak in a whisper; to converse or talk privately
rowel n. A small metal knob on the lash of a scourge or whip
satiate a. Satiated, filled to repletion, glutted, gratified to the full
scammony n. A gum-resin obtained from the tuberous roots of *Convolvulus Scammonia* used in medicine as a strong purgative; also, the dried tuberous root from which the drug is prepared
seely a. Insignificant, trifling; mean, poor; feeble
seld adv. and a. = 'seldom'
semblable a. Like, similar; corresponding, proportional, accordant, suitable; seemly, becoming
semblable n. Something that is like or similar
semblably adv. In like manner, similarly
shawm n. A musical instrument of the oboe class, having a double reed enclosed in a globular mouthpiece
shew v. = 'show'
side a. In 'side gown', reaching or hanging far down on the person; long (cf. n. 'side-coat': a long coat, a greatcoat)
simple n. A medicine or medicament composed or concocted of only one constituent, esp. of one herb or plant; hence, a plant or herb employed for medical purposes
sith conj. From, subsequent to, or since the time that
skill v. To understand, comprehend
sklander v. = 'slander'
slee v. = 'slay'
smoulder v. To smother, suffocate
solace v. To take comfort or consolation, recreation or enjoyment; to cheer, comfort, console; to entertain or recreate
sooth n. Truth, verity
sore adv. So as to cause considerable physical pain or bodily injury; violently or severely; severely, dangerously, seriously; with much suffering; dearly; so as to cause mental pain or irritation; deeply, intensely
sowne v. = 'sound'
spake v. = 'spoke'
spoil v. To pillage or plunder (a country, city, house, ship, etc.); to clear of goods or valuables by the exercise of superior force; to ravage or sack
stablish v. To establish
step n. A trace, vestige; mark or indication left by anything material or immaterial

stert v. = 'start'
stew n. A heated room used for hot air or vapour baths: hence, a hot bath
sturdy a. Of or with regard to countenance, speech, demeanour: stern, harsh, rough, surly
stut v. To stutter
supportation n. Assistance, countenance
supposal n. An act of supposing; something that is supposed; a supposition, hypothesis; an assumption, conjecture
supremity n. Supremacy
sware v. = 'swore'
taste v. To try, examine, or explore by touch; to feel; to handle. To put to the proof; to try, test
therefro adv. = 'therefrom'
thrast v. To push forcibly or violently
touch n. In the phrase 'to keep touch': to keep covenant, keep faith, keep one's promise, or engagement, act faithfully
towardly a. Promising, hopeful, forward; apt to learn, docile. Well-disposed, dutiful, tractable. Favourably disposed, friendly, affable
towardness n. State of advancement or forwardness. Specifically, willingness and aptness to learn; natural aptitude and good disposition; docility, tractableness; forwardness in learning or practice, promise, proficiency
travail v. To torment, distress, harass, afflict, vex, trouble; to weary, tire. To labour at, to perform
trill v. Of tears, water, a stream: to roll, to flow in a slender stream, the particles of water being in constant revolution, with a more continuous motion than is expressed by 'trickle'; to purl
trow v. To trust, have confidence in, believe
tush int. An exclamation of impatient contempt or disparagement
tyrf n. The turn-over, turn-up, or facing of a cap, hood, sleeve, etc.; a cock (of a cap, etc.)
umbrage n. Shade, shadow
undiscrete a. = 'indiscrete'
uneath adv. Not easily; (only) with difficulty; scarcely, hardly
vallary a. Of a crown or garland, 'crowning'; (a Roman antiquity) bestowed as a distinction on the first soldier to mount the enemy's rampart. In the phrase, 'a pair of cards of vallary falsehood' (referring to the two books carried by Gnatho): deceivingly, where 'card of falsehood' may recall 'a false card': a card played in order to take in an adversary; and v. 'false-card': to play a false card; to play a card other than the normal one, so as to mislead an opponent
valour n. Value or worth in material or other respects
vengeable a. Inclined or ready to take vengeance or inflict retaliative injury
venture n. Fortune, luck; chance
visage v. To face or confront; to look upon or at; to regard or observe
vittle n. and v. = 'victual'
volupty n. Pleasure, delight
ware a. Cognizant, informed, conscious; aware
ware v. = 'wore'

wark n. and v. = 'work'
ween v. To think, surmise, suppose, conceive, believe, consider (pa. tense and ppl. 'wend')
whilere adv. A while before, some time ago
whiles conj. = 'while'
white n. The white or light-coloured part of some substance or structure, as flesh, wood, etc.
whoreson n. The son of a whore, a bastard son; but commonly used as a coarse term of reprobation, abuse, dislike, or contempt; sometimes even of jocular familiarity
wit v. To have cognizance or knowledge of; to be aware of; to know (pa. tense 'wist')
withsave v. To grant, permit, or allow, as an act of grace or condescension (cf. 'vouchsafe')
wonderly adv. = 'wonderfully'
wood a. Out of one's mind, insane, lunatic; violently angry or irritated; enraged, furious
woodness n. Madness, insanity
wot v. To know
wrate v. = 'wrote'

www.ingramcontent.com/pod-product-compliance
Lightning Source LLC
Chambersburg PA
CBHW071833270326
41929CB00013B/1986

* 9 7 8 1 7 8 1 8 8 6 2 1 2 *